endorsed for
edexcel

Edexcel GCSE (9–1)
Design and Technology

Trish Colley   Andrew Dennis   Jenny Dhami   Mark Wellington   Timothy Weston

Published by Pearson Education Limited, 80 Strand, London, WC2R 0RL.

www.pearsonschoolsandfecolleges.co.uk

Copies of official specifications for all Edexcel qualifications may be found on the website: www.edexcel.com

Text © Pearson Education 2017
Typeset by Tek-Art, East Grinstead, West Sussex
Illustrations by Tek-Art, East Grinstead, West Sussex
Original illustrations © Pearson Education
Designed by Colin Tilley Loughrey
Cover photo: Getty Images/Yagi Studio

The rights of Trish Colley, Andrew Dennis, Jenny Dhami, Mark Wellington and Timothy Weston to be identified as authors of this work has been asserted by them in accordance with the Copyright, Designs and Patents Act 1988.

First published 2017

19 18
10 9 8 7 6 5 4

British Library Cataloguing in Publication Data
A catalogue record for this book is available from the British Library

ISBN 978 1 29218 458 6

Copyright notice
All rights reserved. No part of this publication may be reproduced in any form or by any means (including photocopying or storing it in any medium by electronic means and whether or not transiently or incidentally to some other use of this publication) without the written permission of the copyright owner, except in accordance with the provisions of the Copyright, Designs and Patents Act 1988 or under the terms of a licence issued by the Copyright Licensing Agency, Barnards Inn, 86 Fetter Lane, London EC4A 1EN (www.cla.co.uk). Applications for the copyright owner's written permission should be addressed to the publisher.

Printed and bound in Italy by Lego S.p.A.

Acknowledgements
For acknowledgements, please see page 342

Notes from the publisher
1.
In order to ensure that this resource offers high-quality support for the associated Pearson qualification, it has been through a review process by the awarding body. This process confirms that this resource fully covers the teaching and learning content of the specification or part of a specification at which it is aimed. It also confirms that it demonstrates an appropriate balance between the development of subject skills, knowledge and understanding, in addition to preparation for assessment.

Endorsement does not cover any guidance on assessment activities or processes (e.g. practice questions or advice on how to answer assessment questions), included in the resource nor does it prescribe any particular approach to the teaching or delivery of a related course.

While the publishers have made every attempt to ensure that advice on the qualification and its assessment is accurate, the official specification and associated assessment guidance materials are the only authoritative source of information and should always be referred to for definitive guidance.

Pearson examiners have not contributed to any sections in this resource relevant to examination papers for which they have responsibility.

Examiners will not use endorsed resources as a source of material for any assessment set by Pearson.

Endorsement of a resource does not mean that the resource is required to achieve this Pearson qualification, nor does it mean that it is the only suitable material available to support the qualification, and any resource lists produced by the awarding body shall include this and other appropriate resources.

2.
Pearson has robust editorial processes, including answer and fact checks, to ensure the accuracy of the content in this publication, and every effort is made to ensure this publication is free of errors. We are, however, only human, and occasionally errors do occur. Pearson is not liable for any misunderstandings that arise as a result of errors in this publication, but it is our priority to ensure that the content is accurate. If you spot an error, please do contact us at resourcescorrections@pearson.com so we can make sure it is corrected.

Contents

Introduction	iv
1 Core content	2
Preparing for your exam 1	78
2 Metals	86
Preparing for your exam 2	124
3 Papers and boards	128
Preparing for your exam 3	156
4 Polymers	162
Preparing for your exam 4	198
5 Systems	202
Preparing for your exam 5	234
6 Fibres and textiles	240
Preparing for your exam 6	270
7 Timbers	276
Preparing for your exam 7	306
Controlled assessment: Introduction	312
Controlled assessment: Investigation	315
Controlled assessment: Design	322
Controlled assessment: Make	329
Controlled assessment: Evaluate	333
Index	337
Acknowledgements	342

WOODKIRK ACADEMY
Rein Road
Tingley
WAKEFIELD
WF3 1JQ

Introduction

Welcome to Edexcel GCSE (9–1) Design and Technology

Building innovative design skills

The new Edexcel GCSE course is a qualification with creative design and making at its heart. Throughout the course, you will be encouraged to take design risks and to innovate through inspiring contextual challenges, helping you to develop the practical skills that you need to succeed in your chosen pathway.

There are many benefits to taking the Edexcel GCSE Design and Technology course.

- There are clear routes to specialisms in material areas that you enjoy and want to study.
- You will have the opportunity to demonstrate innovative design and making skills through the completion of your non-examined assessment.
- If you do well in this course you will be in a good position to progress to further study of design and technology at AS or A level. The content of this GCSE is ideal grounding for these qualifications, and it has been designed using a similar approach in order to make the experience of moving on as smooth as possible.

How you will be assessed

The GCSE course consists of compulsory and optional topics. You will study one compulsory topic, (the core content) and one optional topic from a selection of six material categories.

Your assessment will consist of two separate assessments: an externally examined paper and a non-examined assessment component. Your exam paper will consist of two sections: Section A covers the core content and Section B covers the material category you have chosen. The non-examined assessment takes the form of a project. You will be assessed on your skills in investigating, designing, making and evaluating a prototype of a product.

How to use this book

This book contains all the information you need for the core content and material categories you will be learning about. Each section guides you through the content of the course in a practical and engaging way, making it clear what you will cover and providing useful activities and questions to help you practise what you have learned.

Each topic is covered in full and has a dedicated section to help you with exam questions on that topic. The exam section after Topic 1 (core content) provides useful strategies for the exam.

This book also includes a section dedicated to the non-examined assessment. It covers each of the stages of your assessment – Investigate, Design, Make, Evaluate – and includes all the information you need to succeed at each stage of the process.

Introduction

Features of the book

In this student book there are lots of different features. They are there to help you learn about the topics in your course in different ways, to understand it from multiple perspectives and to get the most from your learning.

- **Learning objectives** – a summary at the beginning of each topic that outlines exactly what you are going to learn.

Learning objectives

By the end of this section, you should know:

- the importance of the evaluative process and criteria when considering the impact of new and emerging technologies
- how design decisions are affected by emerging technologies
- why current and future scenarios need to be fully investigated.

- **Getting started** – an activity or questions to check what you may already know about the topic and to encourage reflection or broader discussion.

Getting started

Electronic systems have developed a lot, and have become an essential part of our everyday life. Think about where you live and consider the following questions:

- Write a list of all of the electronic products you can think of.
- If you could only keep one electronic product in your life what would it be and why?

Think of an idea for an electronic product you would like that does not exist at the moment. What would you like the product to do? Why do you think it would be useful? What sort of people do you think would buy it?

- **Key terms** – there are certain terms that you will need to know and be able to explain. Key words that are explained within the main text are coloured pink and are **bold** to emphasise their importance. They are explained in the nearby Key terms boxes. You will find all of these words put together in an alphabetical glossary at the back of the book.

Key terms

Chuck: is a clamp that will hold cylindrical items, such as drills or mills or a rotating work piece on a centre lathe.

Tungsten carbide: a type of metal made up from tungsten and cobalt, which results in a tool that has greater shock resistance.

- **Apply it** – this feature allows you to practise applying a theory or concept you have learned to a specific task or question.

Apply it

The properties of acrylic make it an ideal material for rear car light covers, but unsuitable for lights on the front of a car. Analyse the parts made from polymers on a family member or relative's car. Consider the properties of polymers that make them suitable for each part.

Introduction

> **Link it up**
> The working properties of flexibility, printability and biodegradability were covered in the core content (Section 1.9) of this book. To remind yourself, look at page 41.

- **Link it up** – these features show you how different parts of your course link together.

- **Summary** – this gives a short conclusion about the key points of the topic you have just studied.

> **Summary**
> **Key points to remember:**
> - Timber is sawn into standard sizes by sawmills.
> - PAR and PSE are planed timber, which has smooth surfaces.
> - Mouldings can be used to add decorative trim to products.
> - Manufactured boards come in standard-sized sheets, in a range of thicknesses.

- **Checkpoint** – the 'Strengthen' questions give you an opportunity to check that you remember and understand the topic you have just studied. You'll have an opportunity to take your learning further with the 'Challenge' questions provided.

> **Checkpoint**
> **Strengthen**
> **S1** What do PAR and PSE mean?
> **S2** Why is most timber sold in multiples of 25 mm?
> **S3** What is a dowel?
> **Challenge**
> **C1** Why is it important for a product designer to use standard-sized timber wherever possible?

> **Exam-style question**
> Use notes and/or sketches to show the process of riveting two sheets of 3 mm sheet metal. **(4 marks)**

- **Exam-style question** – these questions match the style of questions that you are likely to find in the written exams and will give you useful practice as you go through your course.

> **Exam tip**
> Remember that marks will be awarded for understanding of design and technology, not how well you can draw.

- **Exam tip** – hints and tips to aid your learning and help you in the exam.

- **Maths in practice** – helps you to understand new concepts by providing a worked example for new ideas, calculations and questions.

> **Maths in practice**
> *Cross-sectional area*
> To calculate the **cross-sectional area** of a tube, the area of the inner circle must be subtracted from the area of the outer circle. The equation for calculating the area of a circle is:
>
> πr^2
>
> where:
> $\pi = 3.14$ (to two decimal places)
> r = Radius
>
> - Study the diagram opposite illustrating the end of an acrylic tube. Calculate the cross-sectional area of the tube. The tube has an outside diameter of 30 mm and a wall thickness of 3 mm.
>
> Using the above equation to find the area of the **outside** circle, the answer is as follows.
>
> πr^2 = Area of circle
> r = Diameter ÷ 2 = 15
> $3.14 \times 15 = 706.5 \, mm^2$
>
> Note the tube has a wall thickness of 3 mm. This ultimately makes the inside circle 6 mm less in diameter and therefore the radius is given as 12 mm.
> - Use the same equation for the **inner** circle to calculate how much material needs to be removed to calculate the area shaded brown.
>
> πr^2 = Area of inner circle
> $3.14 \times 12 \times 12$ = **452.16 mm²**
> - Finally you need to subtract the area of the inner circle from the area of the outer circle.
>
> Area of outer circle – Area of inner circle = cross-sectional area of tube
> $706.5 - 452.16 = 254.34 \, mm^2$
> The cross-sectional area of the acrylic tube surface = 254.34 mm²

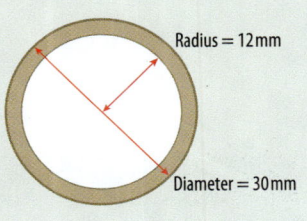

Preparing for your exam

Dedicated exam preparation sections with tips and guidance for success in your written exams. You will find example questions and answers, together with notes and explanations about the quality of the answers shown. This will really help you build your understanding of how to write stronger answers.

Supporting materials

Answers to exam-style questions can be downloaded from the Pearson GCSE (9-1) Design and Technology website at www.pearsonschools.co.uk/edgcsedtsupport.

1 Core content

1.1 The impact of new and emerging technologies

> **Getting started**
>
> What products, services and software have you used this week that are the result of technologies that have become common in the last 30 years? You may want to research this question using the Internet, or discuss ideas in groups.

> **Learning objectives**
>
> By the end of this section, you should know:
> - how new and emerging technologies have had an impact on people, culture and society
> - how developments in industry have affected production and the environment.

New and emerging technologies offer more efficient ways to carry out tasks, which can maximise output, reduce prices and improve the quality of products. However, there are also disadvantages, for example a decline in traditional skills, such as the production of handmade goods.

Industry

Benefits of introducing new technology to industry include:
- cutting costs by changing to more efficient manufacturing methods
- products being brought to market more quickly
- easier manipulation of information to reduce material and stock holding
- a decrease in human error.

Together, these benefits reduce costs and increase revenue, but some changes are not always seen as positive. For example, robotics and computers enable factories to be productive for longer hours, work more safely and improve quality. However, they also reduce the need for manual input, making some lower-skilled assembly line jobs redundant. In some regions, this can cause widespread **unemployment**, particularly if high numbers of people had previously been employed in low-skilled work.

There is an increasing need for employees to take greater personal responsibility for acquiring and updating their skills following the introduction of new technologies. This is known as the **workforce skill set**. All workers need to embrace technology to compete in the labour market.

Demographic movement may occur due to new technologies, for example younger workers moving to jobs involving new or specialist technologies. As a result, some areas or countries lose people and other countries gain them. Table 1.1.1 shows some advantages and disadvantages of demographic movement.

Countries losing people	Countries gaining people
Advantages: • Fewer people to house and feed • Extra income may be sent back home • Reduced pressure on jobs and resources	**Advantages:** • Labour shortages can be overcome • Migrants often prepared to take lower paid jobs • Adds cultural diversity
Disadvantages: • Loss of young and most able people • Loss of those with good education and skills • Families become divided	**Disadvantages:** • Language problems or other barriers to integration • Pressure on housing and health services

Table 1.1.1 Possible advantages and disadvantages of demographic movement

Science and technology parks support new and emerging technologies by enabling businesses to associate with a particular centre of knowledge, such as a university or research organisation. They help the transfer of knowledge, while promoting technology-led economic development in the area. For example, emerging technology firms linked to the USA's Stanford University transformed Silicon Valley into a global centre of technology, finance, education and research. However, science parks are often built on the outskirts of cities and may encroach on green field areas. This can result in habitat loss for wildlife and resentment among local residents.

> **Key term**
>
> **Demographic movement:** the way in which the population's structure changes, for example as a result of an ageing community or migration into an area.

1 Core content

> **Exam-style question**
>
> Explain **one** reason why unemployment in the UK may rise as new and emerging technologies develop.
>
> **(2 marks)**

Enterprise

Small **enterprises** are important to the economy; in 2016 they employed 15.7 million people in the UK, which accounts for 60 per cent of all private sector employment. As new enterprises develop, using new technologies could ensure that they are ahead of the market and attract funding.

Privately owned businesses tend to be relatively small with limited sales, stock and workforce. Strategic decisions are made by the owner(s). An advantage is that they are often sufficiently flexible to easily adopt, adapt and exploit new technologies. However, they may not have enough funds to invest in cutting-edge manufacturing equipment.

Crowd funding is a comparatively new way of launching new products or technologies. It funds a project by raising money from a large number of people who each contribute a small amount of money online. It depends on capturing the imagination of potential funders, using online platforms to coordinate and administer the funds.

Government funding is often available for new businesses that could contribute to the overall economy, making the use of new and emerging technologies easier for them. More than 40,000 UK businesses have taken advantage of business start-up loans since the scheme was launched in May 2012. Local councils may also provide lower-level loans or grants.

Not-for-profit organisations reinvest the money they make in their chosen cause. Many engage with new technologies to help their causes. For example, the organisation Charity: Water worked with Google to develop remote sensor technology to identify when water flows at its projects across the world. Other examples could include healthcare phone apps and reducing admin costs via online communications.

> **Exam-style question**
>
> Explain **one** benefit of crowd funding that can help to promote new and emerging technologies. **(2 marks)**

Sustainability

Sustainable technologies have been driven by environmental awareness and the rising costs of fossil fuels. Companies must balance different, and often competing, needs against an awareness of the environmental, social and economic limitations we face as a society.

Transportation costs

The environmental costs of moving products between locations can be high and transport is one of the biggest energy users. Companies need to develop practices that reduce the use of carbon dioxide, are economically viable and improve quality of life. Solutions could include:

- changing from diesel-intensive lorries to electric vehicles or trains
- making fewer journeys, for example by establishing distribution centres with good links to the end destinations
- designing products that are lighter or with compact packaging, so that more products can fit into the carrier.

> **Key terms**
>
> **Enterprise:** a business, particularly one started by someone who shows **initiative** by taking a **risk** setting up, investing in and running it.
>
> **Crowd funding:** a method of raising funds from many people for an enterprise via online platforms.
>
> **Sustainability:** the ability to meet the needs of the present without compromising the ability of future generations to meet their own needs.

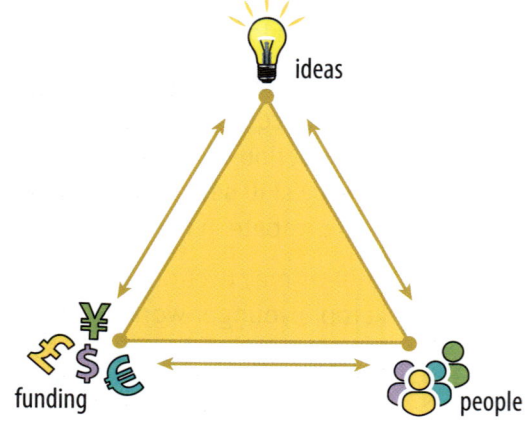

Figure 1.1.1 Cloud funding enables innovation

1.1 The impact of new and emerging technologies

Pollution

Companies have an economic and environmental responsibility to keep **pollution** to a minimum by using new technologies to reuse or dispose of waste without harming the environment, and by being energy efficient and creating less pollution in the first place. Government regulations to encourage companies to reduce pollution include a carbon tax or subsidies for alternative energy resources.

Demand on natural resources

Both natural fuels like coal and gas, and minerals such as tin, copper, iron ore, lead and zinc are finite – if we continue to use them they will run out. Even though new technologies have increased the efficiency of their extraction, companies need to manage the demand for natural resources, for example by developing new sustainable materials, such as biodegradable plastics, that can replace the original materials.

Waste generated

Raw materials are often wasted due to manufacturing inefficiencies. Minimising waste via new technologies makes products sustainable and generates significant cost savings. Here are some strategies companies could adopt.

- **Reducing** the amount of waste produced, for example by using computer-controlled machines to minimise off-cuts and rejects, and sending emails instead of letters.
- **Reusing** products or materials that would otherwise become waste. For example, some ink cartridge suppliers enable used cartridges to be returned, refilled and used again and plastic food containers can be reused around the home.
- **Recycling** allows for materials to be used a number of times. Some newly developed plastics can be melted and reset with no degradation of quality.
- **Recovering** waste generated in factories. This may be in the form of heat energy, which can then be used as a fuel for heating or for boilers to generate steam and power electric turbines.

People

Workforce

Technology, such as the internet, enables some people to choose how they work productively, blurring home and work boundaries. This can have a negative effect on home life and lead to overworking. Companies need a wider skills base to adapt to changes in technology as manufacturing becomes more responsive to changing markets.

Consumers

Consumers are often aware of new technologies, which increases demand but also increases use of scarce resources. Also, some new technologies allow consumers to have input into the design themselves, via things like 3D printing or customising business cards online.

Key terms

Pollution: the release of contaminating substances that are likely to harm the natural environment.

Recycling: the process of converting waste material into other usable products, such as glass bottles made from recycled glass.

Consumer: a person who uses goods and services.

Apply it

Companies are encouraged to use alternative energy resources. Find out which renewable energy resources are most popular in the UK.

Apply it

Think about the technology you could be using in 10 or 20 years' time. How do you think you will travel? How will you work? How will you contact your friends?

Exam-style question

Explain **two** ways in which a shampoo manufacturer could change the packaging of its products to reduce its transportation costs. **(4 marks)**

1 Core content

Children
New and emerging technologies can offer rich opportunities for education and entertainment, developing children's academic and practical skills. For example, the online game Minecraft offers greater creative opportunities than traditional building toys. However, there are concerns that children spend too much time using digital devices at the expense of social and physical activities.

People with disabilities
Assistive technology covers small devices such as pencil grips to larger lifting devices and all-terrain wheelchairs for people with disabilities. Prosthetic limb technology harnesses electrical activity in the body, providing the user with more control. New technology in stem cell therapy can treat cerebral palsy, heart conditions and visual problems but years of trialling are required first.

Wage levels
Companies may need to pay more to attract staff with specialist technological skills. Learning new skills can lead to higher wages, but as some previously high-paid jobs become automated, associated wages may fall.

Highly skilled workforce
Technology leads to the **automation** of routine or repetitive production systems that were previously labour intensive. Demand is growing for highly skilled, highly educated managers and professionals. People with hybrid skill sets, such as technology and project management, are likely to be in demand. Workers must keep developing new technical skills throughout their careers otherwise workers with the necessary skills may be recruited from elsewhere.

Apprenticeships
Even manual trades are enhanced by new technologies. Manufacturers often give training providers new products for testing, encouraging apprentices to use them in their work. Apprentices and their tutors can log evidence and progress online. New technology may create training opportunities for apprentices but no guarantee of employment at the end of their training.

Culture
Technology and **culture** have always been linked. New technologies may support existing patterns of behaviour or evolve to meet the needs of different cultures. Cultures also evolve as technology advances.

Population movement within the EU
Migration is the movement of people from one permanent home to another. Migration is common within the European Union because EU residents are free to choose to live and work in any EU member state. Immigrants can bring energy, innovation and experience of different skills and technologies, filling skills gaps. However, online communication tools may reduce the need for workers to move. After the UK voted to leave the EU in a referendum in 2016, free movement between the UK and the rest of Europe may change.

> **Exam-style question**
> Explain **one** advantage of a company employing migrant workers. **(2 marks)**

> **Exam tip**
> Remember to write about an advantage. Mentioning disadvantages will not get you any more marks.

> **Key terms**
> **Apprenticeship:** a job with training that allows people to gain nationally recognised qualifications.
> **Automation:** using control systems to operate equipment.
> **Culture:** the way a group of people behave, dress, eat and live their lives. Culture can be influenced by anything from religion, tradition and history to local food sources, climate and artistic expression.

Voice recognition software

Screen reader

Eye tracking

Figure 1.1.2 Assisted technology can help people with disabilities carry out tasks at work

1.1 The impact of new and emerging technologies

Social segregation

Although many residential areas are becoming more ethnically mixed, some minority populations have tended to live in clusters, which can lead to social segregation. This leads to reduced contact between different groups, which could create social barriers and ultimately limit access to better education, jobs and technologies.

Society

A society is a large, organised group of people living together. The term applies equally to a village, a country or even a continent. New technologies are influencing the decisions that shape our society. Here are some examples.

- **Changes in working hours and shift patterns**: the internet and mobile apps enable office workers to access systems at convenient times to them and their business. This maximises the labour available, increases productivity and improves morale. This can have a positive or negative effect on home life.
- **Internet of Things (IoT)**: the system of interrelated devices that are connected via the internet is called the Internet of Things. For example, a home's heating or washing machine can be programmed remotely via an app, and many people use smartwatches or bands to track their fitness. Systems can malfunction, such as home alarms not informing the user (remotely via an app) that there was an emergency. Benefits to business include tracking and inventory control, security, factory management and energy conservation. There are concerns that we might become over-reliant on technology and risk personal data being accessed and used fraudulently.
- **Remote working**: when an employee completes work away from their usual workplace, for example at home, at a hotel or on a train. Advances in technology enable employees to access their employer's information and systems easily using remote devices.

Possible advantages	Possible disadvantages
Enables a more flexible work schedule	Could lead to a lack of routine
Less time and money spent commuting	Less workplace social interaction
Work at your own pace as no set hours	Blurs the work–life balance
Technological advances make more work possible	Less IT support may compromise productivity
Fewer distractions	Less face-to-face interaction with customers and colleagues
	Potential security breaches of information

Table 1.1.2 Possible advantages and disadvantages of remote working

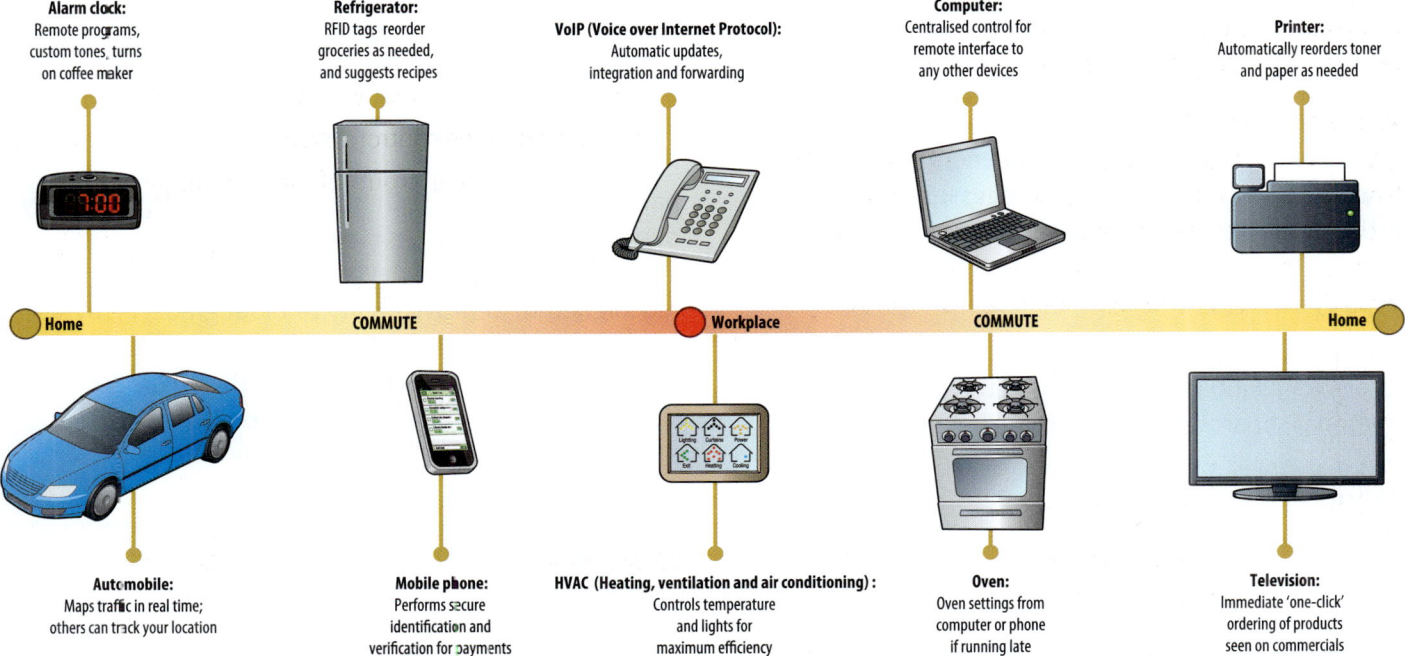

Figure 1.1.3 The growing scope of the internet of things

1 Core content

Video conference meetings

Two-way audio and video telecommunications allow people to connect from two or more sites for a meeting. Often, they can share documents and display information onscreen. Providers such as Skype are making video conferencing widely available for free or at a low cost.

Possible advantages	Possible disadvantages
Meetings and training can take place without leaving the office	May not be as productive as a discussion around a table
Travel costs and the time taken to travel can be reduced or eliminated	Confidential documents may need to be viewed and signed in person
Meetings can be called instantly at multiple locations with little notice	May be a high set-up cost
Speeds up decision making and problem solving	May be difficult to find a suitable time across time zones
	People may not pick up on non-verbal information such as body language

Table 1.1.3 Possible advantages and disadvantages of video conferencing

Environment

Businesses must balance the demand for a wider range of cheaper goods against the needs of the environment. Factors to consider include all the energy, wastes and by-products of manufacturing processes, and disposal of the products after their useful life.

> **Apply it**
>
> Many modern products are more easily recycled than previously. Find out how manufacturers are facilitating material separation and the recycling process.

Pollution

The environmental impact of pollution can be monitored and minimised using emerging technologies, for example by:
- using software to ensure all growth is planned and environmental impacts are predicted
- eliminating outdated, polluting technology
- improving inefficient waste disposal methods
- improving extraction and conversion methods of raw materials.

Waste disposal

Businesses must manage any production waste or try and eliminate it using new technologies, for example by:
- using efficient manufacturing processes
- reusing waste within the same manufacturing process
- recycling waste in a different manufacturing process
- designing products so that the whole or parts of them can be reused or recycled
- harnessing any waste energy such as heat and using it elsewhere.

Materials separation

If useful materials are separated from waste to be recycled and used again, fewer raw materials are required and less material is sent to landfill.

Automated machines separate materials by type (metals, plastics or chemicals, for example). Individual materials need to be separated and reprocessed into the main material with all impurities removed.

Transportation of goods around the world

Local production reduces the need for environmentally damaging transport. As new methods of construction become available, it is easier to reduce the size and volume of products and packaging, enabling more products to be delivered in one shipment.

Packaging of goods

Packaging can be made from metal, glass, plastic, paper, cardboard and other mixed materials, especially paper and cardboard. As new technologies emerge and new materials are developed, packaging can be redesigned to improve ability to biodegrade. Many companies now only use packaging that can be recycled- making it much better for the environment. However, this can sometimes increase the price of a product for consumers.

> **Exam-style question**
>
> Explain **two** ways in which a company that produces televisions could reduce packaging waste. **(4 marks)**

Production techniques and systems

Different production techniques and systems ensure that products are manufactured efficiently and cost effectively.

Technique/system	Description	Example	Advantages	Disadvantages
Standardised design and components	• The same components or modular systems are used across many designs • Usually an individual part, manufactured in large numbers, to an internationally accepted standard	• Electronic (e.g. resistors), or mechanical (e.g. nuts and bolts) components	• Consistent safety and quality • Speeds up product development as parts already exist • Workforce can be easily trained to deal with standard components • Cost saving	• Difficult to customise • Quality of a product may suffer
Just-in-time (JIT)	• Computerised stock control ensures that parts are only received when they are needed in the production process and go straight to the production site rather than being stored	• Car manufacturers (e.g. production line) • On-demand publishing (e.g. photos, greeting cards)	• Can increase efficiency and reduce waste • Enables changes to production runs to meet demand	• Any break in the supply chain holds up production • Cost of more frequent deliveries • Fewer bulk-buying discounts
Lean manufacturing	• Reducing or eliminating waste in design, manufacturing, distribution and customer services	• Eliminating overproduction • Minimising defects • Reducing storage, movement or processing of parts or products	• Multi-skilled teams (cells) are each responsible for part of the production process, which can improve efficiency as workers share their skills and expertise	• Requires time-consuming data analysis • Requires disruptive changes to existing processes
Batch production	• A set number of products are manufactured that are made in limited quantities or for a limited time	• Olympic medals • Books with limited print run	• Could lower capital costs • Reduces inventory/storage space	• Downtime when reconfiguring the production system

Table 1.1.4 Types of production *cont...*

1 Core content

Technique/ system	Description	Example	Advantages	Disadvantages
Continuous production	• Manufacturing of identical high-demand products, 24 hours a day	• Production of sheet materials, such as glass, or standard components, such as nuts and bolts	• Removes the cost of stopping and starting the production process • Materials can be cheaper in high quantities	• Automation can lead to staff redundancy • High-capital input • Low flexibility in changing product/design • A fault in production can stop the whole process
One-off production	• A single, unique product made by skilled workers	• Complex, large-scale products (e.g. a yacht) or smaller-scale crafted products (e.g. specialist furniture)	• High-quality products	• Products are expensive as cost of materials is higher and production is labour intensive • Production times are longer
Mass production	• Efficiently and consistently producing many products at a low cost per unit • Often automated, with parts added in sequence	• Toy manufacture	• Materials can be cheaper in high quantities	• Initial set-up costs can be high • If a production line breaks, manufacture is halted • Repetitive

Table 1.1.4 Types of production

Summary

Key points to remember:
- The nature of industry is changing due to new and emerging technologies.
- Companies are more environmentally aware and many create products that are more sustainable.
- The types of production are changing as technology advances.

Checkpoint

Strengthen

S1 Explain two ways in which new enterprises can be funded.
S2 Describe two ways in which a business can reduce its demand on natural resources.
S3 Describe four ways in which a company can reduce its waste.

Challenge

C1 Explain why robotic technology may increase unemployment and how companies will benefit by increasing the use of robot technology.
C2 Examine the type of work employees completed in a factory in the early 1900s and compare how their work has changed now.

1.2 Evaluating new and emerging technologies to inform design decisions

> **Learning objectives**
>
> By the end of this section, you should know:
> - the importance of the evaluative process and criteria when considering the impact of new and emerging technologies
> - how design decisions are affected by emerging technologies
> - why current and future scenarios need to be fully investigated.

> **Key term**
>
> **Critical evaluation:** a process that identifies positives and negatives from a range of areas to assess the suitability of concepts such as a design, process or material.

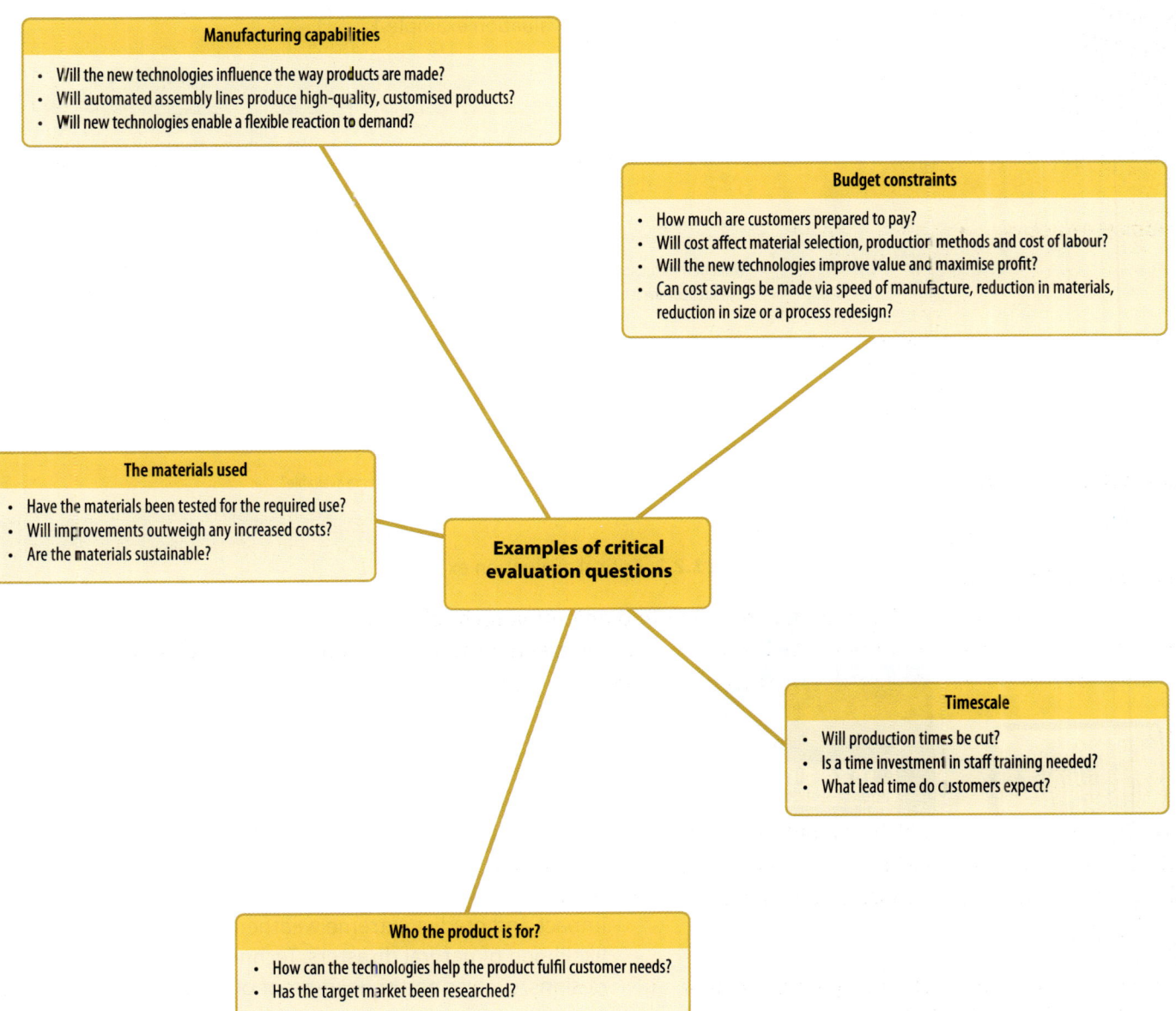

Figure 1.2.1 Questions to ask when **critically evaluating** new and emerging technologies that inform design decisions

1 Core content

> **Exam-style question**
>
> Evaluate the considerations for using new and emerging technologies in the development of a new bicycle for competitive cyclists. **(9 marks)**

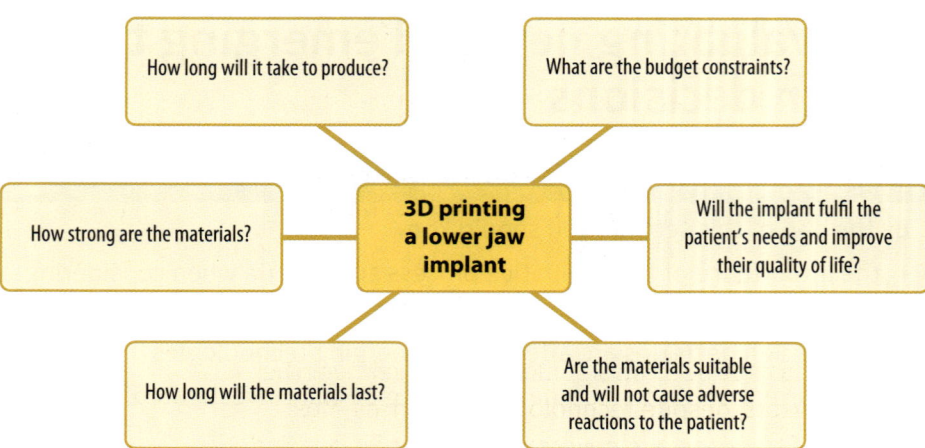

Figure 1.2.2 Critical evaluation example 1

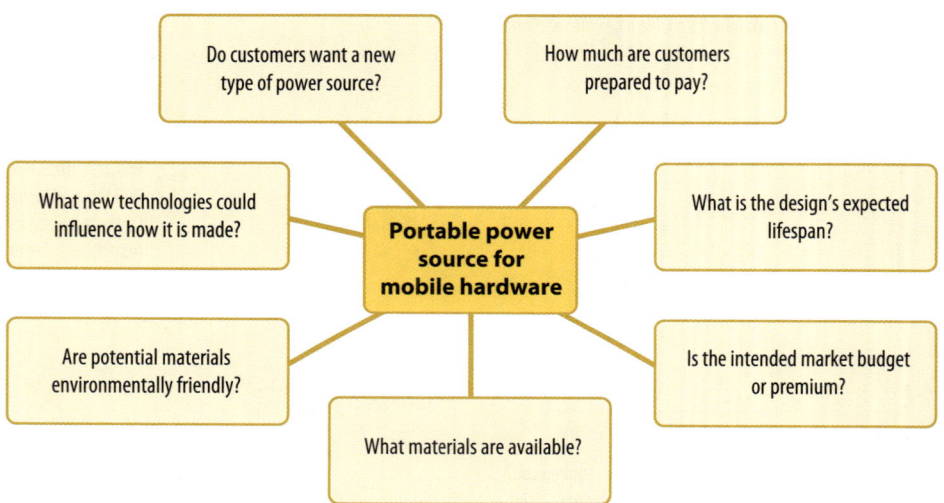

Figure 1.2.3 Critical evaluation example 2

Example of a mobile power source – it is a portable power source

Consideration of contemporary and potential future scenarios

When making design decisions, you must examine possible scenarios. Outcomes could be positive, negative or both. Here are some examples.

- **Natural disasters** such as floods and hurricanes are increasingly attributed to human causes. Advances in technology should help us to reduce our environmental impact and predict extreme weather patterns, evaluating the likelihood of natural disasters. Technology also enables better designs, such as earthquake-proof offices.

1.2 Evaluating new and emerging technologies to inform design decisions

- **Medical advances** such as in biotechnology (examples include artificial organs, implants and prosthetic limbs) and medical equipment (such as magnetic resonance imaging (MRI) scanners to help diagnose illnesses) improve health overall. However, the impact on the population needs to be evaluated and understood. For example, medical advances that allow people to live longer also create a greater need for supporting the elderly.
- **Travel** has not become significantly quicker over the last 50 years, despite technological advances. Most forms of transport are now comfortable, efficient and safe but the environmental impact is still a current and future concern.
- **Global warming** (climate change) is probably caused by the emission of greenhouse gases, especially from burning fossil fuels. Possible solutions are new energies, new low-carbon and zero-carbon technologies and ensuring sustainable development.
- **Communication** is now cheap, quick, global and easy because of the internet, but designers should not assume that the target audience has access to hardware, software, infrastructure and power sources, now or in the future.

Ethical perspectives on new and emerging technologies

Companies that trade **ethically** are not totally driven by profit. They consider their products' wider implications to act fairly and honestly, and not exploit workers or suppliers, or damage the environment.

Key terms

Global warming: an increase in the temperature of the Earth's atmosphere, caused by greenhouse gases.

Ethics: balancing behaviour with moral principles when carrying out an activity.

Apply it

Identify ten companies that use the Fairtrade Foundation Mark. What types of items are identified as Fairtrade?

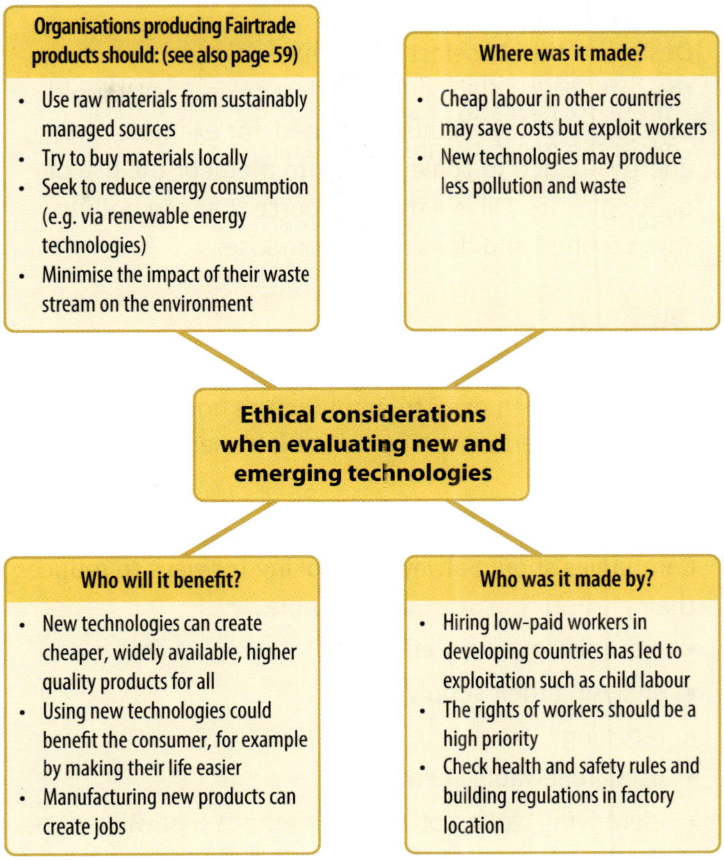

Organisations producing Fairtrade products should: (see also page 59)
- Use raw materials from sustainably managed sources
- Try to buy materials locally
- Seek to reduce energy consumption (e.g. via renewable energy technologies)
- Minimise the impact of their waste stream on the environment

Where was it made?
- Cheap labour in other countries may save costs but exploit workers
- New technologies may produce less pollution and waste

Ethical considerations when evaluating new and emerging technologies

Who will it benefit?
- New technologies can create cheaper, widely available, higher quality products for all
- Using new technologies could benefit the consumer, for example by making their life easier
- Manufacturing new products can create jobs

Who was it made by?
- Hiring low-paid workers in developing countries has led to exploitation such as child labour
- The rights of workers should be a high priority
- Check health and safety rules and building regulations in factory location

Figure 1.2.4 Ethical considerations

Exam-style question

Explain **two** methods that a company could use to relocate its manufacturing operation to a developing country. **(6 marks)**

Exam tip

To get full marks on this type of question, do not repeat yourself – you must give two different reasons.

Environmental perspectives on new and emerging technologies

Any deterioration in the environment threatens natural resources such as food, energy and clean water. Companies must examine their production techniques, materials use, energy consumption and emissions in order to protect the environment.

1 Core content

Use of materials

Designers should select fewer materials and ensure they are recyclable, lighter and less toxic. They should consider the way metals are mined, for example, the energy needed to convert ore into metal or the use of oil for plastics. Oil is a finite resource that can pollute when refined and does not decompose.

> **Apply it**
>
> Look around your home and identify five materials that have been used to manufacture household products. Identify the raw materials that were used.

Carbon footprint

Companies should always be looking for ways to reduce their **carbon footprint**, for example by:

- maximising energy efficiency
- analysing their supply chain
- recycling
- using renewable energy
- identifying carbon offsetting methods that will reduce the overall amount of emissions.

Figure 1.2.5 Your carbon footprint involves all indirect and direct activities in a day

> **Key terms**
>
> **Carbon footprint:** the amount of CO_2 emissions that can be directly or indirectly attributed to an individual's or company's activities. The larger the carbon footprint, the greater the environmental impact.
>
> **Life-cycle analysis:** an analysis of all the environmental impacts related to a product from the extraction of the raw material to its use and disposal.

Manufacture and transportation: energy usage and consumption

The extraction, transportation and emissions of fossil fuels harm the environment. Even renewables impact on habitats and water use, and cause visual and noise pollution. Transporting goods burns petroleum, so companies could use energy-efficient vehicles to distribute products. Making energy cleaner tends to cost more but reduces the cost to the environment.

Life-cycle analysis

A **life-cycle analysis** (LCA) is a systematic inventory of environmental impacts at every stage of a product's life, including:

- raw material extraction and processing
- product / part manufacture and assembly
- product / part transportation and distribution
- product / consumer use
- product disposal or recovery at the end of its useful life.

Governments are moving towards requiring businesses to carry out LCAs so that they can identify opportunities for environmental improvements in the life cycle.

> **Exam-style question**
>
> Explain the steps involved in carrying out an LCA.
>
> **(4 marks)**

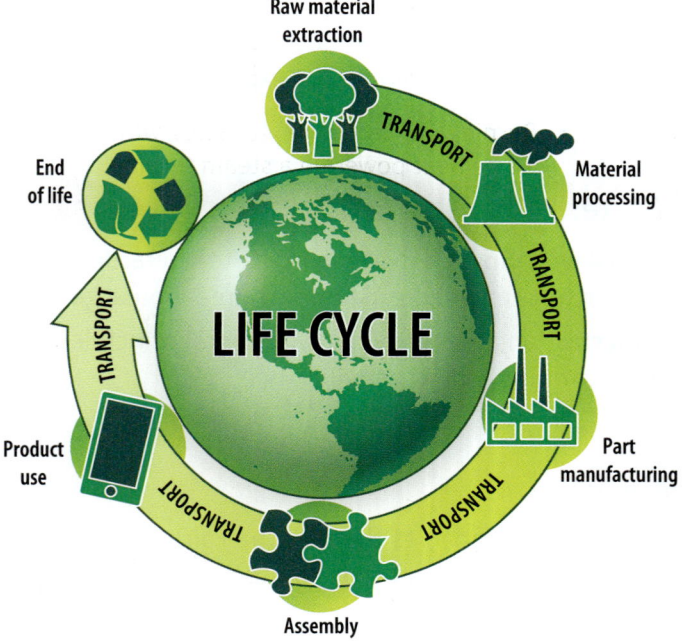

Figure 1.2.6 Key elements of a life-cycle analysis

1.3 Energy: generation, storage and choosing appropriate sources

Learning objectives

By the end of this section, you should know:
- methods of generating energy
- how energy is stored and made available for use
- what factors need to be considered when selecting a power source
- how to discriminate between energy sources and to select appropriately.

Sources, generation and storage of energy

Non-renewable energy sources are fossil fuels that were formed from the remains of animals and plants that lived millions of years ago. They cannot be replenished quickly and will eventually run out.

Link it up

For more on oil see 4.2 *Sources and properties* (pages 162–63).

Source	How it is converted into energy	Advantages	Disadvantages
Coal	• Heat energy and hot gases convert water into steam which powers a turbine to create high-voltage electricity • Smaller amounts used as a domestic heat source	• Stable, large-scale and high-power electricity generation • Relatively cheap to extract and convert • Reliable	• Coal power plants emit pollution such as carbon dioxide, sulfur, mercury, selenium and arsenic • Technologies to reduce coal power plant emissions are expensive • Coal mining impacts significantly on the landscape
Oil	• Processed and split into petroleum products such as petrol, paraffin and diesel • In power plants oil is burnt to heat water and produce steam, which propels turbine blades to produce electricity	• Stable, large-scale and high-power electricity generation • Relatively cheap to extract and convert	• Oil power plants are highly polluting • Oil exploration impacts on the landscape • Oil extraction risks environmental disasters
Gas	• Burning gas can power turbines, with the waste heat powering a steam turbine • Natural gas is used in homes for heating or cooking • It has lower emissions than other fossil fuels – its combustion emits carbon dioxide at half the rate of coal	• Stable, large-scale and high-power electricity generation • Relatively cheap to convert and extract as ready-made fuel • Cleaner than coal or oil	• Burning gases are highly polluting

Table 1.3.1 Advantages and disadvantages of using fossil fuels

Exam-style question

Explain **two** reasons why coal is classed as a non-renewable energy source. **(4 marks)**

Apply it

Fossil fuels are finite. Find out when it is estimated non-renewable energy sources are likely to run out if current usage continues.

1 Core content

Renewable energy sources use natural energy to make electricity. Renewable energy sources produce 20 per cent of the UK's electricity and are important for reducing carbon emissions.

> **Key term**
>
> **Photovoltaics:** using solar cells to generate electrical power by converting energy from the sun.

Source	What it is and how it is converted into energy	Advantages	Disadvantages
Biomass	• Organic matter derived from organisms, such as wood, crops, rubbish, landfill gas and alcohol fuels • Can be used directly via combustion (of wood or biodegradable wastes) to produce heat, or converted to electricity	• Waste from plants and farming can be used	• Large areas needed to cultivate crops • Emits fumes that add to global warming
Biodiesel	• Made from natural elements such as plants, vegetables and fermented waste cooking oil • Can be used in diesel-powered vehicles without modifying the engine	• Uses waste from plants and farming • Does not give off harmful chemicals	• Large areas needed to cultivate crops
Tidal	• Turbines generate electricity from the movement of tidal water • Artificial tidal barrages are constructed across tidal rivers, bays and estuaries, for example – the water is trapped and then released through turbines as the water levels change	• No emissions • Powerful • Tides are predictable and stable • Barrages can have a secondary purpose such as a bridge	• Lower energy output than fossil fuels • Large barrages may have an ecological impact • Expensive to build • Only available in coastal areas
Wind	• Wind turbines use propeller blades, which spin a shaft to create electricity through a generator	• Freely available • Can be used in remote areas • No emissions	• Could restrict shipping traffic when placed in the sea • Wind can be unpredictable • Wind farms are often regarded as unsightly • Expensive to set up
Solar	• Solar (**photovoltaic**) panels convert sunlight into electricity • Solar thermal power plants use the sun's rays to heat a fluid that is circulated through pipes, transferring heat to water and producing steam • Steam is converted into mechanical energy in a turbine, which powers a generator to produce electricity	• Reliable source of power in warmer countries • Homes can have their own electricity supply • More electricity is produced in stronger sunshine	• Could change ecology when large solar farms replace traditional farms • Expensive to set up • Effectiveness of power generation depends on geographical location
Hydroelectric	• A dam traps water that flows through tunnels and turns turbines to make electricity	• Large amount of low-cost power • Can have secondary purpose such as a water reserve	• Expensive to set up • Construction may damage the environment

Table 1.3.2 Advantages and disadvantages of using renewable energy sources

1.3 Energy: generation, storage and choosing appropriate sources

Storage of energy

On a national grid level the supply of electricity must be equal to demand and power companies are continually making adjustments to the supply based on predictable changes such as the timings of the working day, as well as unexpected changes from equipment overloads and storms. Any electricity not used when created must be stored so that there is more flexible and reliable use. This can be in a number of forms that are then used to power systems.

Power systems

A power system is a network of components that supply, transfer and use electric power. These include batteries and cells, solar cells, wind power and mains electricity.

> **Exam-style question**
>
> Evaluate the use of using a wind system for generating electricity in remote countryside. **(9 marks)**

> **Apply it**
>
> Compare the environmental impact of renewable energy sources and non-renewable energy sources. Consider the extraction, conversion, use and geography.

Examples of power systems

Batteries and cells
Use chemical energy to make electricity. Two terminals, one positive (+) and one negative (-). A chemical reaction produces electrons that collect at the negative terminal and when connected in a circuit will flow to the positive terminal. Expensive source of electricity that can lead to chemicals leaching into water and soil if not disposed of correctly.

- Example: cylindrical cell D, C, AA, AAA and AAAA sizes. These are easy to manufacture, small and inexpensive, have good mechanical stability and long life. They are found in medical implants, watches, hearing aids, car keys and memory backup.
- Example: prismatic cell. These are flexible, but can be more expensive to manufacture. They are easy to recharge, but tend to have a shorter life than cylindrical batteries. They are found in mobile phones, tablets and low-profile laptops.

Solar cells
Electronic device that can turn sunlight directly into electricity. Contain two layers of silicon treated to allow electrons to flow when sunlight falls on them. Provide free energy once initial costs are recovered. Non-polluting. Unsightly. Solar farms change the look of the landscape.

- Example: solar panels (photovoltaic cells) on houses to provide local electricity.
- Example: small, thin low-voltage cells can be used cheaply for project work.

Mains electricity
Supplied from power stations through the National Grid. Alternating current (AC) – it flows in one direction and then the other at a rate of 50 times a second. Electricity enters a home at 230 volts and is ready to be used. Items need to be plugged into the mains to be powered. Can be harmful and is produced by dirty energy (nuclear, fossil fuels).

- Example: household equipment, e.g. kettle, television, fridge, hairdryer.

Wind power
Converts the movement of the wind into mechanical power or electricity. A wind turbine consists of a bladed rotor that drives a rotating shaft in a generator to create electricity. A group of wind turbines can produce significant amounts of electricity. Less useful on a smaller scale but small versions can be built at home. A group of wind turbines can produce significant amounts of electricity but is dependent on the strength of the wind.

Figure 1.3.1 Types of power systems

Solar cells used as a power source for a model racing car

> **Apply it**
>
> How many types of battery can you identify around your home? Explain why each type is particularly suited for its purpose.

> **Exam-style question**
>
> Explain **one** reason why solar cells are more environmentally friendly than rechargeable cells. **(2 marks)**

Choosing appropriate energy sources for products and power systems

Here are some examples of factors that designers may need to consider.

- **Portability of the power source:** remote working requires access to devices (computers, phones, medical aids) with a power source that does not need to be plugged into mains electricity. Such devices can be portable and compact as they do not need power converters.

1 Core content

- **Environmental impact:** no entirely 'clean' energy source exists. The impact may be active, like fossil fuel emissions or the destruction of habitats through extraction. Passive impacts include the sound of generators or the appearance of wind farms. Other environmental factors include the impact of transportation or waste disposal.
- **Power output:** a generator's output may vary according to conditions at the power plant, fuel costs or the electric power grid operator. Many renewables do not produce electricity predictably or consistently; for example the output of solar panels relies on the strength of the sunshine, which depends on the time of day and cloud cover. Renewables are therefore often backed up by other forms of electricity generation. A designer must select an electricity supply capable of reliably delivering the required power.
- **Circuit/system connections:** when considering alternative power sources, a designer will need to consider how the circuit or system will be connected to it, for example the use of available plugs, connectors and terminals.
- **Cost:** the choice of the energy supply, for example batteries or a mains electricity power pack, will impact the running costs of the product and so the costs of alternative power supplies must be considered carefully by a designer.

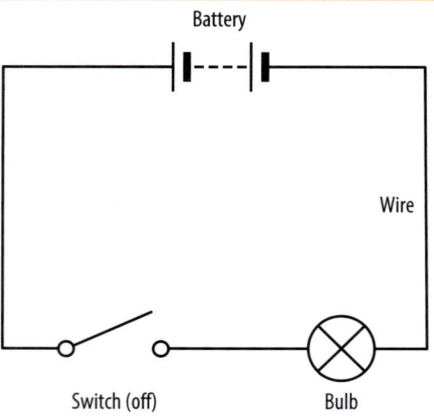

Figure 1.3.2 A simple circuit

Link it up
See Table 1.3.2 for more about how energy sources can impact the environment.

Exam-style question
Explain **two** factors that determine the most appropriate energy source for powering a bedroom desk lamp. **(4 marks)**

Summary
Key points to remember:
- Critically assess new and emerging technologies to be used in manufacturing or the products themselves.
- Consider current and future ethical and environmental factors.
- Life-cycle analyses identify opportunities for environmental improvements during a product's life.
- Energy comes from a range of renewable and non-renewable sources.
- Systems can be powered in different ways and need to be selected appropriately.

Checkpoint

Strengthen
S1 Explain what is meant by 'carbon footprint'.
S2 Describe two environmental disadvantages of using oil as an energy source.
S3 Explain three ways in which companies can help reduce global warming.
S4 Explain two reasons for using solar power instead of coal.
S5 Draw a simple circuit diagram that will power a motor.

Challenge
C1 Work out your carbon footprint for a 24-hour period and describe how you could reduce it.
C2 Explain how a life-cycle analysis may be carried out on a kitchen appliance.
C3 Justify why we still use fossil fuels when the evidence suggests that renewable sources of energy are better for the environment.
C4 Explain the benefits to a customer of batteries that can be recharged after use.

1.4 Smart and composite materials, and technical textiles

Learning objectives

By the end of this section, you should know the characteristics, applications, advantages and disadvantages of:
- modern and smart materials
- composites
- technical textiles.

Modern and smart materials

Modern materials do not occur naturally, but are existing materials that have been altered to improve their properties.

Smart materials are existing or modern materials with physical properties that can be varied by an external input such as temperature, light, moisture, force or electrical current. They sense and respond to conditions in their environment and some can return to their original state when the conditions change.

Table 1.4.1 gives some examples.

Material	Description	Applications	Advantages	Disadvantages
Shape-memory alloys (SMAs)	• Can be plastically deformed (have their shape changed, stretched or crumpled) and will return to their original shape when heated or a current is applied • Examples include nickel-titanium (nitinol), gold-cadmium and iron-nickel-cobalt-titanium	• Glasses frames • Greenhouse window openers • Medical stents • Tweezers and hooks • Orthodontic wires	• Lengthen life of product • Reduced overall size, less complexity	• Expensive • Continuous use can cause metal fatigue
Nanomaterials	• Made of tiny components less than 100 nanometres (nm; a millionth of a millimetre) in at least one direction • May be particles, nanowires, nanotubes or thin films and surface coatings	• Fire-retardant materials • Sunscreen • Tennis rackets • Motorcycle helmets • Car bumpers	• Larger relative surface area can improve their strength, elasticity, magnetic, electrical, thermal conductivity and absorbent properties • Can combine properties, e.g. lightweight but robust and scratch-resistant	• Unusual physical and chemical properties – may need specialist risk assessment relating to health and the environment
Photochromic glass	• Darkens when exposed to light and reverses in the dark • Tiny particles of silver halide are added to glass; these react with ultraviolet light, causing a chemical reaction that changes the glass's colour	• Sunglasses • Plane cockpit windows	• Adapts easily to changing conditions • Can undergo thousands of cycles without performance change	• May be slow to react • User cannot control reaction

Table 1.4.1 Examples of modern and smart materials *Cont…*

1 Core content

Material	Description	Applications	Advantages	Disadvantages
Reactive glass	• Uses electrochromatic technology to change from transparent to opaque by applying voltage while allowing light to pass through from both sides	• Welding masks and goggles • Windows	• Retains heat, so reduces energy bills • Instant privacy without permanent blocking of light	• Expensive • Requires electricity source
Piezoelectric materials	• Generate a small electric charge when compressed (sensors) • Can work in reverse, generating movement when an electric charge is applied (actuators)	• Generating energy • **Sensors**: burglar alarms, keyless car entry, seat belt sensors, keypads, microphones • **Actuators**: for precise position control, e.g. digital cameras, fast-acting valves and nozzles	• Sustainable • Low maintenance • Compact size especially useful in micro-electronics • In actuators, high response speed and can create a large force	• Wear out • Has temperature, load and voltage limitations
Temperature-responsive polymers, e.g. poly N-isopropylacrylamide (PNIPAM)	• Can change physical properties with a change in temperature, so they are useful in many scientific applications	• Can deliver drugs, cells or proteins to patients in a controlled way when mixed with liquid polymer • When injected into a patient, a gel deposit forms; the drug is released in a controlled way when the temperature is increased • Can be used as sensors and gel activators	• Useful in biomedical applications	• Still being researched so wider application may take time
Conductive inks	• Contain pigments that allow small currents to flow through even when dry • Made with silver, carbon, graphite or other precious metal-coated base material • Used in a pen on any suitable material	• Drawing working circuits on polyester, polycarbonates and paper • Improvising or repairing circuits on printed circuit boards • Printing RFID tags for tickets etc.	• Easy to use • Lighter and more economical than traditional circuit boards • Low waste • Ink can be folded, so you can draw a circuit, fold the paper and unfold it to find the circuit still works	• Silver is expensive • Difficult to get circuits right

Table 1.4.1 Examples of modern and smart materials

> **Exam-style question**
> Explain **one** advantage of conductive inks. **(2 marks)**

> **Exam tip**
> This is an 'explain' question. You must give a reason for your answer – do not just give an advantage without an explanation.

1.4 Smart and composite materials, and technical textiles

Composites

A composite consists of reinforcing material(s) and a bonding agent called the 'matrix'. The new material has enhanced properties than the original material(s).

Most composites have excellent strength-to-weight ratios – they are stronger than other materials of the same weight or mass. Table 1.4.2 gives some examples.

Composite	Description	Examples	Disadvantages
Concrete	<ul><li>Made of coarse aggregate (gravel between 14 and 40 mm); aggregate (sand); cement; water</li><li>Proportions depend on the use</li><li>Hardens over time to gain excellent **compressive strength**, but **tensile strength** is low</li><li>Relatively cheap</li><li>Can last 100 years. Additives can prevent attack from seawater or acids</li><li>The tensile strength can be improved by embedding steel rods to form reinforced concrete</li></ul>	<ul><li>Mainly used for construction but it can be used for smaller products such as park benches and bins</li></ul>	<ul><li>Can be damaged by corrosion of reinforcement bars, fire or radiant heat and freezing trapped water</li></ul>
Plywood	<ul><li>Manufactured board of wood **veneers** bonded with glue to produce a flat sheet</li><li>Always has an odd number of layers (at least three) as they balance the stresses around the central core, making it stable in all directions</li><li>The veneers' grain direction runs at 90° to the sheets above and below it, which also increases the stability</li></ul>	<ul><li>Graded for exterior or interior use depending upon the glue's water resistance</li><li>Sheds, cladding, flooring, furniture</li></ul>	<ul><li>Although plywood is strong and stable, some plywood will come apart if the layers become wet</li></ul>
Fibre/ carbon/ glass	<ul><li>Plastic can be reinforced with fine glass or carbon fibres to make a higher strength-to-weight ratio than its component parts</li><li>Loose or woven fibres form a flexible fabric, and are built up in layers with polyester resin</li><li>Reinforced plastic can be sanded for a smooth finish and painted or colour added at the start of the process</li></ul>	<ul><li>**Glass reinforced plastic (GRP)** is easily formed into shapes – it is best suited to large structural items, such as boat hulls, pond liners, car bodies, baths or showers</li><li>**Carbon fibre reinforced plastic (CFRP)** is more expensive than glass fibre but is much stronger – it is used in structural parts such as propeller blades, body armour and golf clubs</li></ul>	<ul><li>Breathing in the fibres can cause respiratory problems</li></ul>
Reinforced polymers	<ul><li>Phenolic resins are combined with cotton fabrics to make inflammable laminated plastic sheets, rods and tubes</li><li>Grades depend on fibre coarseness – all are about half the weight of aluminium, strong, tough and with insulating properties at high temperatures</li></ul>	<ul><li>Non-metallic engineering components like gears and bearings</li><li>Substitute for exterior timber because they are weatherproof and do not need further treatment</li></ul>	<ul><li>Can be expensive</li></ul>
Robotic materials	<ul><li>Materials that couple sensing, activation (movement), computation and communication and can react to their surroundings autonomously.</li></ul>	<ul><li>Vehicles or uniforms that change colour to match their surroundings</li><li>Prosthetics with a sense of touch</li><li>Plane wings that change shape depending on wind conditions</li></ul>	<ul><li>Expensive and complex</li></ul>

Table 1.4.2 Examples of composite materials

> **Key terms**
>
> **Compressive strength:** the ability of a material to resist squashing.
> **Tensile strength:** the ability of a material to resist stretching.
> **Veneers:** slices of wood that are 3 mm or less, used to build up manufactured boards or to protectively coat other woods.

1 Core content

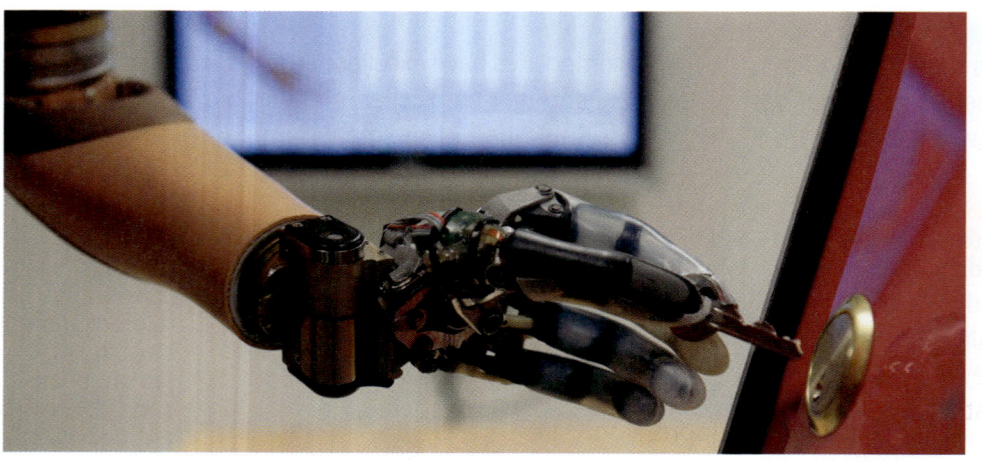

Prosthetics that can 'feel'

> **Exam-style question**
> Give **three** properties of plywood sheeting. **(3 marks)**

> **Apply it**
> Find three uses for plywood. Why do you think it has been used for these purposes?

Composite	Benefits of composite materials
Concrete	• Excellent compressive strength • Good heat and sound insulator • Can be moulded into complex shapes with a variety of surface finishes, so has many applications • Can be manufactured on site, so reduces transport issues • Durable, fire-resistant • Will last for a long time
Plywood	• High strength-to-weight ratio and strong in all directions • High impact resistance, so not easily damaged • Versatile – can be used inside and outside • Economical use of wood as less wastage and available in large sheets
Fibre/carbon/glass	• Low maintenance, durable and good resistance to ultraviolet (UV) light and most chemicals • Able to be formed into most 3D shapes, with added surface texture • Lightweight with an excellent strength-to-weight ratio
Reinforced polymers	• Strong with good wear resistance and excellent machining qualities (will not blunt tools as much as metals) • Good insulator of heat and electricity with low water absorption • Available in a range of forms • Good dimensional stability (does not change shape in heat or moisture-rich environments)
Robotic materials	• Can react to surroundings without connection to a computer • Can react quickly and appropriately by themselves • Can change colour, shape and the load they can carry

Table 1.4.3 Benefits of composite materials

1.4 Smart and composite materials, and technical textiles

Technical textiles

Technical textiles are developed for their functions rather than appearance. They can be strong, lightweight, waterproof, tough, breathable, biodegradable and versatile and are increasingly economical. Table 1.4.4 gives some examples.

Material	Description	Examples	Advantages	Disadvantages
Agrotextiles	• Improve or increase agricultural production • May be made from nylon, polyester, polyethene, polypropene or natural materials like jute and wool • Often biodegradable and offer solar and ultraviolet protection	• Shading • Thermal insulation • Netting • Wind-breaks • Weed suppression	• Durable • Reduces the need for weed killers and pesticides • Can be cheap	• Could change ecosystems by altering natural circulation of water, carbon and other nutrients
Construction textiles	• Developed to improve construction appearance and longevity	• **Structures**: waterproof membrane, concrete reinforcement • **During construction**: hoardings nets, awnings, tarpaulins, canopies	• Strong and light • Resistant to degradation by chemicals, sunlight and acids • Stable in different heat conditions	• May be expensive or hard to source • May degrade over time
Geotextiles	• Used in civil engineering where soil, rock or other geotechnical material needs to be stabilised, filtered, drained or reinforced • Retain their structure in the ground	• Non-woven or woven mats for reinforcing banks or draining flat land	• Do not rot • Deal well with water • Cost effective	• Easily blocked by sediments and organic matter • Ineffective if damaged
Domestic textiles	• Used domestically, even if developed for other purposes	• Cleaning wipes • Furnishings • Wadding • Linings • Carpets • Flooring	• Hardwearing • Stain resistant • Absorbent	• Can be expensive • Fire risk for some textiles • Can be difficult to clean

Table 1.4.4 Examples of technical textiles *Cont…*

1 Core content

Material	Description	Examples	Advantages	Disadvantages
Environmentally friendly textiles	• Use organically grown fibres such as hemp, wool, cotton or bamboo or recycled materials	• Geotextiles • Agrotextiles • Fashion	• Processed with fewer chemicals and naturally more resistant to mould and pests	• Can be expensive
Protective textiles	• Provide protection against heat, harmful chemicals, gases, pesticides and even bullets	• **Clothing:** heat and radiation protection for firefighters, molten metal protection for welders • Tents for severe weather • Parachutes and mountain safety ropes • Disposable chemical protection overalls	• Can be resistant to many external inputs but still breathable and light	• Expensive • Not environmentally friendly
Sports textiles	• Combine function with comfort for high performance • Can be lightweight • Streamlined and breathable • Remove moisture • Sense heart rate • Control bacteria • Block UVA/UVB rays • Resist impact	• Running shoes • Cycling shorts • Rugby tops • Swimsuits	• Can improve athletic performance	• Expensive • Not environmentally friendly

Membrane being laid before a road surface

Table 1.4.4 Examples of technical textiles

Apply it

Why would you want to use a memory foam or a wipe-clean fabric at home?

Exam-style question

Explain **one** benefit of using environmentally friendly textiles to make a pair of school trousers.

(2 marks)

1.5 Mechanical devices used to produce movement

> **Learning objectives**
>
> By the end of this section, you should know:
> - the performance, principles, applications and influence of mechanical devices on product design
> - how mechanisms change movement and increase the mechanical advantage for the user
> - how different components can be used within mechanisms.

> **Apply it**
>
> Identify ten objects that use rotary motion.

> **Exam-style question**
>
> State the type of movement of a car travelling along a motorway.
>
> **(1 mark)**

Mechanisms are devices that can change one form of force into another. They range from simple mechanisms such as a door handle, scissors or a hole punch to complex car engines, bicycles and manufacturing machinery.

Types of movement

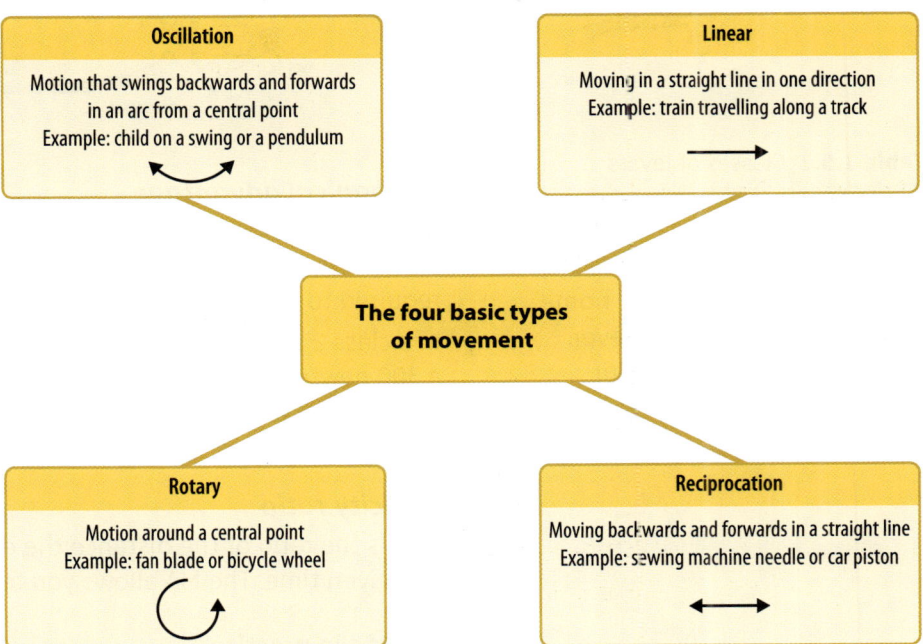

Figure 1.5.1 Types of movement

Classification of levers

Levers are simple mechanisms that create mechanical advantage, for example when moving large objects. Levers have three parts:
- **effort:** the amount of force put in by the user (input)
- **fulcrum:** the point at which the lever pivots
- **load:** the force exerted by the load (output).

> **Key terms**
>
> **Lever:** a fixed rigid beam requiring a fulcrum, load and effort to provide mechanical advantage.
>
> **Force:** a push or pull upon an object that, when unopposed, will change the object's motion.

1 Core content

Class 1, 2 and 3 levers

All levers can be classified into one of three types.

	Class 1	Class 2	Class 3
Reason for mechanical advantage	A large input movement can produce a small output movement but with greater force	A large input movement can produce a smaller output movement with greater force, but the fulcrum is at one end	Limited; the force applied by the user is greater than the output force
Example	Pliers or crowbar 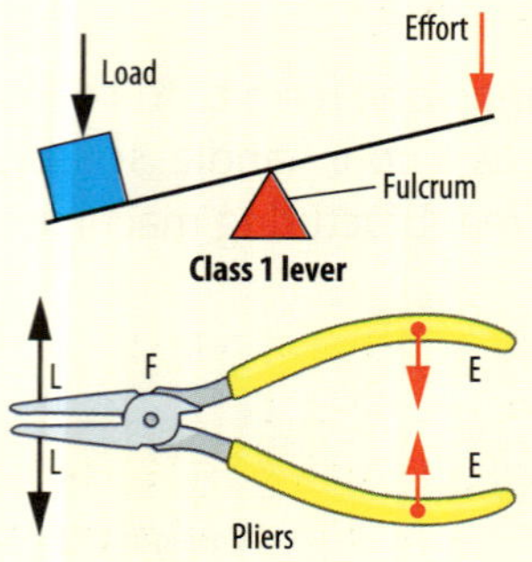	Wheelbarrow or nutcracker 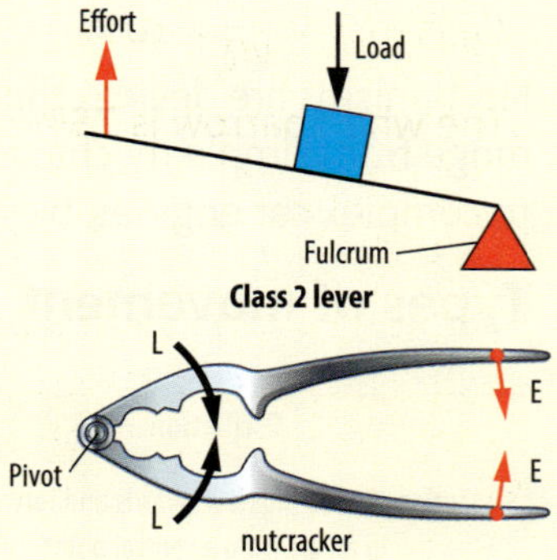	Tweezers or spade 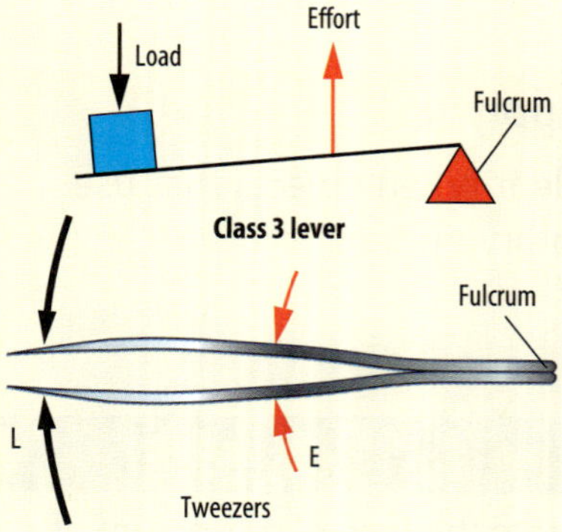

Table 1.5.1 Classes of levers

Apply it

Count the levers in your home. Identify which class of lever they are, and explain your reasoning for your choice.

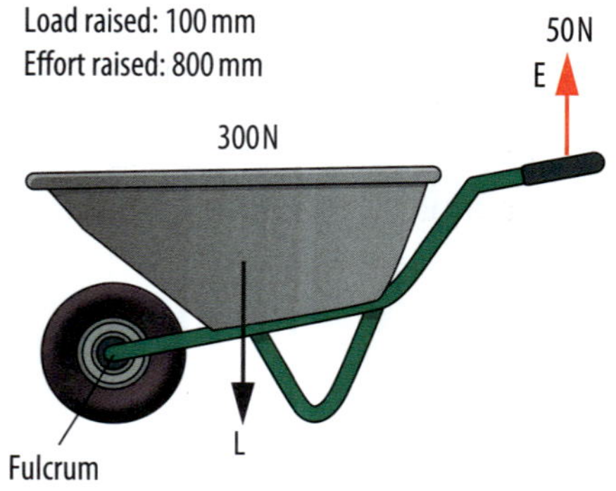

Figure 1.5.2 Class 2 lever

Mechanical advantage

Mechanical advantage (MA) allows a large force to be exerted with small effort. It is calculated by comparing the weight of the load and the effort required to move it.

In a class 2 lever, such as a wheelbarrow, a 50 newton effort is needed to lift a 300 newton load. The lever has a mechanical advantage of 6. The larger the number, the greater the mechanical advantage and the less effort to move the load. MA = load/effort = 300N/50N = 6

Velocity ratio

This is the ratio of the distance the effort has to move compared to the load, in a given time. The MA allows you to lift heavier loads.

> **Maths in practice 1**
>
> **Calculating velocity ratio of a wheelbarrow**
>
> - In the same class 2 lever, the wheelbarrow handles are lifted 800 mm while the load is only raised by 100 mm. What is the velocity ratio?
>
> The wheelbarrow has a velocity ratio of $\frac{800}{100} = \frac{8}{1} = \mathbf{8}$, which means you are lifting the handle eight times as far as the load is raised.
>
> You often need to rearrange the formula in three ways to be able to work out the load, effort or velocity ratio. For example:
>
> $VR = \frac{\text{Distance moved by effort}}{\text{Distance moved by load}}$
>
> can also be written as
>
> $\text{Distance moved by load} = \frac{\text{Distance moved by effort}}{VR}$
>
> or
>
> $\text{Distance moved by effort} = \text{Distance moved by load} \times VR$

1.5 Mechanical devices used to produce movement

Efficiency

No mechanism is 100 per cent efficient as other factors, such as friction, will have an impact. Efficiency is the relationship between the input force and movement, and the output force and movement.

> **Maths in practice 2**
> *Calculating efficiency of the wheelbarrow*
> Calculate the efficiency of the wheelbarrow.
> $$\text{Efficiency} = \frac{MA}{VR} \times 100\% = \frac{6}{8} \times 100\% = 75\%$$
> The wheelbarrow is **75%** efficient.

Linkages

Linkages are levers that allow forces and motion to be transmitted in a certain way, for example by reversing the movement or changing its direction. The same rules on mechanical advantage apply to linkages – they still have an input, a fulcrum and an output that can be adjusted for the desired result.

Bell crank

This is a class 1 lever that can transmit the motion through 90 degrees to allow an input force to be transmitted around a corner. You can see them on bicycle brakes or a sack barrow.

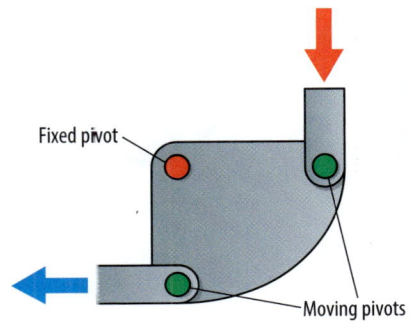

Figure 1.5.3 A bell crank

> **Apply it**
> Draw a diagram to explain how the bell crank system works on a mechanism on a bicycle.

Reverse motion linkage

This is also based on a class 1 lever but it reverses the motion of the input, such as on windscreen wipers or a gear lever in a car.

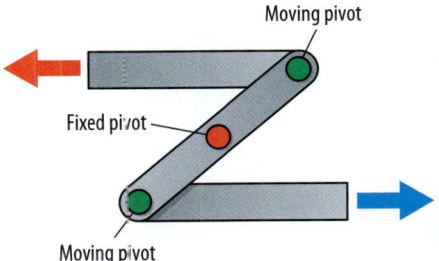

Figure 1.5.4 Reverse motion linkage

> **Exam-style question**
> Explain how you can create a larger output movement from the reverse motion linkage shown to the left. **(2 marks)**

Cams

Cams convert rotary motion into reciprocating and oscillating motion.

Cams with different shapes or profiles are attached to a rotating shaft to provide different outputs that are transmitted to a **follower** held against it. There can be three stages of movement:

- **rise** (moves the follower up)
- **fall** (moves the follower down)
- **dwell** (the follower remains stationary).

Common cam profiles include drop (snail), pear or circular and each is used for specific purposes.

> **Key terms**
> **Cam:** a mechanism for converting rotary motion into reciprocation or oscillating (up and down/back and forth) motion.
> **Follower:** a device that follows the movement of a cam profile to provide a desired output in a connecting part.

1 Core content

	Pear-shaped	**Eccentric/circular**	**Drop (Snail)**
Effect of shape	• Motionless (dwells) for about half the cycle • During the second half it rises and falls	• Circular to give a smooth continuous movement as the follower rises or falls	• Gives a slow rise with a spiral cross-section and then a sudden fall
Example	• Opens and closes valves in a car engine	• In a fuel pump or in steam engines	• Used in hammers/punches or machines needing a sudden drop
	(pear-shaped cam diagram)	(eccentric/circular cam diagram)	(drop/snail cam diagram)

Table 1.5.2 Shapes of cam

> **Apply it**
>
> Draw the profile of a cam that would create a uniform rise and a sudden fall in a cam follower. What is its name?

Followers

Different followers are used for specific purposes, but all slide or roll on the external profile of the cam.

Roller	**Knife edge**	**Flat**
(roller follower diagram)	(knife edge follower diagram)	(flat follower diagram)
• Used when higher speeds are required, such as in engines • Rolling motion reduces **friction** so it will wear better • Has separate parts in the roller mechanism and contends with forces pushing them to the side	• Used when accuracy is required, such as in an embroidery machine, as the cam's profile is followed closely • Suffers from a rapid rate of wear and contends with forces pushing them to the side	• Used when higher load bearing capabilities are required, such as in a steam engine • Has reduced forces pushing it, but suffers from increased friction • The larger surface area means it could rotate, but has larger load carrying abilities

Table 1.5.3 Types of follower

> **Exam-style question**
>
> Explain the movement of a follower while the cam is at the dwell stage of its rotation.
> **(2 marks)**

> **Key term**
>
> **Friction:** the resistance to movement between two surfaces that are trying to slide against each other. Friction generates heat.

1.5 Mechanical devices used to produce movement

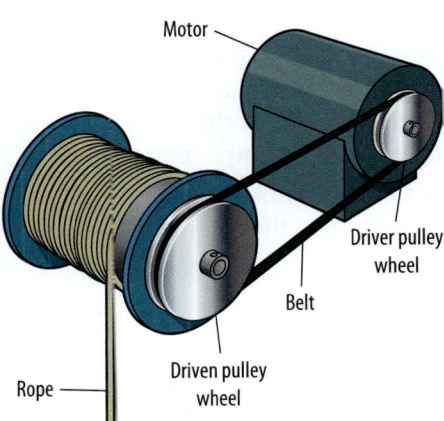

Figure 1.5.5 Example of winch using simple pulley system

Pulleys and belts

Pulleys and belts transmit rotary motion from a driver shaft to a driven shaft and are a drive mechanism for tools such as a pillar drill. A pulley is a wheel with a shaped groove and the belt fits in the groove, connecting two pulleys. Motion is transferred by friction. In this configuration, the driver pulley and driven pulley rotate in the same direction.

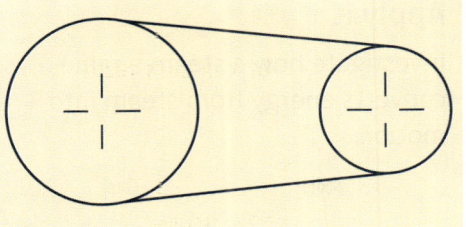

Figure 1.5.6 Graphic symbol of a pulley system

V-belt

V-belts are shaped to increase the force that can be transferred. The V-shape increases the gripping area by having sloping sides. This increases efficiency by reducing any slipping and it also tightens the drive surfaces as it runs, as it wedges into the pulley wheel.

Velocity ratio

When using pulley wheels of different sizes, the smaller one will spin faster. By comparing the size of the two pulleys we can calculate the velocity ratio (VR).

> **Maths in practice 3**
>
> **Calculating velocity ratio in a pulley system**
>
> Calculate the velocity ratio of the pulley system shown below.
>
> $$VR = \frac{\text{Driven pulley diameter}}{\text{Driver pulley diameter}}$$
>
>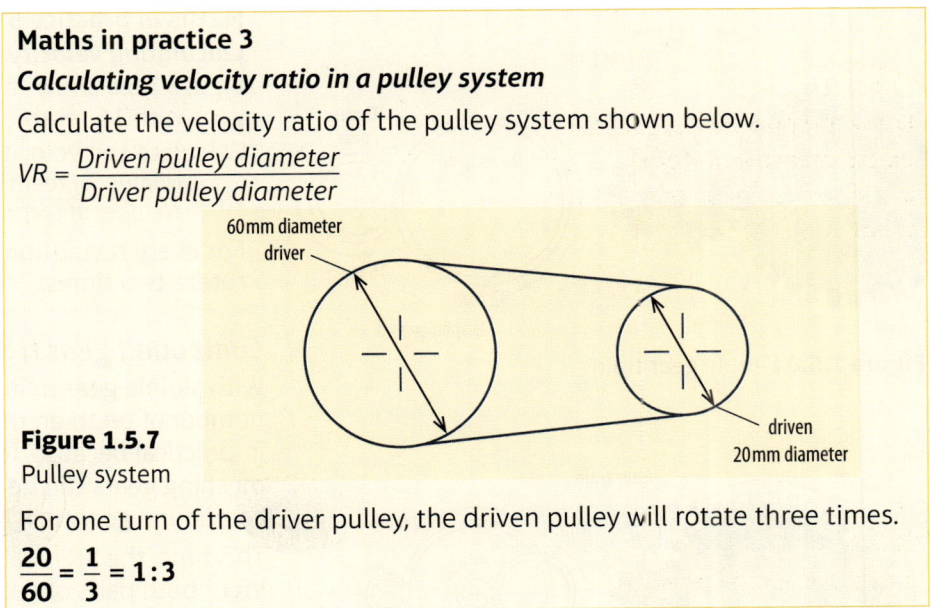
>
> **Figure 1.5.7** Pulley system
>
> For one turn of the driver pulley, the driven pulley will rotate three times.
>
> $$\frac{20}{60} = \frac{1}{3} = 1:3$$

> **Apply it**
>
> Identify the machines in your school workshop that have a pulley system as the drive mechanism. What are the advantages of using pulleys? How can different speeds be achieved?

Input and output speeds

Pulleys are usually connected to a motor or another power source. The input speed is known and the output speed of the pulley system can be calculated.

> **Maths in practice 4**
>
> **Calculating output speed of a pulley system**
>
> In the pulley system above, the input speed is 1800 revolutions per minute (rpm). Calculate the output speed of the pulley system.
>
> $$\text{Output speed} = \frac{\text{Input speed}}{\text{Velocity ratio}} = \frac{1800}{1/3} = \textbf{5400 rpm}$$
>
> The driven pulley is rotating at 1800 rpm and the output speed is 5400 rpm.

1 Core content

> **Apply it**
> Investigate how a steam engine converts energy from steam into motion.
>
>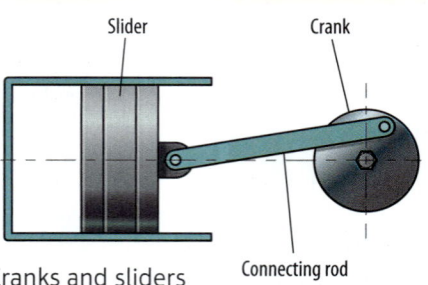
> Cranks and sliders

> **Exam-style question**
> Calculate the length of the crank arm used in a crank and slider mechanism if the slider has a maximum movement of 30 mm.
> **(3 marks)**

Cranks and sliders

These mechanisms convert the rotary motion in a crank to reciprocating motion in a slider. The distance the slider moves depends on the size of the crank arm. The crank arm can be used as the driving force, such as in the crankshaft and pistons of a car or to compress air in the cylinder of a compressor.

The slider can also operate as the driver and turn the crank, for example in steam engines, where the wheels are driven by the pressure of the steam pushing the slider.

The distance moved by the slider is twice the radius of movement of the crank arm.

Gear types

A gear is a toothed wheel fixed to a shaft that connects (meshes) with other gears to change the speed or direction of rotation of a driving mechanism. Gears have an advantage over pulley systems, because the meshing prevents slippage so that greater forces can be applied.

Simple gear trains

A simple gear train is when two spur gears are meshed and fixed on parallel shafts. Simple gear trains reverse the driver gear's direction of the rotation and the driven gear will turn in the opposite direction. When the gears are different sizes (with more or fewer teeth) speeds can be increased or decreased. The amount of change in speed is called the velocity ratio.

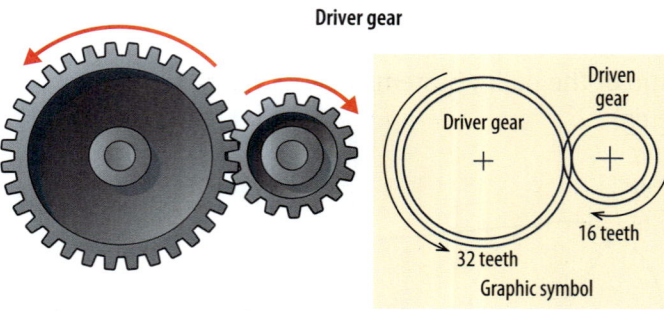
Figure 1.5.8 Simple gear train

> **Maths in practice 5**
> **Calculating velocity ratio of a simple gear system**
> Figure 1.5.8 shows a driver gear with 32 teeth and a driven gear with 16 teeth.
> Calculate the velocity ratio of the gear system.
> $$VR = \frac{\text{Number of teeth on driven gear}}{\text{Number of teeth on driver gear}} = \frac{16}{32} = \frac{1}{2} = \mathbf{1:2}$$
> For every revolution of the driver gear, the driven gear will rotate two times.

Compound gear trains

With simple gear trains, the speed change is limited to the number of teeth on the two gears. A large difference is impractical because, for larger speed changes, several pairs of meshing gears can be combined for a higher velocity ratio. A compound gear train has more than one gear on a shaft.

This time, the VR is calculated by working out the combined VR of both pairs of gears. Figure 1.5.9 shows a compound gear train where gear A is driving gear B (simple gear train 1). Gear B is connected to gear C and spins at the same speed. Gear C then drives gear D (simple gear train 2).

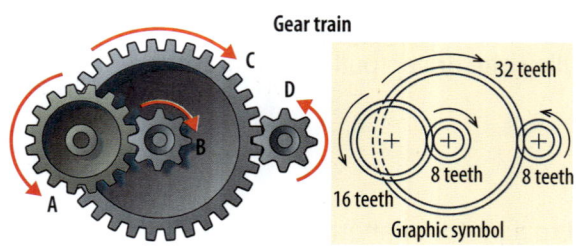
Figure 1.5.9 Compound gear train

> **Maths in practice 6**
> **Calculating velocity ratio of a compound gear system**
> Figure 1.5.9 shows a compound gear train. Gear A drives gear B. Gear B is connected to gear C and spins at the same speed. Gear C drives gear D. Calculate the velocity ratio of the gear system.
> Total VR = VR of gear train 1 (A to B) × VR of gear train 2 (C to D)
> $= 1:2 \times 1:4 = 1:8 = \mathbf{8}$
> For every revolution of the driver gear, the driven gear will rotate eight times.
> Further gears can create a significant speed change.

1.5 Mechanical devices used to produce movement

Idler gear

In a simple gear train of two meshed spur gears, the driver gear and the driven gear rotate in opposite directions. The driver and driven gears rotate in the same direction. It does not have any impact on the output speed.

The velocity ratio is still based on the driver and driven gears.

Figure 1.5.10 Idler gears

Revolutions per minute calculations

Revolutions per minute (rpm) is the number of times a device, such as a gear or wheel, rotates around a fixed axis in 1 minute. The driver gear and driven gears rotate at different speeds, if they are different sizes. This is dependent on the velocity ratio (often called gear ratio in relation to gears).

> **Maths in practice 7**
> *Calculating output of a gear system*
> A driver gear rotating at 100 rpm is connected to a gear system with a gear ratio of 1 : 18. Calculate the output speed of the gear system.
>
> Output speed = $\frac{\text{input speed}}{\text{gear ratio}} = \frac{100}{1/18} = 100 \times 18 =$ **1800 rpm**
>
> The output speed is 18 times faster than the input speed, but the **torque** has been reduced.

> **Exam-style question**
> A designer needs to have an input speed of 800 rpm and output speed of 3200 rpm in a simple gear system. If the driven gear has 20 teeth, calculate how many teeth does the driver gear need to have? **(3 marks)**

> **Key term**
> **Torque:** a measure of a system's turning power.

Bevel gears

These specialist gears can transmit rotary motion through 90 degrees. An example is a hand drill. Bevel gears vary in size to achieve different gear ratios and output speeds. Figure 1.5.11 has a gear ratio of 1 : 3. Two same-sized gears are called mitre gears; they still turn through 90 degrees but the output and input speeds are equal.

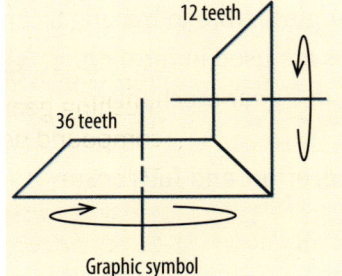

Figure 1.5.11 Bevel gears

> **Apply it**
> Identify another gear mechanism that transfers motion through 90° and find an example of where it may be used.

Rack and pinion

This system uses a gear wheel and a rack to change rotary motion to linear motion or vice versa. Examples are a pillar drill or a car steering system. The rack's movement is determined by the number of teeth on the pinion gear and the number of teeth per metre (TPM) on the rack.

Figure 1.5.12 Rack and pinion

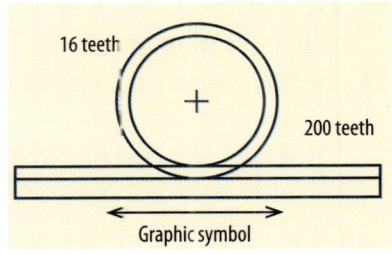

1 Core content

Maths in practice 8
Calculating output movement of a rack and pinion

A pinion gear has 60 teeth and it is meshed with a rack that has 200 teeth per metre. Calculate how far the rack will move for one revolution of the pinion gear.

$$\frac{\text{Number of teeth on pinion}}{\text{Number of teeth on rack per metre}} \times 1 \text{ metre} = \frac{60}{200} = \frac{3}{10} \text{ metre} = \textbf{300 mm}$$

Exam-style question

A compound gear train in Figure 1.5.9 earlier in this topic has two pairs of meshed spur gears. The driver gear is rotating at 3000 rpm. What is the output speed of gear D?

(1 mark)

Summary

Key points to remember:

- Modern and smart materials can react to their surroundings.
- Composite materials combine two or more materials to improve their properties.
- The four types of movement are linear, reciprocation, rotary and oscillation.
- Class 1, 2 or 3 levers change mechanical advantage.
- Linkages transmit force over a distance.
- Cams and followers convert reciprocating movement into linear movement.
- Pulleys can be used in drive mechanisms in a range of products.
- Cranks and sliders convert reciprocating movement into linear movement and vice versa.
- Gears systems can be modified to influence speed and movement.

Checkpoint

Strengthen

S1 Evaluate the use of carbon fibre over glass fibre in making a car body.
S2 Describe three ways that agrotextiles are used in farming.
S3 Explain the purpose of an idler gear in a gear mechanism.
S4 Name the four types of movement.
S5 Draw a class 3 lever and label its load, effort and fulcrum.

Challenge

C1 Sketch a compound gear system with a gear ratio of 50:1 using only the following gears: 100T (teeth), 60T, 50T, 40T, 30T, 10T.
C2 Investigate the drive system used on a bicycle and explain why it is used instead of a pulley or gear system.
C3 Evaluate the advantages of a smart material such as a shape-memory alloy over an electronic sensor system in an automatic window opener.
C4 Identify ways that a decathlon competitor could improve their performance by wearing specialist sports textiles.

1.6 Electronic systems

Learning objectives

By the end of this section, you should know:
- how an electronic system can make a product function
- the role of control devices and components
- some of the input devices and output devices that can be used to make an electronic system.

Electronic systems can have singular or multiple **input** and **output devices**, and sometimes they have a controller between them. The system reads the **input signals** and controls the **output signals** according to the instructions in the **program** it has been given:

INPUT DEVICE → CONTROL → OUTPUT DEVICE

For example, when you use a computer you move a mouse or press buttons on a keyboard. These are input devices that give information to the computer. The computer controller reads the inputs, and its program tells it what to do. The output devices could be the screen, a printer, a laser cutter, or a very complicated robot in a huge factory.

To design an electronic system you need to know about the input devices and output devices you could use.

Key terms

Input device: something that can give an input signal to the system.

Output device: something that responds to an instruction of change in control elements.

Input signal: information given to the system by an input device.

Output signal: an instruction the system gives to an output device.

Program: a set of instructions the system controller has been given to make the electronic system do what it is supposed to do. If a transistor (see page 34) is used, there is no program, just a simple switching action due to the rise in voltage on the base of the transistor above 0.6 volts.

Resistance: an electrical quantity that is a measure of how the device or wire reduces the electric current flow through it.

Sensors

A sensor is affected by the conditions around it. Sensors are good input devices because they can give an input signal to an electronic system.

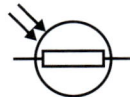

Figure 1.6.1 The circuit symbol used for LDR

Light-dependent resistor

When light falls on the sensing area of a light-dependent resistor (LDR) its **resistance** changes:
- In the light resistance is low, so electricity flows.
- In the dark resistance is high, so not much electricity flows.

Thermistor

A thermistor is a temperature-dependent resistor. Its resistance changes with temperature.
- When it is hot, the resistance is low.
- When it is cold, the resistance is higher.

Some electronic thermometers use a thermistor. As the temperature changes, the system measures the resistance of the thermistor and turns it into a number to display on a screen.

Figure 1.6.2 The circuit symbol used for a thermistor

Apply it

A thermistor can be used in the thermostat of a central heating system. Describe how you think the electronic system that controls central heating keeps a room at the right temperature.

1 Core content

Control devices and components

As well as sensors, there are some other **components** that can be used to give an input signal to an electronic **circuit**.

Single-throw switch

A single-throw switch has a button that switches between on and off. It is a simple control device that the user can operate to turn a circuit on or off.

Figure 1.6.3 The circuit symbol used for a single-throw switch

Resistors

A resistor is a component that can be added to a circuit to change its resistance. This means it can limit the flow of electricity through part of the circuit. Resistors can be used to:

- protect delicate components by stopping too much electricity flowing through them
- help control the flow of electricity around a circuit.

Figure 1.6.4 The circuit symbol used for a resistor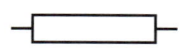

Transistor

A transistor acts like a tiny electronic switch. It has three connections. A small **voltage** at the base connection turns it on and lets a larger **current** flow into the collector and out of the emitter. Transistors are useful in sensing circuits to amplify (make bigger) the small current you get from some sensors. A transistor is a **semi-conductor** that acts like an electronic switch depending upon the voltage across the base and emitter. You can get a single transistor to build into your own circuits. Transistors can be made extremely small by etching them onto silicon wafers known as silicon chips.

Figure 1.6.5 The circuit symbol used for a transistor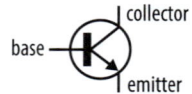

Device	Advantages	Disadvantages
LDRs	Inexpensive	Need to be positioned
Thermistors	Low cost	Need careful placement to be effective
Switches	Wide variety available	May fail mechanically after high usage
Transistors	Easily improve the sensitivity of sensing circuits	Can be destroyed by heat when soldering
Resistors	Available in a wide range of values	A circuit will not work if the wrong value is selected due to incorrect reading of the colour code

Table 1.6.1 Advantages and disadvantages of input devices

Outputs

In an electronic system, output devices are controlled by the system. They can be simple things like lights that are turned on and off or complex things like computer screens that output a lot of information.

Buzzer

A buzzer makes a sound. Buzzers can be useful in a sensing device to give people a warning that something needs their attention.

Figure 1.6.6 The circuit symbol used for a buzzer

Light-emitting diodes

A light-emitting diode (LED) gives out light when electricity is passed through it. LEDs can be small coloured indicator lights or bright enough to light up a room in a house.

Figure 1.6.7 The circuit symbol used for an LED

> **Key terms**
>
> **Component:** an individual piece of a circuit.
> **Circuit:** individual components are joined up with a conductive material so electricity can flow through them and perform a task.
> **Voltage:** the amount of potential electrical force available that could make electricity flow.
> **Current:** the amount of electricity that is flowing through a circuit.
> **Semi-conductor:** a material that allows electricity to flow under certain conditions. It can behave as an insulator or conductor.

Summary

Key points to remember:
- An electronic system has a control program that uses inputs to make outputs happen.
- Light-dependent resistors and thermistors are sensors that make good input devices because their resistance changes as light or temperature change.
- Resistors can be used to help control the current around a circuit.
- Output devices are controlled by the system and have clear functions, like lights and buzzers.

Checkpoint

Strengthen
S1 What are the three main parts of an electronic system?
S2 Name two possible input devices.
S3 Name two possible output devices.

Challenge
C1 Draw a block diagram for a computer, showing some of its input devices and output devices.
C2 Find out the units of resistance and explain how resistance is marked on a resistor.

1.7 Programmable components

Learning objectives
By the end of this section, you should know:
- how flowcharts can be used to create a program
- how to switch outputs on and off in relation to inputs and decisions
- what analogue inputs are and how they can be used
- what delays and loops can be used for in a circuit.

Programmable components are used in a variety of applications, for example alarm systems. In school they allow you to add intelligence to your projects. There are many types of PIC (Programmable Interface Controllers) micro-controllers available, for example the GENIE range. These are programmed and tested by software that makes use of flowcharts.

How to make use of flowcharts

A computer program is usually a set of questions with a yes or no answer. A flowchart is a way of planning a program in an easy to read diagram.

Apply it

How could you change the program so the light goes off again when it gets light?

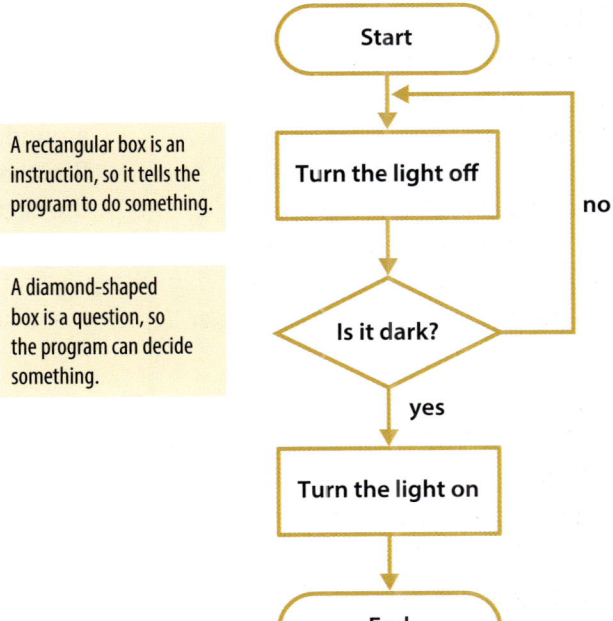

Figure 1.7.1 A flowchart for a simple outside light that comes on in the dark. The light is off to start with, comes on when it gets dark and just stays on forever

1 Core content

> **Key terms**
>
> **Analogue:** a signal that can vary up and down through a range of values.
>
> **Feedback loop:** a loop in a program that goes back to an earlier point to keep repeating that part of the program.

Inputs and decisions: switching outputs on or off

An electronic system uses the questions in its program to make decisions. These decisions tell its output devices what to do. When the control program detects an input, it moves to the next part of the program, and follows the instructions to make an output happen. It is important for a designer to know exactly what they want a product to do, and then break it down into a set of simple steps that can be put into a flowchart.

How to process and respond to analogue inputs

Some sensors give out an **analogue** signal. This means they can give a range of values. LDRs and thermistors are analogue devices. Their resistance goes up and down as levels or temperatures change. This means a system can be programmed to respond to different levels. The outside light has a variable resistor that lets you change the light level at which the light turns on.

How to use simple routines to control outputs

There are some simple routines that can be added to a program to change what happens:

- **Time delay.** A program instruction that says 'wait 10' means the program will wait 10 seconds then go on to the next instruction. You could use this to make a light flash on and off as quickly or slowly as you want.

- **Count.** A program can be told to count how many times it gets an input, and perhaps give an output every ten pushes of a button.

- **Feedback loop.** This sends the program back to an earlier point to do the same thing repeatedly. This is how a system monitors a sensor – it goes around in a loop asking the same question until the answer changes. The flowchart below shows a second feedback loop added to the circuit. Now the light comes on in the dark and goes off when it gets light.

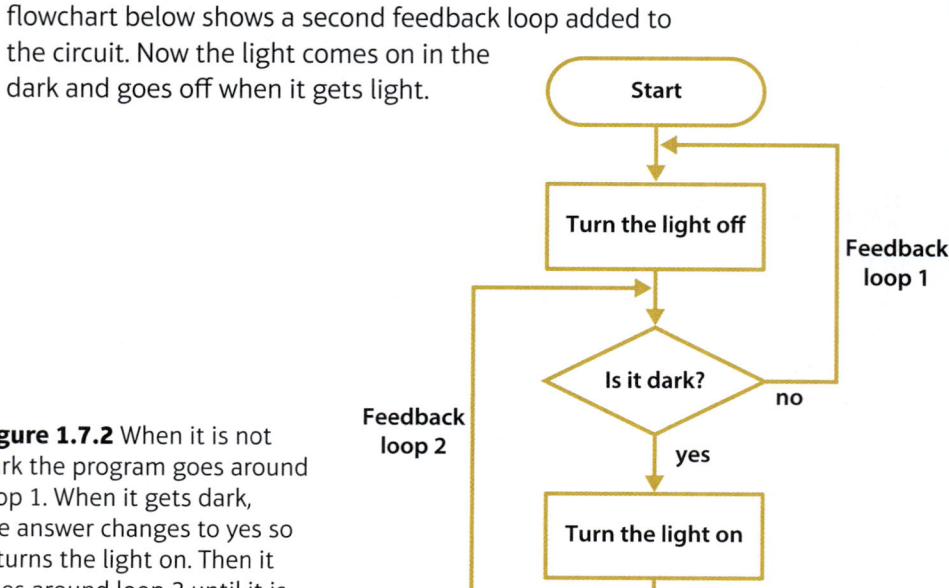

Figure 1.7.2 When it is not dark the program goes around loop 1. When it gets dark, the answer changes to yes so it turns the light on. Then it goes around loop 2 until it is not dark any more. Finally, it goes back to loop 1 and turns the light off

Summary

Key points to remember:
- A flowchart is a good way to plan a computer program.
- A flowchart uses instructions and yes/no questions to create a program.
- Analogue inputs give a range of values to the controller.
- Time delays and counts are useful in a program.
- Feedback loops allow a program to monitor a sensor.

Checkpoint

Strengthen

S1 What do the rectangle- and diamond-shaped boxes in a flowchart mean?
S2 Give two examples of analogue sensors.
S3 What does a feedback loop do?

Challenge

C1 Write a flowchart for a light with a motion sensor that makes the light come on for 60 seconds when someone walks past. (Hint: start by thinking which yes/no questions to ask.)
C2 Write a flowchart for a heating system that keeps a room at a steady temperature.

1.8 Categorisation of ferrous and non-ferrous metals

Learning objectives

By the end of this section, you should know:
- the types, properties, structure and uses of some common metals.

Ferrous metals

Ferrous metals contain iron (ferrite), so most have magnetic properties. Small amounts of other metals or elements may provide other properties. Ferrous metals are vulnerable to rust when exposed to moisture, except for stainless steel and wrought iron.

Apply it

Mild steel can be cut with a hacksaw or drilled. Why are other types of steel able to cut through mild steel?

1 Core content

Type	Properties	Composition	Melting point	Example uses
Mild steel	Tough, ductile, malleable, magnetic, high tensile strength, easily joined, poor corrosion resistance	Iron + 0.1–0.3% carbon	1400°C	Screws, nails, bolts, girders, car body panels
Stainless steel	• Corrosion resistant, hard, tough, sometimes magnetic, resists wear, difficult to cut • Specific properties can be altered by varying the alloyed metals	**Alloy:** Carbon steel + 10.5–18% chromium 8% nickel 8% manganese	1400°C	Kitchenware, sinks, cutlery, medical equipment
Cast iron	Hard skin, brittle, soft core, good in compression, self-lubricating, magnetic	Iron + > 2–6% carbon	1200°C	Machine parts, vices, brake discs, manhole covers

Table 1.8.1 Some types of ferrous metal

> **Key term**
>
> **Alloy:** a mixture of two or more metals or elements, which has improved properties and characteristics.

> **Exam-style question**
>
> Explain **two** reasons why stainless steel would be chosen over mild steel for the bolts on a bicycle. **(4 marks)**

Non-ferrous metals

These do not contain iron, so have a higher resistance to rust and corrosion. They are not magnetic and tend to be more malleable than ferrous metals.

Type	Properties	Composition	Melting point	Example uses
Aluminium	Greyish white: corrosion resistant, malleable, ductile, easily machined, good heat/electrical conductor, excellent strength-to-weight ratio, polishes well	Pure metal	660°C	Aircraft, foil, window frames, engine parts, drinks cans
Copper	Reddy brown: corrosion resistant, malleable, ductile, tough, easily machined, good heat/electrical conductor, good hot or cold working, polishes well	Pure metal	1100°C	Electrical wire, gas and water pipes, printed circuits, roofing
Brass	Yellow: corrosion resistant, easily machined, good heat/electrical conductor, casts well, harder than copper, polishes well	Alloy: 65% copper 35% zinc	900–940°C	Plumbing fittings, door fittings, locks, musical instruments

Table 1.8.2 Some types of non-ferrous metal

> **Exam-style question**
>
> Explain **two** reasons why aluminium would be used for drinks cans in preference to mild steel. **(4 marks)**

1.8 Categorisation of ferrous and non-ferrous metals

Link it up
For information about advantages and disadvantages of metals go to Metals 2.2.

Properties
The mechanical properties of metals define how they react to forces. A large force will deform metal. A temporary change is called elastic deformation and the metal will spring back into shape. A permanent change is called plastic deformation and the metal stays in the new shape. Three properties are **ductility**, **malleability** and **hardness**. All ductile materials are malleable but not all malleable materials are ductile.

Hard materials are often brittle, with a low resistance to impact, and break easily. This property is important for cutting tools such as saws, drills and files. Diamond is the hardest naturally occurring material and is measured at 10 on the Mohs scale (a scale that measures hardness). The mineral, talc is 1, aluminium is 2–2.9 and steels are 5–8.5.

Key terms
Ductility: ability of a material to deform by bending, twisting or stretching; ability to be drawn out without breaking. Ductility in metals increases with temperature.

Malleability: ability of a material to be permanently deformed in all directions without fracture. It increases with temperature.

Hardness: ability of a material to resist deformation, indentation or penetration. Hard materials can resist abrasion, drilling, impact, scratching, and wear and tear.

Apply it
Why is it useful for metals used in the construction industry to have a degree of elasticity when they are in use?

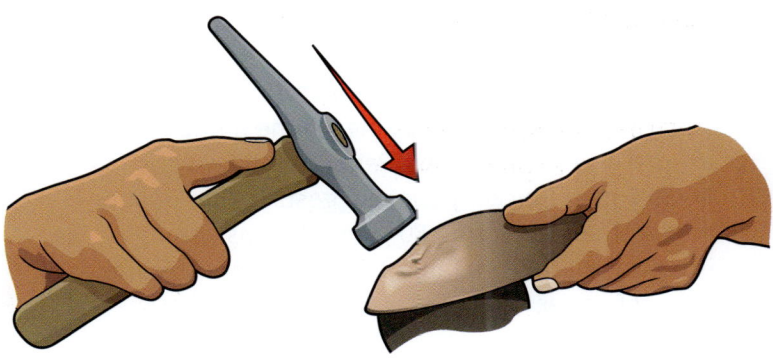

Figure 1.8.1 Malleable materials, such as copper, can be formed into shape by hammering

Summary
Key points to remember:
- Metals are categorised as ferrous or non-ferrous.
- A mixture of two or more metals is called an alloy.
- Metals have useful mechanical properties such as ductility, malleability and hardness.

Checkpoint
Strengthen
S1 Explain two reasons why copper may be suitable for the roof of a building.
S2 Name the element that is added to iron to make mild steel.
S3 Explain what is meant by the term 'malleability'.

Challenge
C1 Mild steel has 0.35% carbon content. Describe what will happen if you increase the carbon content.
C2 Summarise what makes a metal an alloy. Identify two further alloys and explain why the 'new' metal is suited to a particular application.

1 Core content

1.9 Papers and boards

> **Learning objective**
> By the end of this section, you should know:
> - the types, properties, structure and uses of paper and boards.

Paper

Paper consists of fine cellulose fibres, usually from wood but also hemp, flax, cotton or bamboo, pressed together with water and then dried. To achieve the required texture and surface finish, chemicals are added to the pulp – brightening bleaches, for example. It may also be coated with an agent that fills the minuscule pits between the fibres, for a smooth, flat surface with better opacity, lustre and colour-absorption.

In Europe, paper and board is measured in grams per square metre (gsm), which means the number of grams a 1 m × 1 m sheet weighs. Paper usually weighs 80–220 gsm. Thicker paper suggests higher quality – copier sheets are often 80 gsm, whereas writing paper is typically 120 gsm. Table 1.9.1 gives some examples of types of paper.

> **Apply it**
> Paper and card are extremely useful materials that are processed from wood fibres. They come in many different sizes and forms.
> - How many paper products have you used today?
> - Why do you think that some boards are laminated with other materials such as foil?
> - How many different paper sizes do you know?

> **Key term**
> **Paper:** thin, flat material made from natural fibres, weighing less than 220 gsm.

Type	Description	Uses	Advantages	Disadvantages
Copier paper 80 gsm	Thin, lightweight, cheap, bright white paper, with a smooth, bleached, uncoated surface	Writing, printing, drawing	Takes colour well, good surface for pencils, pens and markers, cheap, readily available and in a range of colours	Can be prone to jamming printer feed mechanisms
Cartridge paper 120–150 gsm	Creamy, thick heavyweight paper	General drawing and printing, can be used with watercolour paints without buckling	Accepts most drawing media, opaque	Costs more than copier paper
Tracing paper 60–90 gsm	Thin, smooth and translucent, made by beating to remove air and processing to make a dense, strong paper, usually 60–90 gsm	Art, making copies, envelope windows, overlays on working drawings	Strong, translucent	Can be expensive, limited ink absorption and longer drying time

Table 1.9.1 Properties and structure of examples of paper

1.9 Papers and boards

Board

Papers weighing more than 220 gsm are generally classified as **boards**. Their thickness is measured in microns (μm) which is 1/1000 of a millimetre. A two-ply (layer) board is 200 microns thick. Table 1.9.2 gives some examples of types of board.

> **Key term**
>
> **Board:** thick paper or layers of paper more than 220 gsm.

Type	Description	Uses	Advantages	Disadvantages
Folding boxboard	Stiff layers consisting of: 1. A printable bleached virgin pulp top surface 2. Unbleached yellowish centre layers 3. A bleached inside layer	• Cereal boxes, food and health care packaging, cartons	• Excellent for scoring and bending without splitting • Accepts print well • Inexpensive	• Lower strength than solid white board
Corrugated board	• Two or more layers of fluted paper sandwiched between two paper liners • Available in different thicknesses • Strong and lightweight	• Protective packaging, for example boxes for electrical products and CD sleeves	• Impact resistant, inexpensive, recyclable	• Brown finish does not convey quality • Can deform under pressure • Not water resistant
Solid white board	• Strong, rigid board made from pure, bleached wood pulp • Excellent printing surface	• Book covers, food, cosmetics and medicine packaging	• Strong, rigid, accepts print well	• Can be expensive

Table 1.9.2 Properties and structure of examples of board

> **Apply it**
>
> Collect examples of packaging using the boards in Table 1.9.2. Photograph them and annotate each photograph explaining why you think that material has been chosen for the product.

Properties

Property	Description
Flexibility	• Amount material bends when a force is applied (stiffness), determined by its thickness and weight • Flexural stiffness is resistance to an external bending force • Handling stiffness is the ability to support its own weight
Printability	• Ability to accept a printed image onto its surface (porosity) • Affected by surface properties, such as smoothness or finish, and structural properties, such as bulk or thickness • Not the same as print quality, which is determined by other factors such as alignment of plates on the machinery
Biodegradability	• Ability to be broken down by bacteria or other biological means • Most uncoated paper products are biodegradable because they are made from wood pulp • Compostable means that a material can biodegrade in less than 12 weeks

Table 1.9.3 Some working properties of paper and boards

1 Core content

Apply it

Carry out a printing test on tracing paper, cartridge paper and copier paper. Stamp each one with an ink stamp. Smudge them after 30 seconds and then after a minute. Record your results in the table below.

Smudged after…	Tracing paper	Cartridge paper	Copier paper
30 seconds	Yes/No	Yes/No	Yes/No
60 seconds	Yes/No	Yes/No	Yes/No

Table 1.9.4 Ink drying times

Look at the ink under a magnifying glass. How crisp is each print?

Exam-style questions

The box in the image is used to package CDs to send to supermarkets.

a. Explain **one** reason why this material is suitable for the box. **(2 marks)**

b. Explain **one** disadvantage of this material. **(2 marks)**

Summary

Key points to remember:
- Different paper and board products have different structures and properties.
- Physical properties such as flexibility may affect the quality of the finished product.

Checkpoint

Strengthen

S1 Name three different types of paper.
S2 State an advantage of using folding boxboard.
S3 Explain why printability might affect the quality of a finished product.

Challenge

C1 Describe and compare the properties of two different boards. Evaluate which one would be best for a new perfume package.

1.10 Thermoforming and thermosetting polymers

> **Learning objectives**
>
> By the end of this section, you should know about:
> - the types, properties, structure and uses of thermoforming polymers
> - the types, properties, structure and uses of thermosetting polymers.

Polymers have a wide variety of uses in everyday life. A **synthetic polymer** is usually made from oil-based petrochemicals, but coal and gas can also be used. The crude oil is refined and mixed with other chemicals and can be used to produce many types of polymer.

A wide variety of polymers is available, with engineers continuing to develop the range to meet the requirements of designers and manufacturers. There are two main categories of polymer that you will need to know about: **thermoforming polymers** and **thermosetting polymers**.

> **Apply it**
>
> How many items can you think of that are made from a polymer? Of these, how many polymers can you name? Do you know why polymers have been used to make these items?

Thermoforming polymers

Thermoforming polymers are commonly used to make everyday products. They can offer a wide range of properties that make them suitable for an extensive array of uses. One of the biggest advantages of thermoforming polymers is that they can be recycled, which offers huge benefits to the manufacturer in reducing waste, as well as being attractive to the consumer because it helps to conserve non-renewable resources and prevents more waste going to landfill.

The list of thermoforming polymers available is extensive. You will need to know more about:

- acrylic
- high-impact polystyrene (**HIPS**)
- biodegradable polymers – Biopol®.

You can find out more about these polymers and their uses in Table 1.10.1 on page 44.

> **Key terms**
>
> **Synthetic polymer:** a synthetic material made mostly from oil; normally referred to as plastic.
>
> **Thermoforming polymer:** a material that can be reshaped by application of heat. This type of material can be recycled and made into other products.
>
> **Thermosetting polymer:** a material that cannot be reshaped by reheating. This type of material cannot be recycled.
>
> **HIPS:** high-impact polystyrene: a thermoplastic commonly used for vacuum forming.

1 Core content

Thermoforming polymer	Form	Properties	Common uses	Advantages/ Disadvantages
Acrylic (PMMA: polymethyl methacrylate)	• Sheets, rods and tubes • Available in a wide range of opaque and translucent colours • Also available in a wide range of sizes	• Tough, easily finished, easily cleaned, food safe and can be easily scratched	• Shop signs, rear car lights, baths, fish tanks and menu holders	• Widely available • Common in the school environment as it is easy to cut and finish to a high standard • Can be shaped using heat • Does not need painting • Breaks easily if dropped
High-impact polystyrene (HIPS)	• Sheets, rods and tubes • Available in a wide range of opaque and translucent colours • Also available in a wide range of sizes	• Lightweight, high stiffness, impact resistant but can be easily scratched	• Toys, television parts and refrigerator linings	• Commonly used for vacuum forming, but can be formed using many techniques • Compared to other polymers it has a low melting point • Becomes brittle when exposed to UV light
Biopol®	• Fibre, granules and sheets	• Lightweight, good electrical insulator, degrades over time when in contact with soil, so can safely be disposed of at landfill sites	• Disposable cups, razors, cutlery and other packaging products, surgical stitches and pins	• Degrades in soil and can be disposed of at landfill sites • Can be injection moulded and vacuum formed • Expensive to produce • Has low resistance to impact (e.g. being dropped or having something dropped onto it)

Table 1.10.1 A summary of the different types of thermoforming polymers

Thermosetting polymers

Thermosetting polymers set hard once heated and cooled. Unlike thermoforming plastic, a thermosetting plastic shape, once formed, cannot be altered through reheating. These plastics cannot be recycled and are often used in applications where they will be subjected to heat, chemicals or solvents. The molecule chains in thermosetting polymers set differently once heated and cooled, with cross-linking of the chains preventing further forming and recycling. The types of thermosetting polymers you need to know about are:

- polyester resin
- urea formaldehyde.

1.10 Thermoforming and thermosetting polymers

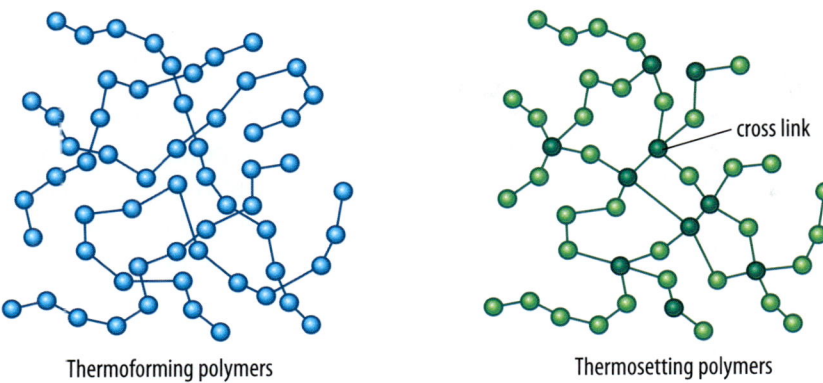

Figure 1.10.1 Structure of thermoforming and thermosetting polymers. Consider how cross-linking of molecule chains prevents the recycling of thermosetting polymers

Thermosetting polymers are widely used to make products that come into contact with heat or electricity. Some examples can be found in Table 1.10.2.

> **Key term**
>
> **Glass reinforced plastic (GRP):** a composite material made from polyester resin and glass fibres. Moulds can be laid up by hand or using a spray-on technique.

Thermosetting polymer	Form	Properties	Common uses	Advantages/Disadvantages
Polyester resin	• Thick liquid for casting and layup • Usually used with a catalyst to harden resin • Can be coloured through use of pigments	• Rigid, brittle, (unless laminated) good electrical and heat insulation, good chemical resistance	• Boat hulls and sports car bodies • Normally formed in conjunction with glass fibre • Can also be cast to form decorative objects	• Can be used with glass fibres (**glass reinforced plastic**) to create lightweight and very strong products • Can be polished to a high finish • Can chip if dropped
Urea formaldehyde	• Powder, granules, preforms	• Rigid, hard, brittle, heat resistant, excellent electrical insulation	• Electrical fittings – plugs, sockets and switches • Used as an adhesive in man-made boards	• Can be coloured using pigments • Can break if dropped

Table 1.10.2 A summary of the different types of thermosetting polymers

> **Apply it**
>
> There are many products in the home that are made from plastic. Make a list of a range of these. What properties ensure the product is successful?

> **Exam-style questions**
>
> a. Explain the difference in structure of thermoforming and thermosetting polymers. **(2 marks)**
>
> b. Explain **one** reason why some children's toys are made from high-impact polystyrene (HIPS). **(2 marks)**

1 Core content

> **Key terms**
>
> **Insulator:** a material with low conductivity preventing electrical current or heat to flow.
>
> **PVC (polyvinyl chloride):** a thermoplastic containing chlorine and carbon.

Properties of polymers

Insulator of heat

Most polymers are excellent **insulators** of heat. They are commonly used to increase the safety of products. For instance, expanded polystyrene cups offer the user's hand protection from hot drinks, while they also help to keep the drink hot for longer. Polymers are also used for handles on saucepans, kettles, hairdryers and electric heaters as other parts of the products can be extremely hot and cause injury.

Insulator of electricity

Most polymers are excellent insulators of electricity and are commonly used in products that contain electrical components. For instance, televisions, computers and electric toothbrushes all use mains electricity for power and charging of batteries but, without adequate insulation around their exterior, could cause serious injury to the user. All electrical products that are connected to mains electricity will have cables shielded by **PVC** and the plug is likely to be made from urea formaldehyde.

Toughness

Most polymers are tough. They can withstand rough handling, making them suitable for a wide range of products in the home, industry, agriculture and school. For instance, wheelie bins, buckets, watering cans, classroom chairs, car wheel trims and car bumpers all have to withstand impact, bumps and scrapes but continue to perform everyday tasks. Some polymers will fatigue and fail to perform following excessive wear.

> **Apply it**
>
> Research the system used to identify which polymers can be recycled. Identify a range of polymers that can be recycled using this system.

> **Summary**
>
> **Key points to remember:**
> - Thermoforming polymers can be recycled.
> - Thermosetting polymers cannot be recycled.
> - Most synthetic polymers are made from crude oil.
> - Polymers include the following materials: acrylic and high-impact polystyrene.

> **Checkpoint**
>
> **Strengthen**
>
> **S1** Name two polymers that are good thermal insulators.
> **S2** List three things often made from thermoforming polymers.
> **S3** Sketch the structure of a thermosetting polymer.
>
> **Challenge**
>
> **C1** Why is it not possible to recycle all polymer-based food packaging?

1.11 The categorisation of fibres, and textiles

> **Learning objectives**
>
> By the end of this section, you should know:
> - the types, properties, structure and uses of different types of fibres and textiles.

'Textiles' refers to all flexible fabrics created from **fibres**, which are fine, hair-like structures that can be made into **fabrics** by weaving, knitting or felting. Fibres are either natural or synthetic.

Natural fibres

Natural fibres from plant sources include cotton, flax, hemp, sisal, jute and coconut. Fibres from animal sources include silk, wool and mohair.

> **Key terms**
>
> **Fibres:** thread-like elements that can be formed into yarns and fabrics.
> **Fabric:** a length of flexible material constructed from fibres.
> **Staple:** the length of a fibre.

	Properties/characteristics/structure	Example applications	Advantages	Disadvantages
Example: Animal – wool	• From an animal's fleece • Made of protein molecules • Produces a short fibre or **staple** with a crimp or kink which, with the scales on the fibre, traps air, creating warmth • May be soft or coarse, depending on sheep breed	• Coats, jumpers, suits, blankets, carpets, upholstery • Grey Faced Dartmoor wool is suitable for carpet and rug making while Merino wool is suitable for fine knitted jumpers	• Warm, absorbent, breathable, durable, repels rain, hangs well, creases drop out	• Dries slowly, susceptible to moth attack, can feel itchy, washes poorly, can shrink, heavy when wet
Example: Plant – cotton	• 'Bolls', the fruit cotton plant's fruit, are machine-harvested • Saw teeth remove waste from the seed pod and the resulting fibre is called lint • Cellulose makes the fibre strong, durable and absorbent • Twenty to 30 layers of cellulose are coiled in natural springs • As the cotton fibres dry they form interlocking flat, twisted, ribbon-like shapes, ideal for spinning	• Towels, denim, socks, underwear, T-shirts, bedding • Shorter fibres make bandages and insulation	• Cool, absorbent, soft, resists abrasion, withstands frequent washing at high temperature, good drape, durable, does not stain easily, static and cling resistant, available in various weights, can be ironed at high temperatures, good colour retention	• Creases easily, burns, shrinks, dries slowly

Table 1.11.1 Summary of the properties of examples of natural fibres

1 Core content

Synthetic fibres

Artificial fibres are usually made using coal, oil and other petrol-based chemicals. Examples include polyester, acrylic, polyamide (nylon), elastane (Lycra) and Kevlar®.

	Properties/characteristics/structure	Example applications	Advantages	Disadvantages
Example: Polyester	• Simple chemical molecules (**monomers**) are joined to form polymers by polymerisation • The polymer chains are spun into a yarn	• Raincoats, fleece jackets, children's nightwear, medical textiles, working clothes	• Strong when wet or dry, dries quickly, resistant to abrasion, soft, hangs well, durable, crease and stain resistant, easy care, can be recycled, resists bacteria	• Damaged by acids, low warmth, poor absorbency, does not breathe, not environmentally friendly
Example: Acrylic	• Formed by polymerisation of at least 85% acrylonitrile or vinyl cyanide • The double bond between the first two carbon atoms is broken and the molecules join in a chain	• Imitation wool knitwear, upholstery fabrics, sportswear, fleece jackets, blankets	• Warm, dries quickly, good drape, durable, crease resistant, easy care	• Poor absorbency, feels stiff, can irritate skin

Table 1.11.2 Summary of the properties of examples of synthetic fibres

---

Key term

Monomer: a molecule that can be bonded to similar molecules to form long chains.

Apply it

1. **Test for durability:** Cut a 100 mm square of fabric into four equal pieces. Wash one at 60°, one at 40° and one at 95° five times. Keep one piece unwashed. Compare the fabrics.
2. **Testing for elasticity:** Cut three different fabrics into 300 mm by 300 mm strips. Stitch a heavy metal nut to the bottom of each. Pin onto a board so that the top edges are level. Mark the starting level of the bottom edge. Leave the board upright overnight then compare the new level with the previous one.

1.11 The categorisation of fibres, and textiles

Woven textiles

Weaving turns yarns into a fabric on a loom, which has an arrangement of warp (vertical) threads held under tension. The edges where the weft (horizontal) threads loop back form a non-fraying edge (selvedge).

	Properties/characteristics/structure	Example applications	Advantages	Disadvantages
Example: Plain weave – calico	• A simple cotton cloth • The warp and weft pass over and under each other, forming a criss-cross pattern that looks the same on both sides • Calico (muslin) is naturally grey • It may be soft or coarse	• Shirts, bags, bedding, textile crafts	• Strong, hardwearing, hangs well, same both sides, cheap to make, good background for printing and applied surface designs	• Firm, varied quality
Example: Twill weave – denim	• The weft yarn goes over two or more warp threads, repeated on the row but steps over one warp thread on the next rows to make a diagonal pattern • Denim is blue in the warp and white in the weft	• Jeans, jackets, curtains, blankets, soft furnishings	• Hardwearing, strong, hangs well, less stiff and more interesting to look at than plain weave	• Frays, thickness makes it hard to use

Table 1.11.3 Summary of the properties of examples of woven textiles

Exam-style questions

1. Explain **one** benefit of using wool felt for constructing the hat shown in the image below. **(2 marks)**
2. Explain **one** disadvantage of using wool felt in a hat. **(2 marks)**

Apply it

What are the advantages and disadvantages of a polyester football shirt over a cotton one?

1 Core content

Non-woven textiles

Fibres are layered at different angles to form a web, joined by either felting or bonding. Bonding joins the fibres with heat, solvents or adhesives, so is cheap to produce but not as strong as woven or knitted fabrics.

	Properties/ characteristics/ structure	Example applications	Advantages	Disadvantages
Example: Felted wool fabric	• Scaly fibres of wool or hair become tangled as they are rubbed together when wet • Heat and pressure are applied to join them	• Pool table surfaces, hats, bags, coats, slippers, appliqué quilts, wall hangings	• Resists chemicals and fire, does not unravel or fray, can be repeatedly compressed and released without deforming, excellent sound insulator, environmentally friendly	• Expensive, no drape, not stretchy, deforms when wet
Example: Bonded fibres/webs	• Does not fray • Weaker when wet • Can be produced in a range of weights • Not very strong	• Fusible interfacing, wet wipes, disposable overalls	• Does not fray, cheap to produce, stable and so retains shape	• Not very strong, does not drape, sometimes weaker when wet

Table 1.11.4 Summary of the properties of examples of non-woven textiles

Knitted textiles

Knitted textiles are constructed from interlocking loops of yarn and are either warp or weft.

	Properties/ characteristics/structure	Example applications	Advantages	Disadvantages
Example: Warp-knitted fabric	• Formed by vertical loops like a series of chains • Can only be produced on a machine	• Swimwear, geotextiles, lace, nets and fleece	• Fairly stretchy, retains heat, does not unravel	• Can lose shape, curls at the edges
Example: Weft-knitted fabric	• A single yarn creates interlocking loops across the fabric • If a loop breaks, a hole forms and ladders • Made by hand or machine	• T-shirts, jumpers, tops, socks	• Stretchy, comfortable, fast production	• Ladders easily

Table 1.11.5 Summary of the properties of examples of knitted textiles

1.11 The categorisation of fibres, and textiles

Properties of fibres and textiles

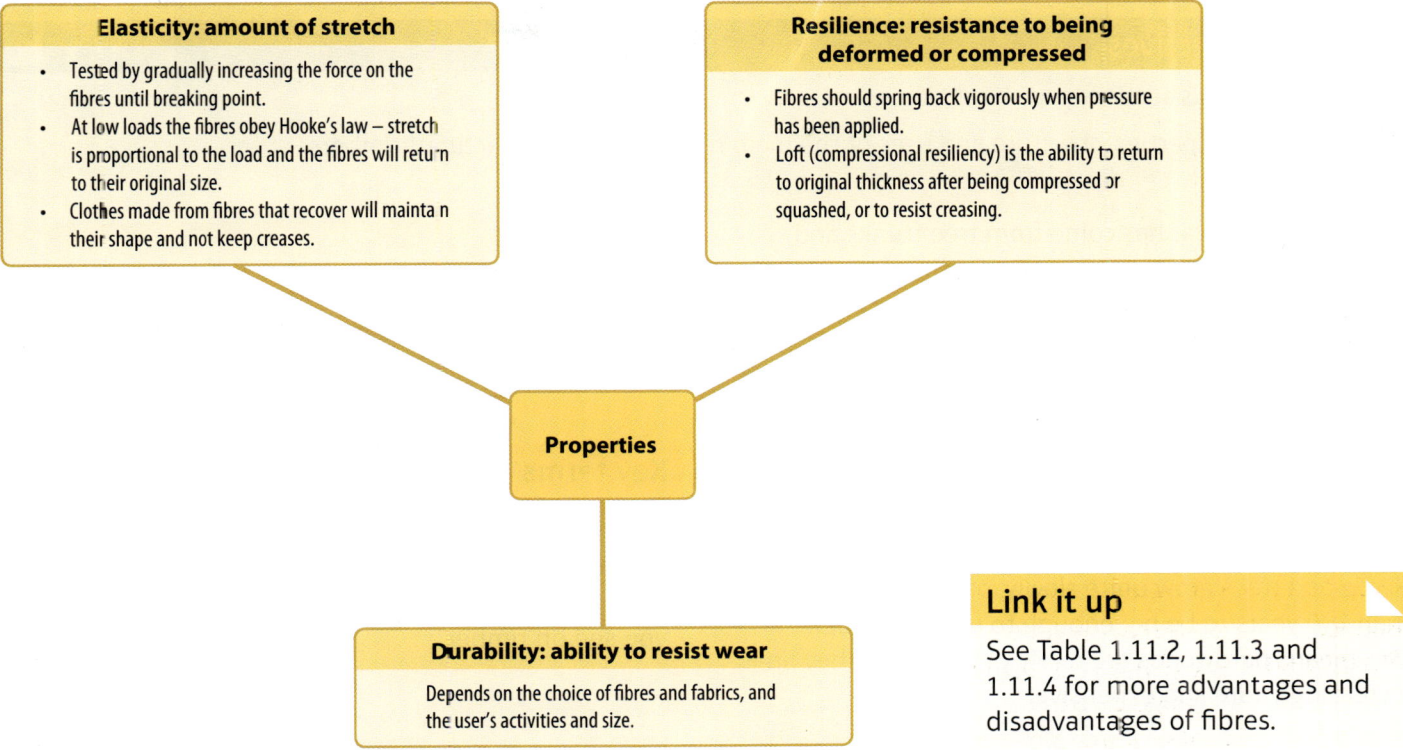

Figure 1.11.1 Properties of fibres and textiles

Link it up
See Table 1.11.2, 1.11.3 and 1.11.4 for more advantages and disadvantages of fibres.

Summary

Key points to remember:

- Natural fibres come from plants and animals.
- Synthetic fibres are artificially made from chemicals.
- The two main types of weave are plain and twill.
- Non-woven fabrics are made by either felting or bonding.
- Knitted fabrics are either warp or weft knitted.

Checkpoint

Strengthen
- **S1** Describe the advantages and disadvantages of cotton.
- **S2** Explain how felt is made.

Challenge
- **C1** Devise a test for the resilience of different textiles.
- **C2** Explain why a test for elasticity would be important when choosing fabrics for swimwear.

1 Core content

1.12 Natural and manufactured timbers

> **Learning objectives**
>
> By the end of this section, you should know:
> - the types, properties, structure and uses of the main natural and manufactured timbers.

Timber is wood that has come from tree trunks and been dried and cut into planks. Timber has been used as a building material for thousands of years to make homes, furniture and tools. Timber is still used a lot as trees grow naturally, their wood is easy to work with and it is relatively strong and lightweight.

Natural timbers: hardwoods

A **hardwood** comes from a broad-leaved tree whose seeds are enclosed in a fruit, such as an acorn. Hardwood trees grow quite slowly, often taking more than 100 years to be big enough to use for timber. This means hardwoods are rarely planted and they are increasingly rare and expensive.

> **Apply it**
>
> Make a list of wooden things you have used. Discuss why you think wood is a good material to make things from.

> **Key terms**
>
> **Hardwood:** comes from a tree with broad leaves.
>
> **Grain:** fibres run the length of a tree trunk, which give it its strength and make the distinctive patterns you see on timber.

Type	Description	Advantages	Disadvantages	Common uses
Oak		• Strong and durable • Has an attractive **grain** when well finished	• Expensive • Becoming rarer • Harder to work with than some woods • Corrodes iron and steel	• Used a lot for building houses and boats in the past • Now used for high-end furniture and wine and whisky barrels
Mahogany		• Has a very attractive finish • Quite easy to work	• Expensive • Environmental problems with sourcing from tropical forests • Oils in the wood can give some people a skin rash or breathing problems	• High-quality furniture, jewellery boxes, windows
Beech		• A tough wood • Does not crack or splinter easily • Hard	• Expensive • Not very resistant to moisture • Not suitable for exterior use	• Toys, cooking implements, solid and laminated furniture
Balsa		• Very lightweight • Easy to cut	• Much too soft and weak for most products	• Model making, primary school projects, surf board cores • Used for rafts in ancient times

Table 1.12.1 Properties of hardwoods

1.12 Natural and manufactured timbers

Natural timbers: softwoods

A **softwood** comes from a tree with needle-like leaves and seeds in a cone. Most softwood trees are **evergreen**, meaning they have leaves all year. Softwood trees grow quite quickly, and can be used for timber after about 30 years. This means they can be grown commercially, which is why softwood timber is a lot cheaper than hardwood timber.

> **Key terms**
>
> **Softwood:** a tree with needle-like leaves and seeds in a cone.
> **Evergreen:** a tree that keeps its leaves all year round.

Type	Description	Advantages	Disadvantages	Common uses
Pine		• Very durable • Easy to work • Quite cheap as it grows quickly enough to be forested • Reasonably strong, lightweight and easy to work with	• Can warp, crack and splinter more than some other woods	• House construction, for roof joists and floorboards • Furniture, doors, interior woodwork
Cedar		• Natural oils make it resistant to water and fungal growth	• More expensive than pine and not as strong	• Outdoor furniture, fences, sheds, boats

Table 1.12.2 Properties of softwoods

Manufactured timbers

Natural timber is a useful material, but because of the size of a tree trunk, it is only available in fairly narrow planks. If you want a large, thin sheet of wooden material, you need a manufactured board. Manufactured boards use timber to make a board that has different properties to plain timber.

> **Key term**
>
> **Veneer:** a thin slice of wood, about 1 mm thick. Used as a decorative surface and to make plywood.

Type	Description	Advantages	Disadvantages	Common uses
Plywood	• A tree trunk is sliced into thin layers called **veneer** • These layers are glued together with the grain lines going in alternate directions	• Flat and structurally strong • Surface looks like wood • Resistant to warping, cracking and twisting	• Quite expensive • Edges can look rather rough • Susceptible to water damage if wrong grade is used	• Building and furniture panels that need some strength
Medium density fibreboard (MDF)	• Wood dust and fibres are mixed with a glue and pressed into flat sheets under extreme heat and pressure	• Cheap (made from waste wood) • Smooth ungrained surface is good for painting or staining • Easy to machine	• Does not look good, so needs coating • Weak compared to real wood or plywood • Tools blunt quickly due to the glue	• Cheap flat-pack furniture, wall panels, display cabinets, storage units

Table 1.12.3 Properties of manufactured woods

1 Core content

> **Key terms**
>
> **Hard:** how well materials resist deformation, indentation or penetration. Hard materials can resist abrasion, drilling, impact, scratching, and wear and tear.
>
> **Tough:** how well a material withstands being hit.
>
> **Durable:** how well a material lasts.

Properties

It is important to know the correct meaning of the words that describe a material's properties. Comparing materials helps to define each material's properties. For example, do not say oak is hard, because there are lots of harder materials. Say: oak is harder than pine.

Hardness

Hardness is the ability of a material to withstand cutting and scratching. Timber is generally quite a soft material. It can easily be scratched and cut with metal tools, which are much harder than wood. Oak is quite hard for a wood. Balsa is very soft for a wood. This should not be confused with the classification of trees as hardwoods and softwoods.

Toughness

Toughness is the ability of a material to withstand being hit. A tough material can be quite soft, and might bend or deform when hit, but not break. Timber is quite a tough material. If you hit it with a hammer it may dent, but not break.

Durability

Durability is the ability of a material to last a long time. Timber that has been dried out and is kept dry is durable. Oak beams in old buildings can be hundreds of years old. However, wood that is left wet can rot quite quickly and won't then be very durable. Some timbers contain natural oils that make them more durable outside. Timber can be treated with preservatives to make it more durable for outside use.

> **Summary**
>
> **Key points to remember:**
> - A biological classification divides trees into hardwoods and softwoods.
> - There are many different types of trees, and the timber from them has different properties. It is important to know their properties to choose the best timber for a product.
> - Manufactured boards are made from wood that has been processed to make it into a large flat sheet.
> - Hard, tough and durable are terms that describe the properties of materials.

> **Checkpoint**
>
> **Strengthen**
>
> **S1** What is the difference between a hardwood and a softwood?
> **S2** What type of timber would you make a coffee table from? Give reasons why you think it is a good choice.
>
> **Challenge**
>
> **C1** What kind of things were often made from oak?
> **C2** Why is beech a good wood to use for a child's toy?
> **C3** Suggest a positive and a negative quality of MDF.

1.13 All design and technological practice takes place within contexts which inform outcomes

Learning objectives

By the end of this section, you should know:
- performance characteristics of a wide range of materials, components and manufacturing processes
- how to discriminate between them and select appropriately.

Selecting the correct materials for a product is a complex process. Designers use a detailed understanding of the properties of materials, and how those materials can be manipulated, to inform their design decisions.

Using materials, components and processes to inform outcomes

Properties of materials and components

When choosing materials or components for a design, manufacturers must consider the **mechanical** or **physical properties** required to ensure that the materials will perform the task.

Key terms

Mechanical properties: elements of a material that resist deformation from external forces or loads.

Physical properties: elements of a material that can be defined and measured, such as colour, size or weight.

Mechanical properties		Physical properties	
Strength	Ability to withstand force, e.g. by resisting squashing (compression) or stretching (tension)	Density	Compactness of a material, defined as mass per unit volume
Elasticity	Ability to return to original shape once deforming force is removed	Electrical conductivity	Ability to conduct electricity
Plasticity	Ability to permanently deform without breaking when subjected to a force	Thermal conductivity	Ability to conduct heat
Malleability	Ability to be permanently deformed in all directions without fracture	Size	Dimensions of the material
Ductility	Ability to be deformed by bending, twisting or stretching	Corrosion	Metal is eaten away as it reacts with oxygen and water in the air. Rust is formed through the corrosion of iron or steel
Hardness	Ability to resist deformation, indentation or penetration	Aesthetics	Appearance of a material, e.g. grain
Toughness	Ability to withstand sudden stress or shocks	Optical	Ability to absorb or reflect light
Brittleness	Inability to withstand sudden stress or shocks	Joining	Ability to be joined to other materials
Durability	Ability to withstand deterioration over time	Magnetism	Attraction to magnetic material
Stability	Ability to resist changes in shape over time		
Stiffness	Ability to resist bending		

Table 1.13.1 Mechanical and physical properties

1 Core content

Link it up

This section provides an overview of performance characteristics of materials and manufacturing processes. Further detail can be found in each material category.

The pictures below are examples of products made from mixed materials.

Figure 1.13.1: Example 1, chocolate box made from folding boxboard and rigid polystyrene

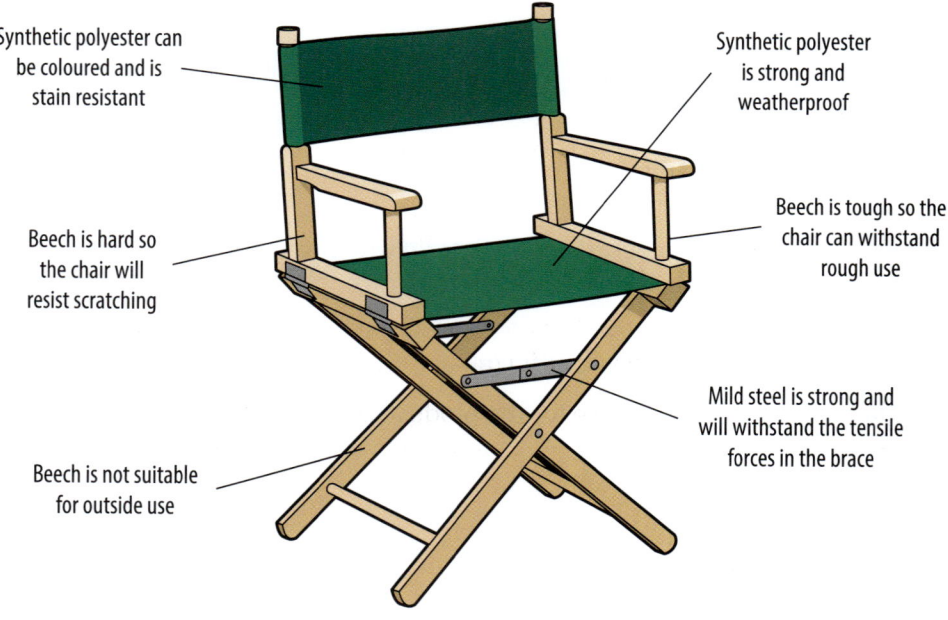

Figure 1.13.2: Example 2, director's chair made from beech, mild steel and synthetic polyester

Exam tip

It is vital that you apply your knowledge and understanding of materials when answering questions about designing products and you should always be able to justify your choices, where appropriate.

Exam-style question

Give **one** property of stainless steel that makes it an appropriate material for cutlery.

(1 mark)

Advantages and disadvantages of materials, components and manufacturing processes

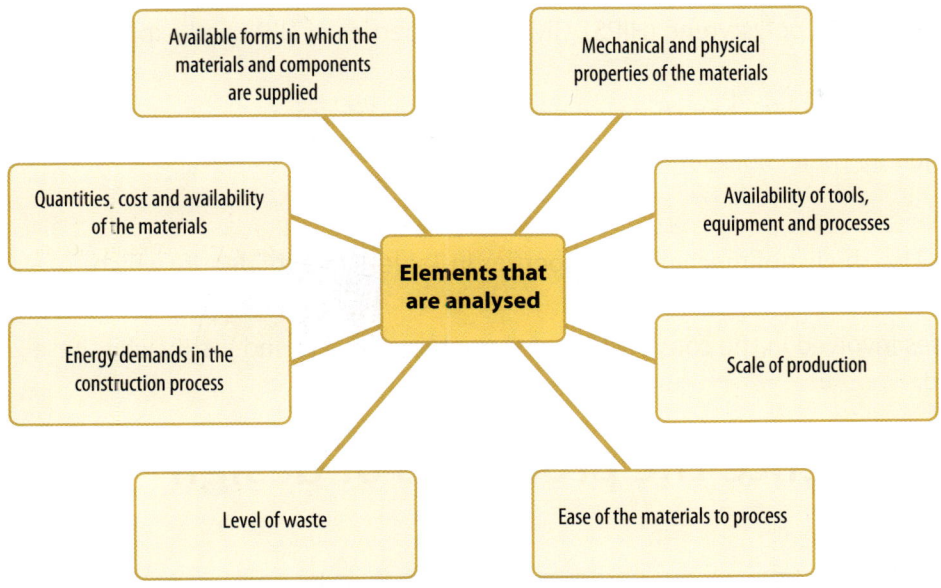

Figure 1.13.3 Before selecting a suitable material, component or process, manufacturers consider a range of elements, as shown above

> **Apply it**
>
> Many components or materials you will use in your chosen material category are only available in certain sizes (standard forms). Why do some suppliers only use standard sizes?

Justifying materials, components and manufacturing processes

The manufacturer can justify why it chose its materials and manufacturing processes in several ways. Below are some examples. This is also covered in section 1.14.

- Producing test pieces to prove that the materials have the desired physical and mechanical properties.
- Producing **prototypes** using manufacturing processes that could be used for the final product to show how it could be made.
- Producing a full economic case for the product, considering factors such as the cost of materials and processing, and hidden costs of manufacturing such as labour, lighting, waste and transportation.
- Evaluating the materials and production methods in relation to the environment and society.

> **Key term**
>
> **Prototype:** a full-size, three-dimensional model of the finished design, created for testing before production is started.

Summary

Key points to remember:
- Designers need to understand the key physical and mechanical properties of materials to inform design decisions.
- Manufacturers need to match materials to appropriate manufacturing methods.
- Businesses need to justify their selection of materials and processes before manufacturing begins.

1 Core content

Checkpoint

Strengthen

S1 Disposable cutlery is made from high-impact polystyrene (HIPS). Give five properties of HIPS and explain why these properties are required in this product.

S2 Explain two factors that companies may consider when choosing a manufacturing process.

S3 Explain two ways a company could justify their choice of manufacturing process.

Challenge

C1 Identify ten products in your home. Use the list of mechanical properties in Table 1.13.1 to identify which properties are important to those products, and why.

C2 Identify the manufacturing processes involved in the construction of these ten products and justify why these manufacturing processes were used.

1.14 Challenges that influence the processes of design and making

Learning objectives

By the end of this section, you should know:
- environmental challenges
- social challenges
- economic challenges
- that designers have to take into consideration in the design and development of new products.

All manufactured items we use have been designed. Designers work to a design brief or a specification, but they must take many other factors into consideration.

Respect for different social, ethnic and economic groups

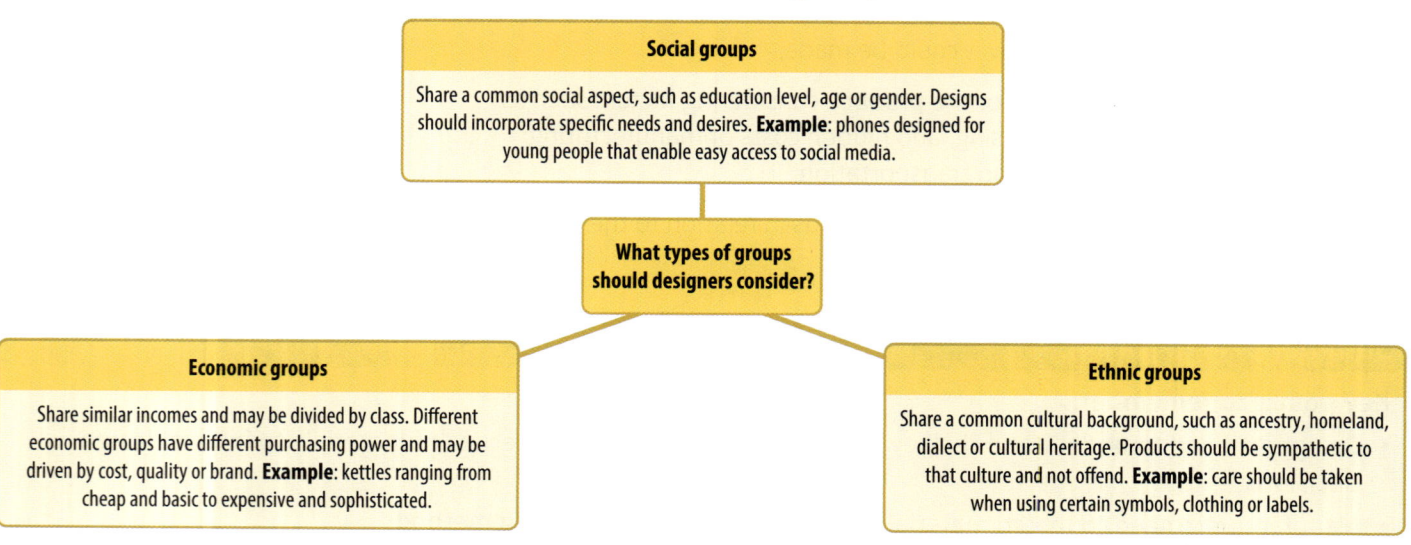

Figure 1.14.1 Designers must understand and respect the preferences of different groups so that they can target their products appropriately

1.14 Challenges that influence the processes of design and making

Environmental, social and economic issues relating to the design and manufacture of products

It is everyone's responsibility to ensure that we live in harmony with our world, within our means. Several bodies and initiatives help to encourage sustainability. Here are some examples:

- **The Fairtrade Foundation** tackles poverty and injustice across the world. It looks after the interests of farmers and producers in developing countries by ensuring they are paid a fair price for their goods. It also looks at working conditions and tries to prevent child or enforced labour and discrimination by gender.
- **Carbon offsetting schemes** allow companies or individuals to try to reduce their carbon footprint or become carbon neutral, for example by planting trees, adopting renewable energy resources or encouraging staff to walk or cycle to work.
- **Product disassembly** enables a product to be recycled, or the parts reused. It also means that products can last longer because they can be repaired or upgraded. When designing products, companies could consider reducing the number of parts, examining how parts fit together and labelling the parts by material for easy separation and recycling.
- **Disposal of waste** is governed by laws at international, European, national and local levels to ensure that the collection, transportation, recovery and disposal of waste has the least impact on the environment.

Consideration of 'green designs'

Global warming and rising energy costs have led to designers thinking about environmental factors when designing products without compromising on function, quality and performance of a design.

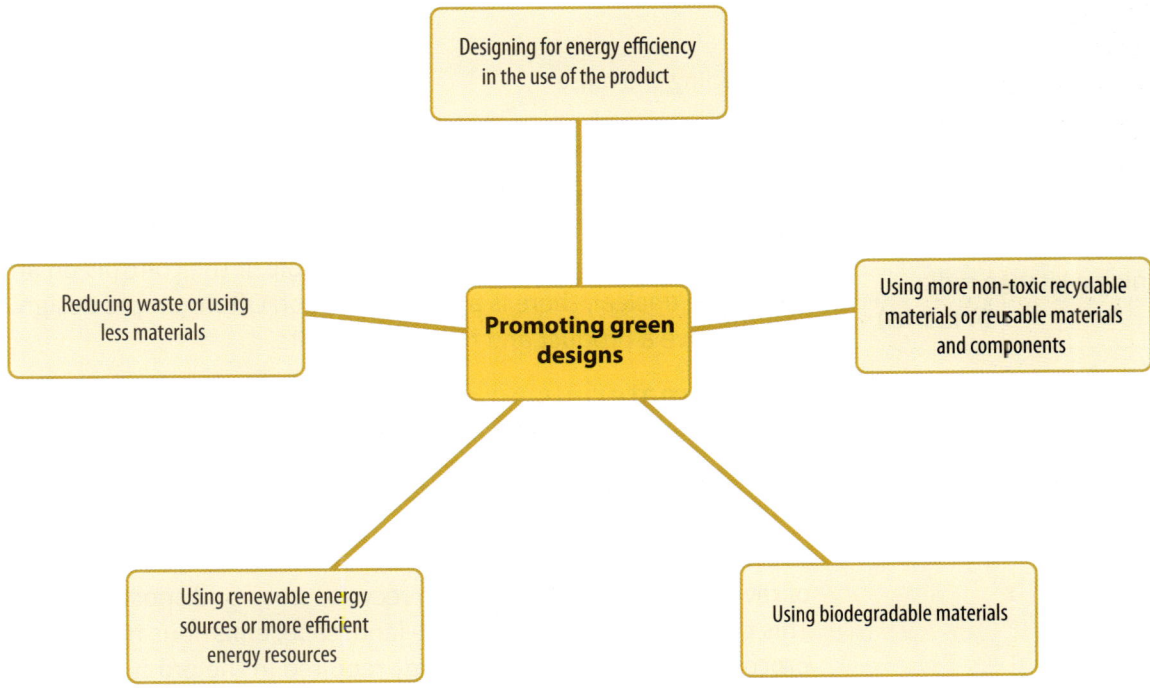

Figure 1.14.2 Examples of green design considerations

1 Core content

Recycling and reusing materials and products

If waste from the construction, use and disposal of a product cannot be eliminated, products should be designed to be recycled or reused. Recycling means that the materials from the product can be reprocessed and used again in a different product. Reusing could mean that a product is refilled, such as printer cartridges or jam jars, or simply used again, like shopping bags.

Potential advantages of recycling and reuse	Potential disadvantages of recycling and reuse
Less waste material to go to landfill	The recycling process can be complex when separating materials
Reduces the demand for new raw materials	Not always cost efficient, as a lot of energy is needed to transport, process and reassemble recyclable materials
Helps reduce global warming caused by emissions from processing raw materials	The recycling process may produce waste and pollutants, creating more environmental problems
Can reduce the need for transportation and mining	Jobs created in recycling industry may be low quality
Jobs can be created in the recycling industry	The quality of the recycled material may be inferior
Money is saved as the materials are used for a second time	

Table 1.14.1 Advantages and disadvantages of recycling and reuse

> **Exam-style question**
>
> Explain **two** ways that human capability would be considered when designing a kitchen radio.
> **(4 marks)**

Human capability

For a design to be successful, it has to meet the needs of the user and operate within their capabilities. Any product that stretches the capabilities of the user is likely to be unsafe. For example, if the controls on an electric heater are unclear, there is a risk of accident. Often, simple design changes can improve a product and reduce accidents.

Cost of materials

This is not just the initial cost of the raw material but also the ongoing costs of maintenance, transportation, recycling and disposal of the material at the end of its life.

The environmental cost also needs to be considered, such as the production of raw materials and the costs to recycle, reuse or dispose of the material. This cost could be damage to the landscape, emissions from conversion processes or the amount of energy required in the production process.

Manufacturing capability

The easier a product is to construct, the lower the manufacturing costs. Factors include the materials used, the required quality or tolerances, the required finish and whether the product can be manufactured using existing processes. Designers can then design for manufacture (DFM) by:

1.14 Challenges that influence the processes of design and making

- using standardised parts and reducing the amount of specialised parts
- simplifying or using repeatable processes
- reducing the complexity of the design or making it **modular**
- designing simple quality control tests
- reducing the tolerance in parts where possible
- designing for disassembly for servicing and repair.

> **Key term**
>
> **Modular:** a design featuring parts of standard sizes so they can be constructed in different ways.

Environmental impact – life-cycle analysis

A life-cycle analysis (LCA) is a systematic inventory that assesses environmental impacts relating to every stage of a product's life. Designers need to calculate all the environmental costs of a product, from extraction, transportation and processing of the raw materials, to manufacture, transportation and distribution of the product, use of the product by the consumer and its disposal or recovery at the end of its life. The LCA makes it easier to identify what areas can be changed to reduce the costs and environmental impact.

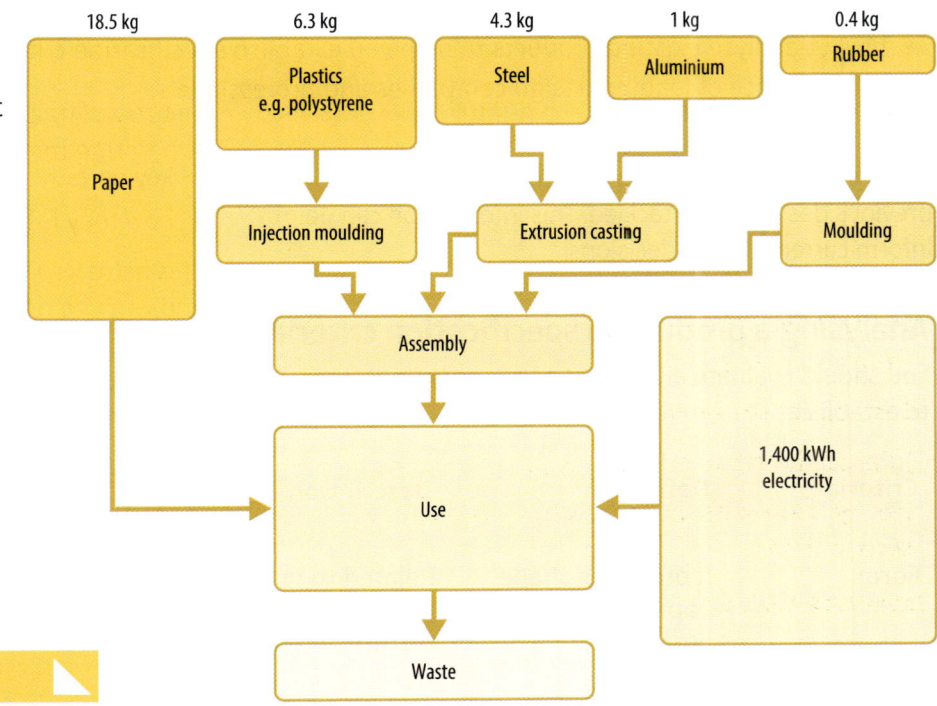

Figure 1.14.3 An example of an LCA for different weights of materials such as paper, plastics and metals

Apply it

Make an inventory of all the environmental impacts in an LCA of a product of your choice.

Summary

Key points to remember:

- Designers must respect different social, ethnic and economic groups.
- Designers need to consider the environmental costs of the design.
- The capabilities of humans and manufacturing methods need to be understood when designing.

Checkpoint

Strengthen

- **S1** Describe four ways that manufacturers could improve their manufacturing capability.
- **S2** Describe four ways that a company could use a 'green design' strategy for manufacturing its products.
- **S3** Explain the term 'life-cycle analysis'.
- **S4** Describe three ways for an individual to offset their carbon footprint.

Challenge

- **C1** Summarise how a manufacturer will use 'design for manufacture' in the design of a new product.
- **C2** Justify why it is important for councils to run a recycling scheme.

1 Core content

1.15 Investigate and analyse the work of professionals and companies to inform design

> **Learning objectives**
>
> By the end of this section, you should know:
> - strategies, techniques and approaches for investigating and analysing the work of others
> - how to analyse existing products to help you establish specification criteria
> - the influence of leading design companies and professionals.

When developing new designs, you must consider how previous designs were tackled. This information can help inform current design decisions.

Analysing a product to specification criteria

You should evaluate all aspects of a product's design to establish:

- key parts
- how they fulfil the design brief and specification.

This helps you to understand the design decisions made and why the final product looks, or works, as it does. A good product analysis will examine a product under certain criteria. In Table 1.15.1 a domestic kettle is used as an example.

Criteria	Definition	Description	Considerations for a kettle's design
Form	A product's shape, appearance and **aesthetics** of a product	Related to product's physical space (size), proportion, weight, colour, texture and tone	Shape, colour, how much space it will take up, comfort to use
Function	What a product is intended to do	How well a product performs for the user	Ease of adding water, ability to know water is at desired level, ability to filter impurities, connection to power source, how well the kettle pours
User requirements	How the product will fulfil the wants and needs of users	• Need to know who the end user is, for example, person with disabilities, child • May need to ask users their preferences	Weight, colour, portability, safety, e.g. automatic switch-off at boiling point
Performance requirements	A product's ability to complete a given task to a measurable standard	• Product is tested and evaluated to ensure it meets relevant standards • Examples of standards are speed, size, distance, quality, quantity, accuracy • Could be a selling point, such as miles per gallon or the sound output of a speaker	Capacity, time to reach boiling point, length of extension cord, carbon output

Table 1.15.1 Specification criteria for a kettle *cont…*

1.15 Investigate and analyse the work of professionals and companies to inform design

Criteria	Definition	Description	Considerations for a kettle's design
Materials and components/ systems	Best materials for making the product	• Depend on the purpose of a product, end user and type or scale of manufacture • Choice of materials also depends on cost, aesthetics, availability and mechanical properties, such as strength, hardness, weight or resistance to heat or chemicals • Can include standardised components such as screws, bolts or circuit boards	Heat insulation, ability to meet strength requirements, cleanability, ability to withstand corrosion, fit to standard UK plug
Scale of production and cost	Relationship between quantity produced and per-unit fixed costs, to ensure an acceptable price and quality for the customer	• Need to identify number of units and production method (for example, one-off, batch, mass or continuous) based on potential demand • Cost will vary due to economies of scale: cost per unit is often less if more units are made • Bulk buying materials or using continuous production can save costs	Materials and processes used, production method, appropriate quality, ideal price, suitability for assembly line manufacture, ability to be broken into components
Sustainability	Environmental impact of a product from manufacture to end of use	• A product's whole-life impact can be identified by completing a life-cycle assessment (LCA; see page 61) • Strict rules encourage products to be sustainable, for example plastic recycling codes or approval by the Forest Stewardship Council	Environmental impact of extraction/processing of raw materials, manufacturing methods, lifetime power consumption, end-of-life disassembly and recyclability
Aesthetics	How we interpret a product as being attractive or pleasing	Related to the way we see, touch, hear, smell or taste an object	• The use of pleasing colours • Smooth to touch • Clear lines with rounded surfaces
Marketability	The ability of a product to be sold	Related to how easily a product will sell in relation to its competitors	• Correct pricing for quality • Extra functionality • Fits with current trends
Consideration of innovation	How a company will look at new ideas and methods in the design of products	How the boundaries of technology are used to improve the design, manufacture, features and functionality of products.	• Improved materials (lighter, stronger) • Advanced manufacturing methods • Exciting new features

Table 1.15.1 Specification criteria for a kettle

> **Key term**
>
> **Sustainability:** meeting the needs of the present without compromising the ability of future generations to meet their own needs.

1 Core content

> **Exam-style question**
> Explain **two** reasons why mass-produced products can be made more cheaply than one-off products.
> (4 marks)

> **Apply it**
> Choose any product and describe how it fulfils its specification under the criteria in Table 1.15.1.

The work of past and present designers and companies

Influential designs are adopted and adapted by other designers. Here are some examples.

Name	Who are they?	Known for	Why they are influential
Alessi	Company, established in Italy in 1921	• Designer and mass producer of functional but visually appealing homeware and kitchen products	• Uses famous designers, such as Philippe Starck, to create iconic kitchen products, such as the spider-like Juicy Salif lemon squeezer and retro kettles, setting a standard for other homeware companies
Apple	Company, established in the USA in 1976	• Producer of consumer electronics and software using cutting-edge technologies, e.g. iPad, iWatch, iPod, iPhone, iTunes	• Ground-breaking design: products looked completely different to anything before • Breaking with tradition and legacy, Apple's iPod made digital music mainstream • A loyal customer base
Heatherwick Studio	Design studio, established in the UK in 1994	• Around 200 designers, architects and makers have worked on projects from perfume bottles to Routemaster buses and Singapore University buildings	• Stretches the boundaries of materials, craftsmanship and artistic thinking, showing that products and buildings can be unusual, experimental and interesting
Joe Casely-Hayford	Fashion designer, born 1956	• Noted for his original but wearable designs that push barriers of conformity, made by master craftspeople using traditional English tailoring methods	• Sets standards for British tailoring that combines style with character and is popular with celebrities
Pixar	Animation studio, established in the USA in 1979	• Among the first to develop computer-animated feature films	• Uses new techniques and technologies to make popular and successful films, including *Toy Story* and *Finding Nemo*
Raymond Loewy	Industrial designer (1893–1986)	• 'The father of modern design' • Emphasised the importance of combining simplicity with functionality, working with more than 200 companies on designs ranging from refrigerators to planes, trains and spacecraft	• Introduced the idea that if two products have the same price, function and quality, the products with better aesthetics will be more popular • His designs are recognisable today, including the Coca-Cola bottle, Le Creuset Coquelle dish and logos for Shell and BP

Table 1.15.2 Examples of influential designers and companies *cont…*

1.15 Investigate and analyse the work of professionals and companies to inform design

Name	Who are they?	Known for	Why they are influential
Tesla, Inc.	Automotive and energy storage company, established in the USA in 2008	• Produces electric cars that don't compromise on power or quality, have zero emissions, are affordable and can be charged at home	• Leads electric car design and technology, including the *Tesla Model X* SUV (2016)
Zaha Hadid	Architect (1950–2016)	• Integrated geometric forms with expressive, sweeping fluid forms • Promoted architecture as a visual art form, with buildings intended to give aesthetic pleasure	• Overcame racial and gender barriers to establish an architecture practice that has designed more than 1000 iconic buildings worldwide

Table 1.15.2 Examples of influential designers and companies

Apply it

Research other products that have been influenced by Raymond Loewy's streamlined design. Explain how they fit into the 'streamlined' philosophy.

Summary

Key points to remember:
- Products can be evaluated under certain specification criteria.
- Many designers have made significant contributions to design and continue to influence today's designers.

Philippe Starck's Juicy Salif lemon squeezer: form over function?

Checkpoint

Strengthen
- **S1** Explain why it is important that companies design sustainable products.
- **S2** Describe two design philosophies at the core of Zaha Hadid Architects' design style.
- **S3** Name the designer whose designs follow the traditions of English tailored clothing but push the barriers of conformity.

Challenge
- **C1** Describe how form could follow function in the design of modern products.
- **C2** Investigate the development of an Apple product and identify technological advances that have improved the product over time. Explain why you think Apple is such an influential company.

1 Core content

1.16 Use of different design strategies

Learning objective

By the end of this section, you should know:
- how to approach and generate different design ideas.

Apply it

Investigate how designers or design companies come up with design ideas.

It is easy to see only one design solution to a problem, but allowing yourself to think like this will mean you miss endless other ideas that could prove to be more successful. Try to keep an open mind especially in the early stage of designing and enjoy the surprise of stumbling across potentially great ideas. Design ideas can be created through different strategies, techniques and approaches; consider the following throughout your designing.

Collaboration

In design companies, it is very rare for only one person to be responsible for the whole of the design process. It is more common for the design process to be a collaborative process, because together people look at problems from different perspectives and generate many more ideas. This means you need to talk to other users or designers and allow them to spark off your imagination in generating your own design ideas.

You could use a design process known as SCAMPER. It was first introduced by Alex Osborn, an advertising executive, in 1953 and developed by Bob Eberle in 1971.

- **Substitute** – could you consider different materials, components or sources of energy?
- **Combine** – could you take successful parts from other ideas to form new ideas?
- **Adapt** – could you incorporate a different function or make use of a different technology?
- **Modify** – could you change the aesthetics, shrink or expand it?
- **Put** to another use – could your design have a second or third function?
- **Eliminate** – could you take away part of your design? Have you over-thought it?
- **Reverse** – could you look at your design completely differently, think about it inside out/upside down, could you move parts around?

Apply it

Find five images of products that have different functions. Swap these pictures with someone else in your class. Challenge yourself to use these products as inspiration to generate design solutions for your design problem. Are you surprised at the ideas that you have created?

User-centred design

User-centred design revolves around putting your users' needs at the centre of every decision that is made throughout the whole designing process. This ensures that the users' opinions are considered at every stage so that the design cannot go off at a tangent or get lost in the design process.

Many web design companies use the 'user-centred design' approach for creating websites, apps and programs. Imagine navigating through a new app that you may have downloaded. Was it easy to understand and get to grips with? If the answer is no, then you have probably deleted it or forgotten that you downloaded it! When designing a new app, a web design company would constantly refer to their users and ask for feedback at every stage, such as for the use of a symbol, a location of a button, a colour chosen or a drop-down menu. This feedback is crucial to the designers to ensure that their app feels natural and predictable for their users to navigate and interact with.

In your classroom, you need to put your user at the heart of your design decisions at every stage of the design process, particularly in the generation of your own design ideas. This could be done by:

- having your user requirements as a starting point for your design ideas
- asking your user to draw out some ideas or making a simple model for you and using these as a starting point to generate more design ideas
- modelling your ideas in 3D to gain user feedback to aid your development
- using **anthropometric data** from your user to influence your design ideas.

> **Key term**
>
> **Anthropometric data:** measurements of the human body.

Systems thinking

Systems thinking is used by designers to solve complex problems, and find solutions. It is an effective way to think about the functions and how users interact with other products and systems. Systems thinking looks at a whole system or product and its individual elements or parts. It looks carefully at how each part or stage contributes and feeds back into the system.

The simplest way is to create a flowchart but start backwards:

1. What do you want your product to do or achieve (the output)?
2. How is it going to achieve that function (the process)?
3. What inputs or energies would it need to do that (inputs)?

Figure 1.16.1 is an example of a design of a drinks vending machine.

> **Link it up**
>
> For more information on how to create systems diagrams, look at page 75. Feedback loops were explained in section 1.7. How could you modify Figure 1.16.1 using feedback loops?

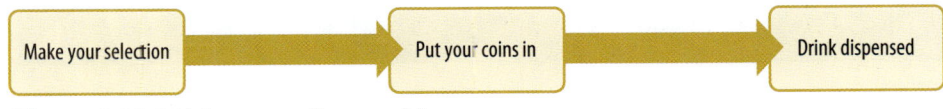

Figure 1.16.1 Using a vending machine

This could then be converted into a systems diagram using the titles 'inputs', 'processes' and 'outputs' alongside the signals for each one. Take note of the addition during the process of coins being counted.

Figure 1.16.2 Inputs, processes and outputs based on using a vending machine

1 Core content

Product designers and engineers commonly use systems thinking in generating their design ideas for products such as mobile phones, baby monitors, kitchen timers and car alarms. Systems thinking helps designers to think about their product/system in a logical manner and stick to the problem that they are solving, especially when the design problem might not be something that they can easily relate to.

Use systems thinking by:

- breaking down the use of the product or system into simple stages
- considering the different options available at each of these stages
- asking your user to describe the stages they would go through when using a particular product or system and asking yourself whether this correlates with your own thoughts.

Apply it

Create a flowchart for making a cup of tea, then develop it into a systems diagram including inputs, processes, outputs and signals.

Exam-style question

Discuss which design strategies a design company might use when designing a pair of headphones. **(6 marks)**

Exam tip

To gain a higher mark on this type of question, the discussion should be well balanced and have a judgement, based on the factors discussed in your answer.

1.17 Using communication techniques to present design ideas

Learning objective

By the end of this section, you should know:
- how to creatively and effectively communicate your design ideas.

Generating and developing design ideas does not have to be simply putting pencil to paper and drawing. There are numerous ways in which to communicate your ideas; you will need to use the knowledge of your design problems, the facilities that your school has and your personal strengths to decide on the most suitable range of methods to present your ideas.

Freehand sketching

Freehand sketching is often used by designers in the generation of their initial design ideas. For example, in the fashion industry, designers may sit down together and start sketching ideas for the new season based on the findings of their trends research. Freehand sketching is an effective way of quickly getting your ideas either in 2D or 3D from your head onto paper. Further along the design process, the freehand sketches can be developed in more depth, often with a different communication technique.

Consider the following in your freehand sketching:

- **different mediums**, for example pencils, ball point pens, fine liners, markers or coloured pencils, depending on which you feel more comfortable working with
- **grid paper or templates**, for example, a human figure outline can sometimes be useful to create scale to your product
- **the use of arrows**: an effective way to show movement within design ideas, for example lids opening and closing or pieces of clothing buttoned or zipped.

Figure 1.17.1 Example of freehand sketching

Apply it

The year is 2099, the season is winter, the trends are bold patterns and zips. Communicate five different design ideas using freehand sketching for either a watch or a winter coat.

Digital photography/media

Graphic designers often use digital photography or media to create and develop their design ideas. Their ideas are often so complex or futuristic that it is easier to create their vision through edited photos and media. Examples could be billboards advertising the releases of films.

Product designers also use photos or images to help create design ideas. One way of doing this would be to use a photograph, place tracing paper over the top and then adapt the image into a product.

Cut and paste techniques

Product designers and fashion designers often use photos/images to help create and inspire their own design ideas. They sometimes copy and paste parts of photographs, existing product images or replications of their own design work to then edit and develop. One way of doing this would be to use a photograph, place tracing paper over the top and then adapt the image into a product/outfit.

1 Core content

> **Key terms**
>
> **Styrofoam:** a modelling foam commonly shaped with a hot wire cutter.
>
> **Stripboard/breadboard:** electronics prototyping board.
>
> **Computer modelling:** using computer-aided design (CAD) software like ProDesktop to visualise your idea.
>
> **Simulation:** a computer model that represents how something would work in real life, such as how the screw on an adjustable spanner could be altered so that it would allow different nut sizes to be tightened or loosened.

3D models

Sometimes drawings are hard for designers to portray and for their users to visualise; this is where 3D models or prototypes can help to represent designers' ideas as something physical. Prototypes could be full size or a smaller-scale version depending on the size and complexity of the idea being developed.

Prototyping could be through a variety of materials; choose the medium that suits your ideas:

- **traditional materials**, such as paper, fabric, cardboard, Styrofoam or HIPS
- **small plastic building bricks**
- **system modelling**, for example stripboards or breadboards
- **computer modelling**, for example 3D printer models and simulations.

A prototype made from breadboard. There are problems with this prototype – can you identify them?

3D drawing

3D drawings allow designers to be able to represent their designs more realistically and encourage designers to think about every angle of their design. Design development naturally occurs when designers move from 2D drawings to 3D drawings, as they often find the opportunity to add parts or features and consider in greater depth how the product would actually be used. Think about the sides of your mobile phone and the buttons, sockets and charging points that you find on it, alongside feedback from users (user-centred design). 3D drawing will have helped the designers to think about where each of these is placed.

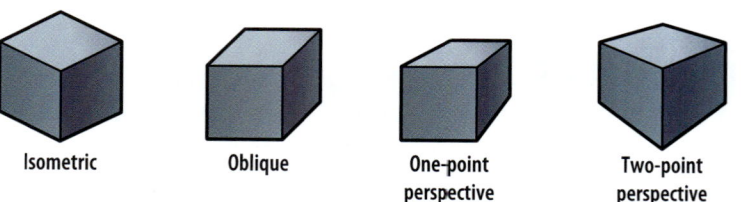

Figure 1.17.2 There are a range of 3D techniques that you could use: have a go at all four and decide which one feels most comfortable for you

1.17 Using communication techniques to present design ideas

Oblique and isometric projections

Both isometric and oblique projections are commonly used by engineers in technical drawings and illustrations and sometimes by architects. Early video games such as SimCity used isometric, or oblique, projection before 3D games were introduced.

SimCity released its first 3D game using isometric projection in 2000 after the 2D version was first released in 1989

Oblique

Oblique projection is the simplest method of creating 3D designs based on 45-degree lines. For support, use oblique grid paper to guide your angles:

1. Draw the front view in 2D.
2. From each corner, draw construction lines projecting out at 45 degrees.
3. On the construction lines, measure half the true length.
4. Draw the back of the product to complete the product.

Isometric

Isometric drawings look more realistic than oblique ones and are based on 30-degree lines. For support, use isometric grid paper to guide your angles:

1. Instead of drawing the 2D front view in oblique, you begin with an edge of the product – draw this as a vertical straight line.
2. From this line, create **construction lines** going off at 30 degrees.
3. Fill in the next vertical lines.
4. From these vertical lines, draw your next construction lines going off at 30 degrees (repeat steps 3 and 4 depending on the complexity of your drawing).
5. Within these construction lines, draw your product.

Apply it

Using construction lines, sketch your mobile phone using either the isometric or oblique technique.

> **Key term**
>
> **Construction lines:** faint sketched lines that help you to build up the rough shape of a product before creating your design within them. They should not be rubbed out.

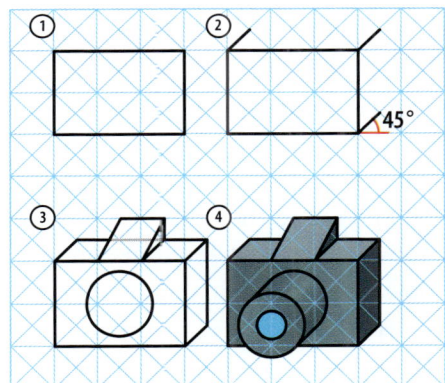

Figure 1.17.3 Example of oblique projection

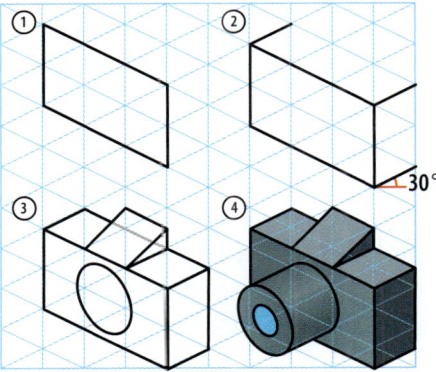

Figure 1.17.4 Example of isometric projection

1 Core content

This London underground platform appears to get narrower in the distance, yet the platform is a consistent width throughout the station

Key term

Vanishing point: a point in the distance where the construction lines project to. It can be positioned to the right or left, above or below, depending on how you would like your image to appear.

Apply it

Draw the entrance hall to your school using one-point perspective. Try to place your vanishing point at a different point to the other people on your table and, once complete, compare the differences in how the images appear.

Perspective drawing

Perspective drawings tend to look more realistic than both oblique and isometric techniques, as they visualise objects in a very similar way to our own eyes.

There are two types of perspective drawing: one-point perspective and two-point perspective.

One-point perspective

One-point perspective is often used in interior design, as it quickly creates an image with a good sense of depth that enables the customer to rapidly visualise the designer's idea. This then allows the designer and customer to work together to develop and adjust the idea to suit the customer's requirements.

One-point perspective is the easier type of perspective drawing.

1. Just like oblique drawing, start by drawing the front view in 2D.
2. From each corner, create construction lines to a point in the distance called a single **vanishing point**.
3. Draw your next vertical lines between your construction lines.
4. Join up your vertical lines with horizontal lines (keep these faint).
5. Draw your product within these lines.

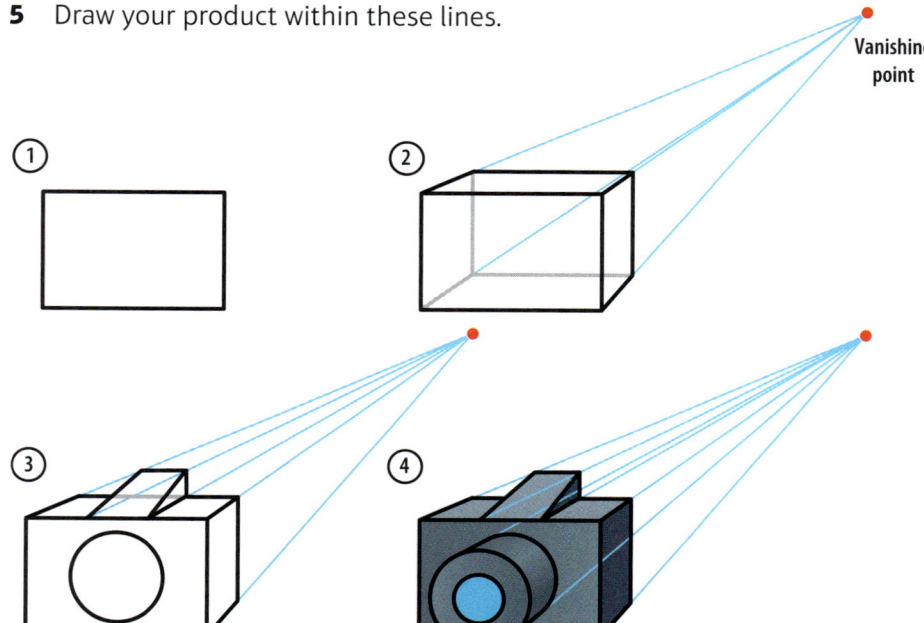

Figure 1.17.5 Example of one-point perspective drawing

Two-point perspective

Two-point perspective is often used by architects when developing their ideas in 3D, as it gives a speedy realistic interpretation. Like interior designers, the architects can work alongside their customer to develop their ideas to the customer's requirements.

1.17 Using communication techniques to present design ideas

Two-point perspective uses two vanishing points either side of the object to produce a more realistic representation of the product.

1. Just like isometric drawing, you begin with an edge of the product – draw this as a vertical straight line.
2. From each corner, create construction lines to two vanishing points.
3. Draw in your next vertical lines between the construction lines.
4. From these vertical lines, draw construction lines going off to the vanishing points.
5. Draw in your product between your construction lines.

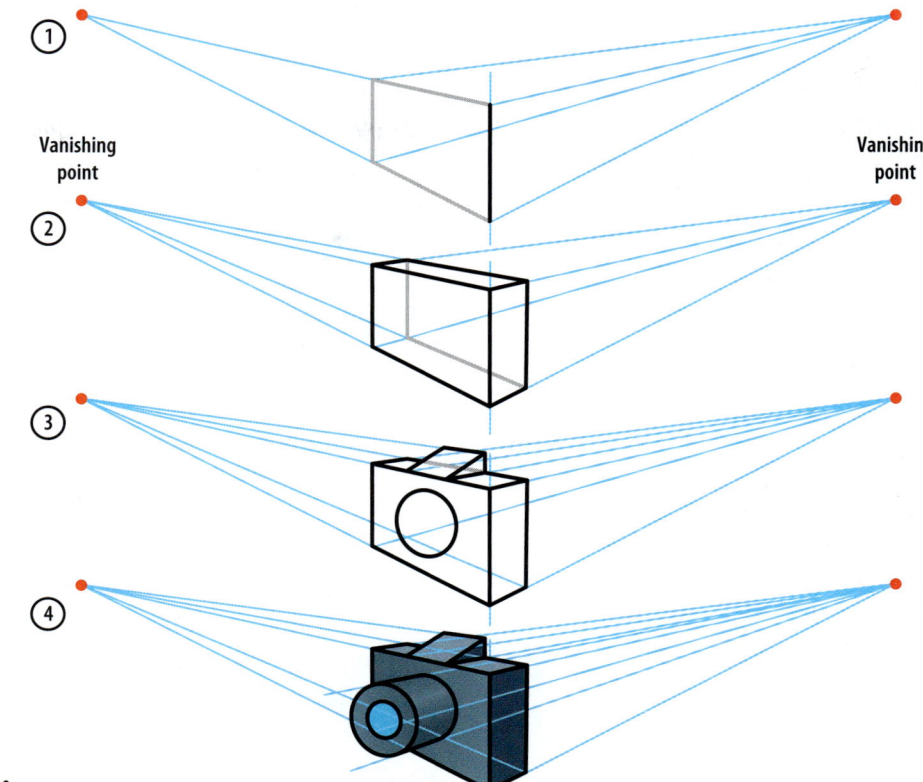

Figure 1.17.6 Example of two-point perspective drawing

Orthographic and exploded views

Designers tend to use both orthographic and exploded views during design development or final concept drawings, as they show the product in greater detail than an initial idea. They not only help the designer to get their head around how exactly the design will be made and what materials it will use, but also allow others looking at their designs to fully understand them without the need to ask the designer for clarification. This is crucial for manufacture.

Orthographic views

Orthographic projection is used to show the detail and measurements of the product clearly from a range of angles so that a stranger could use the drawing to work out the shape and dimensions for manufacture. A furniture designer would be a perfect example of someone who may use orthographic projection.

To create an orthographic projection, you draw the front view, side view and plan view of your product in 2D. You can either draw them out by hand or generate the views using various CAD programs from your CAD model. You can use first angle projection or third angle projection – although the views may appear the same, the order that they are laid out differ.

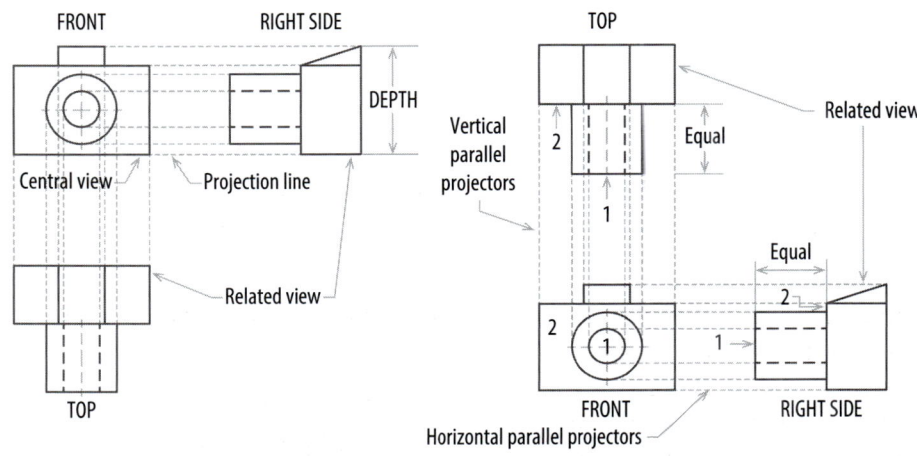

Figure 1.17.7 First and third angle projections for orthographic projection showing all sides of the product

1 Core content

> **Key terms**
>
> **Disassemble:** to take apart a product so that you can identify the parts that it consists of.
>
> **Patent:** a licence that is applied for to protect the way that a design works. Once a product has been patented, no one else can use that exact design for a similar product.
>
> **Ergonomics:** designing products that take into account the strengths and limitations of people so that the product fits well, reduces effort and increases performance.

Exploded views

Exploded views are an effective way of demonstrating what is inside a product. These enable designers to think about the materials, the components and the way that the product is assembled. Exploded views show how the product would look if it were to be **disassembled**. You often find exploded views in the drawings that make up a **patent**.

Assembly drawings

Assembly drawings are used by designers to inform manufacturers and customers about how to assemble their product correctly. Ikea uses assembly drawings in its instructions for flat-pack furniture so that customers can assemble items by themselves at home. The assembly drawings show how parts fit together and which component goes where. You will often find them labelled with a key to the parts or components. Each part is numbered and named. There are usually several sheets with dimensioned detail drawings for each part. Each part can then be made and assembled by looking at the assembly drawing.

Systems and schematic diagrams

As described earlier, systems diagrams tend to be used for electronics projects, showing how the system will function with regard to inputs, processes and outputs. This is an effective way to create design ideas before moving to schematic diagrams, which show the detail of how they will actually function. Schematic diagrams tend to be drawn by engineers to show exactly what components will be in the circuit, alongside how they will be connected. A successful schematic diagram will clearly show component names and values and provide labels to explain the intended purpose. They may be either hand drawn or drawn using a computer program such as SmartDraw.

Figure 1.17.8 An exploded diagram of a shoe, showing the layers of fabrics and materials that make up a finished shoe to make it ergonomically comfortable

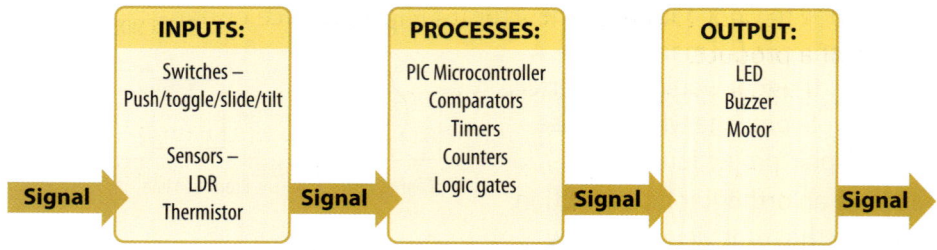

Figure 1.17.9 Use this systems diagram to help you consider the options at the input/processes/output stages when you are designing your product, before moving on to the schematic diagrams

> **Apply it**
>
> Choose a product from your classroom and have a go at drawing it using either an exploded diagram or an orthographic projection.

1.17 Using communication techniques to present design ideas

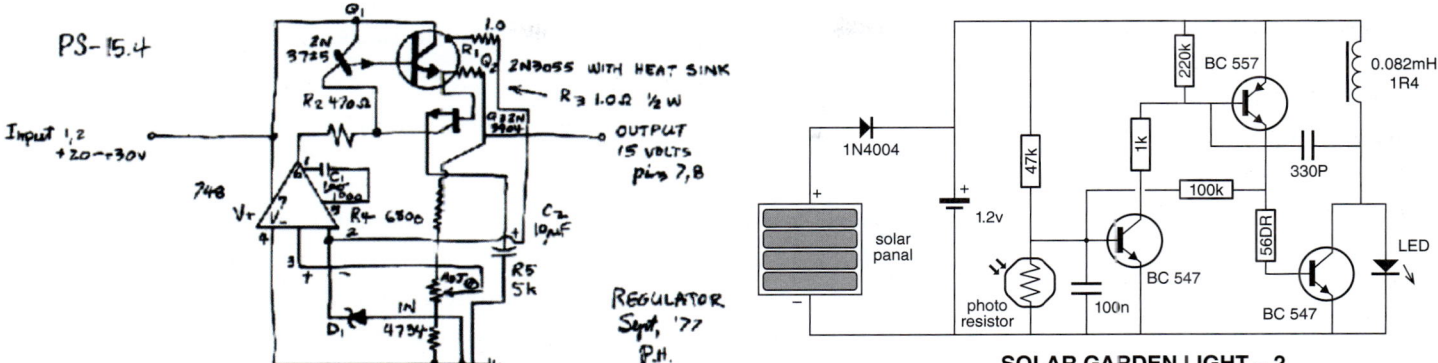

Figure 1.17.10 A hand drawn and computer drawn schematic diagram showing the required electronic components

Computer-aided design and specialist drawing programs

Computer-aided design (CAD) is now commonly used by designers in a variety of ways. CAD can be used to create design ideas, develop designs and to model and test something to be later made in **CAM**. CAD is often preferred by designers because the design looks realistic and professional to present to users or investors. Some of the ways designers use CAD include:

- **CAD freehand sketching:** programs such as Adobe Photoshop, 2D Design and Pro Sketch are commonly used by graphic and product designers to either draw out their design ideas from scratch or enhance some of their sketches.
- **2D modelling:** graphic and product designers commonly use programs such as 2D Design or Adobe Illustrator to create 2D designs that can be sent to the laser cutter (CAM) to produce either a model or part of a product.
- **3D modelling:** product designers and engineers commonly use programs such as ProDesktop to create 3D designs that can then be turned into models, actual parts or even whole products through 3D printers or **CNC** routers.
- **System design:** electrical engineers commonly use programs such as Yenka Technology and PCB Wizard to build and test a system. This allows ideas for components and layout to be changed electronically, rather than wasting components during testing.

> **Key terms**
>
> **CAM:** computer-aided manufacture, such as using a laser cutter or 3D printer.
>
> **CNC:** computer numerically controlled, for example using a CNC router.

Figure 1.17.11 CAD freehand sketching using Photoshop to build up professional looking design ideas

75

1 Core content

CAD can be used to build a system as well as to test it. This allows ideas for components and layout to be changed electronically, rather than wasting components in testing. For example, in textile design, Pro Sketch may be used to create concepts for an outfit.

Record and justify design ideas clearly
Annotated sketches

Designers from all areas and backgrounds commonly use annotations alongside each of the communication techniques above. The annotations help them to explain their ideas and enable anyone looking at their work to be able to understand their ideas without the need to speak to them directly. This is really important in the design process, as designs will need to be passed on to other people who would also need to be able to read them.

For example, a fashion designer would sketch out their final concepts for a new season's coat with annotations detailing the types of materials to be used. That would then get passed to the manufacturing team who would be specialists in tooling and machinery but are unlikely to be specialists in fabric, making the annotations crucial.

Annotations vary at different stages of the design process but tend to refer to the following:

- Design justifications:
  - user and design requirements
  - positives and negatives of each design
  - ergonomics – would your user be able to use/operate/wear the item comfortably?
  - sustainability considerations.
- Manufacturing details:
  - materials and components
  - dimensions
  - manufacturing process and techniques
  - sources of energy, for example batteries, mains, solar or wind-up.

> **Exam tip**
>
> For question (a), remember to give a linked justification to back up the reason you choose.

> **Exam-style questions**
>
> a. Explain **one** reason why annotations are important when a designer passes their concepts to a manufacturer. **(2 marks)**
>
> b. Explain **one** benefit and **one** drawback of freehand sketching versus CAD modelling. **(4 marks)**

Summary

Key points to remember:
- Decide on suitable design strategies for your design problem or scenario.
- Choose a range of suitable communication techniques for your design problem or scenario.

Checkpoint

Strengthen

S1 Name two different design strategies that designers sometimes use.

S2 List five things that a designer might annotate on their designs.

S3 Choose a suitable communication technique and sketch out a product that you might find in your design and technology classroom.

Challenge

C1 Consider the advantages and disadvantages of collaborative designing.

C2 Discuss the potential differences in communication techniques for the following products:
   a) pop-up children's book
   b) interior of a wedding venue
   c) clothing for a triathlon athlete
   d) system for an Amazon locker.

Preparing for your exam 1

Exam strategy

What to expect in the exam

The examination is designed to test your knowledge and understanding of the core content and the material category you have chosen. Throughout the course you will need to practise exam-style questions in all areas. Preparing carefully for your exams is important in order to get as many marks as you can.

The paper consists of two sections: Section A assesses your knowledge on the core content and Section B assesses your knowledge on your material category.

Section A: Core (1DT0)
Section A is worth 40 marks and contains a mixture of different question styles, including open-response, graphical, calculation and extended-open-response questions. There are 10 marks allocated to calculation questions.

You should know about:

- the impact of new and emerging technologies
- how the critical evaluation of new and emerging technologies informs design decisions
- how energy is generated and stored in order to choose and use appropriate sources to make products and power systems
- developments in modern and smart materials, composite materials and technical textiles
- mechanical devices that produce movement and change forces
- how electronic systems provide functionality to products and processes
- programmable components and flowcharts
- categorisation of the types and properties of:
  - ferrous and non-ferrous metals
  - papers and boards
  - thermoforming and thermosetting polymers
  - natural, synthetic, blended and mixed fibres, and woven, non-woven and knitted textiles
  - natural and manufactured timbers
- contexts in which design and technological practice takes place
- environmental, social and economic challenges of designing
- the work of certain past and present designers
- using different design strategies to generate ideas
- how to develop, communicate, record and justify design ideas.

Section B: Material categories
This section is worth 60 marks and contains a mixture of different question styles, including open-response, graphical, calculation and extended-open-response questions. Topics 2–7 in this Student Book cover the different material categories covered in Section B of the exam.

Preparing for your exam 1

There are 5 marks allocated to calculation questions in Section B. The material categories are divided into:

- 1DT0/1A – Metals
- 1DT0/1B – Papers and boards
- 1DT0/1C – Polymers
- 1DT0/1D – Systems
- 1DT0/1E – Textiles
- 1DT0/1F – Timbers

Whatever the material category, you should know about:

- its design contexts
- its sources, origins, physical and working properties and the materials' social and ecological footprints
- the way in which the selection of the material is influenced
- the impact of forces and stresses and how the materials can be reinforced and stiffened
- stock forms, types and sizes in order to calculate and determine the quantity of the materials required
- alternative processes that can be used to manufacture the materials to a different scale of production
- specialist techniques, tools, equipment and processes that can be used to shape, fabricate, construct and assemble a high-quality prototype
- appropriate surface treatments and finishes that can be applied to the materials.

> **Exam tip**
>
> Sample answers for questions given in Section B of the exam can be found on the following pages:
> - Metals: pages 125–127
> - Papers and boards: pages 157–161
> - Polymers: pages 199–201
> - Systems: pages 235–239
> - Textiles: pages 271–275
> - Timbers: pages 308–311

Revision tips

- Ensure you start revising in plenty of time. You will find it easier to remember facts you have revised several times over a few weeks than those you have tried to memorise at the last minute.
- Make clear and well-ordered notes about all the sections.
- Work through all sample assessment materials, past papers and textbook questions available from Pearson.
- Identify the areas where you are likely to get mathematical questions and practise arithmetic and numerical computation, handling data, graphs, geometry and trigonometry.
- Discuss the course with your teacher and peers as it will help your understanding.
- Use online or other resources to extend your understanding of the design and technology context.

Exam tips

- The total time for your paper is 1 hour 45 minutes. This works out at about 1 mark per minute (about 40 minutes on Section A and 60 minutes on Section B), with 5 minutes left over to check your answers. You could plan to have more time at the end but try not to rush through the questions, as you are more likely to make a mistake.
- You must answer all the questions. If you are stuck on one, leave it and come back at the end.
- The number of marks awarded for each question will tell you how many separate points you need to make in your answer.

Preparing for your exam 1

Understanding the questions

The questions will use command words that require a certain type of answer. Familiarise yourself with common command words and read the question carefully before answering it.

Command word	Instruction
Calculate	Work out a numerical problem using mathematical processes or formulae. You may get points for using correct formulae, using correct stages of calculation (by showing your workings) and getting the correct outcome.
Discuss	Identify, explore and investigate the issue, situation, problem, concept or argument within the question, using reasoning. This type of question does not require a conclusion.
Evaluate	Measure the value or success of something and provide a substantiated judgement or conclusion. Review information and bring it together, drawing on evidence such as strengths, weaknesses, alternatives and relevant data.
Give/State/Name	Recall and write down one or more pieces of information.
Explain	Provide an answer and reason(s) qualifying the answer, such as why something can be considered to fulfil a need, provide a purpose or communicate an intention. Your answer must contain some reasoning or justification, and it may support a statement.
Use notes and/or sketches to show	Using graphical depiction with annotation, give an account of a process, showing its stages in the correct order, or give an account of something, showing a series of features, points or trends. The number of points and the depth of answer required will be indicated by the mark allocation.

Table 1.1 Common command words

Preparing for your exam 1

Sample answers with comments

The following questions give some examples of how to interpret the different command words.

Question 1: Calculation question

A nutcracker is going to be used to crack open a nut, with an applied load of 12 N, as shown in Figure PE1.1.

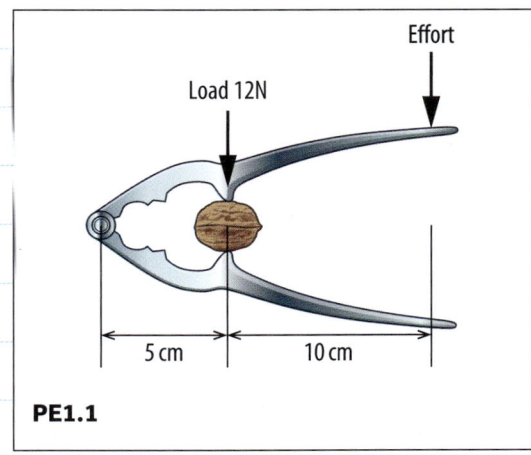

PE1.1

Calculate the effort required to crack open the nut in this example of a lever. (3 marks)

> **Exam tip**
>
> You will need to use your maths skills in the exam. The formula you need may be given in the question but it helps to be familiar with formulae that are likely to come up.

Student answer

Force (E) × distance of effort
= force (L) × distance of load

Force (E) × 10 = 12 × 5

Force (E) = $\frac{12 \times 5}{10}$

Force (E) = 6 N

Verdict

Although the student used the correct calculation, and recognised that the load was 5 cm away from the fulcrum, they incorrectly assumed that the effort was only 10 cm away from the fulcrum. The correct substitution into the formula should have been Force (E) × 15 = 12 × 5, which would make the force (E) 4 N.

Preparing for your exam 1

Question 2: 'Discuss' question
Discuss the effects of a manufacturing company investing in video conferencing in their global operation. (6 marks)

Exam tip

'Discuss' answers need to be fairly detailed, exploring aspects of the situation by reasoning or argument.

Student answer

1. There are many advantages of using video conferencing – for example, managers of a company can save time by speaking to staff abroad without having to travel. There are also no travel costs, making it cheaper to contact staff.

2. Decisions which could take a long time to make via email could be made much quicker during a video conference. Also, physical examples of products or parts can be shown in real time.

3. However, there are also disadvantages. There may be set-up costs linked to video conferencing, and time zones may make meetings inconvenient for some staff.

Verdict

The student has given six good answers that explore aspects of the concept. Care needs to be taken not to repeat answers. In this case, although the answer discusses time twice, the first point relates to time lost through travelling and the second relates to the speed the decision can be made, so the answers are different.

Question 3: 'Evaluate' question
Evaluate the use of wind-generated electricity as an alternative to fossil-fuelled power stations. (9 marks)

Exam tip

'Evaluate' answers need to look at the strengths and weaknesses of a proposition and then draw a conclusion.

Student answer

Wind power is a clean technology that does not produce harmful emissions like fossil fuels when burnt. Wind is a renewable form of energy so it will not run out, unlike fossil fuels. The power from wind farms can be connected directly into the electricity from where the energy is generated, while fossil fuels need to be transported to where they will be used. In conclusion, wind energy is more environmentally friendly, it will be available in the future and the electricity is more easily distributed from where it is created.

Verdict

This is a good answer. The student has made several well-balanced evaluations of the two concepts and drawn a reasoned conclusion on the benefits of wind power.

Preparing for your exam 1

Question 4: 'Give'/'Explain' questions

The light switch on the right is made from a thermosetting polymer.

1. Give the name of a suitable thermosetting polymer from which to manufacture the switch. (1 mark)

2. Explain **two** benefits of using thermosetting polymers. (4 marks)

Exam tip

This is a combination of a 'give' question and an 'explain' question. You do not need to get the first part right to gain marks in the second part. 'Explain' questions require you to give reasons why you have chosen your answers.

Student answer

1. Urea formaldehyde
2. (a) Heat resistant
   (b) Hard

Verdict

In part 1, the student correctly identified a suitable thermosetting polymer.

In part 2, the student does not give the full justification required. They could have written the answer in the following way.

2. a) Thermosetting polymers are heat resistant and so will not be affected by the heat of the electricity or melt in a fire.
   b) They are also hard meaning they are resistant to scratching when used so will look good for longer.

Question 5: 'Explain' question

The materials that products are made from are chosen because of their characteristics. The picture below is a child's toy train.

Explain **one** benefit of using beech to manufacture the toy train. (2 marks)

Exam tip

This type of question requires one benefit. However, this needs to be explained: why is this a benefit?

Student answer

Beech is a good material to use because it does not splinter easily, which means it would be safe for small children to play with without hurting themselves.

Verdict

The student answered the question as required.

Preparing for your exam 1

Question 6: 'Give'/'name' (short answer question)

Figure PE1.2 shows a graph of the carbon emissions based on a life-cycle analysis (LCA) of two hand drying options.

a) Name the hand dryer that has additional carbon emissions during materials production. **(1 mark)**

b) Give **one** reason why dryer B has additional carbon emissions after materials production. **(1 mark)**

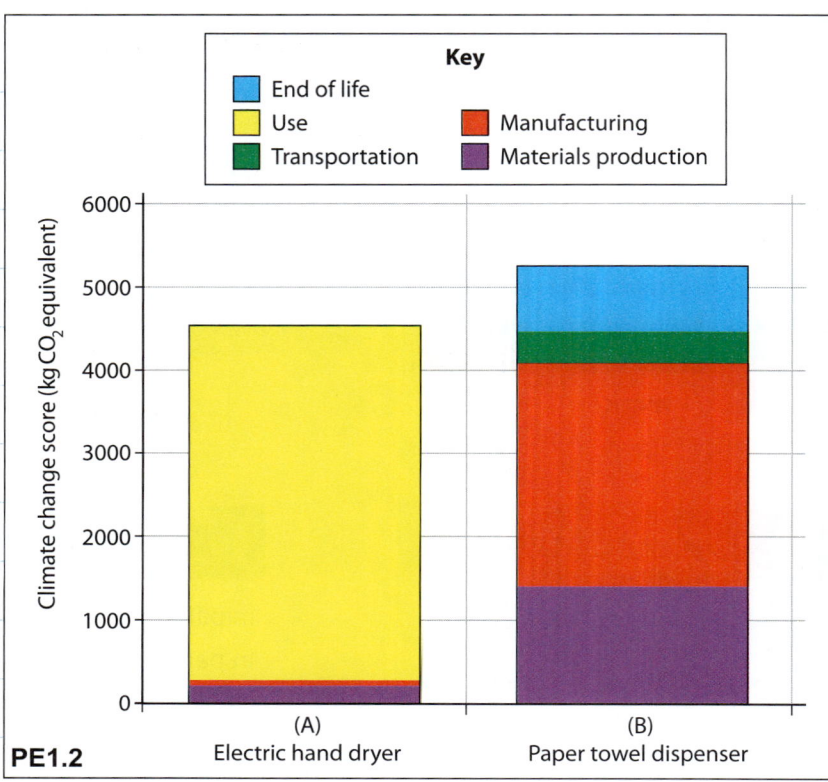

PE1.2

> **Exam tip**
>
> This type of question requires you to draw conclusions from key information displayed in a certain format.

Student answer

1. Paper towel dispenser.

2. Paper towels need to be supplied to the dispenser throughout its life and not just in the construction of the dispenser.

Verdict

The student has answered this question well.

Preparing for your exam 1

Question 7: 'Use notes and/or sketches to show' question

Use notes and/or sketches to show the structure of plywood. (2 marks)

Exam tip

It is important to annotate (label) sketches as the detail is not always clear in a sketch and the marks awarded can come from written or the drawn information.

Student answer

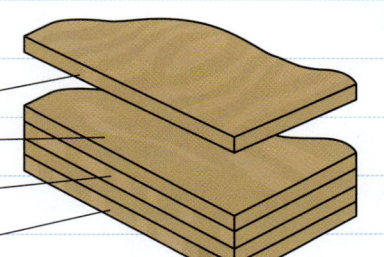

- Laminate
- Thin laminates bonded with adhesive
- 90° alternate layers
- Odd number of layers

Verdict

This is a good answer. The annotation states what is not clear from the sketch – that glue and thin laminates are used. The sketch shows the grain directions at 90 degrees to each other and that there is an odd number of layers.

Pearson Education Ltd accepts no responsibility whatsoever for the accuracy or method of working in the answers given.

2 Metals

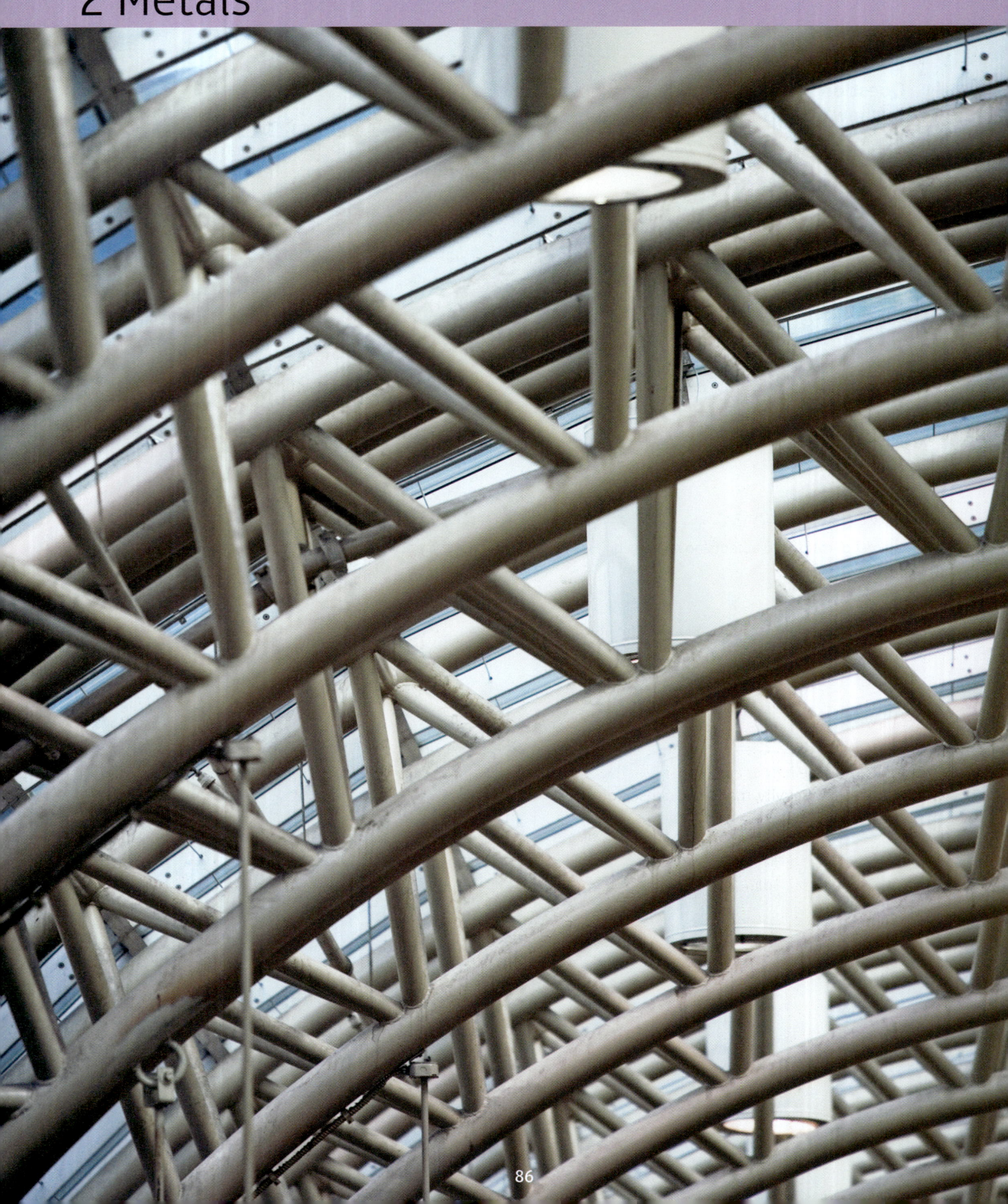

2.1 Design contexts

Getting started
How many different metals can you name?
Find an item of metal jewellery, a bolt and a saucepan. Do you know which metals they are made of, and why?
Do you know where metals come from and what ecological issues are related to their use?

Metals offer many design opportunities, from small components to decorative items and large, functional products. It is useful to know how metals differ, the properties that make them suitable for different uses and the different manufacturing processes.

2.2 Metals sources, properties, social and ecological footprints

Learning objectives
By the end of this section, you should know:
- the advantages, disadvantages and applications of different metals
- how physical and working characteristics influence the selection of individual metals
- the origins of different metals and the implications of extracting and processing them.

Ferrous metals
Table 2.2.1 describes the properties of high-carbon steel and tungsten steel.

Material	Properties	Composition	Melting point	Uses
High-carbon steel	Very hard, difficult to cut, less **ductile**, can be hardened and tempered, good conductivity, magnetic, dense, tough	Iron + 0.8–1.5% carbon	1800°C	Chisels, plane blades, saws, drill bits, hammers, screwdrivers
Tungsten steel	Good strength, resistant to corrosion, not magnetic, tough, stable at high temperatures, good conductivity, dense	Iron + 1–18% tungsten	1650–3695°C	Nozzles in rocket engines, high-speed cutting tools, light filaments

Table 2.2.1 Examples of ferrous metals

Link it up
See pages 37–39 for more information about ferrous and non-ferrous metals.

Key term
Ductile: something that can be deformed by bending, twisting or stretching. Ductility in metals increases with temperature but heating may weaken them.

2 Metals

Non-ferrous metals

Table 2.2.2 describes the properties of tin, 7000 series aluminium alloys and titanium.

Type	Properties	Composition	Melting point	Uses
Tin	Soft, ductile, malleable, high corrosion resistance, low melting point, weak	Pure metal	232°C	Food packaging, solder
7000 series aluminium alloys	High strength, poor corrosion resistance, heat treatable	Aluminium (main metal) with various quantities of zinc, magnesium and copper	660°C	Aircraft frames, bicycle frames, car wheels, climbing equipment
Titanium	Corrosion resistant, strong, tough, stiff, low density	Pure metal	1668°C	Small gears, coatings, replacement human joints

Table 2.2.2 Examples of non-ferrous metals

> **Key term**
>
> **Malleable:** something that is able to be permanently deformed in all directions without fracture. It increases with temperature.

> **Apply it**
>
> Research the new materials introduced in Tables 2.2.1 and 2.2.2 (high-carbon steel, tungsten steel, tin, 7000 series aluminium alloys and titanium) and find a specific example of the use of each one, other than the examples given above.

> **Exam-style question**
>
> Explain **two** reasons why tin would be a suitable metal for lining the inside of food cans. **(6 marks)**

Sources and origins

Metal	Ore-bearing rock	Main sources
Iron	Magnetite, haematite	USA, Russia, Sweden
Steel	Iron ore	China (also main manufacturer/processor)
Aluminium	Bauxite	USA, France, Australia
Copper	Chalcopyrite	USA, Chile, Zambia, Russia
Tin	Cassiterite	Indonesia, China

Table 2.2.3 Where the ferrous and non-ferrous metals are resourced or manufactured and their geographical origin

The physical characteristics of ferrous and non-ferrous metals

All metals have some properties that can be measured against other materials (see Table 2.2.4).

Working properties of ferrous and non-ferrous metals

The working properties define how a material will behave or respond to external influences:

- **durability:** withstanding deterioration over time
- **toughness:** withstanding sudden stress or shocks
- **elasticity:** bending without fracture when subjected to a force
- **strength:** withstanding forces which can be compressive or tensile
  - **tensile:** resisting pulling forces without stretching
  - **compressive:** resisting pushing forces without being crushed.

Social footprint

Trend forecasting

Identifying trends in the metals industry ensures that supply fulfils demand and relies on the availability of existing metals and new alloys. It also looks to the ability of metals to be recycled and monitors the finding of new sources. Steel is likely to be the most important metal due to its low cost and customisable properties, but new aluminium alloys are gaining popularity.

Impact of extraction and material production on communities and wildlife

Large communities often grow where significant ore reserves have been discovered. Mining and processing operations bring employment to the area. This, however, has an impact on the landscape with the loss of habitats for wildlife and plants, through deforestation and the destruction of countryside.

Recycling and disposal

The process of extracting metals from ores is complicated, high in energy costs and produces substantial waste. Although bauxite (aluminium ore) is the most widely available ore it requires several refining processes that add to the cost of production. Steel is currently the most processed metal, as the ore is widely available and the conversion process is relatively straightforward. All metals can be recycled, which should reduce the demand on raw materials and reduce raw ore processing costs.

Ecological footprint

The extraction and processing of metal ore is having a significant impact on the world's natural resources (see Table 2.2.5 on page 90).

Conductivity	- The ability to allow the flow of electricity, or the rate that heat can pass through a material
Magnetism	- The ability to repel or attract other magnetic materials
Density	- Weight in grams per cubic centimetre or kilograms per cubic metre. - Density is the compactness of a substance or material. - Things feel 'heavier' if they have a higher density

Table 2.2.4 Physical characteristics of metals

2 Metals

Sustainability	• Although 25% of the Earth's crust is made up of metal ores, ores are a finite resource and can run out. • Metals need to be recycled wherever possible.
Extraction and erosion of the landscape	• Clearing areas for open-pit and underground mining damages the landscape. • Loss of habitats. • Deforestation of cleared areas can lead to soil erosion.
Processing	• Processing ores requires vast energy inputs. • Relatively small amounts of metal are produced from large amounts of ore.
Transportation	• Transportation links are required to get to the raw materials and to process them. • New road links are also needed to transport materials from the processing sites and the heavy goods vehicles are energy hungry (they use a lot of pollutant as fuel, such as diesel).
Wastage	• Processing ore into metal creates significant waste material that needs to be disposed of. • Waste materials also need to be treated to remove any impurities.
Pollution	• Release of toxins and carbon dioxide into the atmosphere through processing contributes to global warming. • Release of contaminants into the water course or into the soil. • Noise and vibration from heavy machinery and mining processes.

Table 2.2.5 Ecological impacts of metal ore extraction

Summary
Key points to remember:
- Ferrous and non-ferrous metals have different properties.
- The working properties of both include ductility, malleability, hardness, durability, toughness, elasticity and strength (both tensile and compressive).
- Understand that the ecological impacts of metal ore extraction are important.

Checkpoint
Strengthen
S1 What are the properties of high carbon steel?
Challenge
C1 Explain four different ecological impacts of metal ore extraction.

2.3 The way in which the selection of metals is influenced

Learning objective
By the end of this section, you should know:
- how different factors will influence the choice of materials for a specific application.

Choosing the right metal for a product involves analysing factors beyond just processing the metal to include aesthetic (how it looks) and external factors such as the environment, economics, availability and social implications.

2.3 The way in which the selection of metals is influenced

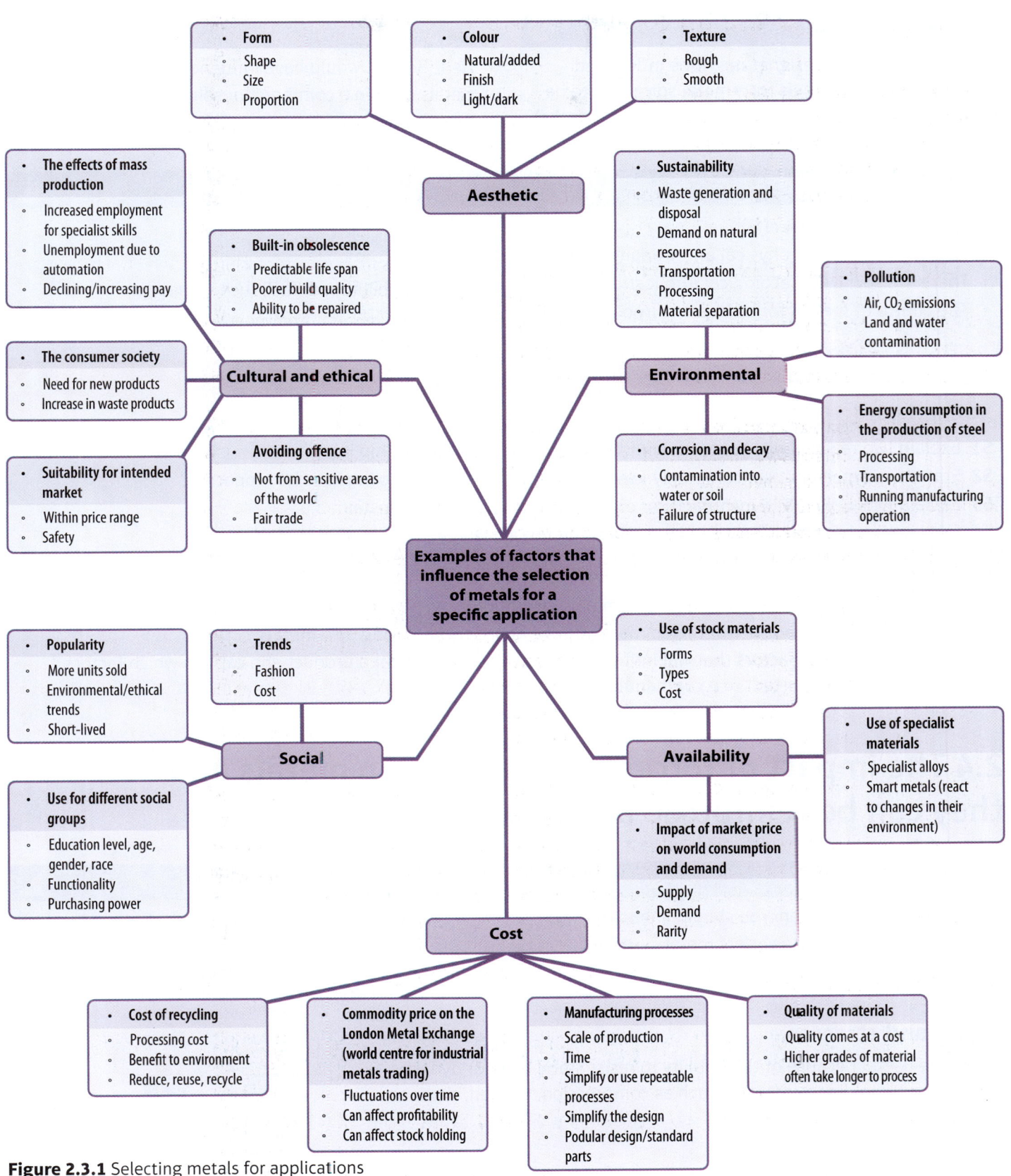

Figure 2.3.1 Selecting metals for applications

2 Metals

> **Exam-style question**
>
> Explain **two** ways a designer might be influenced when selecting materials for a metal spice rack to be sold at a craft fair. **(4 marks)**

> **Apply it**
>
> Identify what would have influenced the choice of metals used in a common household product of your choice.

> **Summary**
>
> **Key points to remember:**
> - Metals have specific physical and working properties.
> - There are social and ecological implications in the extraction and processing of metals.
> - The choice of metals for different purposes is influenced by many external factors.

> **Checkpoint**
>
> **Strengthen**
>
> **S1** Explain two reasons why titanium would be used for a replacement hip joint.
> **S2** State two metals that are commonly used to alloy with aluminium to improve its properties.
> **S3** Explain two ways that a manufacturer could make a product more sustainable.
> **S4** Explain three aesthetic factors that might influence a designer's choice of materials.
>
> **Challenge**
>
> **C1** Explain the effects on a community of a mining operation moving into the area.
> **C2** Investigate the reasons why recycled metal may be cheaper than using new metals.
> **C3** Summarise the key factors that will influence the choice of metals for a product and explain which factors would be most important to a car manufacturer.

2.4 The impact of forces and stresses on metals and how they can be reinforced and stiffened

> **Learning objectives**
>
> By the end of this section, you should know:
> - how forces and stresses affect metals
> - ways to strengthen the metals mechanically or physically.

Forces and stresses

Metals are useful because of their ability to resist static (still) or dynamic (moving) external forces or loads, such as compression, tension, shear or electrical or magnetic forces.

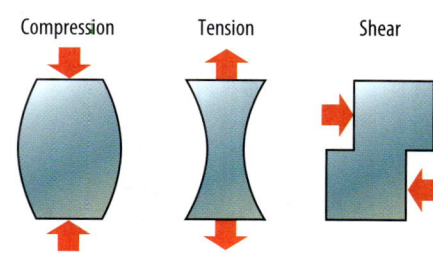

Figure 2.4.1 Types of force and stress

2.4 The impact of forces and stresses on metals and how they can be reinforced and stiffened

Force/stress	Definition	Example of item subjected to this force/stress
Compression	A force that tends to squash or shorten	Chair or table legs, the columns in a building
Tension	A force that tends to stretch or lengthen	Cables in a suspension bridge, wire in a crane
Shear	A force that acts in opposite directions	Paper or blades of grass cut by scissors or garden shears
Electrical	Ability to conduct electricity and allow the flow of electrons	Electrical cables (copper, steel), contacts in circuits, battery parts
Magnetic	Metals that contain iron are attracted to magnets	Motor parts, speakers, electro-magnetic locks, lathe chucks

Table 2.4.1 Types of force and stress on metals

Apply it
Investigate the principles of a motor and explain how a magnet and electrical energy are used to create the movement.

Reinforcement/stiffening techniques

Reinforcing or stiffening metal by hardening, tempering or changing its carbon content or physical form will maximise its structural properties.

Technique	Description
Hardening	• Some steel (with a certain percentage of carbon) can be hardened by heating and quenching in water (see Section 2.6, page 102) but it increases brittleness
Tempering	• Reduces steel's brittleness and increases its toughness once it has been hardened (see Section 2.6, page 102)
The effect of carbon content	• Changing the amount of carbon in steel can significantly change its hardness and toughness • Mild steel has 0.15–0.35% carbon – it is a tough metal used in construction or furniture frames • High-carbon steel has 0.8–1.5% carbon – it is very hard but more brittle and is used for cutting tools
Work hardening	• When metals are bent, rolled or hammered, their crystal structure becomes distorted (work hardened) • This makes it more difficult to work and it becomes brittle and may crack (see Section 2.6, page 102)

Table 2.4.2 Examples of reinforcement/stiffening techniques

2 Metals

> **Key terms**
>
> **Flange:** horizontal section of a beam.
> **Web:** vertical section of a beam.
> **Cantilever:** projecting beam fixed at only one end.

I, U, T and C beams

Beams are used in construction for carrying large loads across a gap. Designers often try to maximise their load-carrying capabilities and minimise their weight by using certain cross-sectional shapes. Horizontal parts are called **flanges** and vertical parts are called **webs**.

Beam type		
I		Most common and efficient form with large supporting flanges to spread load over larger area
U		Has twice the supporting load-carrying capability provided by the two webs
T		Weaker than 'I' beam due to the single flange but often used inverted with reinforced concrete flooring to support the blocks
C		Used when a single flat face is needed but the **cantilever** reduces load-carrying efficiency

Table 2.4.2 Load-carrying beams

> **Exam-style question**
>
> Explain **one** reason why an 'I' beam might be used in preference to a 'T' beam.
> **(2 marks)**

Summary

Key points to remember:
- Metals react to external forces and stresses acting on them.
- Metals can be reinforced or stiffened to improve their ability to carry loads.

Checkpoint

Strengthen

S1 Explain the effect of increasing the carbon content from 0.15–0.8% in steel.
S2 Explain why a 'C' beam has reduced load-carrying capabilities.

Challenge

C1 Draw a diagram to show how a 'T' beam could be used to support a concrete floor in a building.
C2 A beam supported at either end will be subjected to compressive and tensile forces. Draw a diagram to show where these two forces will be located.

2.5 Stock forms, types and sizes to calculate and determine the quantity of metals required

> **Learning objectives**
>
> By the end of this section, you should know:
> - about stock forms, types and sizes of metals
> - how to select appropriate stock forms and types
> - how metals are graded into different sizes.

Designers and manufacturers need to understand the advantages, disadvantages and applications of using stock forms of metals for their products.

Stock forms/types

Metals used in the workshop and industry are generally available in standard forms, a practice which is cost effective and gives designers ready-made shapes to incorporate into their designs.

Form	Description	Use	Diagram
Bar	- Has a solid cross-section - Available in different shapes including square, round, half round, hexagonal, flat, angle and channel	- General purpose construction work	
Sheet	- Comes as flat sheets ranging in thickness from 0.6–3 mm	- Washing machine casing, radiators	
Plate	- Sheet metal more than 3 mm thick	- Heavy-duty work, ship hulls	
Pipe/tube	- Has a hollow section - Shapes include square, rectangular, round and hexagonal	- Water pipes, general construction work where reduced weight is important	

Table 2.5.1 Stock form types *Contd...*

2 Metals

Form	Description	Use	Diagram
Castings	• Liquid metal is poured into a mould and sets into shape	• G-clamps, workshop vices, anvils	
Extrusions	• A metal billet (small bar) is pushed through a die to make the desired cross-sectional shape	• Complex cross-sectional shapes, window frames	
Wire	• A strand of metal is drawn through a plate to make the desired cross-sectional shape	• Electrical wire, brake cables	
Powder metallurgy	• Powdered metal is heated at just below its melting temperature and compacted into specified shapes	• Bearings, gears	

Table 2.5.1 Stock form types

> **Exam-style question**
>
> Explain **two** reasons why a company might prefer to use stock forms of metal when manufacturing a washing machine. **(4 marks)**

Sizes

Metals are available in a range of sizes to suit different applications.

Gauge

Sheet metal comes in a range of thicknesses that can be graded by a number called its gauge. The gauge number typically ranges from 1 to 30 and as the number increases, the material thickness decreases.

Gauge	Thickness (approximate)
5	5.4 mm
10	3.25 mm
15	1.8 mm
20	0.91 mm
25	0.5 mm

Table 2.5.2 Gauge numbers for different metal thicknesses

2.5 Stock forms, types and sizes to calculate and determine the quantity of metals required

Cross-sectional area
Calculating the cross-sectional area of a metal enables you to calculate the weight and design in adjustments. The cross-sectional area is found by cutting a section through the metal and measuring the solid shape.

Maths in practice 1
Cross-sectional areas
Use these formulas to work out cross-sectional areas. Note that the radius is half of the diameter.

- **Area of a square or rectangle** = length × width
- **Area of a circle** = πr^2 (i.e. 3.142 × radius × radius)
- **Area of a triangle** = half the length of the base × perpendicular height

Hint: break irregular shapes into squares, rectangles, triangles or circles

- What is the area of this irregular shape? Each grid square represents 10 cm × 10 cm.

Area = area of square A + area of rectangle B + area of triangle C + area of rectangle D

= 30 × 30 + 10 × 20 + ½ × 10 × 10 + 40 × 10

= 900 + 200 + 50 + 400

= 1550 cm²

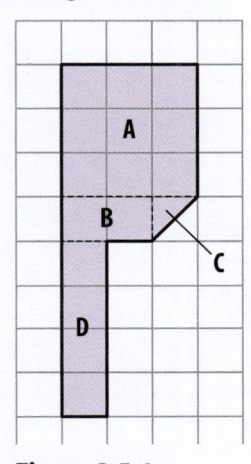

Figure 2.5.1 Irregular shape

Diameter
Solid tubes come in different stock forms that are measured by the diameter (Ø) of the cross-section.

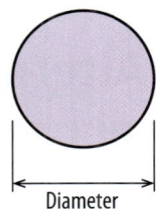

Figure 2.5.2 Measuring diameter

Wall thickness of tubes
Tubes have an internal and external diameter. It is important to know both diameters and the gauge when designing with tube. By subtracting the internal diameter from the external diameter, you can calculate the wall thickness. This will also be its gauge.

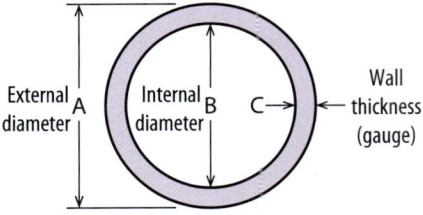

Figure 2.5.3 Calculating tube wall thickness

Exam-style question
Calculate the cross-sectional area of the three metal forms in Figure 2.5.4. **(5 marks)**

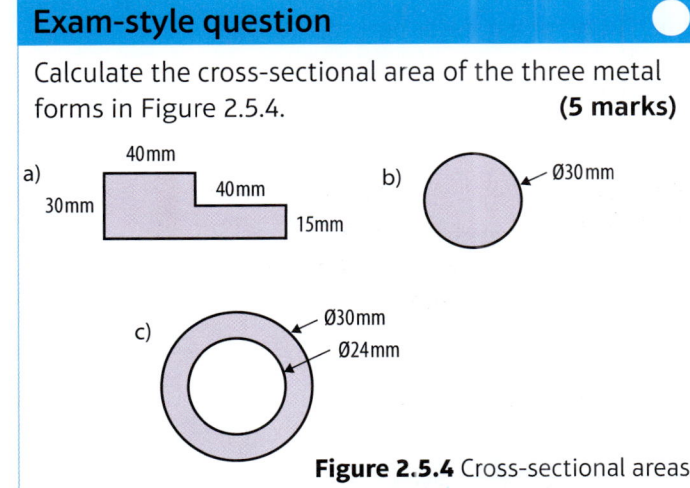

Figure 2.5.4 Cross-sectional areas

Summary
Key points to remember:
there are different uses for the different forms of ferrous and non-ferrous metals.

Checkpoint
Strengthen
S1 Give a short description of extrusions, and the uses of them.

Challenge
C1 How are metals graded into different sizes?

2 Metals

2.6 Alternative processes that can be used to manufacture metal products to different scales of production

> **Learning objectives**
>
> By the end of this section, you should know:
> - how metals are processed for specific purposes
> - how scales and methods of production will vary depending on demand.

Metals can be joined and shaped in several ways depending on the required scale of production. The choice of processing method will have an impact on profits as machinery and equipment can be very expensive.

Processes

Forging

Forging involves heating metal to soften it and then hammering it into shape. It can be completed on a small scale, such as the work of a blacksmith, or by applying greater forces (drop forging) using large machinery for a greater output.

Forged metal is stronger than cast metal as the hammering creates a tight grain structure. It is also tougher and has good wear resistance.

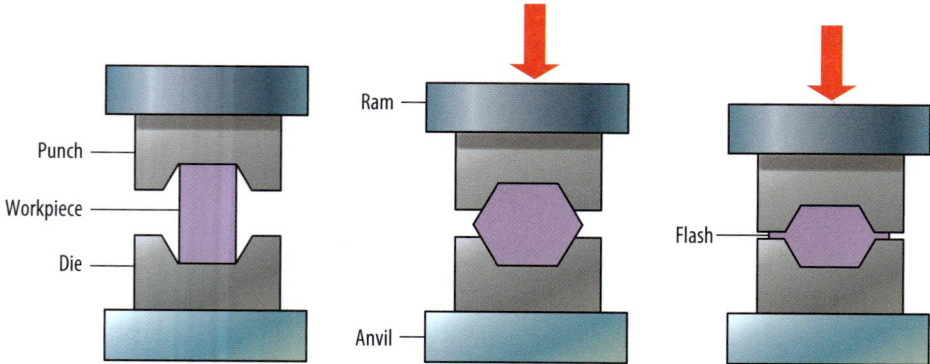

Figure 2.6.1 Drop forging

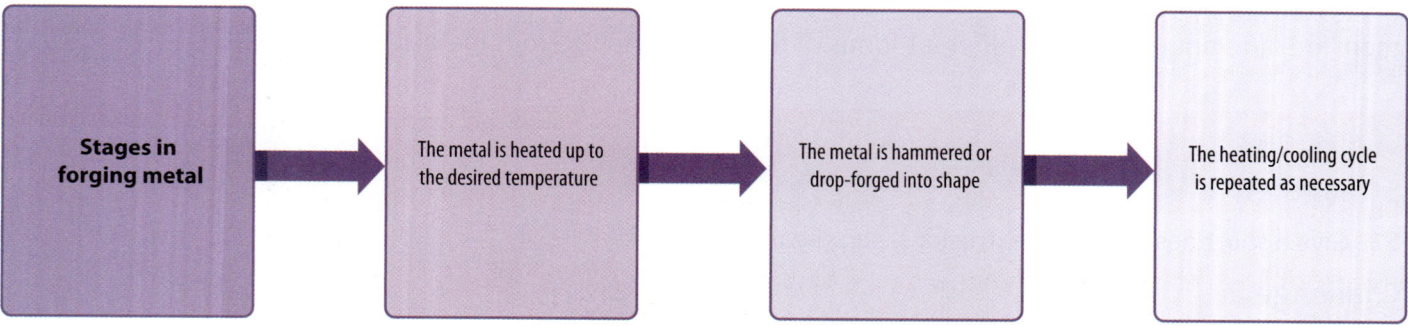

Figure 2.6.2 Forging metal

2.6 Alternative processes that can be used to manufacture metal products to different scales of production

Casting
When casting, the metal is heated to a molten state and then poured into a mould to create the desired shape using either sand casting or die casting.

Sand casting
The quality of finish depends on the quality of the mould and the type of sand used. Sand casting is generally used for larger objects such as tank tracks, vices or G-clamps, where the quality of finish is not the highest priority. It is usually completed in small quantities as the mould has to be re-made after each casting.

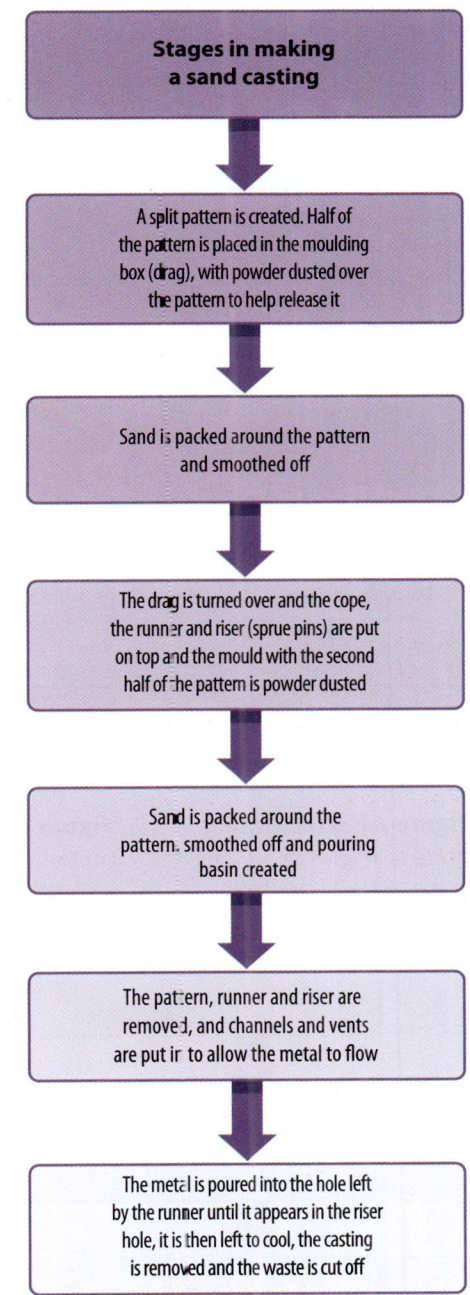

Figure 2.6.4 Stages of sand casting

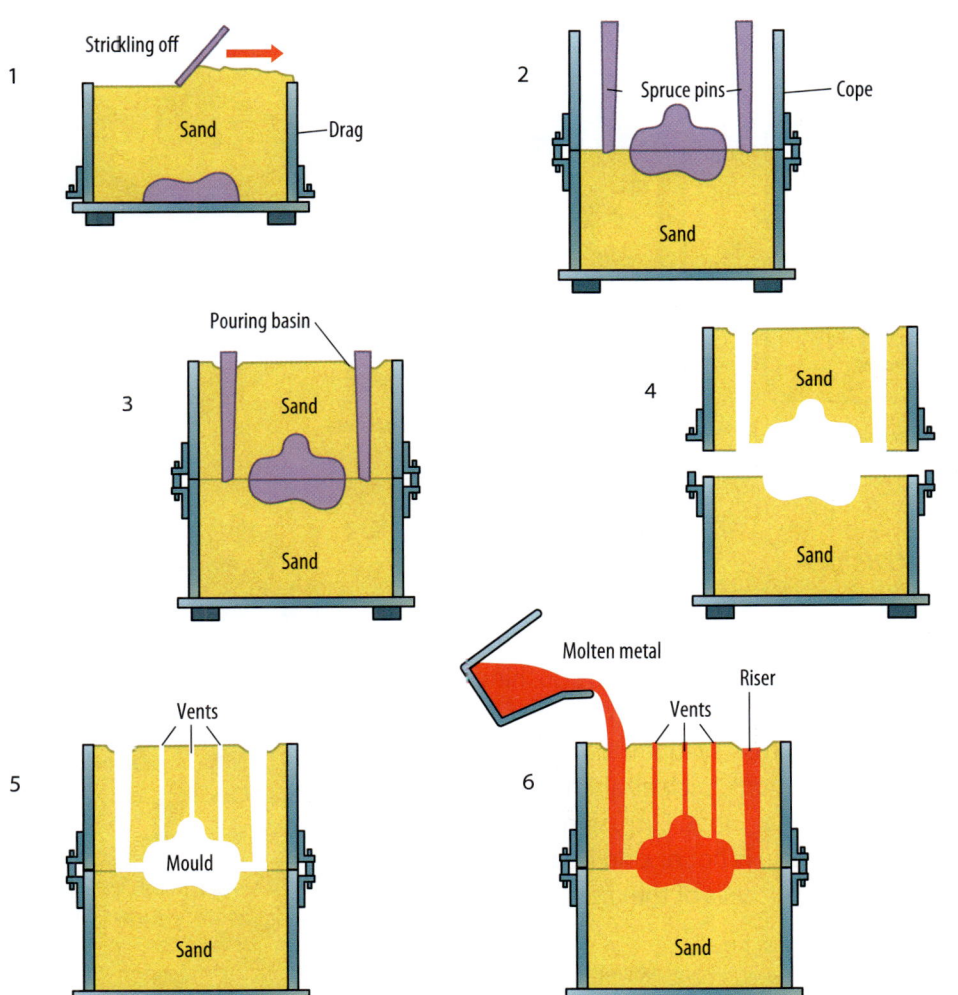

Figure 2.6.3 Sand casting

Die casting
This is generally used for smaller products such as toy cars or small parts in household machinery as the process is repeatable at a high quality in large quantities. A die is a shaped piece of metal, often with a hole in it that uniquely matches the shape of the product to be cast.

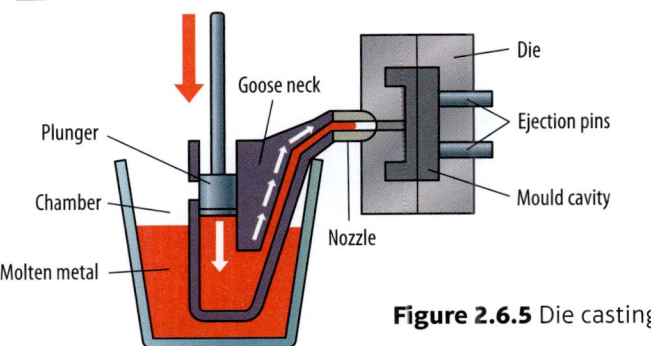

Figure 2.6.5 Die casting

99

2 Metals

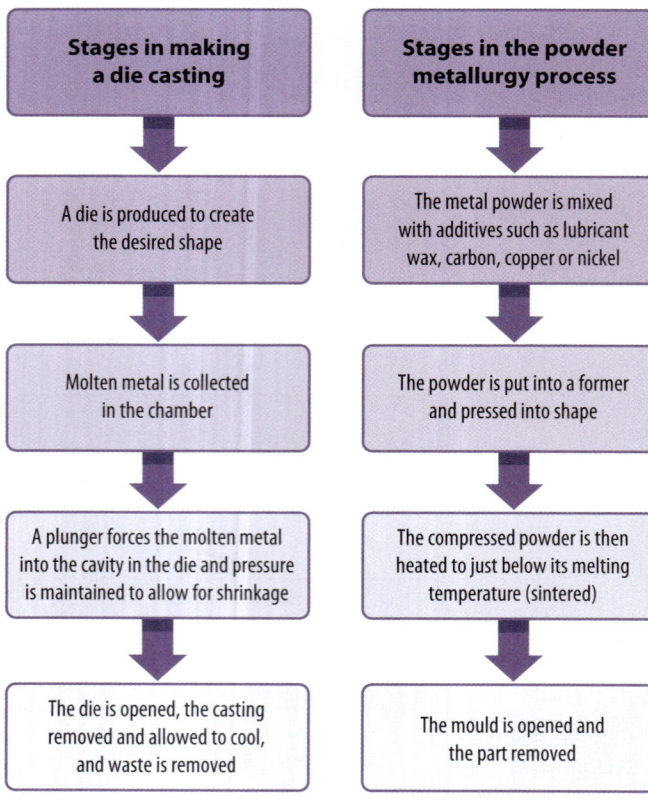

Figure 2.6.6 Die casting process

Figure 2.6.7 Powder metallurgy process

Powder metallurgy (sintering)

This is the process of forming powdered metal into specified shapes at just below its melting temperature. The mix of metal powders can contain additives to improve the properties of finished products, such as bearings and engine parts.

Stamping

Stamping is used to cold-form a metal sheet into a three-dimensional shape. It is commonly used to manufacture car body panels or for casing on kitchen appliances.

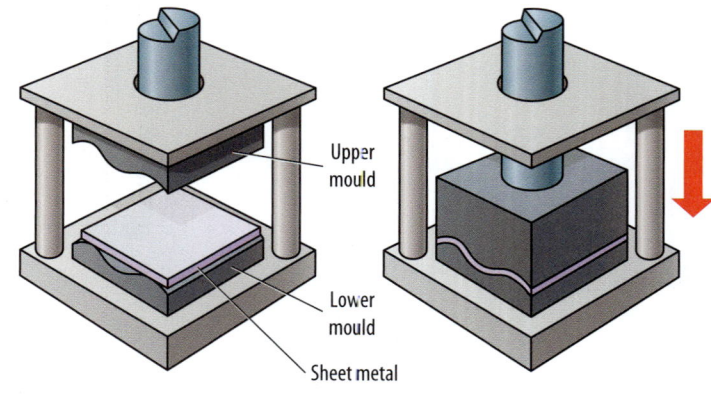

Figure 2.6.8 Stamping

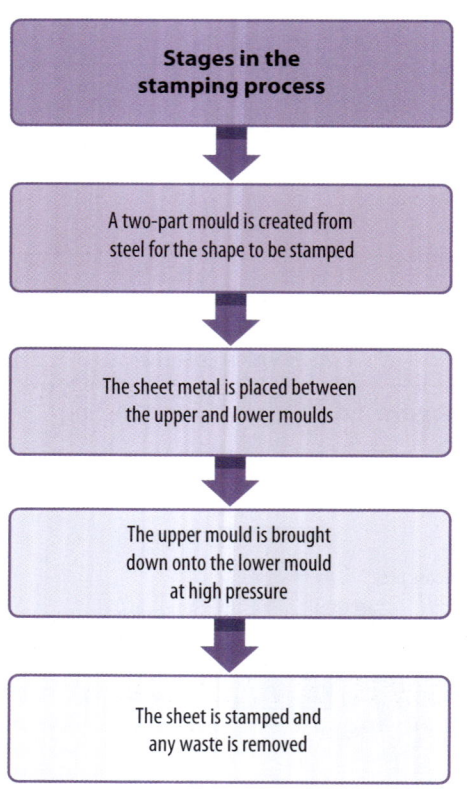

Figure 2.6.9 Stamping process

Extrusion

Extrusion is the process of producing a defined cross-sectional shape with a good finish. The shape is achieved by pushing the metal billet through a die. Extrusion often has complicated cross-sections that are used in many applications, such as aluminium window frames or metal tubes. Extrusion can be done when the metal is hot or cold depending on the relative softness of the metal.

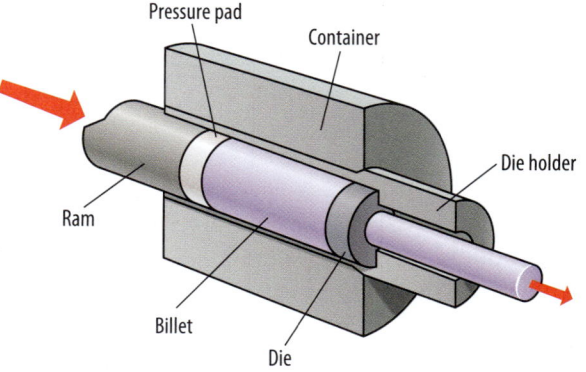

Figure 2.6.10 Extrusion

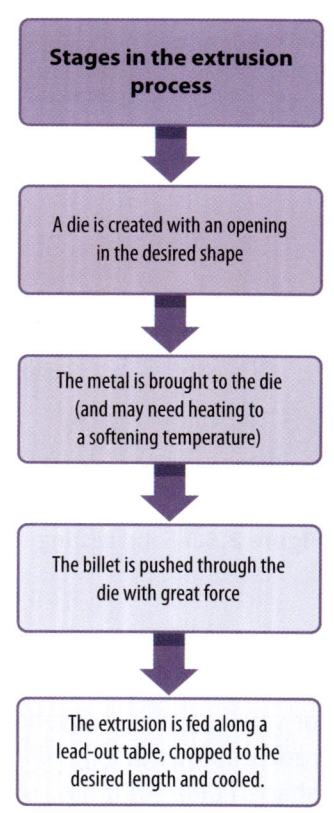

Figure 2.6.11 Extrusion stages

2.6 Alternative processes that can be used to manufacture metal products to different scales of production

Welding

Welding fuses two metals by melting them together. The joint produced is as strong as the parent material. The most common techniques are arc (electrical) and oxy fuel (acetylene) welding.

In industry, robots carry out many welding processes and, to reduce costs, parts may be spot welded (welded at a number of separate points) to give a line of localised welds that will provide sufficient strength, e.g. to join car body panels.

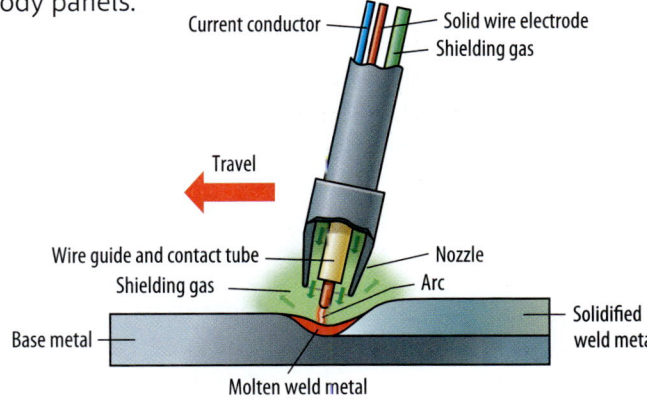

Figure 2.6.12 Arc welding

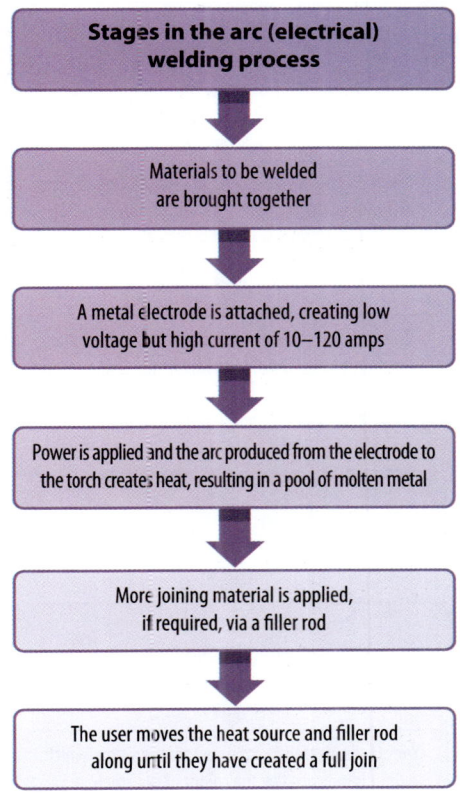

Figure 2.6.13 Arc (electrical) welding process

> **Exam-style question**
>
> Use notes and/or sketches to show the process of sand casting. **(4 marks)**

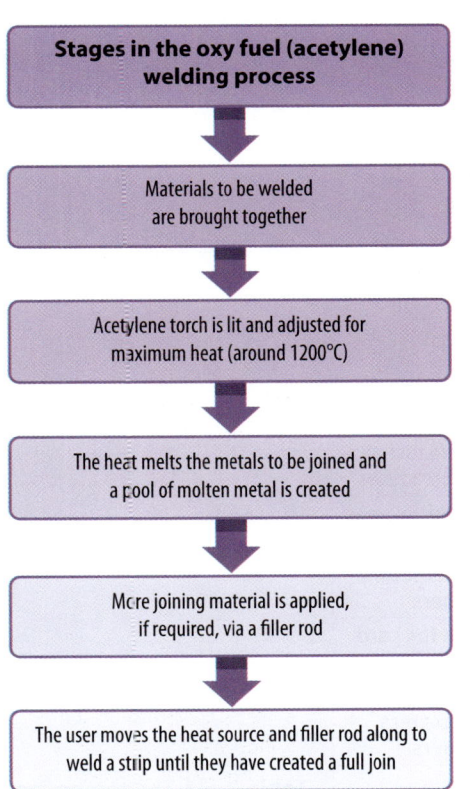

Figure 2.6.14 Oxy fuel welding stages

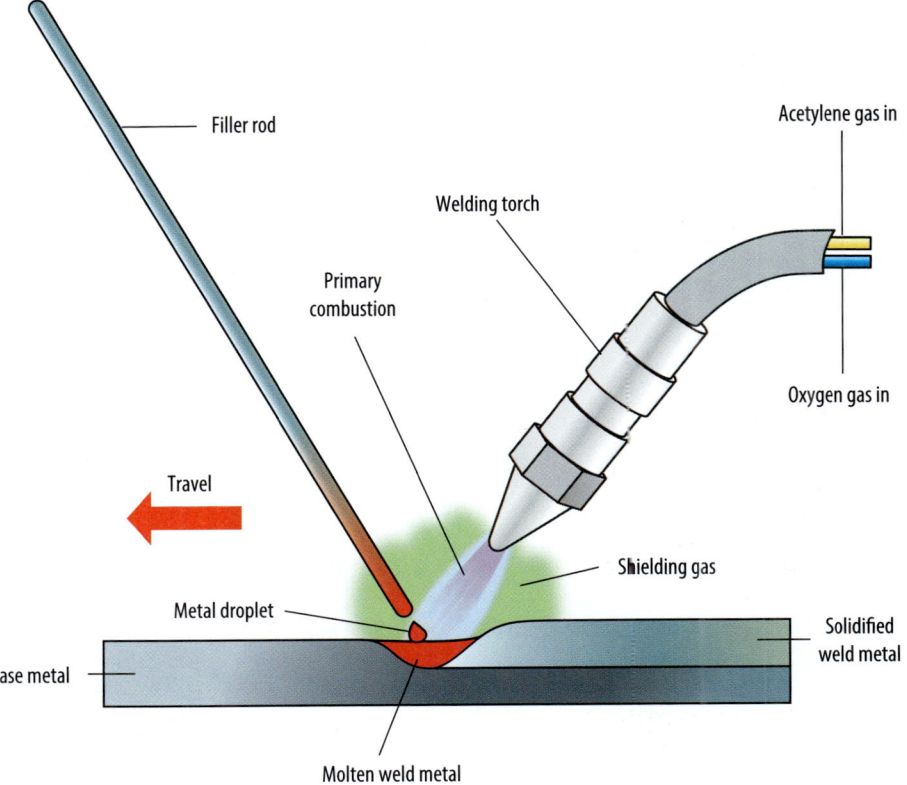

Figure 2.6.15 Oxy fuel welding

2 Metals

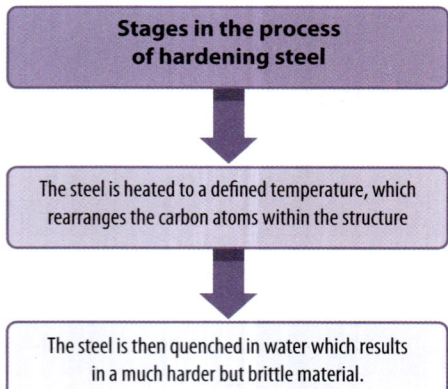

Figure 2.6.16 Hardening stages

Hardening

The properties of metals can be changed by heating and cooling in a defined way (hardening and tempering). Metals can also harden after being worked and will need to be annealed (reformed) to reduce internal stresses. Case hardening is a third method of hardening metal but this only affects the outer surface. The hardness of steel also varies depending on its carbon content with mild steel having approximately 0.1–0.3 per cent carbon content and high-carbon steels having approximately 0.55–0.95 per cent carbon content.

Tempering

Hardening steel by heating and quenching in water rearranges the carbon atoms within the steel structure and locks the steel to a new structure. The material is much harder but brittle. It is therefore important to temper the steel to reduce brittleness and increase toughness.

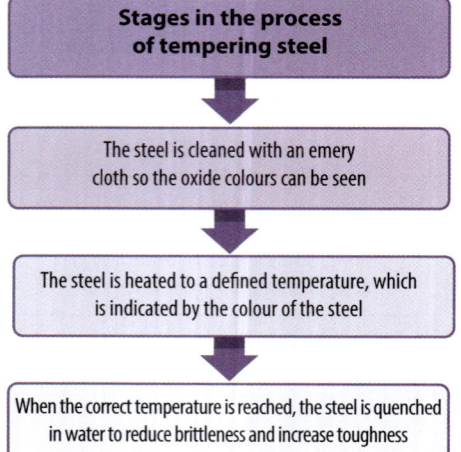

Figure 2.6.17 Tempering stages

Work hardening and annealing

When metals are bent, rolled or hammered, their crystal structure becomes distorted and the metals become work hardened. This makes the material harder to work and it becomes brittle and may crack. To prevent this, the metal needs to be annealed to release the internal stresses.

Apply it

Research the advantages and disadvantages of each of these processes. Consider:
- the cost of equipment
- which types of metal they suit and do not suit
- the amount of waste and energy consumption
- relative accuracy and speed
- the size of production runs.

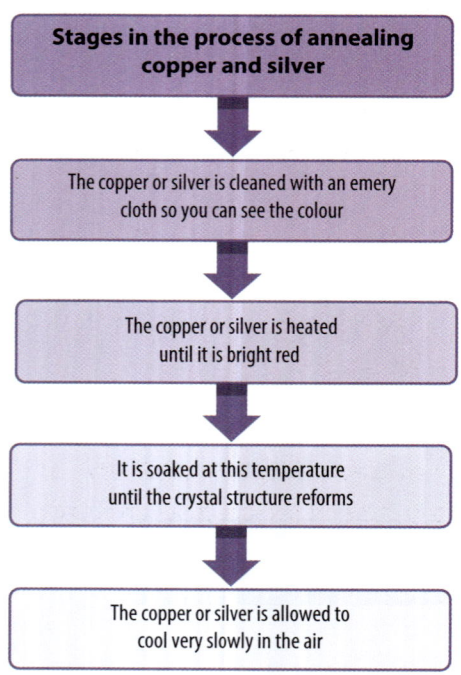

Figure 2.6.18 Annealing copper and silver

Temperature (°F)	Temperature (°C)	Colour of heated carbon steel	Examples
600	316		Scrapers, spokeshaves
560	293		Screwdrivers, springs, gears
540	282		Cold chisels, centre punches
520	271		Taps ≤ 1/4 inch
500	260		Axes, wood chisels, drifts, Taps ≥ 1/4 inch, nut taps, thread dies
480	249		Twist drills, large taps, knurls
460	238		Dies, punches, bits, reamers
450	232		Twist drills for hard use
440	227		Lathe tools, scrapers, milling, cutters, reamers
430	221		Reamers
420	216		Knives, hammers

Table 2.6.1 The tempering colours of steel

2.6 Alternative processes that can be used to manufacture metal products to different scales of production

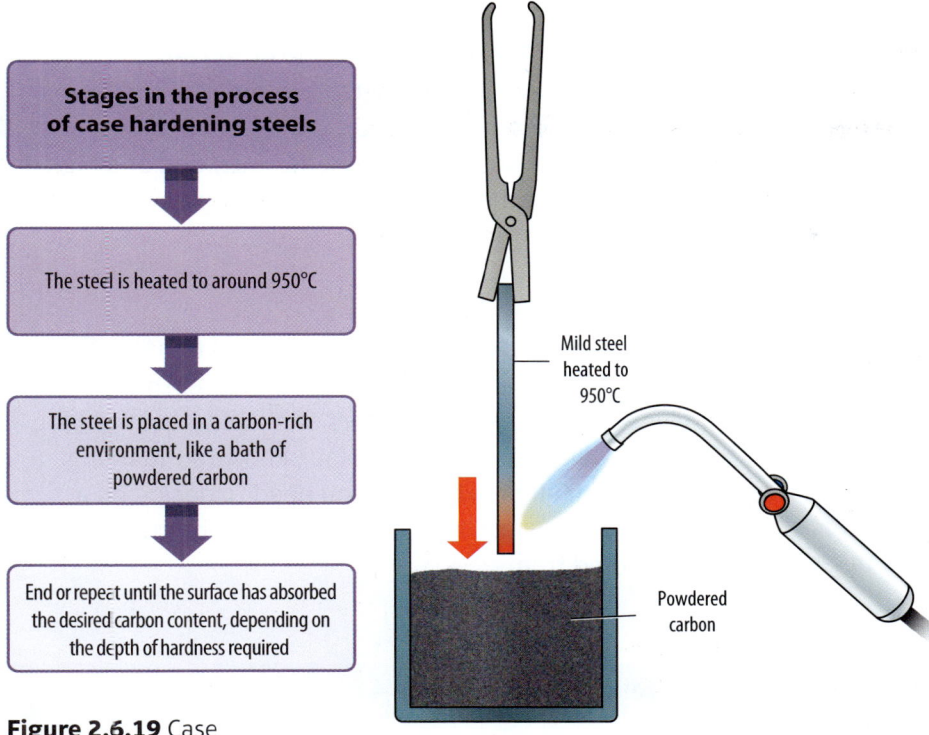

Figure 2.6.19 Case hardening steels

Figure 2.6.20 Case hardening

Case hardening

Case hardening is the hardening of mild steels by increasing the carbon content on the outer surface. This will increase the hardness of the surface and improve the steel's wear. Examples of this are bearing, gear or cam surfaces where the wear only occurs on the outer surfaces, or for tools that may need sharpening so the depth of hardness needs to be greater.

Scales of production

The choice of manufacturing process will depend on many factors. The scale of production, based on demand, is important and will have a large impact on the cost effectiveness of the manufacturing process.

Scale of production	Potential advantages	Potential disadvantages
One-off e.g. a custom motorcycle	• Each product is unique • Workers tend to be highly skilled • Products often higher quality • Client-led	• Expensive • Higher cost of materials • Production times are longer as they are labour intensive
Batch e.g. metal hinges and locks	• Set number of products manufactured, so suited to products that are made in limited quantities • Workers are more flexible to respond to demand • Can allow more customer choice • Cheaper, as relatively more units are made	• Storage of the batches • Repetitive work • Time and money lost in changing production set-up
Mass e.g. cars and car parts	• Large quantity of products at low unit cost • Often automated, so fewer workers needed • Costs are lower due to the economies of scale	• Repetitive work for remaining workforce • High initial tooling and set-up costs • Breaks in production are expensive
Continuous e.g. continuous casting of steel	• Production lines run 24 hours a day, seven days a week, so there is less down time • Thousands of identical products are manufactured with minimum input • Meets high level of demand and highly automated • Materials can be bought more cheaply due to economies of scale	• Repetitive work for remaining workforce as they are just 'minding' machinery • Initial tooling and set-up costs are high

Table 2.6.2 Scales of production

2 Metals

> **Exam-style question**
> Give **one** method of production that is most suitable for manufacturing a large quantity of metal furniture at low cost. **(1 mark)**

> **Apply it**
> Make a list of all the areas where a company will save costs if they choose mass production, compared to batch production.

> **Link it up**
> For more information about marking out, see page 226.

Techniques for high-volume production

When manufacturing in metal it is important to look for ways to improve accuracy and the level of output so that products are made more efficiently and at a higher quality. This can be achieved by adopting a number of key manufacturing methods.

Marking-out methods

To mark out outlines on metal you need to use different methods to accurately scratch the surface. This may not give a clear mark so engineers often use a quick drying spirit liquid that is blue in colour, known as 'marking blue'. With all marking out, you need to decide on a datum face, which is where all subsequent marks can be measured from.

Tool	Uses	Details
Scriber	Used for marking lines	
Odd leg calipers	Used to mark a parallel line to an edge	
Engineer's square	Used with a scriber to mark lines at 90° to the edge	The square is pushed up against the scriber then the mark is made across the work — scriber, square
Centre punch	Used to create an indent for the exact centre of a hole for drilling, or a series of 'dots' along a curve to indicate where a line is to be cut	

Table 2.6.3 Tools used in different marking-out methods *Cont…*

2.6 Alternative processes that can be used to manufacture metal products to different scales of production

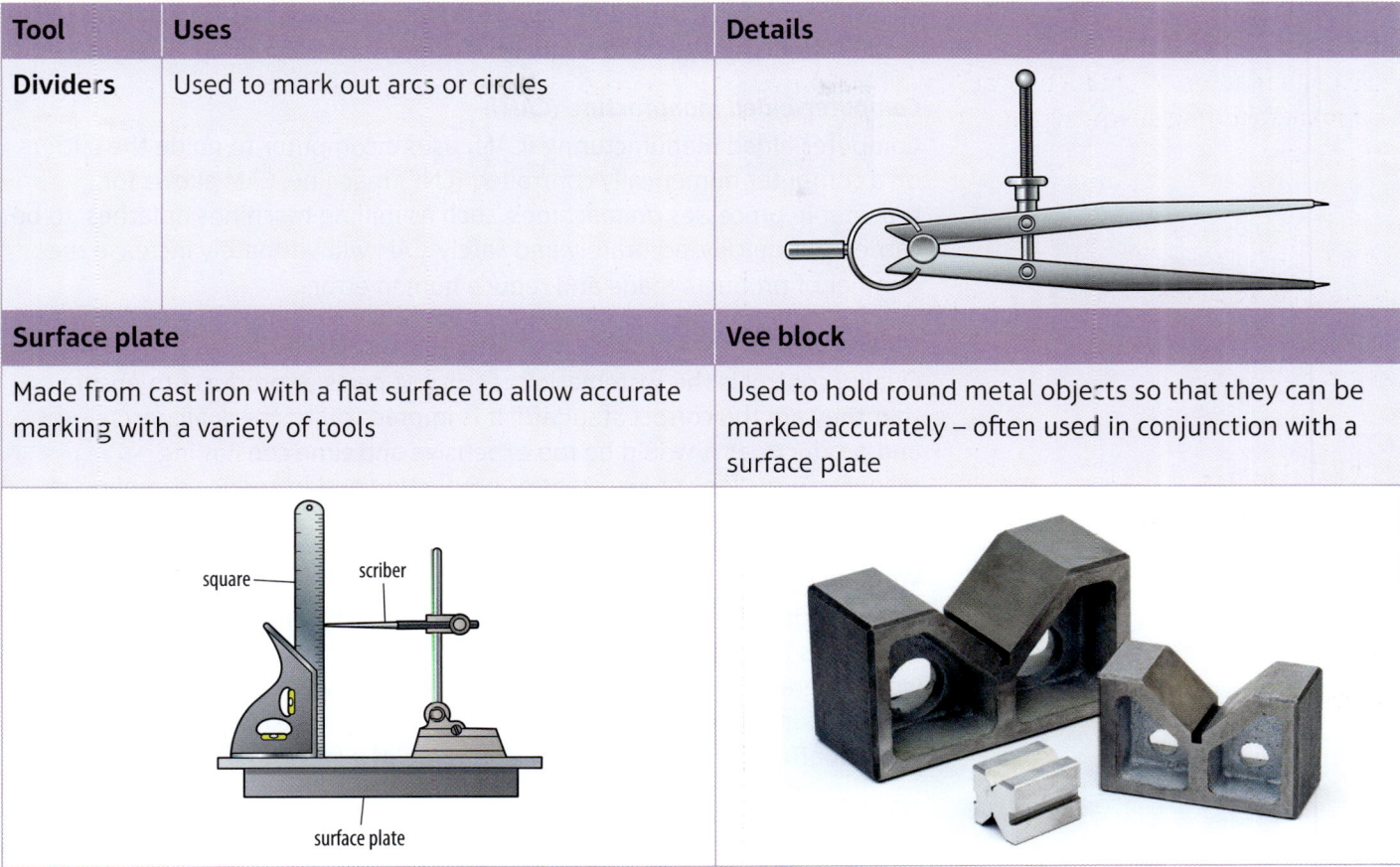

Tool	Uses	Details
Dividers	Used to mark out arcs or circles	
Surface plate		**Vee block**
Made from cast iron with a flat surface to allow accurate marking with a variety of tools		Used to hold round metal objects so that they can be marked accurately – often used in conjunction with a surface plate

Table 2.6.3 Tools used in different marking-out methods

Ensuring quality when producing in quantity

Jigs
A jig is a device for holding work in place that helps when carrying out repetitive manufacturing methods. The jig holds the work in the same position and then the cutting tool is guided to the correct place, such as a jig for drilling accurate holes in a metal bar.

Fixtures
Fixtures are similar to jigs, but they are fixed in position to line up with the tools being used. An example of this would be a vice clamped to the table of a milling machine or pillar drill.

Templates
Templates are used if you need to mark out the same points, or shape, onto metal a number of times. The template is made to the exact size of the shape to be cut or the location of holes. It can then be fixed to the metal surface each time.

Patterns
Patterns are replicas of the product to be cast, which are used in the sand-casting process. They are often slightly larger to cater for shrinkage. The quality of the pattern is directly related to the quality of the casting made – it can be made from cheaper material that is easier to work and can be used many times.

Moulds
When casting (sand or die), the mould is the hollow container that the molten metal is poured into. This can be sand, in the case of sand casting, and once the metal has been poured into the mould, it will then cool, harden and be removed from the mould, having taken the shape of the original pattern. In die casting, the mould/die will be machined from a steel block.

Sub-assembly
Sub-assemblies are a number of components that have been assembled and used as an individual component in a larger product. This means that the sub-assembly is built to a uniform specification, quality tested in its own right

2 Metals

and can be replaced in its entirety. An example of this could be a standard DVD module that is inserted into a variety of different desktop computers.

Computer-aided manufacture (CAM)
Computer-aided manufacturing (CAM) uses a computer to guide the cutters on a computer numerically controlled (CNC) machine. CAM allows for repeatable processes on machines, such as milling machines or lathes, to be carried out quickly, accurately and safely. CAM will ultimately increase the number of products made and reduce human error.

Quality control
Quality control is the systematic checking of parts or products to ensure that they are the correct standard. It is impractical to check all parts and products, as it would be too expensive and time consuming, so manufacturers look at key areas of production and introduce sampling in order to maximise the checks made in relation to cost.

Working within tolerance
Tolerance is the level of accuracy that a manufacturer sets on any product made. It is important to set a tolerance, so that parts will fit together and work. Tolerances on some products will be extremely high, such as in the manufacture of engines, but other products may have a wider tolerance without affecting quality, such as the frame of a swing.

Minimising waste
Materials tend to come in standard sizes and manufacturers need to ensure that they plan the cutting of the material to suit stock sizes and maximise the available material. If a manufacturer is cutting a number of pieces from a sheet of steel, large savings can be made if parts are cut efficiently.

Maths in practice 2

Calculating waste

A manufacturer needs to cut out four 'L' shaped pieces of steel from a strip that is 50 mm wide.

- Calculate how much metal will be saved if the manufacture changes the cutting method from A to B.

Area of one 'L' shape = 50 × 50 − 30 × 25 = 1750 mm^2

Area of four 'L' shapes = 4 × 1750 = 7000 mm^2

Method A
Area of strip used = 4 × 50 × 50 = 10,000 mm^2

Method B
Area of strip used = 2 × (50 + 25) × 50 = 7500 mm^2

Amount of metal saved = 10,000 − 7500 = **2500 mm^2**

Figure 2.6.21

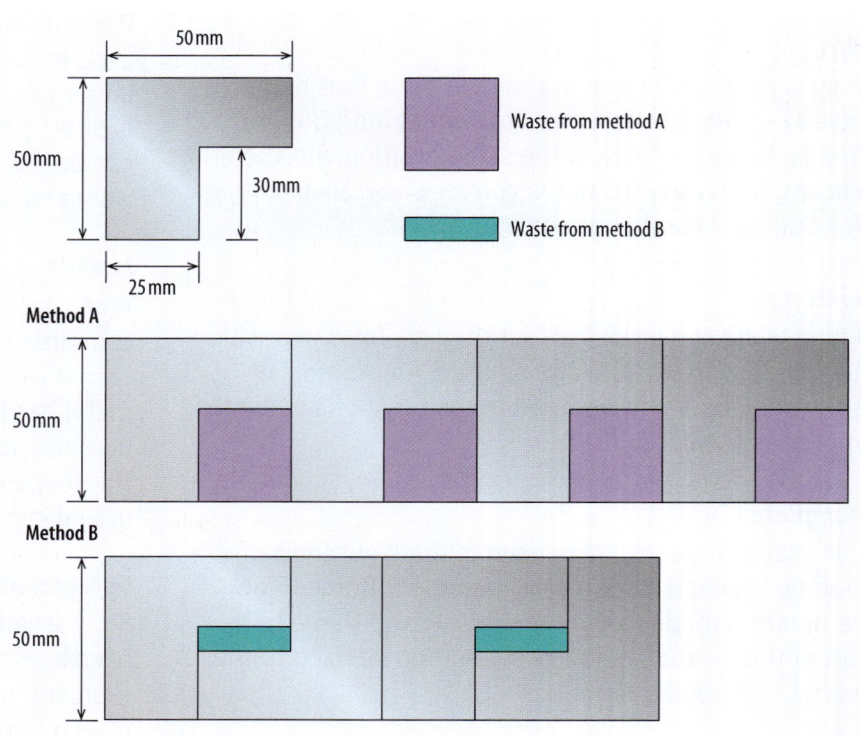

Summary

Key points to remember:
- Processed metals come in a range of shapes, sizes and forms.
- Metals can be processed by forging, casting, stamping, welding, extrusion and powder metallurgy.
- The hardness of metals can be changed, depending on the type of metal and strength properties needed.
- The scale of production should match the quality and quantity required.

Checkpoint

Strengthen

- **S1** State the maximum thickness of sheet steel.
- **S2** Describe how you would calculate the wall thickness of aluminium tube.
- **S3** Explain what is meant by the term 'gauge' when referring to sheet metal.
- **S4** Explain two reasons why die casting would be used in preference to sand casting for manufacturing a toy car.
- **S5** Explain what is meant by mass production.

Challenge

- **C1** Examine the design of a set of crutches, and justify why it is important for a manufacturer to have considered the internal and external dimensions of the tube.
- **C2** Summarise the process of turning metal into a wire.

2.7 Specialist techniques, tools, equipment and processes that can be used to shape, fabricate, construct and assemble a high-quality metal prototype

Learning objectives

By the end of this section, you should know:
- how to select the process for shaping materials
- how to fabricate metals by reshaping or joining them
- how to assemble component parts using temporary methods.

The ways metals are processed depend on the scale of production, levels of accuracy required and skills of the workforce. Designers need to choose the most appropriate manufacturing methods based on the advantages and disadvantages of the tools and processes available.

2 Metals

Tools and equipment

A wide variety of tools and equipment is available to shape, fabricate, construct and assemble ferrous and non-ferrous metals into prototypes.

	Description	Examples	Advantages	Disadvantages
Hand tools	Held in the hand, do not need an external power source	Saws, tin snips, (see page 111) files, twist drills, hammers	Relatively cheap, easy to source, do not need an energy source	Only as accurate as the user, time consuming, not as safe as other methods, more highly skilled users required
Machinery	Has complex mechanism and usually requires power	Bandsaw, powered hacksaw, guillotine, pipe benders, pillar drill	More accurate than hand tools, provides greater mechanical advantage to perform the task, saves time	Higher cost, increased potential for serious injury
Digital design and manufacture	Tools connected to a computer system that can make calculations, process data and provide real-time feedback to the user	CNC lathe (see page 75), milling machine, drilling machine	Very accurate, saves time and can operate 24/7, repeatable process from program, high levels of safety	Expensive, loss of skill level

Table 2.7.1 Types of tools and equipment

> **Apply it**
>
> Explain why using a CNC machine is likely to be safer than doing the work by hand. Then, describe four advantages of using CNC machines in the manufacture of washers for a bicycle wheel.

Shaping

Shaping metals into the form required to build a prototype will involve several processes that can cut, deform or reform the metal.

Filing

Files are made from high-carbon steel and are used to remove small amounts of metal. Files are characterised by their length, shape and cut.

The cut relates to the type of work that is to be carried out. Files are classified into grades:

- **Rough or bastard** are used for coarse work and softer metals.
- **Second** is a general purpose file.
- **Smooth or dead smooth** are for fine work and finishing.
- **Dreadnought** has curved teeth for rapid removal of soft metals, such as aluminium and copper.
- **Needle files** are smaller and are used for precision work.

2.7 Specialist techniques, tools, equipment and processes

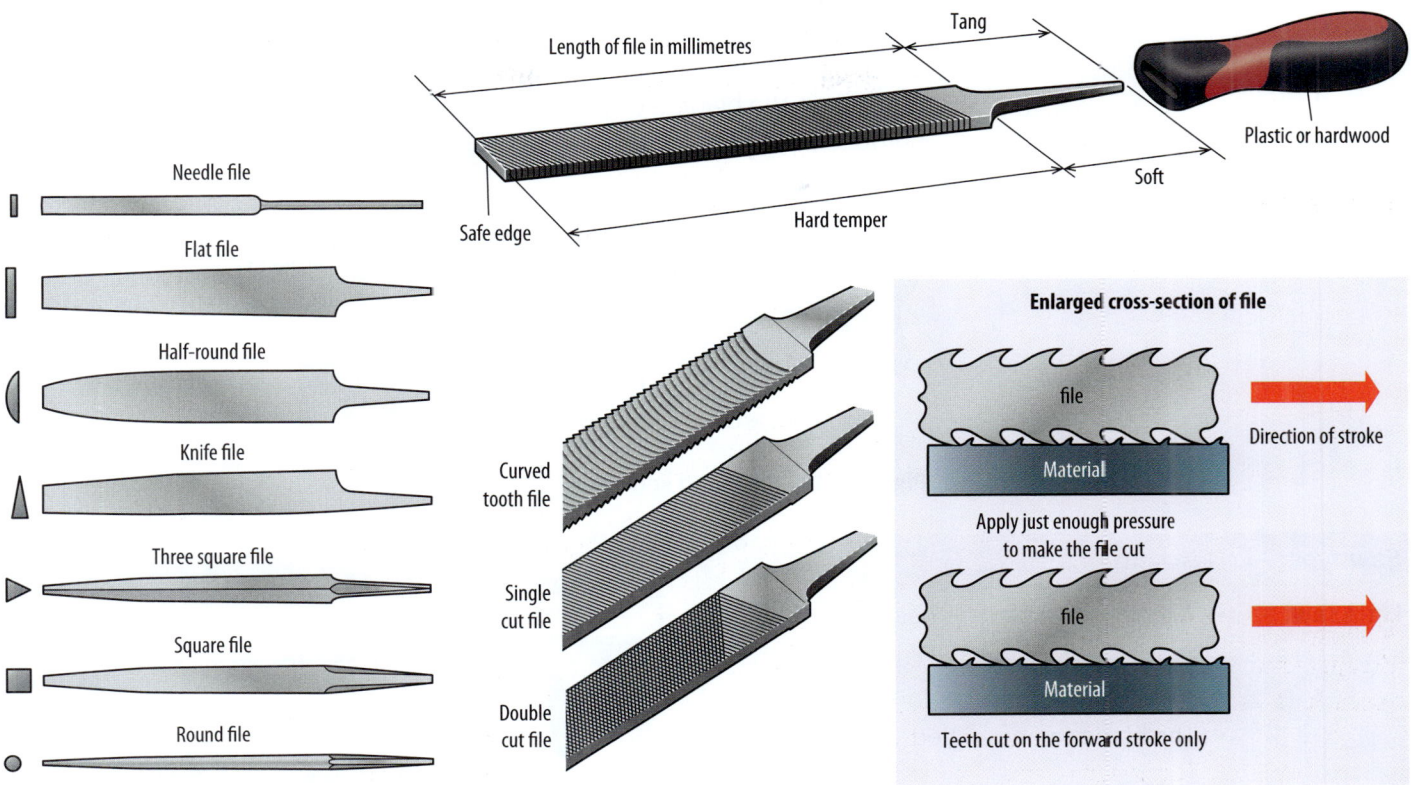

Figure 2.7.1 Types of file

Files are generally used in two ways.

1. **Cross filing** removes larger amounts of waste by filing diagonally down the length of the material.
2. **Draw filing** is a finishing method after cross filing by filing along the length of the material.

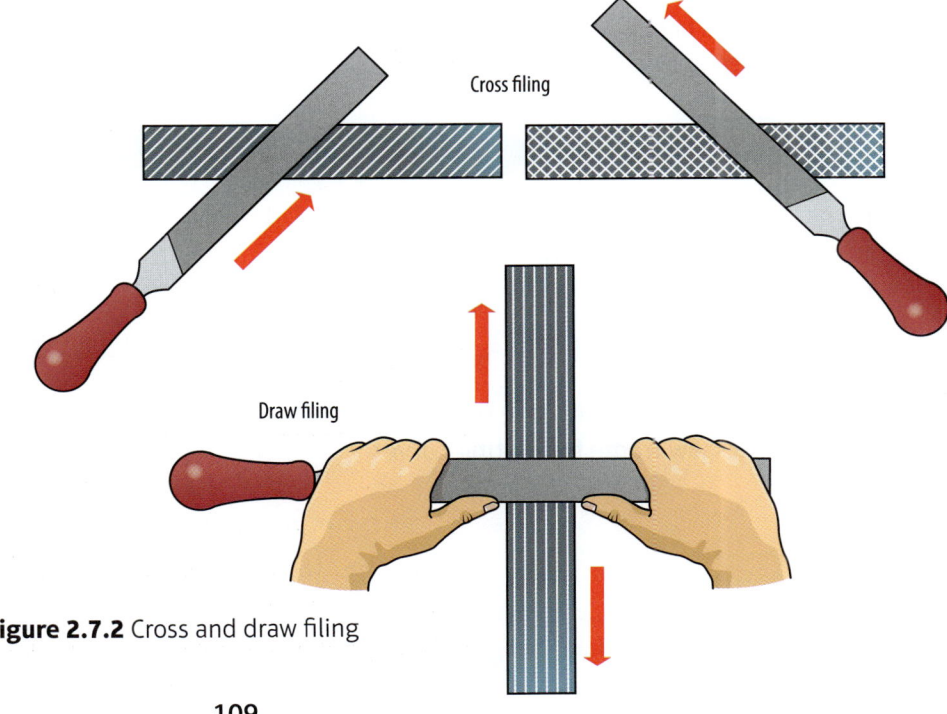

Figure 2.7.2 Cross and draw filing

109

2 Metals

Cutting

Cutting (sawing) uses the teeth on the saw blade to drive a wedge into the metal to force the waste material to split off. The teeth will cut a groove wider than the blade (kerf) so that the blade does not jam. The pitch is the number of teeth per section of the blade.

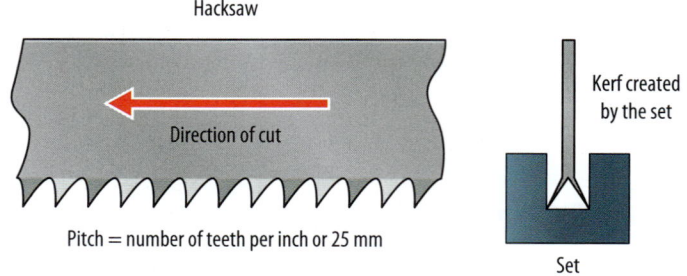

Figure 2.7.3 Pitch and kerf

Saw type	Description	Details
Hacksaw	• A replaceable blade is held in tension • Teeth face forward and cut on forward stroke • The blade can be angled	
Junior hacksaw	Like a hacksaw but with fine teeth for cutting thin material	
Piercing saw	Thin blade with fine teeth for cutting curves in thin metal	
Abrafile	Toothed circular blade that fits into a hacksaw frame for cutting curves	

Table 2.7.2 Types of hand saws for cutting metal

2.7 Specialist techniques, tools, equipment and processes

Metal saws can also be powered, for example:

- **Jig saws** are used for cutting some sheet metals.
- **Powered hacksaws** can cut steel up to 15 mm.
- **Bandsaws** are fitted with metal-cutting blades.

Shearing

Shearing metal uses two cutting edges that come together and pass by each other in a shearing action, like a pair of scissors. There are two methods of shearing, depending on the thickness of the material.

Drilling

Drills make holes by using a wedge action to cut away the material. In a workshop, drilling is normally carried out on a hand drill, portable power drill or a drilling machine called a pillar drill. When drilling metal, larger drills need to run at slower speeds so they do not have reduced cutting ability and overheat.

Type	Uses	Details
Tin snips	• Hand tool for cutting thin sheet metal • Can cut intricate shapes	
Guillotine	Used for cutting thicker sheet material in straight lines	

Table 2.7.3 Types of tools for shearing metal

Drill type	Twist drills	Machine countersink	Counter bore
Uses	Cutting straight holes	Has a 90° angle to create a seating for the screw head	Cutting flat bottomed holes to recess bolt heads
Features	Shank, Flute, Cutting edge, Point, Spur	Counter bore, Pilot hole	Counter bore, Pilot hole

Table 2.7.4 Types of drills bits for metal

2 Metals

> **Key terms**
>
> **Chuck:** is a clamp that will hold cylindrical items, such as drills or mills or a rotating work piece on a centre lathe.
>
> **Tungsten carbide:** a type of metal made up from tungsten and cobalt, which results in a tool that has greater shock resistance.

Turning

Centre lathes 'turn' cylindrical metal bars to reduce their thickness or to shape them. Work is held in a **chuck** (clamp) that is rotated while the tool is held firmly in a tool post. As the work rotates against the cutting tool, the 'wedge' action cuts away the material. The tools are made from high-speed steel (special steel with high wear resistance) or may have replaceable **tungsten carbide** tips. Rotation speeds are set depending on the thickness of the bar and the speed of rotation. A lubricant eases the cutting process, cools the metal and flushes away the swarf (waste).

Centre lathes can have CNC capability.

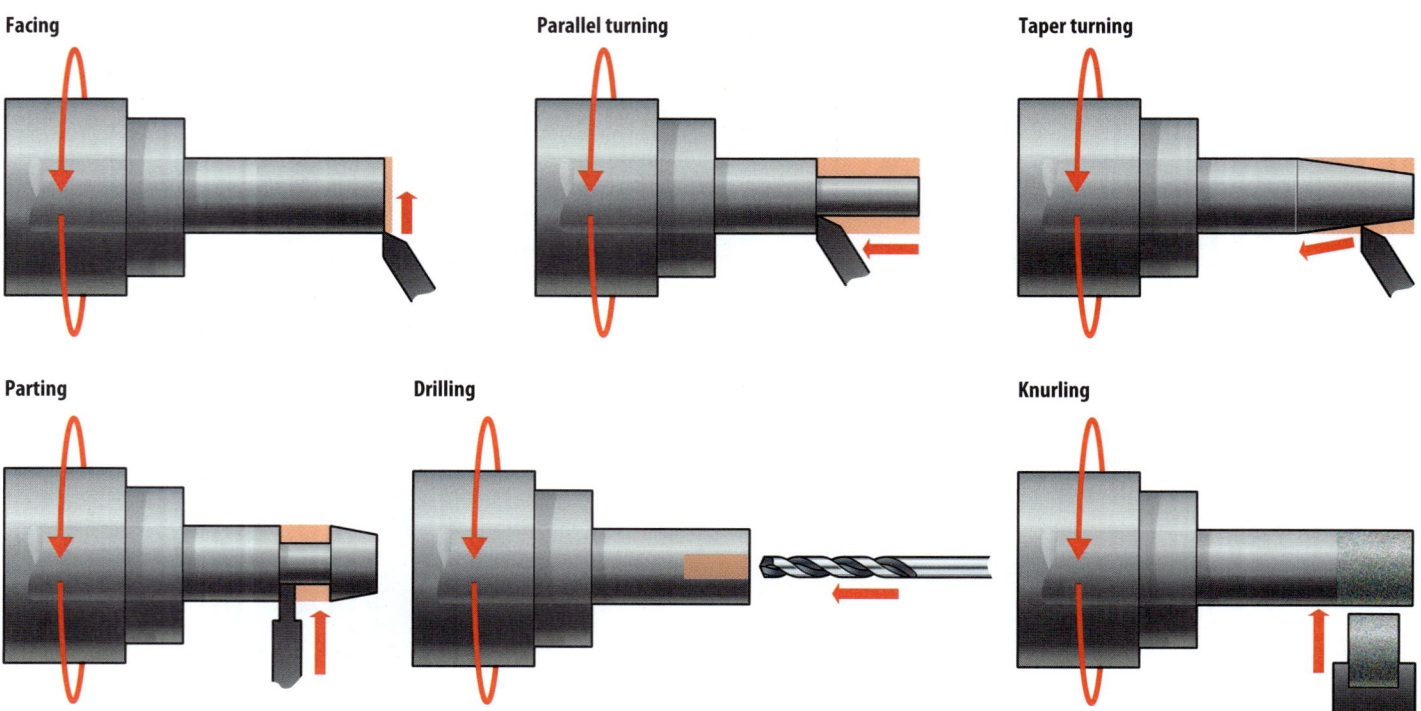

Figure 2.7.4 The six main operations of turning to produce desired cuts

> **Exam-style question**
>
> Use note and/or sketches to show the process of turning the aluminium drawer handle shown in the diagram below on a centre lathe. **(4 marks)**
>
>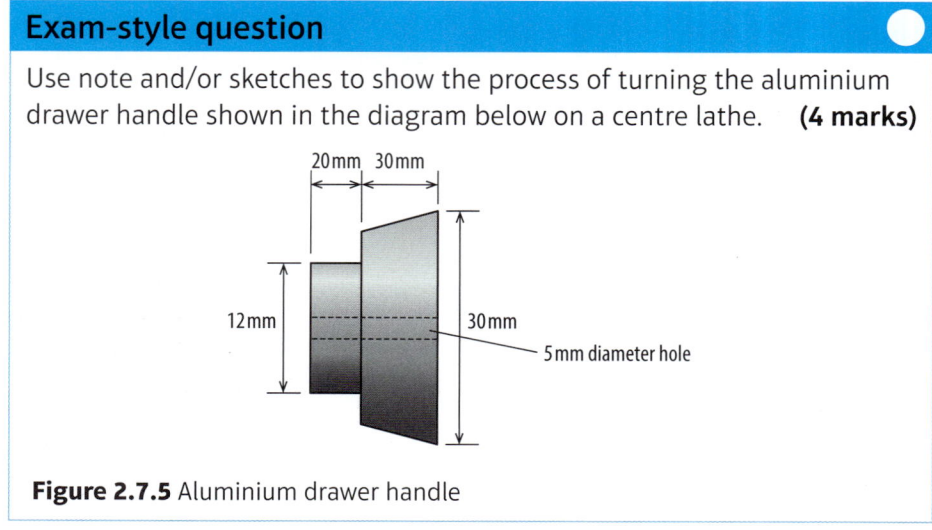
>
> **Figure 2.7.5** Aluminium drawer handle

2.7 Specialist techniques, tools, equipment and processes

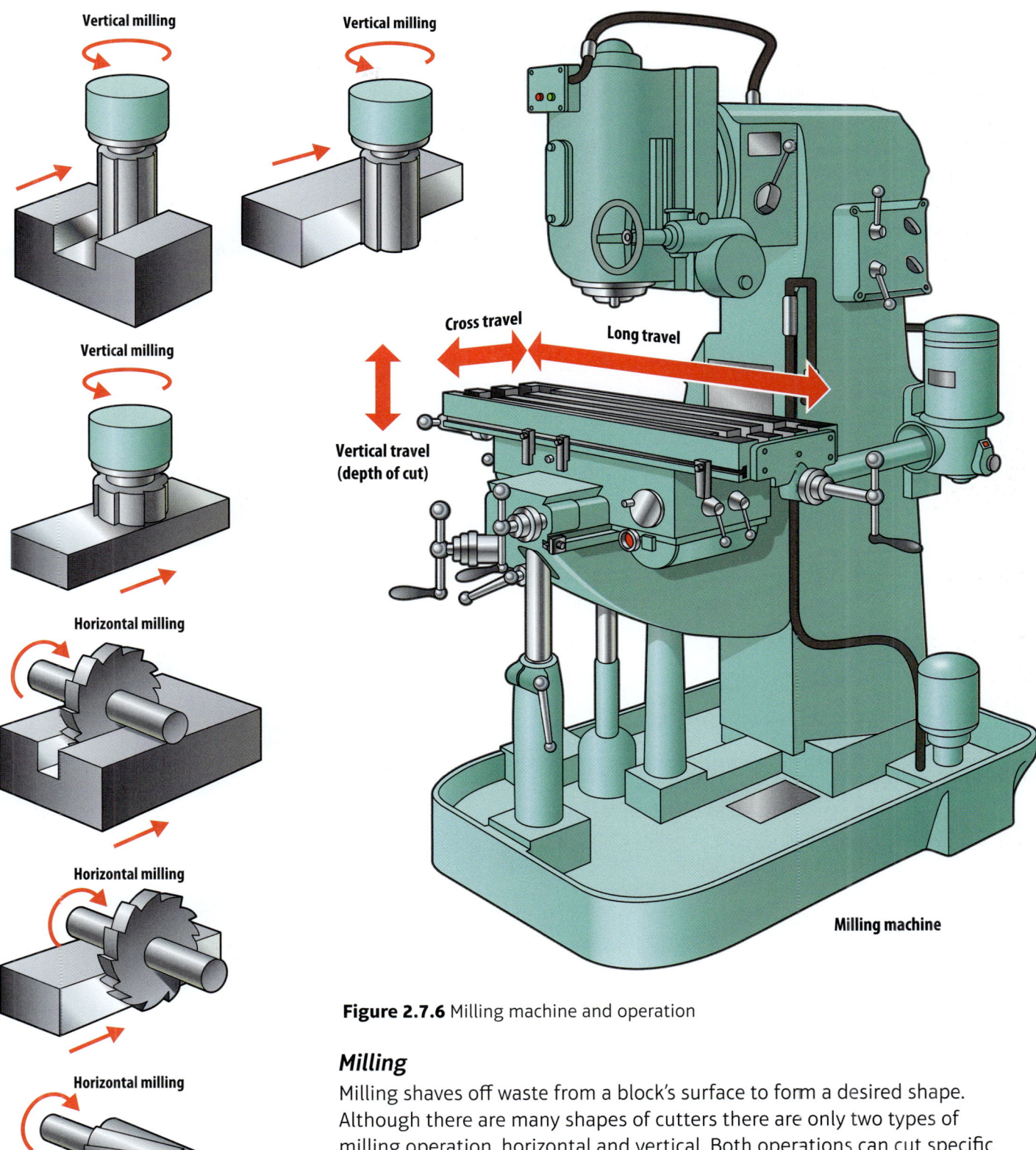

Figure 2.7.6 Milling machine and operation

Milling

Milling shaves off waste from a block's surface to form a desired shape. Although there are many shapes of cutters there are only two types of milling operation, horizontal and vertical. Both operations can cut specific shapes into solid metals.

Milling machines can be computer numerically controlled (CNC).

2 Metals

> **Link it up**
>
> You have already looked at forging, presswork, stamping and annealing in Section 2.6, pages 98–102.

Bending

Metals can be bent by:

- forging
- sheet metalwork
- tube bending
- presswork/stamping.

Beaten metalwork

Beaten metalwork is the term for curved malleable metals such as dishes, bowls and trophies. The metal can be beaten into shape with mallets and hammers. During this process the metals will work harden and need to be annealed.

Process	Description	Details
Hollowing	Stretches sheet material into a bowl shape with a bossing mallet and hollows the metal into a sand-filled leather bag	
Sinking	Stretches the material, giving a defined edge, which is put against a block and forced into the desired shape	
Raising	Creates tall-sided shapes. The action increases the thickness of the metal, which needs to be hit above the stake to force it to thicken	
Planishing	A finishing process that evens out the surface by removing blemishes. Planishing hammers are polished to give a high-quality finish	

Table 2.7.5 Examples of bending processes

2.7 Specialist techniques, tools, equipment and processes

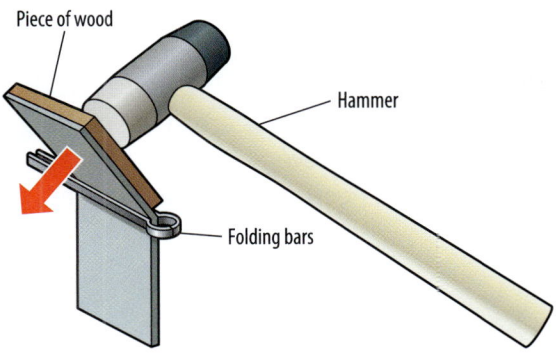

Figure 2.7.7 Sheet metalwork

Sheet metalwork
Sheet metalwork creates a more defined shape from sheet materials on a small scale by forcing the metal around folding bars or by using a vice. On a larger scale it works by using a folding machine to make straight lines or rollers to create curves.

Tube bending
Tube bending uses shaped formers or rollers to bend tubes into curved shapes without the material buckling.

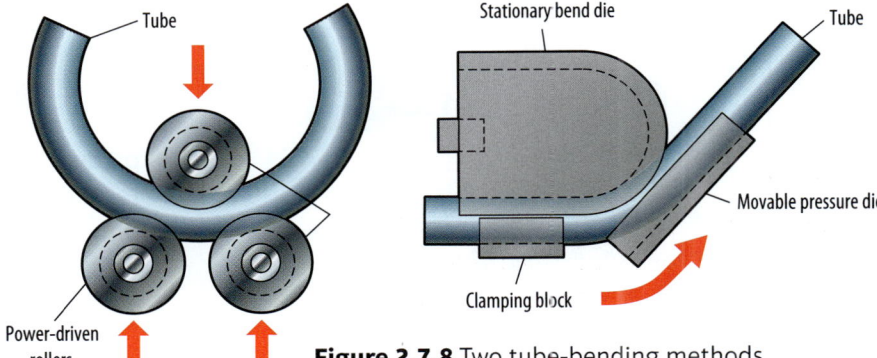

Figure 2.7.8 Two tube-bending methods

Link it up
The processes for reforming metals were covered in Section 2.6 on page 102. For more information on welding and casting, see pages 101 and 105.

Abrading/grinding
Abrading tools remove small amounts of waste by filing or using abrasive papers or grind wheels. Abrasive powders are either bonded to a backing or formed into a specific shape.

Type of abrasive	Description	Details
Wet and dry paper	• Made with silicon carbide • When wet the waste is washed away and it also acts as a lubricant • Has very fine to medium grade	
Emery cloth	• Made with aluminium oxide, flexible cloth-backed abrasive in medium to coarse grit	
Disc/angle grinder	• Electric or pneumatic, with a disc made from an abrasive powder, such as aluminium oxide, silicon carbide or ceramic grains	

Table 2.7.6 Common abrasive/grinding methods for metal

2 Metals

Fabricating/constructing

Fabricating or constructing metals involves processes such as bending, joining or reforming to change them into the desired structures.

Brazing

Brazing permanently joins metal using an alloy with a lower melting point. Brazing is a strong method of joining metals by using a different alloy and is ideal for steel.

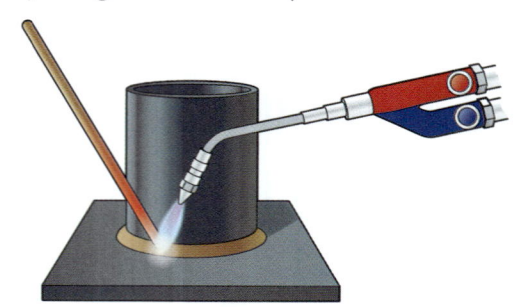

Figure 2.7.9 Brazing

Soldering (hard)

Hard soldering joins metals with low melting temperatures, such as brass or copper. The process is the same as brazing, but the hard solders are in the melting range of 625–800°C, enabling several joints to be made on a complex product that needs to be assembled in stages.

Punching

Punching produces identical shapes, such as chain links or washers out of sheet metal. The process requires short-term large forces. The punching process can be carried out in two ways: piercing (when the shape punched out is wastage) and blanking (when the shape punched out is kept).

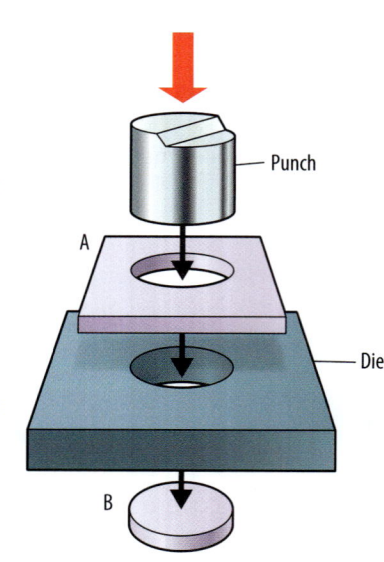

Figure 2.7.11 Punching

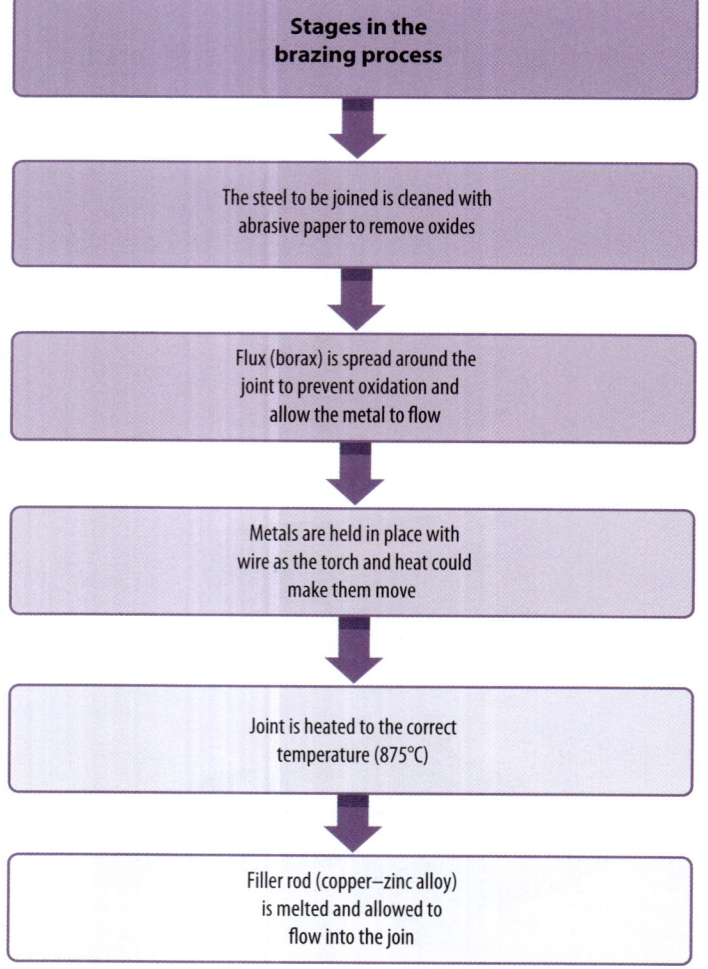

Figure 2.7.10 Brazing process

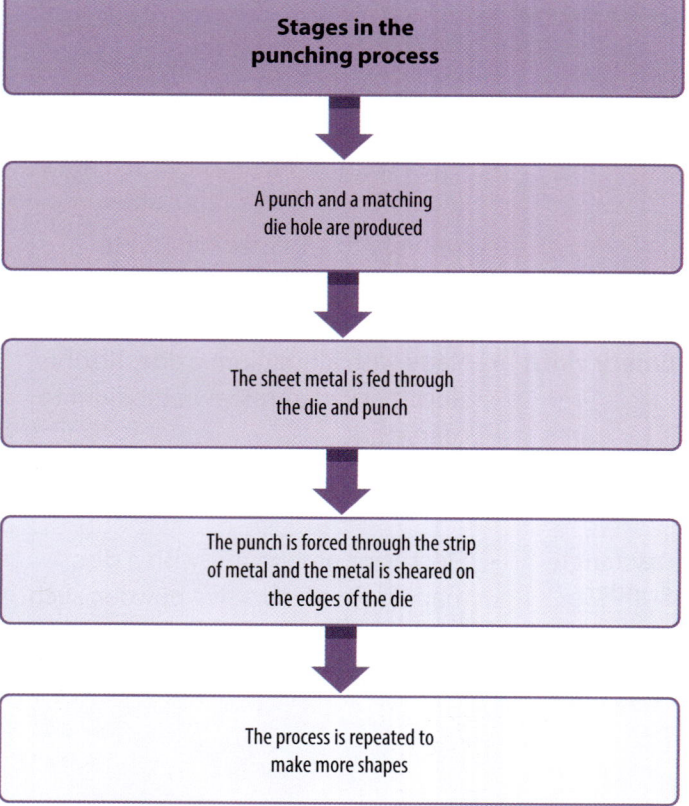

Figure 2.7.12 Punching process

2.7 Specialist techniques, tools, equipment and processes

Riveting: snap and pop

Riveting is a quick method of joining sheet materials. The choice of rivet (metal pin) is important and depends on the strength required in the joint, the metals being joined and the ability to access both sides of the parts being joined.

Snap rivets are made from aluminium, copper or soft mild steel and can be countersunk, flat or round head.

Pop rivets are ideal when you have access to only one side of the joint and are quicker to insert. However, the rivet is hollow and is not as strong as a snap rivet.

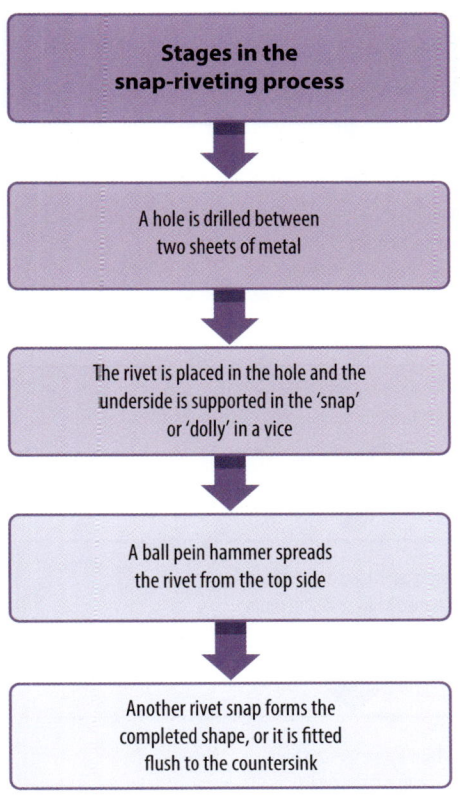

Figure 2.7.13 Snap-riveting process

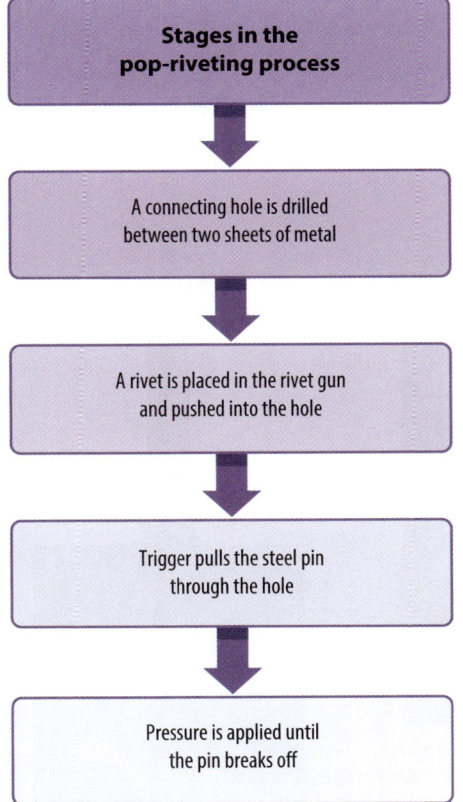

Figure 2.7.14 Pop-riveting stages

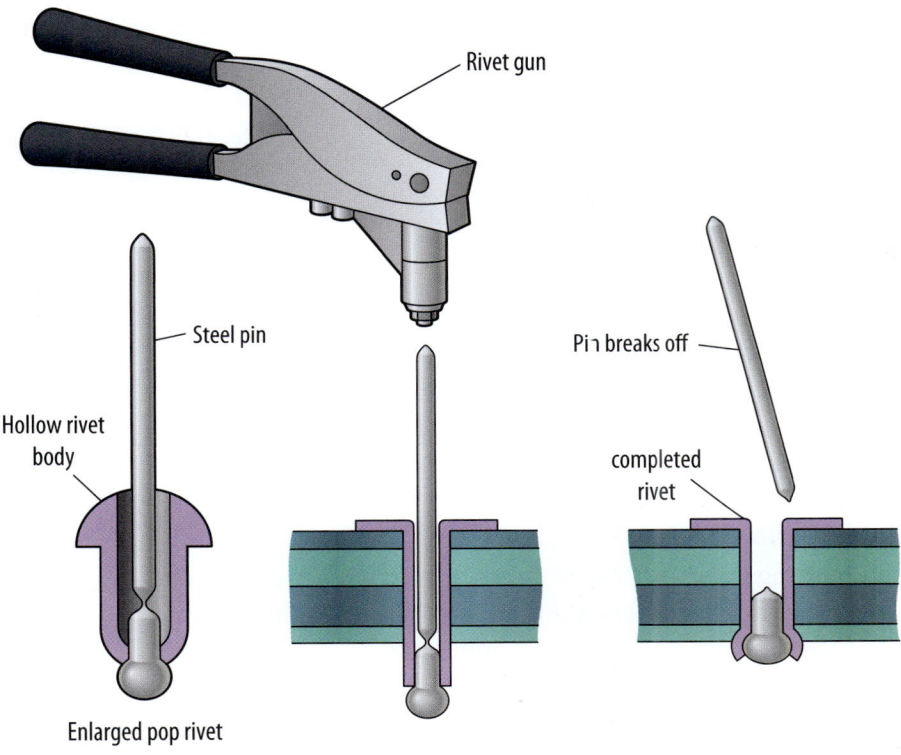

Figure 2.7.15 Pop riveting

Exam-style question

Use notes and/or sketches to show the process of riveting two sheets of 3 mm sheet metal. **(4 marks)**

Exam tip

Remember that marks will be awarded for understanding of design and technology, not how well you can draw.

2 Metals

Wastage
Many metal processes, such as sawing, piercing, stamping, drilling or turning, involve the removal of material. Waste should be reused or recycled where possible.

Addition
Metal fabrication often involves adding component parts to create a product. Manufacturers need to look at the most effective method based on cost, strength and process. Additional processes include riveting, adhesives, welding and brazing, which can be carried out in the factory or, for large structures, parts are made separately and added on site.

> **Link it up**
>
> For more information on other fabricating and constructing methods, such as welding and stamping, see pages 100 and 101. For sheet metalwork see page 115.

Assembling
Joining metal using standard components can make the product cheaper, and easier to assemble and dismantle in the future.

Tapping/threading
Screw cutting is the process of either putting a thread in a hole (tapping) or putting a thread on a bar (threading). Both processes will require lubrication to produce accurate and smooth threads.

Tapping cuts an internal (female) thread using a tap wrench and a sequence of taps called taper, plug and bottoming.

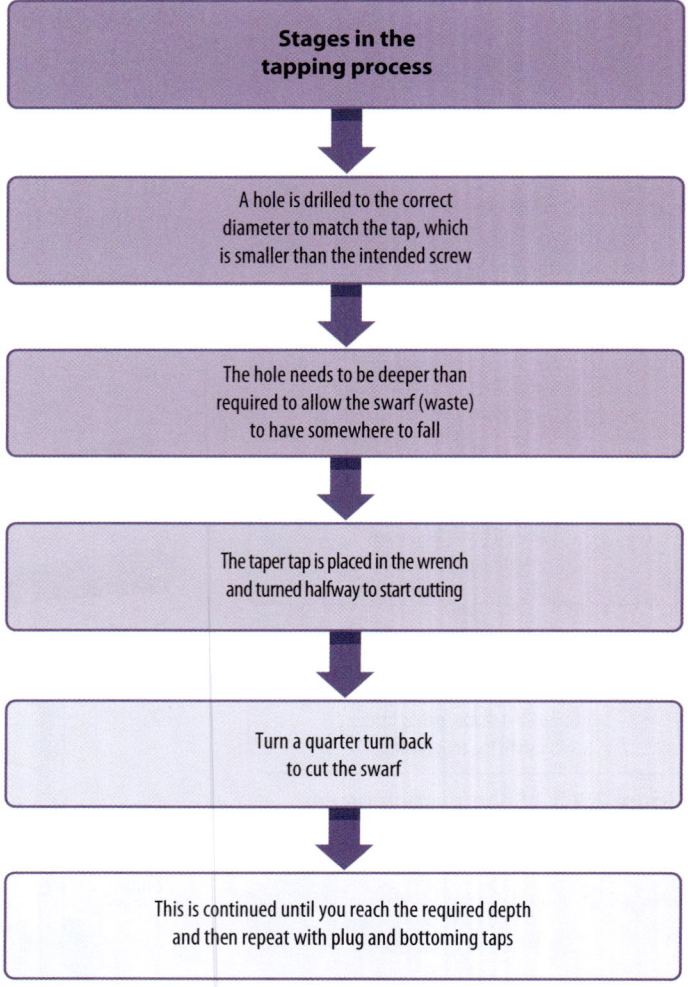

Figure 2.7.17 Tapping process

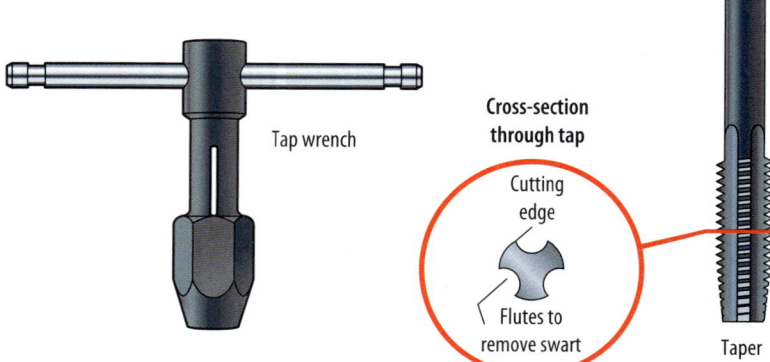

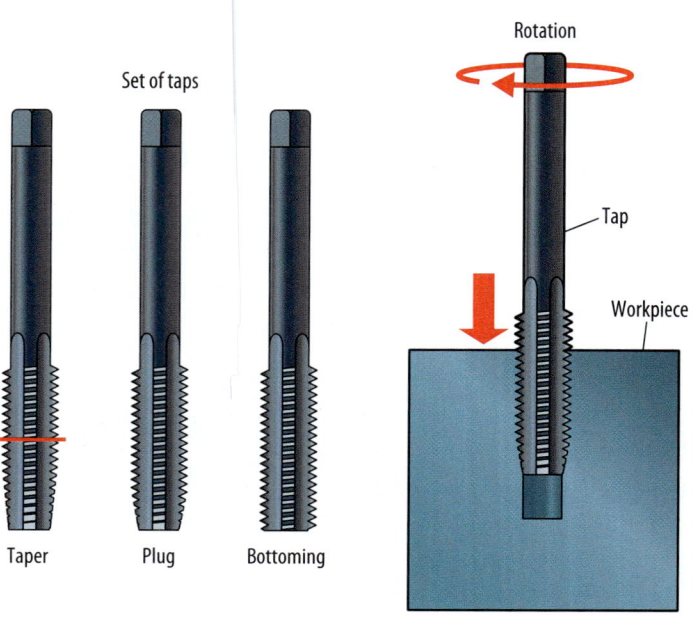

Figure 2.7.16 Tapping

2.7 Specialist techniques, tools, equipment and processes

Threading cuts an external (male) thread using a die stock and a suitable die.

'Drunken' thread: the die is not square to the axis of the rod

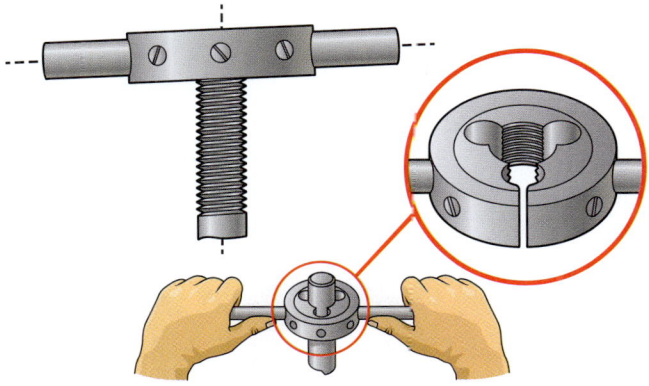

Figure 2.7.18 Threading

Fastening

Nuts, bolts and washers are all classed as temporary fastenings as they can be easily undone to allow items to be dismantled. They are all standard components that match the ISO (metric) screw threads.

> **Apply it**
>
> Investigate other areas of design and technology that are affected by the ISO (metric) system and find out why the standard is important.

Nuts

A nut fits onto a threaded bar or bolt and will have a matching thread form. Nuts come in a range of types for specific purposes.

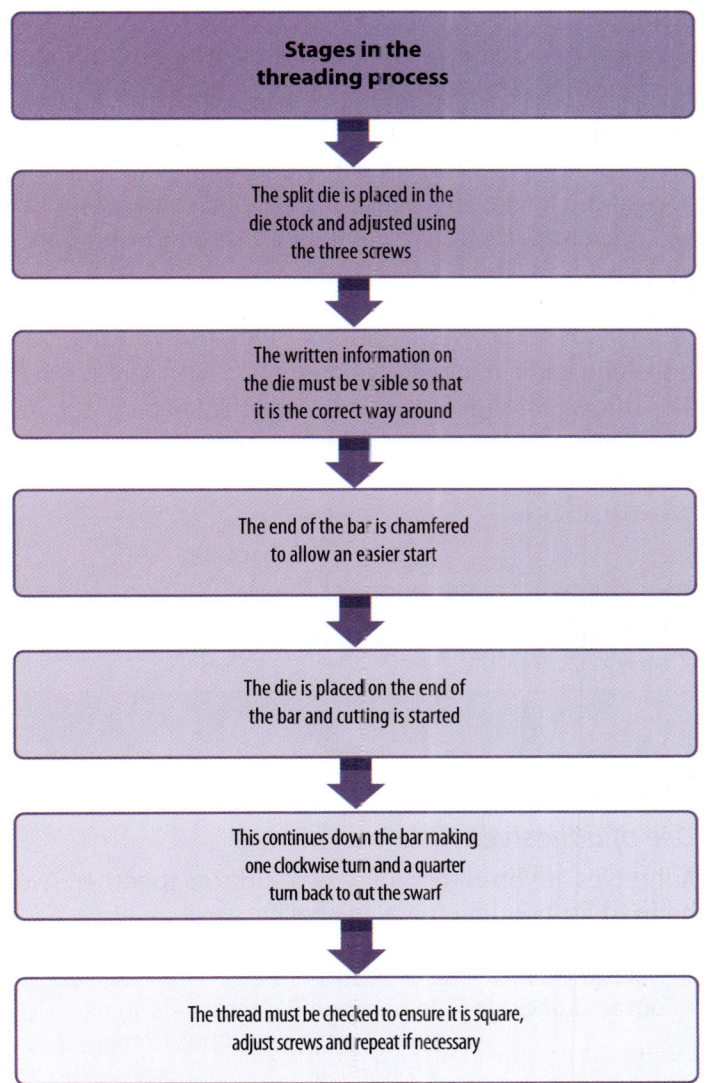

Figure 2.7.19 Threading process

Type of nut	Features	Details
Standard hexagonal nut	• General purpose • Six sides, needs tools to be tightened but can loosen with vibrations	
Wing nut	Can be fastened without tools but will loosen with vibrations	
Nylon locking nut (nyloc)	Prevents the nut loosening through vibrations as it has a plastic insert, but needs tools to be tightened	

Table 2.7.7 Types of nut

119

2 Metals

Bolts

Bolts are strong and generally made from high-tensile steel. They have square or hexagonal heads and are classified by length in addition to the ISO metric sizes.

Washers

These protect surfaces when the bolt rotates when tightened. They also spread the load over a wider surface and some washers, such as lock washers, will prevent parts from coming loose through vibration.

Machine screws

Machine or set screws are another temporary fitting, but are smaller than bolts and come in a range of diameters with threads in the ISO metric sizing. The thread goes up to the head, and the shape of the head varies to fit a range of tools. The screws are mainly made from steel or brass.

Bolts are strong and generally made from high tensile steel

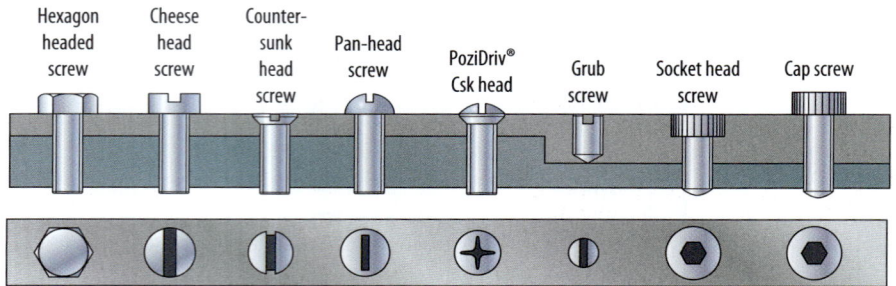

Figure 2.7.20 Types of screw

Different types of washers (spring and plain washers)

> **Exam-style question**
>
> Give **one** mechanical fittings that could prevent a nut from working loose on a bicycle wheel. **(1 mark)**

Use of adhesives

Adhesives are used for gluing two surfaces together. Two types of glue can be used for bonding metal in specific ways.

Type of adhesive	Features	Application	Example uses
Contact adhesive	Joins dissimilar materials, joins on contact so no repositioning, economical	Applied to both surfaces to be joined, left to dry and then brought into contact	Sticking laminates to surfaces
Epoxy resin (e.g. Araldite®)	Two parts, joins dissimilar materials, expensive in quantities, takes a long time to fully cure (1–2 days), brittle, water resistant, good gap filling	Equal amounts of hardener and resin mixed together, applied to parts to be glued, hardening (chemical reaction) begins immediately	Setting stones in jewellery

Table 2.7.8 Types of adhesive

Summary

Key points to remember:

- the way metals are processed depends on three things: the scale of production, levels of accuracy required and skills of the workforce.

Checkpoint

Strengthen

S1 Identify tools that are suitable for shaping, fabricating or assembling.

Challenge

C1 Explain the tapping process in detail.

2.8 Appropriate surface treatments and finishes that can be applied to metals for functional and aesthetic purposes

Learning objectives

By the end of this section, you should know:
- how to apply finishing techniques to ferrous and non-ferrous metals
- about the advantages and disadvantages of different finishing techniques.

Surface finishes and treatments

Surface finishes and treatments are used to enhance the aesthetics of metals (appearance) or, in the case of steel, to form a protective layer to prevent degradation through rusting.

All metals first need to be chemically cleaned or degreased using white spirit or paraffin to allow the finish to adhere to the surface.

Finish	Description	How applied	Advantages	Disadvantages
Paint	- Creates a coloured barrier on the surface of metals - Specialist paints can provide additional properties, such as heat resistance	- Brush, roller or spray - For best finishes, a zinc chromate or red-oxide primer, undercoat and top coat are also applied	- Quick, easy and cheap - Requires no specialist equipment or skills	- Needs regular maintenance - Waste paint can be difficult to dispose of
Dip coating	- Provides a relatively thick layer of plastic - Often used on handles for tools such as pliers, or racks and crates	- The powdered plastic has air blown into it - The metal is heated to above the melting point of the plastic (230°C) and then dipped into the powder - The plastic melts and as the metal cools it solidifies into an even coating	- Little waste - Even coating	- Equipment can be expensive - Not suitable for delicate work

Table 2.8.1 Examples of surface finishes and treatments *Cont…*

2 Metals

Finish	Description	How applied	Advantages	Disadvantages
Electroplating	• Covers the base metal with a thin layer of other metals such as gold, silver, tin, chromium, copper and zinc, taking on their colours • Suitable for decorative purposes	• This electromechanical process allows ions from one metal to attach to the base metal • The metal is suspended in a solution of metallic salts and is negatively charged (cathode), while the metal to be deposited is positively charged (anode)	• Gives base metals lustre without the cost • Corrosion resistant	• Equipment can be expensive • Solution is not environmentally friendly • Hard to get an even layer
Anodising	• Improves or thickens the natural oxide barrier of some metals, such as aluminium • Different dyes can be used to change the colour • Uses include cameras, sports gear and window frames	• Metal is placed in a sulphuric acid, sodium sulphate and water solution • The metal is the positive electrode (anode) and lead plates are negatively charged (cathode) • The electric current builds up a tough oxide layer, which is fixed in boiling water	Durable and low maintenance	Limited colour selection
Galvanising	• A zinc protective layer on steel that is not affected by scratching, because the zinc corrodes quicker than the exposed steel, so reforms • Often used as the primary layer on car panels	Steel is dipped in molten zinc, which is heated to 450–460°C and solidifies in a thin layer on the surface of the metal	Durable and low maintenance	• Equipment can be expensive • Limited to a few base metals
Powder coating	• A thick, even protective paint layer • Most white electrical goods (e.g. fridges and freezers) are powder coated	• The powder is positively charged and sprayed onto the negatively charged metal • The powder sticks to the metal and is baked to melt the powder to form an even finish	• Little waste • Even coating • Wide range of colours available	Difficult to apply a thin layer

Table 2.8.1 Examples of surface finishes and treatments *Cont...*

2.8 Appropriate surface treatments and finishes

Finish	Description	How applied	Advantages	Disadvantages
Lacquering	• A clear cellulose or varnish that will prevent tarnishing, rusting or oxidising, allowing the natural colour of the metal to show • Particularly suitable for decorative products such as jewellery	Brush, roller or spray	• Keeps original colour • Can be attractive	• May not be durable • Requires several coats
Polishing	Improves the finish of the metal and removes surface marks from finishing processes	Using different compounds that have fine grits embedded in them depending on the material or finish required, the metal can then be buffed with a cloth or on a machine buffing wheel or mop	Easy, with several methods available	Requires a secondary process, such as lacquering, to maintain the finish

Table 2.8.1 Examples of surface finishes and treatments

Apply it
Find objects in your home that each demonstrate one of the finishing processes in Table 2.8.1 and explain why each finish was chosen.

Summary
Key points to remember:
- metals can be processed by shaping
- metals can be fabricated by heat processes and by deforming
- metals can be assembled using machine screws, nuts, bolts, washers and adhesives
- surface finishes can improve the appearance of the metal and protect it.

Checkpoint
Strengthen
S1 Describe the process of tapping a hole in aluminium.
S2 Explain two differences between welding and brazing.
S3 Describe the process of electroplating a steel door.
S4 State the finish you would apply to a metal if you still want to see its colour.

Challenge
C1 Examine the processes of stamping and punching and write down how they differ from each other.
C2 Describe all the stages of smoothing the edge of a metal bar that has just been cut with a hacksaw.

Preparing for your exam 2

Exam strategy

What to expect in the exam

The examination is designed to test your knowledge and understanding of metals. Throughout the course you will need to practise exam-style questions that will challenge you in all areas. Preparing carefully for your exams is important if you are to fulfil all of the criteria the examiners will be looking for.

Section B: Material categories – Metals
This section is worth 60 marks and contains a mixture of different question styles, including open-response, graphical, calculation and extended-open-response questions. Five marks are allocated to calculation questions in this section.

For metals, you should know about:

- Design contexts
- The sources, origins, physical and working properties of ferrous and non-ferrous metals and their social and ecological footprints
- The way in which the selection of ferrous and non-ferrous metals is influenced
- The impact of forces and stresses on ferrous and non-ferrous metals and how they can be reinforced and stiffened
- Stock forms, types and sizes in order to calculate and determine the quantity of ferrous and non-ferrous metals required
- Alternative processes that can be used to manufacture ferrous and non-ferrous metal products to different scales of production
- Specialist techniques, tools, equipment and processes that can be used to shape, fabricate, construct and assemble a high-quality ferrous and/or non-ferrous metal prototype
- Appropriate surface treatments and finishes that can be applied to ferrous and non-ferrous metals for functional and aesthetic purposes.

Revision tips

- Ensure you start revising in plenty of time before your exam. You will find it easier to remember facts you have revised several times over a few weeks than those you have tried to memorise at the last minute.
- Make clear and well-ordered notes about your chosen material category.
- Work through all sample assessment materials, past papers and textbook questions available from Pearson.
- Identify the areas in which you are likely to get mathematical questions and practise the sections on arithmetic and numerical computation, handling data, graphs, geometry and trigonometry.
- Discuss the course with your teacher and peers as it will help your understanding.
- Use online or other resources to extend your understanding of the design and technology context.

Preparing for your exam 2

Sample answers with comments

The following questions give some examples of how to interpret the different command words.

Question 1: Calculation question

A student is going to manufacture a pencil holder. It will be a cylinder made from one strip of aluminium and a base made from a circular disc of aluminium. Both pieces of aluminium are 2 mm thick, as shown in Figure PE2.1.

Calculate the area of the aluminium sheet required for the pencil holder. (5 marks)

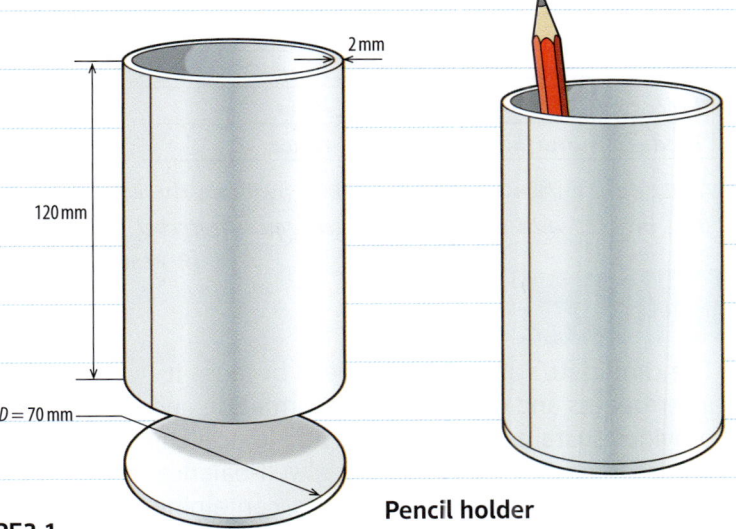

PE2.1

Pencil holder

Student answer

Area of base = $\pi \times r^2$ = 3.14 × 35² = 3846.5 mm²

Area of curved strip = 120mm × circumference of base ($\pi \times D$) = 120 × 3.14 × 70 = 26,376 mm²

Total area = 26,376 + 3846.5 = 30,222.5 mm²

Verdict

The student correctly separated the problem into the component parts to find the area of the strip and the circular base and then added the two answers together to get the total.

Question 2: 'Explain' question

This image shows a kitchen stool made from aluminium. The kitchen stool must be comfortable to use. Analyse the kitchen stool. Explain two ways in which the kitchen stool meets or fails to meet the criterion of being comfortable to use. (4 marks)

Student answer

The kitchen stool is comfortable because it has a curved shape at the back that fits the shape of the user, and also a curved shape on the seat that fits the shape of the person sitting on the stool.

Verdict

The candidate gave two answers but they were similar and focused on one aspect of comfort – the curved shape. The answer would be improved by including a second/different way that comfort would be achieved, such as the use of a cross rail which supports the feet.

> **Exam tip**
>
> When analysing a product, imagine the product in use and how you might use it.

Preparing for your exam 2

Question 3: 'Evaluate' question

The mild steel bracket to support the hanging basket shown in Question 7 is to be sold in the United Kingdom. This table shows information about the mild steel bracket:

Raw material	Iron ore
Material	Mild steel
Source of material	China
Processed	China
Product manufactured in	France

Analyse the information in the table. Evaluate the mild steel bracket with reference to its ecological footprint.

(9 marks)

Verdict

The candidate's answer is at level 3 because it interrogates and deconstructs information and provides sustained connections and logical chains of reasoning. The answer shows a well-balanced appraisal of the information/issues, containing judgements that show a thorough awareness of the inter-relationships between factors and competing arguments. A conclusion is presented that is fully supported by relevant judgements.

Question 4: 'Explain' question

Explain *two* environmental effects of producing steel. (6 marks)

Verdict

The first two points are valid as they focus on the extraction and transportation of the raw material to make the steel. Answer 3 is not valid as the student focused on the manufacturing of products after the steel had already been processed, so it did not answer the question.

Question 5: Give/state/name (short answer question)

Give the name of the fixing shown above. (1 mark)

State *one* reason why this fixing could be used on a bicycle axle. (1 mark)

Student answer

The material is extracted as iron ore and the mining of the ore is very damaging to the landscape. The ore has to be processed into mild steel and this uses up a large amount of energy. It will also create a large amount of greenhouse gases and pollution. Both the source of the material and where it is processed are in China, which could save on transportation costs. Transporting the finished mild steel to France will use up more fuel, such as diesel. The mild steel will then have to be moved again to the UK after the bracket has been manufactured. If the bracket was manufactured in the UK, it could reduce the transportation costs. Overall the extraction of materials, processing and transportation of the product to the end user causes a high amount of ecological damage. The manufacturer could try to offset this by planting trees, by using more environmentally friendly transportation methods, or by removing the extra stage in France.

Exam tip

When answering an 'evaluate' question, you must look at the positives and also the negative sides of the argument and come to an overall judgement.

Student answer

1. The extraction of the iron from the ground in the form of an ore will cause environmental damage due to the cutting down of forests and loss of habitats.
2. The transportation of the ore to the processing plant will require a large amount of energy to run the lorries and pollution in the form of exhaust fumes is created.
3. Steel is very difficult to cut and large machinery is needed to manufacture products which will use a lot of energy.

Student answer

1. Nyloc nut.
2. These are used to prevent the fixing from coming loose.

Verdict

This is a good answer to the question. No explanation is needed as each part is only worth 1 mark.

Preparing for your exam 2

Question 6: Identify (short answer question)

Aluminium is extracted from bauxite. The graph represents the amount in tonnes that has already been extracted and a prediction for future extraction.

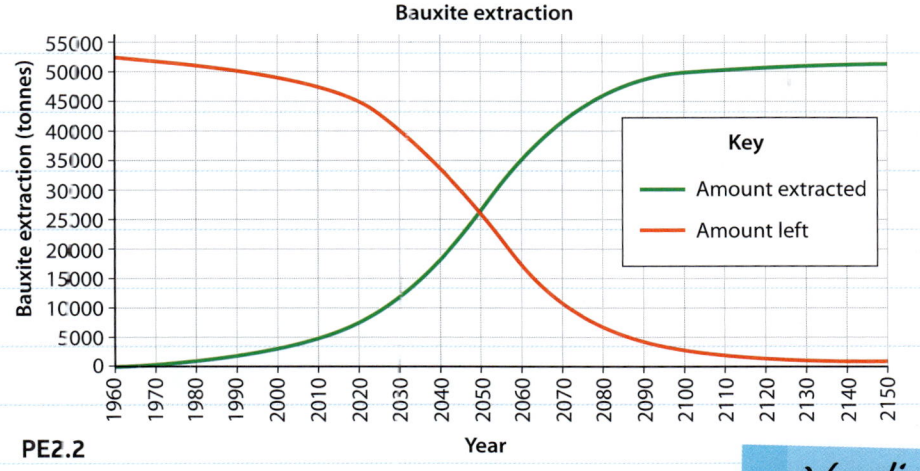

PE2.2

1. Identify the decade during which the amount extracted exceeds the reserves that are left. **(1 mark)**
2. Describe **two** ways that aluminium extraction could be slowed down. **(2 marks)**

Student answer

1. 2040–2050
2. a) Have a better system for recycling aluminium so that less raw material is used.
   b) Develop alternative materials that can replace the use of aluminium in products.

Verdict

This is a good answer. The student correctly identified the crossover was before 2050, and gave two ways in which the current supplies could be extended.

Question 7: 'Use notes and/or sketches to show' question

The diagram below shows a design solution and some additional information for a mild steel bracket to support a hanging basket.

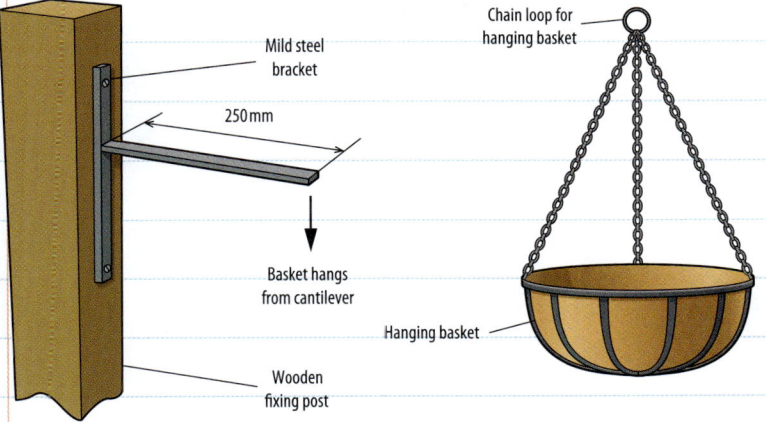

The mild steel bracket needs to be improved to include the specification points listed below.
To support a hanging basket, the bracket must:
- hold the chain loop and prevent it from sliding off the bracket
- hold the increased weight of the basket when full of plants and water
- eliminate any sideways movement when mounted on the wooden post.

Use notes and/or sketches to show how the mild steel bracket could be modified to include these three specification points. You will be marked on how you apply your understanding of design and technology, not your graphical skills. Use the outline of the original design solution to show your modifications. **(6 marks)**

Student answer

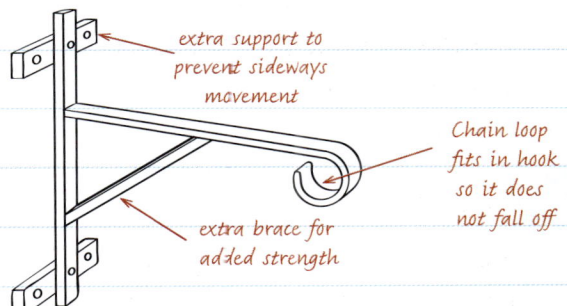

Verdict

The candidate gave three good improvements to the design. The first is a hook shape to hold the chain loop of the basket in place without easily coming out. The bracket has also been made stronger by the addition of the triangulated brace. Finally, the back plate has been widened so the mounting screws can be positioned side by side to increase stability.

Exam tip

When answering a design question, try and identify the simplest solution and do not over-complicate the answer. Make sure you label your design clearly.

3 Papers and boards

3.1 Design contexts

Getting started
We are surrounded by printed materials: from cereal packets to fast food flyers, letters and posters. How many different paper and board products do you have at home?

While you are designing and developing or modifying graphic products, you will have certain materials in mind. To make the right choices you need to understand that the following factors affect the performance, look and cost of the finished product.

- **Physical characteristics:** what does it look like? How does it behave?
- **Manufacturing processes:** for example, should it be printed, die cut and finished?
- **Performance requirements:** for example, how many forces will the product be subjected to?
- **The social and environmental impact:** does producing the material damage the environment or cause problems for nearby communities?

3.2 The sources, origins and properties of papers and boards and their footprints

Learning objectives
By the end of this section, you should know:
- the origins of some papers and boards
- the properties of a larger range of paper and board products
- that the papers and boards you choose have social and ecological footprints.

Paper, board and packaging laminate

As we saw in Section 1.9, paper and board is measured in grams per square metre (gsm), and board is paper that is more than 220 gsm. Its thickness is measured in microns.

Maths in practice 1
Calculating the weight of paper

To calculate the weight of paper, you need to divide the weight of the paper by the area.

- A sheet of a newly developed paper is 2 m² and a mass of 100 g. Calculate its weight in gsm, showing your working.

$$\text{Weight} = \frac{\text{mass of sheet}}{\text{area of sheet}} = \frac{100 \text{ g}}{2 \text{ m}^2} = 50 \text{ gsm}$$

Link it up
Copier, cartridge and tracing paper, and folding boxboard, corrugated board and solid white board were covered in the core content (Section 1.9) of this book. To remind yourself, look at pages 40–41.

3 Papers and boards

Material	Description	Advantages	Disadvantages
Bond paper 50–100 gsm	• High quality, durable writing and printer paper • Stronger but rougher than copier paper • Not bonded with glue – the name comes from having originally been used for important documents such as government bonds	• Good quality and range of colours	• More expensive than copier paper
Heat transfer printing (sublimation) paper 70–140 gsm	• Used for coloured printing with sublimation inks • Not too absorbent • Dye particles in the ink stay on top of the coating while the water is absorbed into the paper	• Produces full colour, good-quality printed images	• Expensive
Foil-lined board 1000–3000 microns	• Laminated board consisting of a layer of foil (usually aluminium) and a layer of board • Used in food packaging	• Strong • Foil provides an excellent moisture barrier • Aluminium does not react with food	• Expensive
Packaging laminate, e.g. Tetra Pak® 220–300 gsm	• A laminate consisting of six layers, four of which are polyethylene, interspersed with paperboard and aluminium foil (properties found below) • Combines the properties of the constituent materials to package long-life food	• Maintains nutritional value and flavours of food in ambient temperatures	• Expensive • Not recyclable in some areas
Packaging laminate, e.g. paperboard 224+ gsm	• Strong paper-based material generally thicker than paper • Used for packaging, book and magazine covers and postcards	• Stable, strong, smooth printing surface	• Absorbs water
Packaging laminate, e.g. polyethylene 3.5–500 microns	• A common, flexible plastic layered with foil or other plastics, particularly in food packaging, to prevent preservative gas escaping	• Excellent moisture barrier, enables the paperboard to stick to the aluminium foil	• Does not biodegrade quickly • Plastic layer often from oil
Packaging laminate, e.g. aluminium foil 6.35–15 microns	• The aluminium in packaging laminates is processed from the ore bauxite to create flexible packaging, particularly for food	• Protects against oxygen and light	• Making aluminium is an energy-hungry process

Table 3.2.1 Properties and structure of examples of paper, board and packaging laminate

3.2 The sources, origins and properties of papers and boards and their footprints

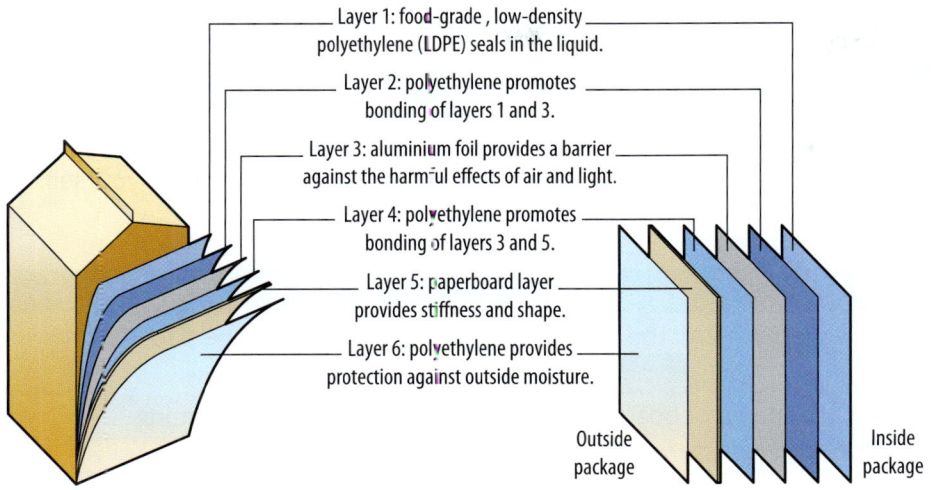

Figure 3.2.1 The six layers of Tetra Pak® are made from paperboard, polyethylene and aluminium foil

Apply it
Collect examples of printed products made using the materials in Table 3.2.1. Label each one to explain why those materials were used for that purpose.

Sources and origins of paper and boards

Materials	Origin
Pulp, paper and cardboard	China, USA, Japan, Germany, Canada, Finland
Rice paper	Eastern Asia (primarily China and Vietnam)

Table 3.2.2 Origins of different paper and boards

Physical characteristics of paper and board
The main physical characteristics of paper and board are their **density**, **transparency** and **texture**.

Paper density is its mass divided by its volume. Paper density ranges from tissue paper at 250 kg/m^3 to 1500 kg/m^3 for some speciality papers. Copier paper is about 800 kg/m^3.

Transparency or opacity describes the amount of light transmitted through a material. Highly opaque paper does not allow much light to pass through, unlike translucent paper, such as tracing paper. This can be important when printing on both sides of a page, as low-opacity paper will allow the reverse side printing to show through.

Texture is a paper's finish and feel, and ranges from smooth to heavily textured or 'laid'. Examples are smooth wove paper for writing on and linen paper, which looks and feels like fine linen fabric with its subtle embossed texture in a crosshatch pattern. Watercolour papers are heavily textured to absorb the water from the paint and create an illusion of depth in paintings.

Exam-style question
Study the picture of the milk container.

a Give **one** method of making the drinks container stronger.
(1 mark)

b Explain **two** reasons why these materials used to make up the drinks container are suitable for storing drinks.
(4 marks)

Key terms
Density: weight in grams per cubic centimetre or kilograms per cubic metre. Density is the compactness of a substance or material.

Transparency: the amount of light transmitted through a material.

Texture: tactile quality of a material; how it feels, for example coarse, smooth, silky.

3 Papers and boards

Working properties of paper and boards

> **Link it up**
>
> The working properties of flexibility, printability and biodegradability were covered in the core content (Section 1.9) of this book. To remind yourself, look at page 41.

Property	Description
Weight	Expressed in grams per square metre (gsm): the higher the number the heavier the paper
Surface finish	The smoothness or roughness of the paper or board surface – for example, papers for printing photographs onto are very smooth and glossy to give a crisp, sharp image
Absorbency	The amount of water absorbed by the surface of paper and boards, which can influence the printability and the setting rate of water-based adhesives
Printability	The ability to accept a printed image onto its surface (porosity). It is affected by structural factors such as thickness or bulk, and surface properties like absorbency or smoothness. This is not the same as print quality, which is determined by other factors such as alignment of plates on the machinery

Table 3.2.3 Working properties of paper and boards

> **Apply it**
>
> Collect 10 cm by 10 cm samples of a range of papers and boards. Observe them under a microscope. Bend them and assess their ability to flex from excellent to poor.
>
> Put a sample over a beaker and secure it with an elastic band. Use a pipette to drop 5 ml of water onto the surface. Wait for 1 minute. Observe how much water has been absorbed.
>
> Using a soft pencil, draw a line on each paper and board. Look at the quality of the line. A broken and shaky line would indicate a rough surface finish. Assess the finished surface from rough to very smooth.
>
> Complete Table 3.2.4 to show the working properties of folding boxboard. Then complete the properties for five more types of paper and board.
>
> | Material | Flexibility | Printability | Biodegradability | Weight (gsm) | Surface finish | Absorbency |
> |---|---|---|---|---|---|---|
> | Folding boxboard | | Excellent | | 225–350 | | |

Table 3.2.4 Working properties of popular papers and boards

Social footprint

Trend forecasting

Designers need to know what customers will buy months or even years ahead.
- Trend forecasters compile mood boards and colour palettes of emerging trends for packaging and interiors, and many brands subscribe to trend forecasting websites to gain information about what might be trending in the future.
- Trade shows showcase new developments in packaging and printing technologies or advances in production or finishing techniques.

Impact of logging and material production on communities and wildlife

- Paper and board are made from hardwood and softwood fibres. Harvesting trees can threaten **biodiversity**, destroy wildlife habitats and cause soil erosion so crops cannot be grown, and create water pollution.
- Transporting timber to the processing plant can generate carbon dioxide emissions and air pollution.
- Processing pulp can lead to noise pollution from heavy machinery and air pollution from dust. This can cause respiratory problems in those living near the plant.
- The manufacturing process requires a lot of water, so rivers are sometimes diverted, affecting ecosystems and communities. Waste water effluent can pollute water courses.
- Excess waste wood fibre needs to be disposed of via landfill or incineration.

Recycling and disposal

A huge amount of paper and board is used in the UK: more than 12.5 million tonnes every year. The average person uses 38 kg of newspapers per annum. However, two-thirds of paper in the UK is recycled, making it one of the most recycled materials. Recycled paper produces 73 per cent less air pollution than if it was made from raw materials. Recycled paper reduces energy consumption by 28–70 per cent compared to using virgin pulp, as most of the energy used in papermaking is to turn wood into paper. Recycled paper produces fewer polluting emissions to air and water; oxygen, rather than chlorine, is generally used to bleach recycled papers (if bleaching is necessary), which reduces the amount of chlorinated compounds released into the environment.

Paper and board can generally only be recycled seven times before the fibres become too short to be useful and need to be mixed with new wood fibres, so we have an ethical responsibility to reduce our paper use.

Paper-based items also contribute to the litter on Britain's streets, despite the increase of recycling bins in town and city centres in the last few years. The UK is often cited as being one of the worst countries in Europe for litter.

Reduction of packaging materials

The increase in online shopping has created a huge demand for cardboard packaging, and the amount of material used is often far more than is necessary to protect the product inside. It's also less efficient for many companies because of the excess space large boxes take up in warehouses.

Many companies are committed to reducing the amount of materials used for packaging while still keeping the products inside safe. Marks & Spencer devised Plan A which, among other ecological commitments, aimed to reduce non-glass packaging by 25 per cent. This reduction in packaging reduces energy use and waste.

Brand identity

A brand identity is the way that a company wants customers to perceive it. This may include its logo, marketing messages, customer service and reputation.

> **Key term**
>
> **Biodiversity:** the variety of plant and animal life in a habitat.

> **Apply it**
>
> Find out how many disposable coffee cups are used a year in the UK:
> - What proportion of used cups are recycled?
> - What could be done to improve the recycling rate of these cups or reduce the number wasted?

3 Papers and boards

> **Key term**
>
> **Consumerism:** how a business protects or promotes the interests of its customers and/or those who use its products.

One element of this is how a company deals with **consumerism**. Businesses are dependent on customers for their income, so they want customers to have the best experience of them and their products. However, consumerism can also relate to unnecessary consumption of products, so is associated with waste and greed. Companies need to balance these ideas within their brand identity. For example, they can promote changes to their packaging, as reducing waste and responding to customer requests could make customers more likely to buy their products.

The changing packaging of products over time

Figure 3.2.2 McDonald's packaging has changed over the past 60 years

> **Apply it**
>
> Describe the changes in styles of the packaging shown in Figure 3.2.2. How have the products evolved? Investigate the packaging evolution of:
> - OXO cubes
> - Kellogg's breakfast cereals.
>
> Produce a report detailing the changes over time to the brand identity and packaging.

Product packaging evolves over time, responding to developments in new materials, processes and consumer demands. The evolution of McDonald's packaging, as shown in Figure 3.2.2, is partly related to available materials. Originally only paper packaging was used but the development of plastic suitable for moulding allowed the first push-on lids. McDonald's is committed to using as many recycled materials as possible and is working towards 100 per cent sustainable, renewable and recyclable materials by 2020. It already uses wood fibre from forests certified as sustainable by the Forest Stewardship Council (FSC) and the Programme for Endorsement of Forest Certification (PEFC).

Ecological footprint

Human activities consume resources and produce waste. Sustainable development usually includes considering environmental, social and economic factors.

Sustainability

It is important to consider whether paper is a sustainable material in terms of these environmental, social and economic factors.

The environmental impact of producing and using paper and board is considerable. Factors such as the modern printing press and the mechanised harvesting of wood have led to paper and boards becoming very cheap materials, with associated high levels of consumption and waste. The pulp and paper industry is attempting to take a more sustainable approach to production methods, but demand remains unsustainably high.

Harvesting and erosion

Most paper comes from forest trees, which can result in large areas being cleared at once (**deforestation**). A more responsible way to manage forests can be seen in some parts of the USA, where paper is often made from small trees thinned from forests at intervals of around 15 years. Thinning improves overall forest health by preventing infestations of pests, such as beetles, and decreasing fire risk.

Our demand for paper products has risen by 400 per cent in the past 40 years, with 35 per cent of harvested trees being used for paper manufacture. Plantation forests can be a **monoculture**, which means that trees of only one species grow there. This can lead to a reduction in the range of wildlife living in those forests. Such practices also affect people who depend directly on forests, as it depletes resources such as food.

We tend to think of deforestation as a problem only in developing countries but wood chipping to produce paper pulp is a sensitive environmental issue in Australasia. In New Zealand the government stopped the export of woodchips from native forests after environmentalists campaigned to preserve natural habitats.

Processing

Processing wood into fibres can cause noise pollution and damage, as well as emitting dust particles into the environment. It can even redirect watercourses. However, processing plants provide employment for the local community.

Transportation, wastage and pollution

Transporting raw materials to the processing plant can cause increased CO_2 emissions, due to fossil fuel use. This gas contributes to global warming.

Toxic chemicals are used in paper making, particularly chlorine compounds for bleaching the paper and solvents for softening the wood fibres. Fossil fuels used in the production of paper pulp, and in operating the mills used to press the paper, can result in CO_2 emissions and other air pollutants. Waste effluent from a paper processing plant contains solids, nutrients and dissolved organic matter which, when present in high levels, pollute water.

Water pollutants from paper production can include:
- toxic chlorine compounds like dioxins
- organic materials that consume oxygen during decomposition
- sulphur dioxide that contributes to lake acidification
- air-polluting nitrogen compounds
- phosphates that boost algae growth.

> ### Link it up
> Many of these issues also apply to timber. For more information, see Section 7.2, page 281.

> ### Key terms
> **Deforestation:** removal of trees so that land can be put to other uses.
> **Monoculture:** production of a single type of crop.

3 Papers and boards

3.3 Selection of papers and boards

Learning objectives

By the end of this section, you should know:
- that there are various factors affecting the selection of materials, including aesthetics, environmental issues and availability.

Many factors need to be considered when selecting materials for a specific application.

Aesthetic factors

Form: the thickness, physical properties and size of the stock forms. E.g. rigid but pliable high-quality board has been chosen for the complex net.

Colour: varies depending on the use of the product and appeal to target customer. E.g. in this chocolate box, muted tonal colours suggest quality.

Surface graphics: the material's ability to accept surface graphics will be crucial to the success of the final product. E.g. a test piece would have ensured a crisp, clean print quality with no colour seepage. This box is also die cut.

Texture: feel can influence the market placing of the product. E.g. the matt, slightly textured surface of the board helps to convey the sense of a high-quality product.

Figure 3.3.1 Aesthetic factors in material selection

A compostable disposable coffee cup

Environmental factors

Sustainability

When designing products, designers should research the range of possible materials to ensure that the environmental impact of the processing, material production, product production, use and disposal of the chosen material have the smallest environmental impact possible. Materials made from plants are generally considered more sustainable than those derived from crude oil, as their source can be regrown. The image on the left shows a compostable cup made by British company Vegware from biodegradable polymers that have been derived from plants.

3.3 Selection of papers and boards

Pollution

The designer should choose the product that creates the least pollution when constructing and disposing of the product.

Genetic engineering

The yield of usable wood fibre from trees can be increased by genetically modifying their levels of **lignin** to reduce pulping costs. Chemically modifying the lignin makes it easier to break down without affecting the material's strength.

Availability factors

Use of stock materials

These are easy to order, widely available and are ready for immediate use – saving time and costs. Manufacturers can guarantee a good-quality finish because they know how the materials will accept print, fold and join, and fit their machines as their properties, sizes and quality are consistent.

Stock finishes are gloss, dull and matt. Gloss papers are coated to give them a lustrous appearance, are less opaque, have less bulk and are cheaper than other finishes. Most magazines and flyers are printed on gloss paper. Dull papers are low in gloss, while matt paper is flat-looking to give a publication an elegant feel – they are normally more expensive.

Specialist materials

Designers need to research how specialist material could, for example, fold, accept print and join. Their thickness or finish may not fit in standard machinery, so a bespoke setting may need to be applied. An example of a specialist material would be a gold foil-flecked handmade paper for a limited edition book insert. The impacts of using specialist materials could include inflated costs; however, they could also suggest better quality.

Cost factors

Every process has an associated cost. Here are some examples.

- **Quality of materials:** the higher the quality of the materials, the higher the cost of producing the product and these costs are passed on to the customer. The cheapest material may not be the best option in the end if the print quality is poor because of the paper or board stock.
- **Decorative techniques:** this includes die cutting (see page 147), embossing and hot foil blocking, which will all add to the unit costs.
- **Manufacturing processes:** these can also influence the cost. For example, **laser printing** is cost effective for short runs of posters and leaflets but for larger volumes a process such as **offset lithography** produces higher-quality products that are cheaper per unit. The number of colours also affects the cost as one-colour prints are cheaper than full colour. Other manufacturing processes that add costs include cutting, folding and assembly.
- **Commodity price:** this is the cost of the paper or board used in the product. It will be bought in bulk, making it cheaper than smaller amounts. The cost of delivery would also need to be factored into this price.
- **Cost of recycling:** the cost of using recycled materials in comparison to the cost of production from raw materials should be considered. Recycling paper saves both energy and resources, but the costs of specialist materials, transport and equipment may be higher.

Social factors

Different materials appeal to different social groups and depend on their use and perception. For example, lower-quality materials would be used as a flyer for a club night than for a wedding invitation.

For some products, the packaging is as important a symbol of the product's brand identity as the product itself. For example, much research was undertaken to develop Apple's distinctive iPhone packaging. Boxes for perfume bottles are also often distinctive and attractive, for example Issey Miyake's diamond-shaped box. These become attractive and collectible in themselves.

Certain paper products can become popular such as Pokémon and football cards and stickers. This impacts upon demand.

> **Key terms**
>
> **Lignin:** the naturally-occurring polymer that makes the cell walls of usable wood fibre.
>
> **Laser printing:** a type of printing popular in offices that uses toner (dry powder) instead of ink.
>
> **Offset lithography:** a method of printing used for high volumes, such as magazines and newspapers.

3 Papers and boards

Cultural and ethical factors

Avoiding offence
Printed material can sometimes be designed to provoke a reaction, such as controversial campaign posters. However, generally designers need to research carefully the cultures that their products will be placed in so as not to unnecessarily cause offence through the misuse of colour, meaning or imagery.

Suitability for intended market
The market should be researched early on, considering the wants, needs and priorities of those likely to buy the product. Some customers may prioritise sustainability while others are motivated by cost.

Use of colour and language
Different colours have different associations in the world, for example, red is considered lucky in China but is the colour of mourning in South Africa. Language on printed materials should be carefully checked for both accuracy and meaning, and to ensure it is appropriate.

The consumer society
Many customers want products quickly and easily, and often have little regard for the effects of waste on the environment. For example, large quantities of convenience food packaging for supermarket sandwiches and ready meals is often unnecessary.

The effects of mass production
Mass production is often the most cost-effective way to produce many identical products. It makes products available at cheaper prices, making them more accessible. Disadvantages include cheap products leading to a throwaway society, resulting in depletion of resources and increased habitat destruction. Unskilled jobs are also harder to find due to automated production methods.

Built-in product obsolescence
By its nature, food packaging is only required for a short time; however, the materials used can be too robust and not break down easily. Some coffee shops are encouraging the use of reusable ceramic mugs, which have a longer lifespan, to reduce the use of unrecyclable paper cups. Electronic media means that short-lived posters and flyers are less common than they once were.

> **Apply it**
>
> Would you be more attracted to a product if its packaging was ethically responsible? Carry out research into materials used by Vegware to give you an idea.

> **Exam-style question**
>
> Look at the image of the disposable coffee cup.
>
>
>
> a Name the type of materials used for the body of the coffee cup. **(2 marks)**
>
> b Explain **one** reason why the properties of these materials make them suitable for this product. **(2 marks)**
>
> c Explain **two** benefits of using papers and boards to manufacture disposable coffee cups, rather than polymers. **(4 marks)**

> **Summary**
>
> **Key points to remember:**
> - Different types of papers and boards have different working characteristics and physical properties that influence their use.
> - Designers and manufacturers must balance the social, cultural and environmental impact of the materials in their products with customer requirements.

Checkpoint

Strengthen

S1 Compare the properties of Tetra Pak® with bonded paper.
S2 Describe the structure of foil-lined board.
S3 Explain why businesses care about reducing packaging materials.
S4 Explain how a paper mill affects local communities.

Challenge

C1 Evaluate the impact of harvesting trees for wood pulp on neighbouring communities.
C2 Investigate genetic engineering of paper materials. Why are some people opposed to it?

3.4 Forces and stresses

Learning objectives

By the end of this section, you should know:
- that materials will undergo forces when processed and used
- that different techniques can be used to reinforce materials.

Papers and boards are subjected to many forces when used in products. Their ability to withstand these forces determines if it is a successful choice.

Force/stress	Definition	Application to paper and boards
Bending	A force that moves the material into a curve or an angle	• The ability to bend is important when paper has to be fed into machinery. • For boards, stiffness prevents cartons from bulging when full, enables them to be stacked and protects the contents. Flimsy paper could cause feeding problems in larger sheet presses. A sheet that is too stiff will cause problems in copier machines, as it will be unable to bend around feed rollers. • Stiffness is measured in mNm (millinewton metre). It is the force required to move the free end of a 38 mm wide vertically clamped sample 15° from its centre line when load is applied 50 mm away from the clamp. The higher the value of the force needed, the stiffer the paper or board.
Torsion	A force that twists the material (torque)	• Papers and boards can be tested for their resistance to torsion. Cardboard boxes will undergo twisting when moved. They need to be resistant to tearing to protect the contents.
Shear	A force that acts in opposite directions	• Tearing paper exerts a shearing force. The tearing strength is the force needed to continue to rip an existing tear. After several tests, the average is taken. Tear strength can be improved by blending in fibres resilient to tearing or by improving the construction of the product to alleviate weak spots. Longer paper fibres make it more resilient to tearing. Tearing resistance is measured in mN (millinewtons). Papers can be given a tear index value.
Compression	A force that tries to squash or shorten by decreasing the thickness of a material by increasing the force applied to it	• A paper's ability to change its surface contour and to conform to and make contact with the printing plate or blanket during printing is important. The paper or board's ability to 'bounce back' or recover is called resilience.

Table 3.4.1 Types of force and stress on paper and boards

3 Papers and boards

> **Exam-style question**
>
> Name the type of force that relates to twisting a material.
>
> (1 mark)

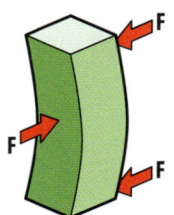 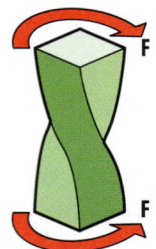 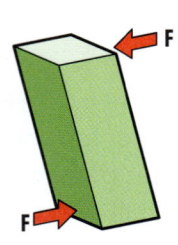 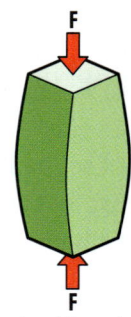

Bending: A force that moves the material into a curve or an angle.

Torsion: A force that twists the material.

Shear: A force that acts in opposite directions.

Compression: A force that tries to squash or shorten by decreasing the thickness of a material as a result of an increase in pressure.

Figure 3.4.1 Types of force and stress

> **Apply it**
>
> The picture below shows a child's cardboard chair and footstool. Sketch a side view and indicate using arrows where forces will act when the child sits down.

A chair and footstool made from cardboard

Reinforcement techniques

Reinforcement means to strengthen or enhance the stiffness of a material. Different techniques can be used to strengthen card and paper structures. These include adding overlapping or double layers, particularly on corners or sides of boxes, bracing structures using triangular pieces (or ribs) and adding bracing.

- **Laminating** builds up material by adding layers. Paper and card are often already laminated with layers of fibre and can be further laminated with plastic film, foil or other types of paper. This will improve the qualities and strength of the base material, making it more resistant to shear forces.
- **Encapsulation** is to contain paper within two layers of plastic with a sealed edge. This makes the item strong and waterproof, making it last longer. Examples of encapsulated sheets include maps and menus.
- **Corrugated board** consists of a fluted inner board sandwiched between two smooth unbleached containerboard sheets. They can be constructed of a single fluted layer with one or two sides or doubled or tripled to make thicker, stronger boards that will resist compression.
- **Corrugated card** is an example of **sandwich construction**. Another is foam board, which consists of an inner layer of polystyrene or polyurethane foam clad on each side with white clay-coated paper. It is a strong and lightweight material that is easily cut with a sharp craft knife or picture framing mat cutter. It is used for mounting prints and photographs or for interior design and architectural models.
- **Packaging laminates** are used for different purposes, for example:
  - Tetra Pak® provides hygienic packaging for food. It consists of a multi-layered board that takes on the properties of the contributing layers (see also page 128).
  - Portabio® is a cellulose-based metallised film applied to a base board. It is more sustainable than other films and is easily recycled and biodegraded.
  - Metallic and holographic finishes to board or paper are used on packaging for high-quality products such as perfumes.
  - One type of laminate layer is designed to convert microwave energy into radiant heat to promote browning and crisping of microwaved food.

> **Key terms**
>
> **Laminating:** to make a material by bonding layers together.
>
> **Encapsulation:** to contain an object in another material.
>
> **Sandwich construction:** composite materials made by attaching two thin, stiff outer pieces to a lightweight but thick core.

> **Apply it**
>
> Look at a drinks carton and delaminate it into its constituent layers.

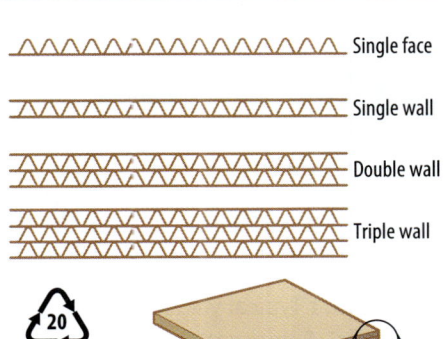

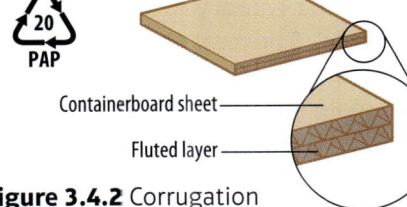

Figure 3.4.2 Corrugation

Summary

Key points to remember:
- The types of force and stress on paper and boards are bending, torsion, shear and compression.
- Reinforcement means to strengthen or enhance the stiffness of a material.

Checkpoint

Strengthen

S1 State the difference between tension and shear forces.
S2 Name three reinforcing techniques.

Challenge

C1 Evaluate the flexibility of three papers and boards and suggest a use for each.

3 Papers and boards

3.5 Stock forms, types and sizes: calculating quantities required

> **Learning objectives**
> By the end of this section, you should know:
> - that materials are produced in set sizes, called stock sizes, such as A4
> - that there are B and C series of stock sizes too.

Stock forms/types

Weights

Paper is sold by weight, but the buyer also needs to know the size of the paper or number of sheets so that they can calculate how many products will be produced using the quantity they buy. The basis weight determines the area of paper the buyer gets for a given weight. When the basis weight is expressed as ream weight (weight per 500 sheets), the buyers know how much paper they are getting for a given weight.

Grade	gsm
Newsprint	40–50
Tissue paper	22–25
Bond paper	50–100
Paperboard	220–300

Table 3.5.1 Typical values of paper grades (accepted trade tolerance ±5 per cent)

The main advantage of standard weights is that paper suppliers and printers all use the same system. It can, however, be quite tricky to work out how much paper you need to complete a job if you only know the area of the work.

Laminates

The thinnest common laminate is 0.04 mm, followed by 0.08 mm, 0.1 mm and 0.2 mm. The thickness will affect the rigidity of the finished product. Paper and thin card also come in rolls (webs) that allow printing of longer objects, such as banners and products that need to be printed quickly in high quantities, such as newspapers.

Bond paper

Bond paper is commonly used for letterhead, business forms, writing, typing and copying. It is durable, with a high surface strength to withstand writing and corrections. It is stiffer than copier papers and can be produced with or without a watermark. The highest-quality bond papers have a high cotton content.

Sizes

Common A sizes

The metric system of paper and card sizing, defined by ISO 216, is shown in Figure 3.5.1. All 'A' sizes are half the previous size, with A0 being the largest, with an area of 1 m². The International Organization for Standardization sets out the common paper sizes used and 161 countries adhere to this standard.

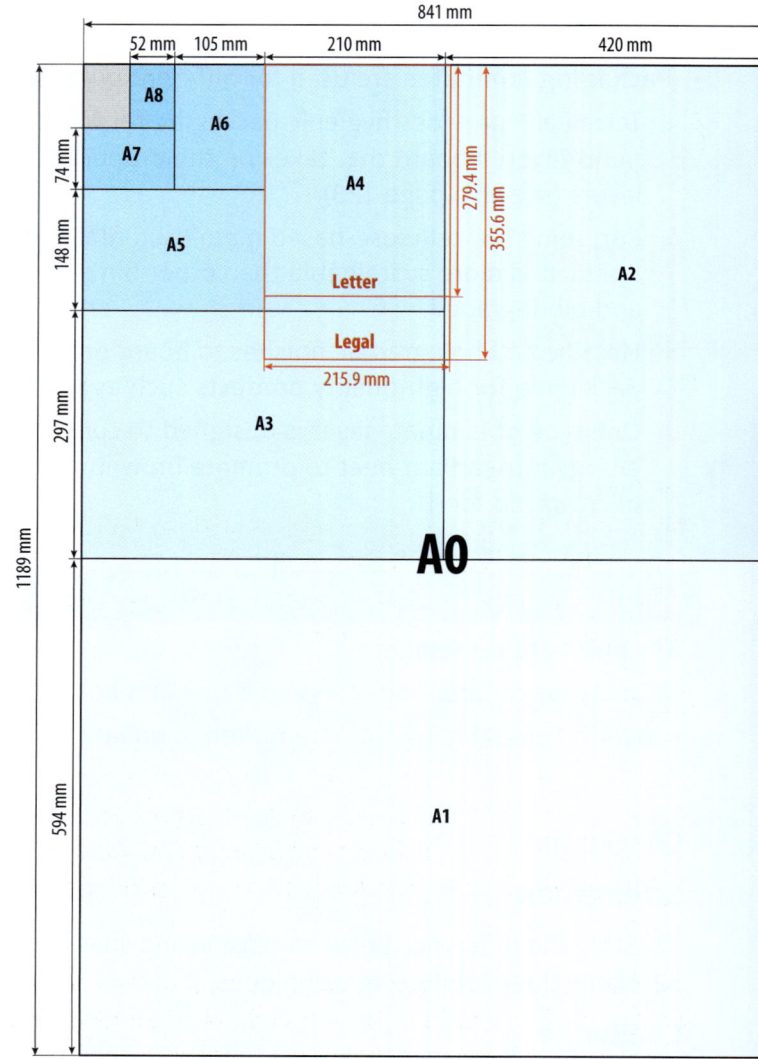

Figure 3.5.1 Comparative A sizes of paper

3.5 Stock forms, types and sizes: calculating quantities required

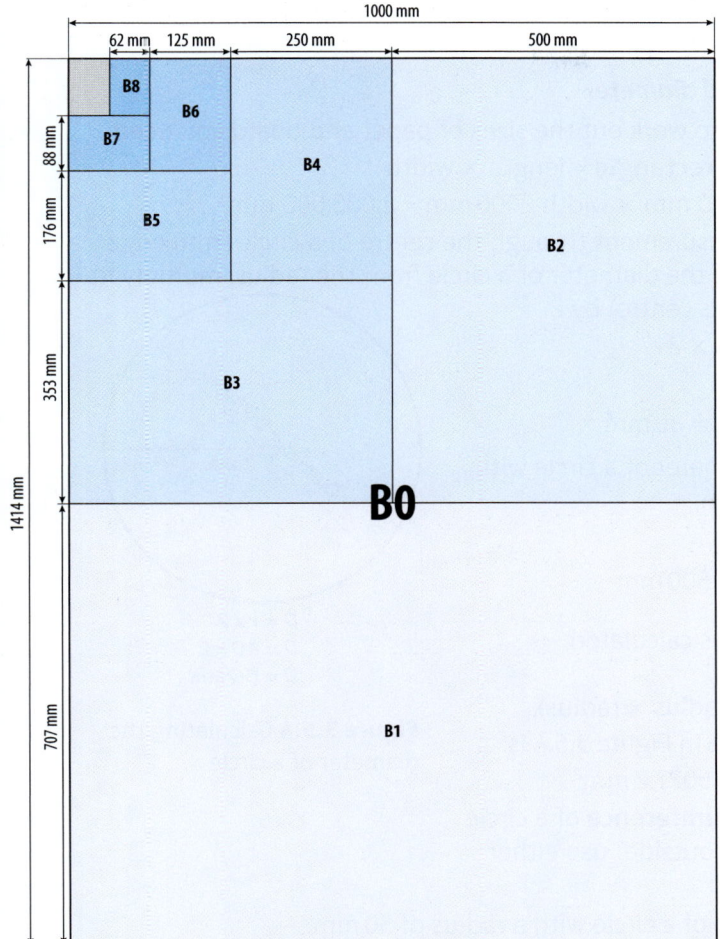

Figure 3.5.2 Comparative B sizes of paper

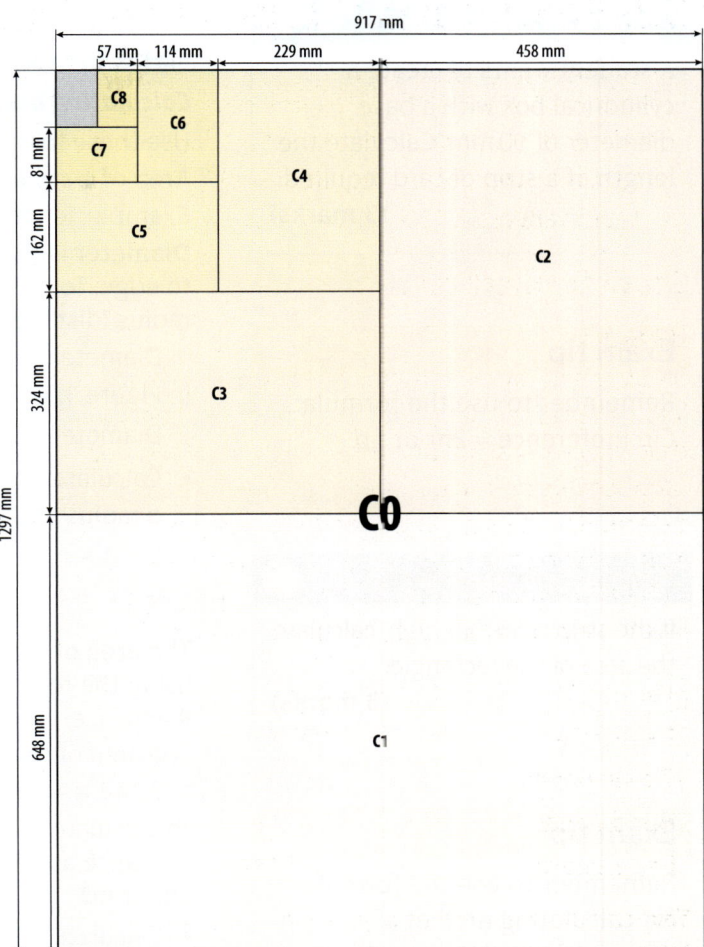

Figure 3.5.3 Comparative C sizes of envelope

B series

The sizes of B series paper are also defined by ISO 216 and are shown in Figure 3.5.2. The B series sizes are halfway between the A series sizes. The printing industry uses B sizes to set printing presses.

C series (envelopes)

Envelope sizes are called the C series and are defined in ISO 269. The area of C series sheets is the geometric mean of the areas of the A and B series sheets of the same number. This means that C4 is slightly larger than A4, and slightly smaller than B4. A letter written on A4 paper fits inside a C4 envelope.

The advantages of using standard sizes are that they are widely available, they fit in printers and they are understood internationally. However, it limits creativity and bespoke work, and the sizes are not adopted by all countries.

Foolscap

Foolscap is 203 × 330 mm and was the traditional paper size used in the British Commonwealth before ISO 216 standard A sizes. It is not used now so you would only normally come across it in archives of historical documents.

Letter size

Letter, 216 × 279 mm, is an American paper size also adopted by Canada and Mexico. You will see it as an option in software when setting document paper sizes.

3 Papers and boards

> **Exam-style question**
>
> A student wants to create a cylindrical box with a base diameter of 50 mm. Calculate the length of a strip of card required.
>
> **(3 marks)**

> **Exam tip**
>
> Remember to use the formula: Circumference = $2\pi r$ or πd

> **Exam-style question**
>
> If the strip is 50 mm high, calculate the area of the rectangle.
>
> **(3 marks)**

> **Exam tip**
>
> Remember to use the formula for calculating area of a rectangle, which is length multiplied by width.

Calculating area and diameter

Maths in practice 2

Calculating area and diameter

Use these formulas to work out the sizes of paper and board you need.

Area of a square or rectangle = length × width

Example: length 1000 mm × width 2000 mm = 2,000,000 mm²

Diameter is the measurement through the centre of a circle from edge to edge. To calculate the diameter of a circle from the radius, multiply its radius (distance to its centre) by 2.

Diameter = radius × 2

In Figure 3.5.4

Diameter = 2 × 40 = 80 mm

- Calculate the diameter of a circle with a radius of 250 mm.

$D = 2 \times r$

$D = 2 \times 250$ mm = 500 mm

The **area of a circle** is calculated using the formula
$A = \pi r^2$ (i.e. 3.142 × radius × radius).
The area of the circle in Figure 3.5.4 is:
3.142 × 40 × 40 = 5027.2 mm²

To calculate the **circumference** of a circle (distance around its outside) use either $2\pi r$ or πD.

- Calculate the area of a circle with a radius of 50 mm.

$A = \pi \times 50$ mm × 50 mm

$A = 3.142 \times 2500$ mm²

$A = \mathbf{7855}$ **mm²**

Now you try:

Calculate the circumference of a circle with a radius of 70 mm.

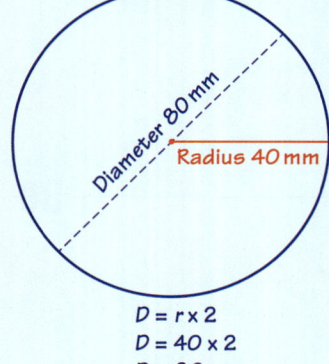

$D = r \times 2$
$D = 40 \times 2$
$D = 80$ mm

Figure 3.5.4 Calculating the diameter of a circle

Summary

Key points to remember:
- A paper or board's ability to withstand stress and forces determines if it is a successful choice.
- Products can be reinforced to withstand these forces.
- Papers and boards come in stock forms, weights and sizes.

Checkpoint

Strengthen

S1 Explain one advantage of using a stock form of paper.

Challenge

C1 Evaluate the advantages and disadvantages of using the different grades of paper.

3.6 Alternative manufacturing processes for different scales of production

> **Learning objectives**
>
> By the end of this section, you should know:
> - that there are seven different techniques for printing onto materials
> - that there are different scales of production from one-off to continuous
> - that there are methods of ensuring quality products are produced.

Deciding on the best manufacturing process for paper and card will depend on the quality required, as well as the scale of production.

Printing

The type of printing method you choose influences the final quality of your project. Table 3.6.1, on page 147, shows some of the manufacturing processes you could use.

Digital printing

Printing from a PC to a laser or inkjet printer is often the easiest option for small-scale document production at home, at school or in the office. Digital printing is quick, straightforward and immediate, but not economical as long print runs and the inks, or toner, are expensive.

Photocopying

Photocopiers are commonly used to produce multiple copies. A photocopier uses a six-stage process:

1. A cylinder inside the machine is electrostatically charged, then a beam of light travels across the document. The white areas reflect the light back.
2. The areas on the drum that correspond to the white areas become conductive (allowing electricity to run through them), whereas the black areas of the image remain negatively charged.
3. The photocopier has a positively charged fine powder called toner, which is attracted to the negatively charged areas.
4. An image made of powder is formed on the drum.
5. The image is transferred onto paper and fused by heat.
6. The drum is cleaned off and the process repeats for more copies.

Photocopiers can produce multiple copies quickly, and can automatically staple and collate documents. They are also commonly available. However, the electrostatic image fades over time and photocopiers are not cost effective for long print runs.

Letterpress

Raised metal letters locked into rigid frames are covered in printing ink then pressed onto paper in printing presses. Letterpress used to be the standard printing process but is now only used on low-volume production of books and stationery. Letterpresses give high-quality, crisp prints, but are less flexible, slower and more expensive than other methods and the plates need maintenance.

Example of letterpress printing

Offset printing (offset lithography)

Offset lithography works on the principle that oil and water do not mix. A four-stage process is used.

1. The print design is transferred using an oil-based emulsion to a printing plate made of flexible aluminium, or a polymer, fixed to a plate cylinder in the press.
2. Rollers apply water to the cylinder. It is repelled by the emulsion but attracted to the blank areas of the cylinder.
3. Ink is applied that only sticks to areas covered in emulsion.
4. A rubber blanket cylinder transfers the ink from the printing plate to the paper. The paper does not come into contact with the metal plates.

3 Papers and boards

The design can be built up using individual print units or a different plate for each of the four process colours: cyan, magenta, yellow and the key colour, black (often abbreviated to CMYK).

Offset machines can feed cut sheets or rolls of paper known as web fed. Web offset is where a continuous roll of paper is fed through the printing press. Pages are separated and cut to size after they have been printed. It is used for high-volume publications such as books, magazines, newspapers, catalogues and brochures. Offset printing is fast, flexible and provides good-quality material, but it has high set-up costs and can only be used for printing on flat surfaces.

Flexography

Flexography is similar to letterpress printing but uses cylindrical plates. The cylinders rotate and the raised design picks up quick-drying, semi-liquid ink from a roller that prints onto the fed paper. It can be used on corrugated cardboard, cellophane, plastic, label stock, fabric and metallic film. It is suitable for printing continuous patterns, such as for gift wrap and wallpaper, onto webs or rolls of paper.

Using rolls of material allows large orders to run with few interruptions for reloading. However, flexographic printers cannot print fine detail and there are high set-up costs.

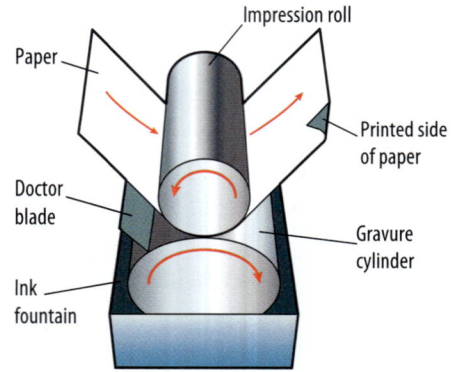

Figure 3.6.1 Gravure process

Gravure

The image is engraved onto a copper plate, which is mounted on a cylinder. The metal plate rotates into a bath of ink, which collects in the sunken sections and is transferred to the paper. It is used for large runs for such items as directories and magazines. The finished result is high quality and the ink is fast drying. However, the cost of producing the plates makes the overall costs significantly higher than other printing methods.

Screen printing

Screen printing can be used to print small quantities of items such as posters, display boards, fabrics, wallpaper, and control panels of electronic products. To produce the screen, fine mesh is stretched over a wooden frame and stapled into place. A stencil is made from either paper or, more commonly, chemicals using a photographic method. The printing ink is placed at the bottom of the screen and moved over the mesh with a squeegee to force it through onto the paper below. It is possible to make multiple prints with the same screen, but you need a separate screen for each colour, so multi-coloured patterns are costly. Screen printing cannot produce fine high-quality images.

Apply it

Investigate the printing options for making a flyer for a club night. If you are going to produce 500 copies, which printing method would be the most cost effective?

Other processes

Process	Application	Advantages	Disadvantages
Cutting by hand	• Paper and board can be cut and scored using scissors, scalpels and craft knives • A cutting mat and safety ruler should be utilised when using knives	• Easy to use, readily available equipment	• Can be inaccurate and slow
Cutting with machinery	• Laser cutters and die cutters accurately cut paper and board • Lasers require a suitable software package to design the shape to be cut • Die cutters (or dies) are steel outlines that are pressed into the paper or board to stamp out shapes	• Accurate cutting, repeatable	• Laser cutting gives a burnt edge • Die cutters vary in cost
Intermediate modelling	• Used for mocking up ideas for paper and card packaging prototypes	• Can quickly and cheaply give an idea of the finished product's proportions	• Can be flimsy • Needs to be to scale to get the correct effect
Frame modelling	• Paper is rolled into tubes and constructed into strong structures • Bridge designs can be constructed and tested using weights • The Japanese architect Shigeru Ban uses cardboard tubes to design fully functioning buildings	• Quick and easy to do	• The tubes need to be cut accurately to create accurate parallel structures • Cardboard tubes can be tough to cut
Test modelling	• Test models are used to try out ideas and tested for performance	• Can quickly and cheaply give an idea of the finished product's proportions	• Can be flimsy • Needs to be to scale to get the correct effect

Table 3.6.1 Types of product manufacturing processes using paper and/or board

> **Apply it**
>
> Investigate the work of Shigeru Ban. Make a fact file on his career and most famous works. Describe how he has exploited the properties of paper and board in his work.

3 Papers and boards

Scales of production

Table 3.6.2 summarises four methods as they apply to paper and board.

> **Link it up**
>
> Scales of production were covered in the core content (Section 1) of this book. To remind yourself, look at pages 9–10.

	Definition/Application	Advantages	Disadvantages
One-off	• A high-quality, expensive item made once for a specialist market or clientele, e.g. bespoke birthday card, hand-painted artwork, mono print	• High-quality, exclusive items	• Expensive to make and buy • Needs highly trained, specialist workforce • Labour intensive
Batch	• Produces up to 20,000 identical products before production moves to a different product, e.g. limited edition screen prints	• Cheaper production costs	• Needs design, pattern making and sampling skills • Repetitive tasks • Requires training • Lost time changing production line after each run
Mass production	• Produces a high volume of identical products, usually on a production line, e.g. cereal boxes	• Materials bought cheaply in bulk keeps costs low • Can be automated, requiring only a small semi-skilled or unskilled workforce	• Expensive to set up • Needs a large storage area • Jobs taken by machines
Continuous	• Constantly produces a high volume of identical products, e.g. toilet paper	• Low unit costs • Only small workforce is needed	• Expensive to set up and restart production if something goes wrong • Only suitable for simple products with few components

Table 3.6.2 Scales of production using paper and board

Techniques for quantity production

Larger quantities of products can be made by hand or using a larger-scale manufacturing process. Photocopying is one example – see page 145.

Technique	Description	Advantages	Disadvantages
Marking-out methods	• Paper and board can be marked out by hand using a pencil, ruler and set square • A metre rule and bow compass are also useful to mark reference points and lines • French curves are templates for curved shapes	• Immediate, quite quick to do	• Requires some skill and accuracy

Table 3.6.3 Techniques for quantity production *Cont…*

3.6 Alternative manufacturing processes for different scales of production

Technique	Description	Advantages	Disadvantages
Fixtures	• A rigid mechanical device that clamps the work against cutting tools	• Fast, accurate cutting of consistent quality, with no need to mark out each time • Interchangeable	• Only cost effective for more than about 200 units
Jigs for folding	• A type of fixture that can also guide the tool	• Fast, accurate folding of consistent quality, with no need to mark out each time • Interchangeable	• Only cost effective for more than about 200 units
Templates and patterns	• Pre-cut shapes to draw around, e.g. box nets • Packaging templates can be downloaded and adapted in software packages	• Easy, saves time spent marking out	• Not as fast as some other methods
Stencils	• Made from thin card, vinyl or plastic with shapes cut out • Can draw, spray paint or stipple paint through a lettering stencil • Can be bought in or made especially	• Repeatable design	• Stencil sometimes slips, spray paint can get underneath the stencil if not adhered properly to the material • Webs are needed on some shapes to stop them falling out, e.g. the centre of the A
Computer-aided manufacture (CAM)	• A programmable machine attached to a computer, e.g. digital printers, dye sublimation printers and laser cutting in schools, and computerised plotters and cutters, large-scale digital printers and large-scale laser cutting machines in industry	• Accurate • Can operate 24/7 • Easy to make changes	• Equipment is expensive • Training needed to learn how to use software • Jobs taken by machines
Quality control	• A system of quality checks during manufacturing, e.g. checking **registration marks**, **crop marks** and **colour bars** • A 'proof' copy is initially made with the desired colour saturation levels • The proof is approved by the client and subsequent prints are compared to the proof to make sure that all the colours are set to the right level • If prints differ, the machines are adjusted	• Produces high-quality products • Results in less material wastage and happier customers due to improved quality and reliability of the products purchased	• Extra time taken • Cost of quality control staff • Wastage if pieces are rejected

Table 3.6.3 Techniques for quantity production *Cont…*

3 Papers and boards

Technique	Description	Advantages	Disadvantages
Working within tolerance	• A measure of accuracy – how much larger or smaller you can cut within a tolerance of + or – a set number of mm	• Accurate sizing	• Takes care and skill • Wastage if badly cut pieces are rejected
Efficient cutting	• Carefully planning the placement of templates or dies so that they touch without overlapping by rotating or flipping shapes	• Minimises waste	• Takes time and consideration

Table 3.6.3 Techniques for quantity production

Key terms

Registration mark: a circle with a cross through it on the edge of printed material. Printed using all four colours, it should look black. If any colours are slightly offset (out of register) then the mark will look blurred and the machine needs to be reset.

Crop marks: small lines that show exactly where the finished page will be cut during the finishing process. Also known as a trim mark.

Colour bars: a strip of the four CMYK colours printed outside the trim area, used for colour quality control.

Maths in practice 3

Minimising waste

- How many 60 mm equilateral triangles can be cut from an A3 piece of paper? (Remember: an A3 piece of paper is 297 × 420 mm).

Number of triangles in each 'odd' row = 420 ÷ 60 = 7

Number of triangles in each 'even' row = 6

Number in each pair of rows = 7 + 6 = 13

Height of each triangle = 52 mm (draw a 60 mm equilateral triangle to measure its height)

Number of pairs of rows = 297 ÷ 52 = 5.71…

There are 5 full pairs of rows, so:
5 × 13 = **65** of the 60 mm equilateral triangles on one A3 sheet.

Figure 3.6.2 Equilateral triangles

Summary

Key points to remember:
- Choosing a print method has cost and quality implications.
- Different processes can be used to manufacture paper and board products to different scales of production.

Checkpoint

Strengthen

S1 Name four different types of printing.
S2 Name a printed product that would be made using continuous production.
S3 Explain why colour bars are used when printing.

Challenge

C1 Describe what a blurred registration mark would mean to the quality of the finished product.
C2 Give examples of where working to strict tolerances would be necessary and explain why.

3.7 Specialist techniques used for high-quality paper and board prototypes

> **Learning objectives**
> By the end of this section, you should know:
> - that a range of hand and machine processes can be used to create high quality products
> - the difference between serif and sans serif letter forms.

Tools and equipment

It is important to choose the right techniques, tools, equipment and processes to shape, fabricate, construct and assemble your high-quality prototypes.

Hand tools

Hand tools are generally cheap and easy to buy and have immediate results, if used with skill. As with all tools, they should be used with care as they can be dangerous and are only as accurate as the user.

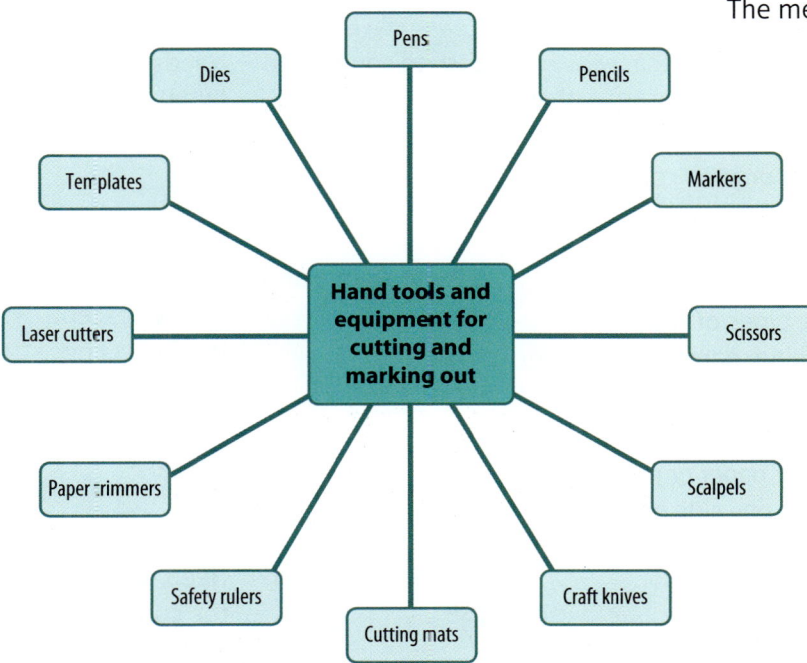

Figure 3.7.1 Types of hand tools for paper and board

Machinery

Using machinery achieves professional results more quickly and accurately. However, machinery may be expensive, and users need training to operate it effectively and safely. Machinery that can be used for prototypes includes drills, small-scale die cutting machines and scroll saws.

Digital design and manufacture

Specialised software can design patterns or whole products, which are downloaded to a digital machine. That can be as simple as an inkjet printer or as complex as a laser cutter or a large-format printer and knife cutter. All require training on appropriate software and how to set up the machinery. The outcome is accurate and high quality but the machinery can be expensive, and cutter plotters and lasers need to be risk assessed.

Shaping

Paper and board need to be shaped to fit their purpose. The methods depend on the end use.

Shaping, folding and manipulation

Paper and board can be formed by creasing and scoring using low-cost, easily available tools. Scoring uses a knife, or straight edge, lightly along a fold line to make a cut that does not go all the way through. The paper or board will fold away from the score with a crisp edge.

Creasing is using a blunt tool to compress the paper or card along a fold line to aid folding. Packaging dies use a combination of cutting bars with a sharp 'v' edge and creasing bars with a rounded top to make fold lines. Formers, bending jigs and scoring aids can also be bought. You can fold paper against a straight edge, such as a ruler, to achieve a crisp finish or use a bone folder, which is a creasing tool. Paper and card can also be manipulated into shape by scoring, curling and pressing.

Notching

This is cutting out a slot in sheet material or a piece in tubing. It can be used to reduce bulk at corners and aid folding or to make slot-together components.

Modelling

When designing your product, you will progress through a range of modelling techniques from initial sketch models to working high-quality prototypes.

3 Papers and boards

Fabricating/assembling/constructing

When making paper and board structures, you need to consider how you will join the various elements and how to choose the best method. Sometimes they will be permanently fixed in place with glue, but you may want to be able to undo the pieces or design an object that can move freely. Remember to use **marking-out tools** to plan the assembly, as it may be difficult to take the model apart if you make a mistake. See Table 3.63, on page 148 for further information.

Temporary or removable components	Application	Advantages	Disadvantages
Split pins	• Creating a fixed or moving pivot on pop-up mechanisms or moving shop displays	Easy to apply, cheap, reusable	Requires some pre-planning to ensure the mechanism works
Mapping pins	• Modelling card mechanisms in conjunction with a cork board • Can temporarily hold card in place to check for fit	Easy to apply, cheap, reusable	Can be fiddly and fall out
Stapling	• A U-shaped, sharp-ended thin wire that is driven into paper or card with a stapler, which bends the legs • Attaches papers or joins corners of cardboard boxes	Easy to source and use	Needs some force to get through thick materials
Taping	• Used to join paper and card • Many different types of tape available: masking, parcel, clear sticky tape, brown paper tape and double-sided tape • They are a film of paper or plastic film with adhesive on one side or both	Easy to source and use	Difficult to remove except from masking tape which is designed to be low tack
Adhesives	• Liquid to stick components • Options include PVA (polyvinyl acetate), glue sticks (acrylic polymer), hot glue	Easy to source and use	Need to ensure the correct type is used for the materials
Paper engineering	• Manipulating paper, ultimately to make 3D pop-up scenes in books and cards	Looks very effective if done right	Requires skill and practice

Table 3.7.1 Types of assembling components

Apply it

Find out about the children's pop-up book artists and paper engineers Robert Sabuda and Jan Pieńkowski. Try out some ideas for pop-up cards.

You can **strengthen** the model by layering materials, adding ribs or laminating other materials to the paper and board. See section 3.4 for more information.

3.7 Specialist techniques used for high-quality paper and board prototypes

Dissimilar materials

Another element to consider is how you can use **dissimilar materials** to paper and board, such as adding acetate windows to packaging, vacuum-formed inserts, stickers and temporary components. They may have different properties and not bend or fix in the same way as the other materials in the product.

Lamination

Similarly, you could use **lamination** to apply different coatings to paper and board, for example:

- aluminium is used for **insulation** and as a bacterial barrier
- plastic film or wax for waterproofing
- greaseproof paper for containing products that can be baked.

Lettering

Typography is about letter style and design. The type of font, font spacing and colour that you choose can determine whether a product looks sleek and modern or unprofessional and dated.

There are three types of letterform:

- **Serif** typefaces have 'feet'; an example is Times New Roman. They are seen as traditional typefaces.
- **Sans serif** are plain typefaces, without embellishment; an example is **Helvetica**. These are seen as more modern, partly because they are easier to read on screen which has increased their popularity over the last two decades.
- **Script fonts** look handwritten and flow such as the one in the Coca-Cola logo.

Text size is measured in points. One point is 1/72 of an inch, which is about 0.35 mm. A 50 pt letter is about 17.5 mm high.

Kerning is the space in between the letters. This can be reduced or enlarged to give different effects or to fit more words on a line to avoid awkward line breaks.

Binding

Documents or mock-ups of books need to be bound so the pages do not fall out. Hand-stitching is easy if pilot holes are made in the paper or card with a sharp tool. Comb binding machines and combs are readily available in most offices and create a book that opens fully with pages that turn easily. For a more professional finish you could ask a specialist book binding service to apply thermal tape for you. Case binding is used to produce hardback books. The pages are stitched in a complex arrangement and then glued to a hard outer cover.

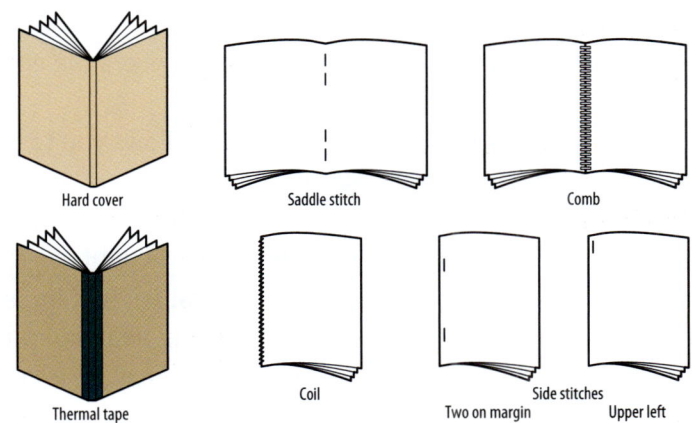

Figure 3.7.2 Types of binding

> **Apply it**
>
> Collect different typefaces from publications such as magazines, free font websites and local papers. Sort them into serif and sans serif typefaces. Consider which types of product each would be appropriate for.

Summary

Key points to remember:

- Specialist tools such as hand tools and machinery are used to shape, fabricate and construct prototypes.
- It is important to consider the best method of joining together all the different elements of the prototype.

Checkpoint

Strengthen

S1 Name an example of a sans serif typeface.

Challenge

C1 Describe and compare the different ways of cutting paper and board.

3 Papers and boards

3.8 Surface treatments and finishes for papers and boards

> **Learning objectives**
>
> By the end of this section, you should know:
> - the types of finishing techniques and surface treatments that can be applied to paper and board.

Surface finishes and treatments

Before or after the product is assembled, it may need to be decorated or finished. Here are some common techniques.

Material	Description	Advantages	Disadvantages
Varnishing/UV varnishes	• Varnish is a clear ink with a gloss, satin or matt finish • A flood varnish covers the entire printed page • A spot varnish allows you to highlight specific areas • Ultra-violet (UV) flood or spot coatings are dried using UV light	• Conveys a sense of quality • Flood finish may improve the product's longevity	• Adds cost to the process • UV varnishes are difficult to apply in non-commercial settings
Hot foil blocking	• Pre-glued metal foil is stamped onto the surface using heat and pressure • Holograms can be applied in this way for security printings such as on banknotes and music event tickets	• A cost-effective way to add metallic colour to part of the printed product	• Adds cost to the process
Edge staining	• Dye is applied to the trimmed edges of a book, on all three unbound edges, only on the side edge, or only on the top edge • Edge stains in a spatter pattern are known as sprinkled edges	• Unusual finish • Conveys a sense of quality	• Adds cost to the process
Embossing	• Raising the surface of the paper, often using steel dies	• High-quality, tactile finish	• Adds cost to the process
Packaging laminates and films	• Laminate films can be PET (PolyEthylene Terephthalate), LDPE or PP (Polypropylene) • They accept high-definition prints and are combined with papers and boards to create robust full-colour packaging • They provide practical advantages such as puncture resistance, barrier capabilities and qualities suitable for frozen foods or use in ovens and microwaves	• Can reduce packaging materials by making the package stronger	• Difficult to recycle as they have to be separated

Table 3.8.1 Types of surface finish

3.8 Surface treatments and finishes for papers and boards

Exam-style question

A student wants to make the box below in thin card in school.

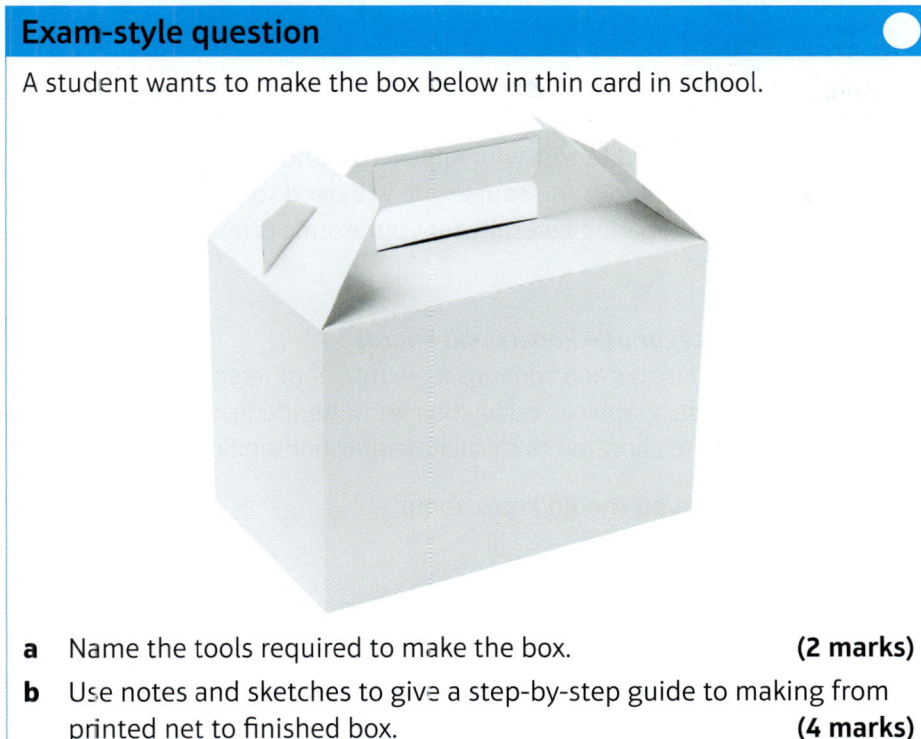

a   Name the tools required to make the box. **(2 marks)**
b   Use notes and sketches to give a step-by-step guide to making from printed net to finished box. **(4 marks)**

Summary

Key points to remember:
- Surface treatments and finishes are applied to papers and boards for decorative purposes or to change their properties.
- These treatments may be physical or chemical.

Checkpoint

Strengthen

S1 Name four different types of finish.
S2 Explain why embossing would increase the cost of a product.

Challenge

C1 Investigate different ways of binding documents.

Preparing for your exam 3

Exam strategy

What to expect in the exam

The examination is designed to test your knowledge and understanding of papers and boards. Throughout the course you will need to practise exam-style questions in all areas. Preparing carefully for your exams is important to get as many marks as you can.

Section B: Material categories – Papers and boards

This section is worth 60 marks and contains a mixture of different question styles, including open-response, graphical, calculation and extended-open-response questions. Five marks are allocated to calculation questions in Section B.

For papers and boards, you should know about:

- design contexts
- the sources, origins, physical and working properties of papers and boards, and their social and ecological footprints
- the way in which the selection of papers and boards is influenced
- the impact of forces and stresses on papers and boards and how they can be reinforced and stiffened
- typical stock forms, types and sizes used in order to calculate and determine the required quantity of papers and boards
- alternative processes that can be used to manufacture papers and boards to different scales of production
- specialist techniques, tools, equipment and processes that can be used to shape, fabricate, construct and assemble a high quality paper and board prototype
- appropriate surface treatments and finishes that can be applied to papers and boards for functional and aesthetic purposes.

Revision tips

- Ensure you start revising in plenty of time. You will find it easier to remember facts you have revised several times over a few weeks than those you have tried to memorise at the last minute.
- Make clear and well-ordered notes about all the sections.
- Work through all sample assessment materials, past papers and textbook questions available from Pearson.
- Identify the areas where you are likely to get mathematical questions and practise arithmetic and numerical computation, handling data, graphs, geometry and trigonometry.
- Discuss the course with your teacher and peers, as it will help your understanding.
- Use online or other resources to extend your understanding of the design and technology context.

Preparing for your exam 3

Sample answers with comments

The following questions give some examples of how to interpret the different command words.

Question 1: Calculation question

Figure PE3.1 shows a net of a CD sleeve made from card. Calculate the area of card wasted each time a sleeve is cut out. Give your answer in mm². **(5 marks)**

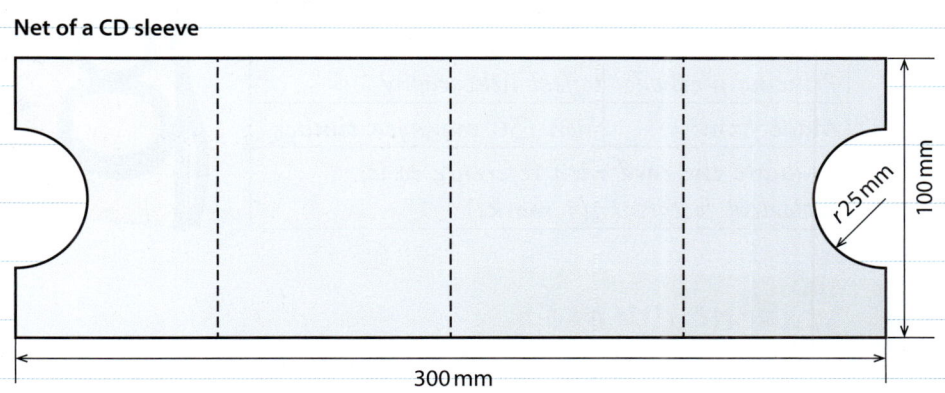

Figure PE3.1

Student answer

a) Area of a circle = π × r²
r = 25 mm   π = 3.14
Area = 3.14 × 25 mm × 25 mm
     = 3.14 × 625 mm²
     = 1962.5 mm²
Area of card wasted each time = 1962.5 mm²

Exam tip

You will need to use your maths skills in the exam. The formula you need may be given in the question, but it helps to be familiar with formulas that are likely to come up.

Verdict

The student has the correct answer, but they have not explained in their working that they have concluded that they needed two semi-circles, which is the same as calculating the area of one full circle. Make sure that you read questions carefully as they may give further instructions as to the units the answer would need to be expressed in, e.g. mm², cm² or m², and to how many decimal places.

Question 2: 'Explain' question

Explain two benefits to the manufacturer of a die-cut and printed card of carrying out quality control checks during manufacture. **(4 marks)**

Exam tip

'Explain' answers need to be fairly detailed, exploring aspects of the situation by reasoning or argument.

Student answer

1. Consistent quality of product would be achieved by eliminating inferior products during the checking stages.
2. Less waste would be produced meaning potentially increased profits for the company.

Verdict

The student has given two good answers that explore aspects of the quality control and its impact on the manufacturer. The student could expand on the answers given, by adding in examples.

Preparing for your exam 3

Question 3: 'Evaluate' question

The birthday card pictured has been designed to be sold by a large high street store. Analyse the table below.

Country of origin:	China
Added feature:	ribbon trim
Printing method:	offset lithography
Made from:	non-FSC managed timber

Evaluate the card with reference to its ecological footprint. (9 marks)

Exam tip

'Evaluate' answers need to look at the strengths and weaknesses of a proposition and then draw a conclusion.

Student answer

Offset machines provide a full colour, high quality result. They can be fed using either cut sheets or rolls of paper known as web fed. The advantages of using this system are that it produces good quality images quickly. The disadvantages are that there are quite high set-up costs as a different plate for each of the four printing colours, cyan, magenta, yellow and black would need to be set up as this card is a full colour print. The energy needed to run four separate machines would be high compared to a simpler process. This could have environmental implications depending on where the manufacturer sources their energy from for example from renewables or from burning fossil fuels. Harmful solvents may also be used to clean the plates of the machinery.

The card is produced in China which means it has to be packaged and transported a great distance before further distribution to the high street store. Most ships and road transport use fossil fuels further increasing the environmental impact of this card.

Lastly the card is produced from timber which is not FSC certified. This means that the timber has come from a forest that is potentially not well managed and maybe has not been replanted at all. This could lead to soil erosion and loss of wildlife habitats.

Overall, I think that the ecological footprint of the card is quite high. This could be reduced by producing it locally and by using printing inks and solvents that are not harmful to the environment. On a positive note the card is made from a sustainable material that can be recycled.

Verdict

This is a good answer. The student has raised ethical issues relating to transportation of the card from its country of manufacture to its retail outlet, the source of the materials used and energy consumption of the printing process.

Question 4: 'Name' or 'Explain' question

The pop-up book pictured has complex paper structures. Name **two** methods that could be used to cut out the shapes of the book. For each method explain **one** advantage to the manufacturer. (6 marks)

Preparing for your exam 3

> **Exam tip**
> This is a combination of a 'Give' question and an 'Explain' question. 'Explain' questions require you to give reasons why you have chosen your answers.

> **Verdict**
> In part 1, the student correctly identified two suitable methods.
>
> In part 2, the student does not give the full justification required. They could have written the answer in the following way:

> **Student answer**
> 1. Die cutting or by hand using a scalpel and cutting board.
> 2. Die cutting is accurate and repeatable. Hand cutting would produce a unique one-off piece.

Die cutting is capable of mass producing accurate, complex shapes that are stamped out of card using a sharp steel blade that has been bent into shape. There are a number of varying heights for the cutters resulting in cuts and folds.

Question 5: 'Give/name' (short answer question)

A local nightclub wants to start a teen night. It is going to print the leaflet in Figure PE3.2. Give a suitable method of printing a flyer for a club night like the one on the right. **(1 mark)**

> **Exam tip**
> This type of question requires specific information but it does not need to be clarified further.

> **Student answer**
> Offset lithography

> **Verdict**
> The student answered the question as required.

Figure PE3.2

Preparing for your exam 3

Question 6: Identify (short answer question)

Figure PE3.3 shows a design of a seed packet that needs to be improved to include the following specification points.

The seed packaging must:
- appeal to children to encourage them to grow and eat vegetables
- be easy to open
- be re-sealable if not all the seeds are used in one go.

Use notes and/or sketches to show how the design could be modified to include these points **(6 marks)**

Figure PE3.3

Student answer

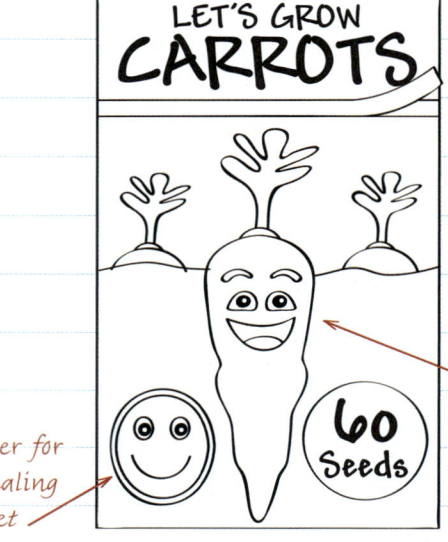

Verdict

The student has answered this question well. Each of the specified criteria have been covered to good effect.

Question 7: 'Use notes and/or sketches' to show question

Use notes and/or sketches to show the difference between serif and sans serif typefaces. **(4 marks)**

Exam tip

It is important to annotate (label) sketches as the detail is not always clear in a sketch and the marks awarded can come from written or the drawn information.

Student answer

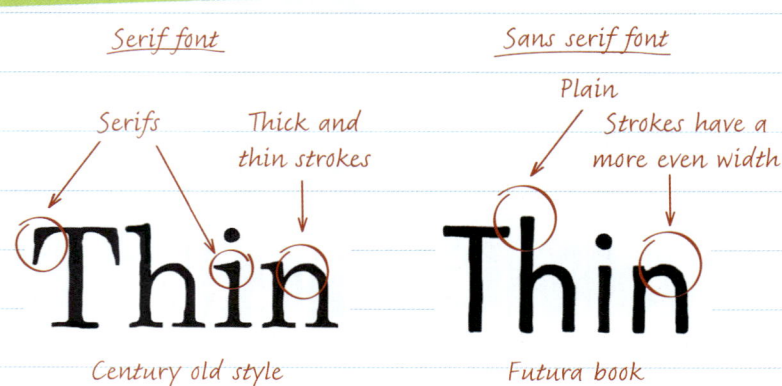

Figure PE3.4

Verdict

This is a good answer. The annotation clearly states the attributes of each typeface.

Preparing for your exam 3

Question 8: 'Explain' question

Describe one working property of Tetra Pak® that makes it suitable for a milk carton. (3 marks)

Student answer

Tetra Pak maintains the nutritional value and flavours of the food in the package in ambient temperatures by acting as an impermeable barrier.

Verdict

The answer is correct, as the properties described relate to the use of Tetra Pak® laminate in relation to a milk carton. You could also explain what each material contributes to the laminate, such as foil providing a barrier against air and light.

Pearson Education Ltd accepts no responsibility whatsoever for the accuracy or method of working in the answers given.

4 Polymers

4.1 Design contexts

Getting started

As already mentioned in Topic 1.10, polymers have a wide variety of uses in everyday life. Think about the home environment and consider the following questions.

- How many of your personal possessions are made from polymers?
- Of these, how many polymers can you name?
- Do you know the properties of some of these polymers?

Count how many items made from polymers you can identify in your home. Select one and complete a detailed product analysis. Consider how the item has been made.

Learning objective

By the end of this section, you should know:

- a range of contexts where polymers are essential to the success of a product.

Most synthetic polymers are made from oil-based petrochemicals. However, alternatives that use natural and sustainable sources are becoming increasingly available. Designers and engineers use a wide variety of polymers every day to make commonplace products we take for granted: toothbrushes, toothpaste tubes, shower gel containers, hair brushes and hairdryers.

There are two main categories of polymer that you need to know about: thermoforming polymers and thermosetting polymers. You will also need to learn more about biodegradable alternatives.

Design contexts

The first polymer 'Bakelite' (a phenol-formaldehyde resin) was invented in 1907. It was mostly used to case electrical components in radios and other electrical devices, but it was also used to manufacture toys and jewellery. Bakelite was non-recyclable and this concerned environmentalists. Over the last 100 years, the list of polymers has expanded. At first, products made from polymers only used a limited range of manufacturing processes, but the number of techniques available today makes it possible to make complex products.

Polymers are now used in:

- **medicine:** for artificial limbs, tablet coatings, blister packs, syringes and heart valves
- **household goods:** kitchenware, laptops and personal music players
- **building materials:** including home insulation.

The list is endless. With crude oil being a **non-renewable resource**, it is becoming increasingly important for polymers to be recycled and cause less impact on the environment in which we live.

Key terms

Bakelite: a thermosetting phenol-formaldehyde resin.

Non-renewable resource: natural resources, such as crude oil, that take millions of years to form and are used up more quickly than they can be replaced.

Apply it

Do some research to find out how consumers can responsibly dispose of products that are made of polymers.

4 Polymers

Summary

Key things to remember:
- There are two main categories of polymer: thermoforming polymers and thermosetting polymers.
- When they were first invented, polymers were non-recyclable. Now, however, polymers made from renewable resources are being used so they do not cause as much environmental damage.

Checkpoint

Strengthen
S1 Name two products that are made of polymers.
S2 Describe the benefits of using polymers compared to more traditional materials.

Challenge
C1 Why have polymers become more popular for the production of products?

4.2 Sources and properties

Learning objectives
By the end of this section, you should know:
- the types, properties and structure of thermoforming polymers and thermosetting polymers not considered in Topic 1.10
- the components and manufacturing processes associated with polymers
- the advantages and disadvantages of using polymers for different applications
- the social and ecological footprints of polymers.

Link it up
Thermoforming polymers were covered in the core content section of this book. To remind yourself, look at pages 43–46.

Thermoforming polymers are used in many different products. When designing a product, the designer will need to select the most appropriate polymer for the task. Designers will need to factor in many **design constraints** such as cost, manufacturing methods and material properties. In this section you will learn about other polymers that are commonly used in everyday products.

Key term
Design constraint: limitation on the design and manufacture of the product.

Thermoforming polymers

Thermoforming polymer	Form	Properties	Common uses	Advantages/disadvantages
Polyvinyl chloride (PVC)	Powder, granules and sheet	Chemical and weather resistant	Window frames, cable insulation, pencil cases and drainage pipes	• Can be formed using a wide range of techniques • Needs UV stabilisers to stop material fading in sunlight
Acrylonitrile-butadiene-styrene (ABS)	Granules, tube and sheet	High impact strength, lightweight, hard and durable	Computer casings, mobile phones, safety helmets and car bumpers	• Excellent impact strength • Can be formed using a wide range of techniques • Can be coloured using pigments • More expensive than alternative materials
Polyethylene terephthalate (PET)	Granules and sheets	Lightweight, strong and food safe	Food packaging, bottles, electronic component coatings	• Excellent visual clarity • Can be coloured using pigments
Urethane/polyurethane	Liquid, sheet, foam and granules	High-load resistance, high-wear resistance, flexible and good electrical resistance	Bags, varnish, wheels and furniture foam	• Can be made into very thin sheets to produce carrier bags • Governments have imposed a charge for carrier bags to reduce landfill and promote reuse
Fluoroelastomer	Sheet and tube	Heat, chemical and solvent resistant	Heat shrink tubing, car hoses, chemical-resistant gloves, gaskets	• Can be used to tie wiring looms together • Differently sized material is required depending on amount of shrink fit required
Rigid polystyrene (high-density polystyrene)	Granules and sheets in a wide range of colours	Lightweight, food safe, heat resistant	Food packaging, such as coffee cups	• Can be recycled at school where equipment available • Difficult to recycle if contaminated by food
Expanded polystyrene	Beads, sheets and blocks	Lightweight, buoyant, tough but breaks easily	Packaging, swimming floats, cups, sound insulation, heat insulation, beads in bean bags	• Can be vacuum formed • Excellent thermal properties that are useful in drinking cups • Difficult to recycle if contaminated with food
Styrofoam™ (extruded polystyrene – EPS)	Sheets	Lightweight, buoyant, heat insulation and can be easily shaped using workshop tools to make models	Fast-food packaging, packaging of audio-visual equipment, silk flower holders	• Can be easily formed using school workshop tools and equipment • Cutting by hot wire requires good ventilation due to fumes

Table 4.2.1 A summary of the different types of thermoforming polymers

4 Polymers

What are the advantages or disadvantages of Styrofoam™?

Apply it

The properties of acrylic make it an ideal material for rear car light covers, but unsuitable for lights on the front of a car. Analyse the parts made from polymers on a family member or relative's car. Consider the properties of polymers that make them suitable for each part.

Thermosetting polymers

Link it up

Thermosetting polymers were covered in the core content section of this book. To remind yourself, look at pages 44–45.

Key term

Composite material: a material made from a combination of two or more materials.

Thermosetting polymers are commonly used as a resin glue to bond particles and sheets of timber together in manufactured boards. Polyester resin is also combined with glass fibres to form glass reinforced plastic (GRP), a **composite material**. The glass fibre strands are fixed in place once the polyester resin is hardened and toughened. GRP is very strong and lightweight. The direction of the glass strands is random and this is what provides GRP with uniform strength. GRP is commonly used in low-production products such as sport cars and boats as it can be formed into many shapes. A polyester gel coat resin is used to give the GRP a smooth finish. The gel coat layer can also be coloured using pigments. Urea formaldehyde is used in the moulding of products, such as an electrical wall socket. It is also used as an adhesive in manufactured boards.

Sources and origins of polymers

Most synthetic polymers are made from crude oil. Oil is a non-renewable resource, most of which is found deep in the ground. Oil rigs are used to drill for oil in the rock below the sea. On land, pumps are used to extract oil from wells. The largest oil-producing nations are Russia, Saudi Arabia and the United States.

4.2 Sources and properties

Oil contains many **hydrocarbons** that need to be cracked into smaller particles to make polymers. This process is carried out at oil refineries throughout the world. Crude oil is transported by pipeline, or large ships, to refineries where polymers are made. In the UK, most oil refineries can be found close to the coast where ships can unload and pipelines from oil rigs come ashore.

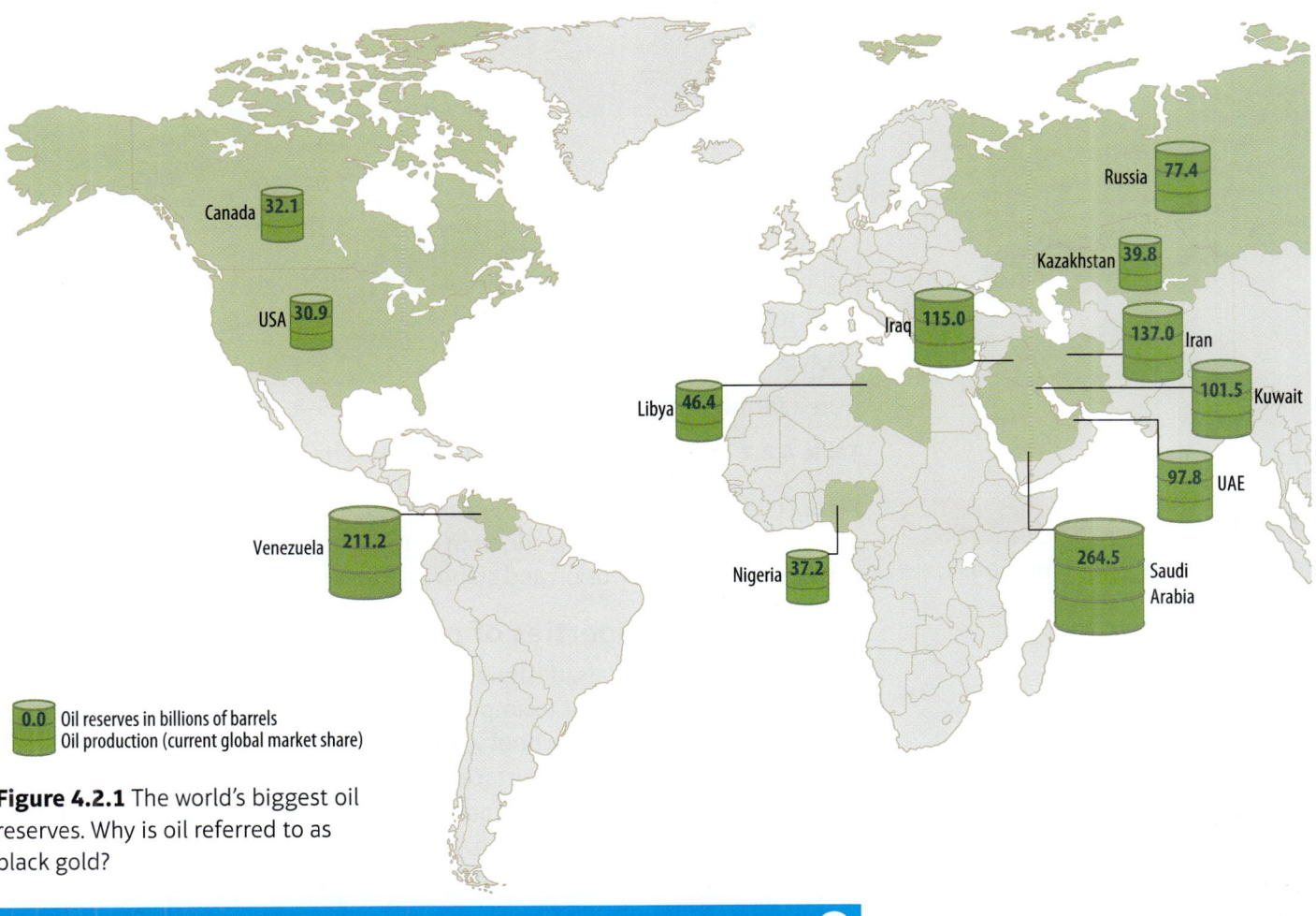

Figure 4.2.1 The world's biggest oil reserves. Why is oil referred to as black gold?

Exam-style question
Explain **one** reason why oil refineries are often found near the sea.
(2 marks)

Exam tip
Focus on the command word 'Explain'. Consider the transport of oil to the refinery from the source of extraction.

The physical characteristics of polymers
When choosing materials to make different products you will need to consider what properties are required. When selecting a polymer where the product needs to float, the density needs to be less than $1\,g/cm^3$. The durability of polymers is more difficult to calculate. Tests that replicate wear are used to make **qualitative** comparisons.

Key terms
Hydrocarbon: a compound consisting of hydrogen and carbon.
Qualitative: measuring results by quality.

167

4 Polymers

Type of polymer	Density (g/cm³)
Acrylic	1.20
High-impact polystyrene (HIPS)	1.03–1.06
Polystyrene (PS)	0.96–1.04
Styrofoam™	0.05
Biopol®	1.06
Polyvinyl chloride	1.47
Acrylonitrile-butadiene-styrene	1.0–1.05
Polyethylene terephthalate (PET)	1.38
Urethane/polyurethane	1.20
Fluoroelastomer	1.8
Polyester resin	1.3–1.7
Urea formaldehyde	1.5–1.6 g/cm³

Table 4.2.2 The density of thermoforming and thermosetting polymers

> **Key term**
>
> **Durable:** how well a material lasts.

Products designed to last more than a year, such as home appliances, motorbikes and computers, need to be made from **durable** materials. Polymers are often used, as they resist corrosion and stand up to everyday wear and tear.

The working properties of polymers

When selecting materials, designers need to consider how they will need to perform in daily life. For example, Styrofoam™ is a suitable material for modelling prototypes in a school workshop, but it would not be suitable for a product that needs a hard surface and can resist scratching. High-impact polystyrene is harder than Styrofoam™ and offers good plasticity in that it can be easily shaped to make different forms. Styrofoam™ is tough: it can resist impact and absorb energy without fracturing. ABS is also used in products that need to be tough. For example, a car bumper made of ABS needs to withstand small knocks without deforming and causing damage to other parts of the car. ABS is also strong in tension and compression, and is used in chairs to create rigid structures that withstand the weight of those sitting on the chair as well as misuse through swinging on two legs. The plasticity of polymers also makes them easy to shape. See Table 4.2.1 on page 165 for further properties of polymers.

> **Exam-style question**
>
> Explain **two** reasons why polymers are an appropriate material for the manufacture of products that need to float. **(6 marks)**

> **Link it up**
>
> Other working properties of polymers are covered in Section 1.10 in Topic 1, see page 47.

The social footprint of polymers

Trend forecasting

Between 2011 and 2016 there was a 1.3 per cent increase in the use of **flexible packaging** and a 2.3 per cent rise in the use of **rigid packaging** (source: PIRA) worldwide. During this period, there was a higher demand for **bioplastics** due to consumer demand for greener products, government initiatives, new production capabilities, an increase in oil prices and the development of material properties. Flexible polymer packaging alternatives are replacing the need for glass and metal packaging. Flexible packaging is lighter in weight, easier to transport and considered more cost effective to produce. Asia currently has the highest growing market for polymer-based packaging. There has been an increase in the use of PET for packaging of soft drinks, food and personal care products. The wall thickness of polymer packaging has decreased significantly during the last 20 years, with drinks bottles being some 27 per cent lighter in weight. It is expected that there will be continued growth in the use of polymers in southern and central America, Africa and South Europe.

The global polymer industry for car manufacture is expected to exceed a value of $22 billion by 2019 (source: Research and Markets). There is an increased demand for lighter and stronger materials that meet government legislation and will improve fuel efficiency. With a growing demand for vehicles in emerging and developing countries, the demand for polymers is very likely to increase.

This expected trend means that there will be a need for materials that can be recycled, as well as lighter alternatives and increased use of bioplastics, which reduce reliance on oil. As the price of oil is volatile, manufacturers may look at alternatives to a purely synthetic-based material.

The impact of extraction and material production on the environment

The building of oil rigs, drilling sites on land and refineries can lead to deforestation or disturbance of the environment in the sea. This can make animals and sea life seek out other habitats as their homes and food supplies have been destroyed.

The extraction of oil from the seabed and land can cause significant damage to the environment. On land, it can lead to deforestation. Where legislation is not strict, waste products can be disposed of in rivers – lead, cadmium and mercury are just a few of the chemicals released. Such pollution can cause health problems for people living near oil drilling fields and oil distribution pipes can leak if not maintained, having a devastating impact on local wildlife. The impact of drilling for oil and deforestation can also lead to an increase in CO_2 into the atmosphere.

Drilling at sea also risks damage to the environment, as any leaks can affect sea and bird life. Pipes that lie at the bottom of the seabed are more difficult to repair when damaged and leaks can often go undetected.

> **Key terms**
>
> **Flexible packaging:** pouches, bags and films.
>
> **Rigid packaging:** pots, tubs, trays and bottles.
>
> **Bioplastics:** a type of plastic that is made from biological substances, not petroleum.

4 Polymers

A bird covered in oil: oil spills can have a devastating effect on wildlife

The impact of extraction and material production on wildlife

Oil leaks from pipes or spills from ships can have a devastating impact on wildlife: birds, fish and sea mammals. The oil covers the body of the animal in a thick layer, which in birds can affect flight. It can even break down the waterproofing or insulating properties needed in feathers or fur, causing hypothermia. Other sea life can die due to dehydration or starvation as the oil prevents them from feeding in their normal habitats. Oil can also wash up on beaches, killing animals that feed in these areas. It can also destroy nesting areas for turtles and cause poisoning of animals higher up the food chain.

Ease and difficulty of recycling and disposal

It is possible to recycle most thermoforming polymers, but thermosetting polymers need to be disposed of at landfill sites. Where polymers are used to package food, the containers will need to be thoroughly cleaned before being sent for recycling to avoid contaminating the process. Most households in the UK will have access to a means of disposing of polymer-based products.

Most recycling plants can separate and recycle polymer, metal and card-based products. Polymers disposed of at landfill sites can take more than 500 years to decompose, whereas it is also possible to use some polymer waste that cannot be recycled as fuel.

> **Exam-style question**
>
> Evaluate the ecological footprint of a plastic disposable cup.
>
> **(9 marks)**

> **Exam tip**
>
> When answering 'Evaluate' questions, you are advised to plan your answers. Consider your main points, give examples, explain each and make links to the question. You can remember this using the acronym PEEL:
>
> **P**oint
>
> **E**vidence/Example
>
> **E**xplain
>
> **L**ink

Figure 4.2.2 Symbols used for identifying and recycling of polymers: how many of these do you recognise?

4.2 Sources and properties

The ecological footprint of polymers

At its simplest, the ecological footprint is the amount of the environment required to produce the goods and services necessary to support a particular lifestyle.

Sustainability

Synthetic polymers are not naturally a sustainable material. As polymers are made from oil, they contribute to the depletion of non-renewable materials. For a polymer to be considered sustainable, it must be able to be recycled or reused forever. Some polymers are not recyclable, while those that are need to be disposed of responsibly if they are to be made into other products. In the UK only 29 per cent of polymers are currently recycled, but this is to increase to 57 per cent by 2020 to meet a government target.

Oil exploration and extraction

It is the job of geologists to find sources of oil reserves. This is an expensive process and can be costly if drilling for oil is unsuccessful. Survey ships are used to find oil below the sea, using compressed air to send shock waves into the bed rock. The waves are reflected back to sensors dragged behind the ship and the results of the reflected waves allow geologists to plot the seabed and identify oil reserves. A similar system can be used on land, but instead of compressed air it uses vibrations to send shock waves into the ground.

As oil reserves run out there is a need to drill deeper or in more hazardous conditions, such as ice and snow. This increases the risks of endangering workers and causing oil leaks.

> **Link it up**
>
> For more information on the potential effects of oil leaks on wildlife, see page 170.

Processing

Oil is processed in a petroleum refinery. Here hydrocarbons are separated into components that can be used for fuels and polymers as well as other materials. Long hydrocarbon chains are cracked to make monomers, which are then polymerised to make polymer resins. These are then further processed with additives and dyes ready for moulding.

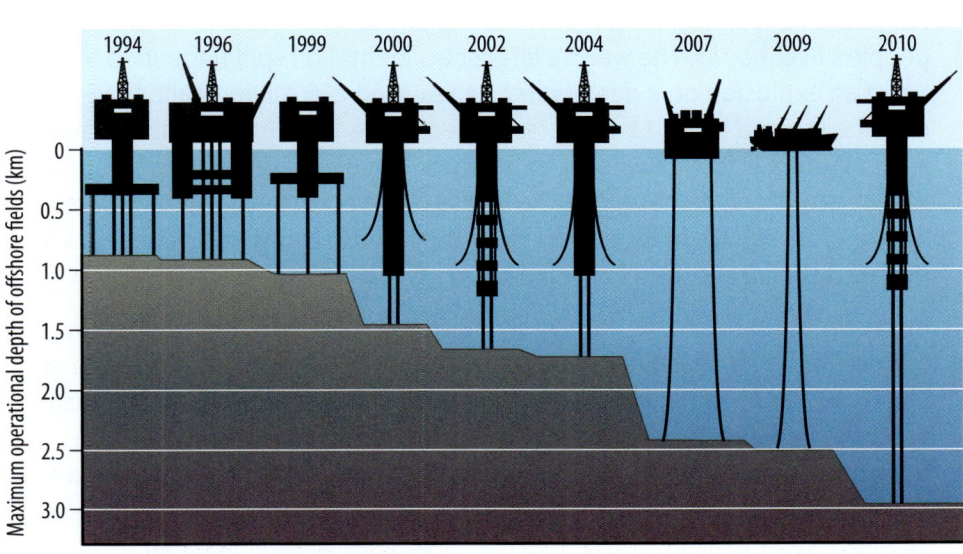

Figure 4.2.3 Maximum drilling depths at sea: with resources depleting, it has become necessary to drill deeper for oil

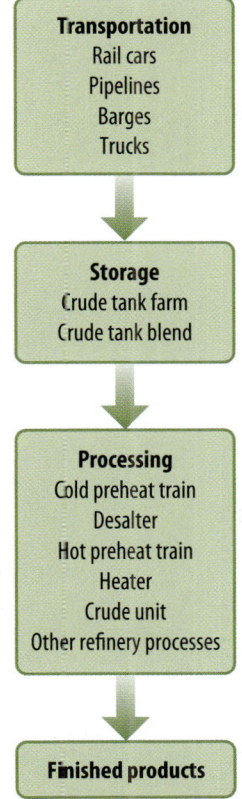

Figure 4.2.4 The process of making products from oil: consider which aspect of this process is the largest contributor to damaging the environment

4 Polymers

> **Apply it**
>
> Discuss the impact of transportation and suitability on land usage.

Transportation

Oil is transported to refineries by oil tankers or by pipes that run under and over ground. Polymers are transported from refineries as pellets or resins ready for forming. The pellets are usually transported by lorry or train to factories that use forming techniques to make products or stock material.

Polymer resin pellets: pellets are heated and formed into products

Wastage

Flash material removed after forming products can be recycled if products are made of thermoforming polymers. The waste is ground and chipped into pellets that can be mixed with new polymer material. Vacuum-formed waste material can also be recycled.

Flash material removed from products made from thermosetting materials cannot be recycled. This material will usually end up at landfill.

Pollution

Pollution from oil can have a devastating effect on the sea, wildlife and people's livelihoods. The world's largest accidental oil spill happened in 2010 when an explosion on a deep-water rig released 210 million gallons of oil into the sea and killed 11 workers. The leak lasted for three months, having a devastating effect on wildlife in the area. The oil company tried to prevent the spread of the damage, but the leak is believed to have killed wildlife in a zone of 80 square miles surrounding the rig. The company that owned the rig faced the largest fine for pollution in US history.

It is estimated that more than 8 million tonnes of plastic are dumped in our oceans every year. Such waste can be seen in large slicks referred to as plastic soup or is broken down into tiny pieces that are then eaten by fish and other wildlife, particularly birds. This causes fish to become ill, with the consequences eventually passing up the food chain. Larger items can become entangled around marine animals.

Microbeads found in cosmetic products such as exfoliators are often also made from polymers. They are too small to be removed when water is treated at sewerage works, so eventually end up in the sea. Microbeads are toxic when ingested by sea life. Countries including the UK and the USA are introducing bans on microbeads.

> **Key term**
>
> **Flash material:** excess material left on the product after forming.

4.2 Sources and properties

When crude oil is extracted, toxins can be released and oil disposed of. This can have an impact on local wildlife.

Where oil is drilled on land, areas are cleared for new roads and drill camps.

Pollution is created by refining oil into plastic through the burning of fossil fuels to power the plant.

Where oil is shipped or transported by pipelines, there can be leaks into the environment, which pollute waterways and kill wildlife.

Figure 4.2.5 Impact diagram of making plastics

Summary

Key points to remember:
- Oil is extracted from the ground through use of drilling rigs and pumping stations.
- Oil is transported to refineries through pipelines and tankers.
- Flexible polymer packaging is replacing traditional packaging alternatives.
- There is demand for lighter and stronger polymers.
- Oil leaks can have a devastating impact on the environment, wildlife and people.

Checkpoint

Strengthen

S1 Name three available forms of polymer.
S2 Describe the trend forecast for use of polymers.
S3 Discuss the implications of having to drill deeper for oil at sea.
S4 Explain the impact of plastic waste in the sea.

Challenge

C1 Consider the issues associated with having a universal system for identifying products made from polymers that can be recycled.
C2 What strategies could the UK government employ to meet its goal for recycling polymers by 2020?

4 Polymers

4.3 Selecting polymers

> **Learning objectives**
>
> By the end of this section, you should know:
> - the influences upon the selection of thermoforming polymers and thermosetting polymers
> - how aesthetic considerations, environmental factors, availability factors, cost factors and social factors influence the selection of polymers.

Aesthetic factors

Polymers can be formed into many complicated or simple shapes. Different manufacturing processes require the polymer to be supplied in a variety of stock shapes and sizes. The manufacturing method, stock shape and size can all influence the aesthetic qualities of the manufactured product. Some polymers are naturally dull in finish while others are glossy.

Form

The shape of products depends mainly on the forming technique chosen. Vacuum-formed products can be identified through designs that have an internal and external shape that follows the same form. Other manufacturing techniques offer more intricate detail and complexity. Injection moulding is used where products require different internal and external forms. Products made using this technique may also have fixing points or over mouldings, like those on toothbrushes. Polymers can be used in sheet form to create shop window signage, or can be used in thin sheets to form carrier bags or wrapping products. Some thermoforming polymers have what is known as a plastic memory and when heated will return to their original shape.

Colour

Polymers are available in many colours. It is possible to specify a colour to match the exact customer requirements, as long as enough of the material is ordered. Polymers such as acrylic are available in transparent, clear, frosted, pearlescent, opal, fluorescent and sparkle finishes, and in a variety of different colours. The polymers are coloured during manufacture using pigments. This results in the material being coloured throughout, not just a surface. Using this technique makes it more difficult to see scratches and defects on the material's surface.

It is possible to use special 'smart' pigments to enhance the colour properties of polymers. Phosphorescent and thermochromic pigments can be used where applications require items to glow in the dark or change colour with temperature, such as baby feeding spoons.

Texture

The texture of polymers can be altered to suit their use. Through different forming techniques, texture can be applied to add grip, improve appearance and make products easier to clean. For example, if using a torch, the user will want the grip to be textured so that it doesn't slip out of the hand. If purchasing a radio, you may want a textured handle for grip, but another texture to improve the appearance of the product over alternatives. When purchasing kitchenware, you will want items that have a smooth finish and are easy to clean.

> **Exam-style question**
>
> Explain **two** ways in which the aesthetic properties of polymers are affected by user requirements. **(4 marks)**

Environmental factors

When deciding on which polymer to use for a product, designers need to consider the life cycle of the product. If it will be used only once, then a material that is readily available and easy to recycle should be used. Where products are to be used for longer periods, a designer may be able to justify the choice of material based on other factors such as physical properties and cost.

Sustainability

Crude oil is a non-renewable resource, and it is important for designers to consider the life cycle of products when choosing materials. Where possible thermoforming polymers should be used as these can be recycled, but where this is not possible and other properties are required, the designer may have no choice but to use a thermosetting polymer. Certain groups of consumers will demand that the products they buy are more sustainable. There is a growth in the market for products to be made from recycled materials, even though the cost of such items is likely to be more expensive.

Apply it
Research what impact the government scheme to reduce plastic bag usage has had on the amount of waste going to landfill.

Pollution
Pollution from polymers is a major concern. Spillages of oil and polymer waste have a detrimental effect on wildlife in oceans with loss of life due to contamination of food sources and drowning. There is another significant problem on land as a large proportion of polymer products are disposed of at landfill sites. In 2014, 7.6 billion single use plastic bags were disposed of in England. Customers are now encouraged to use long-life alternatives, such as cotton or jute, or pay for bags which were once free.

Biodegradable polymers – Biopol®
Biopol® is an environmentally friendly alternative to other synthetic polymers. It is made from plant and vegetable extracts using fermentation. The process of fermentation is slower than making polymers from crude oil, but as it naturally breaks down in soil producing no toxins, it is highly suited to short-life disposable items. It is more expensive than polymers made from crude oil, has limited resistance to impact and is unsuitable for holding chemicals.

Availability factors
There are many stockists of polymer materials. They are usually cut to a size that is convenient to aid delivery and storage of materials. Most non-specialist materials can be ordered and delivered a few days later.

Use of stock materials
Polymers are available in many forms. Thermoforming polymers are available as powders, granules, sheets, rods, bars and tubes. A designer may choose to use a stock material such as sheet acrylic to manufacture products if the volume to be made does not justify the use of moulding techniques and the use of other available stock forms of the material. The stock forms and sizes available restrict the way in which a designer can design and make products. For example, if a product requires an acrylic sheet of thickness 3.5 mm and this is not available, it would need to be manufactured at a very high cost. Instead, the designer may have to redesign the product to match the stock sizes available and in this case, it would be acrylic 3 mm in thickness.

Use of specialist materials
Where a specialist finish or size of material is required, small batches of the material can be manufactured at a higher cost. The cost of the material could be extremely high and result in a designer changing their plans but, where there is no choice, a specialist material may be required. Specialist materials can include those whose size is not of normal stock availability, but also include specific textured and coloured finishes. Materials that include thermochromic or phosphorescent pigments, or other, will need to be made to customer requirements. Recycled polymers can also be made into sheet material for specialist use.

Exam-style question

Explain **one** advantage and **one** disadvantage of using Biopol® instead of oil-based polymers.
(4 marks)

Exam tip

Consider the amount of time needed to make Biopol® and how it can be disposed of.

Link it up

For more information about available stock forms and sizes, look at page 182.

4 Polymers

> **Apply it**
>
> The cost of crude oil has increased from $53.89 to $61.30 per barrel between 2005 and 2015. Consider why the cost of oil changes and why at one point in the last 10 years it cost $132 per barrel.

Effect of global oil supply and price

The cost of oil is measured in dollars per barrel. Its cost depends on several factors including political influences, conflicts, supply and demand. The cost of extracting oil is also dependent on the amount of money invested in finding a suitable site, the time spent drilling, and the cost of energy and equipment. The cost of transporting oil to refineries also should be considered.

A shortage in oil can cause the cost to rise as communities compete to buy what is available. Oil is essential as fuel for transport, heating and electricity as well as making polymers. Without it we wouldn't be able to run cars, make products or power our factories. When supply is high, the cost of oil falls as there is surplus stock available. Conflicts and disputes between countries can also make it harder to transport oil, reducing supply and ultimately increasing costs. Labour supply can also have an effect on the availability of oil. If oil refinery workers go on strike to protest about wages or working conditions, this will limit the amount of oil to leave fuel depots and refineries.

Being a non-renewable resource, the trend is for the cost of oil to increase as supplies will eventually run out.

Cost factors

The final cost of a product made from polymer will depend on many factors. Polymers are not priced equally due to the difference in properties, cost of production and demand.

Quality of material

The quality of material is judged on how well it compares with other materials depending on how it performs its role. For example, if a designer were to compare the use of HIPS and ABS for a casing on an electronic gadget they would need to consider the circumstances under which the product would be used. If it is likely to be dropped or knocked repeatedly, then the designer may opt for the more expensive ABS material, but if the product was to be kept safe on a desk, HIPS may be sufficient. In selecting the best material, the designer will need to balance cost against quality. The designer may be aiming the product at a higher end of the market, or making the product more widely available.

Manufacturing processes

The cost of tools and complexities for making products is dependent on a number of factors. If only making a few items, there is not a need for expensive tooling, but in doing so the skill level and time making such products could be extremely high. For example, polystyrene can be formed using a wide range of processes, such as vacuum forming and injection moulding, whereas urea formaldehyde is unsuitable for vacuum forming but can be formed using injection or compression moulding.

> **Key term**
>
> **Tooling:** machinery used for shaping materials, usually by cutting, drilling, shearing, and moulding.

4.3 Selecting polymers

Materials/processes	Vacuum forming	Injection moulding	Extrusion	Compression moulding	Rotational moulding	Blow moulding
Acrylic	Yes	Yes	Yes	No	Yes	Yes
Polystyrene	Yes	Yes	Yes	No	Yes	Yes
PVC	Yes	Yes	Yes	No	Yes	Yes
ABS	Yes	Yes	Yes	No	Yes	Yes
PET	Yes	Yes	Yes	No	Yes	Yes
Urea formaldehyde	No	Yes	Yes	Yes	Possible	No

Table 4.3.1 The manufacturing processes available for different polymers

Polymer treatments

Adding treatments or additives to polymers can improve processing during manufacture, make them safer to use, increase strength, make them degrade quicker, improve aesthetics and improve durability. There are a wide range of treatments and additives available of which some are described in Table 4.3.2.

Additive/treatment	Function
Fire proofing	Flame retardants are used to prevent ignition or prevent spread of flames
Anti-static	Prevents build-up of static electricity on a surface
Biodegradable plasticisers	Help the product to degrade quicker in soil
Blowing agents	Used to create foams by putting gases in the material
Fillers	Natural materials used to improve strength and add bulk to the material
Light stabilisers	Reduce degradation caused by UV light
Plasticisers	Help to make the material more flexible and softer
Pigments	Used to add colour to the polymer
Reinforcement fibres	Used to add strength and stiffness

Table 4.3.2 The function of additives to polymers

Link it up

For more information on oil commodity price, look at page 176.

Social factors

When we purchase and use products, we often need to consider what influences our decisions. Social influences such as religion, family and wealth may contribute to the decisions we make.

Use for different social groups

The groups that we belong to may influence the products we purchase. You have probably bought similar items to your friends or have had to buy

4 Polymers

a certain piece of sports equipment that has been recommended by your coach. To compete at a higher level in sport, or to achieve a higher grade on a musical instrument, it is likely that you will require better and more expensive equipment to remain competitive. These items will be made more accurately and of higher-quality materials.

Trends and fashion

The home in the 1970s was very different to that of today. Everyday chores took much longer to complete and not every household could afford the luxury of a freezer or even a telephone. The development of plastics helped to change this and by the end of the 1970s such products became more widely available as technology improved and manufacturing became more efficient. Sales of plastic toys like Action Man and Barbie hit record heights. Tupperware was sold in high volume as a better method of food storage and a means of preventing waste. At the time televisions were seen as a piece of furniture and were packaged in a wooden box, but as plastics were further introduced into the design, different-shaped and coloured products became available. PVC was widely used as an alternative covering for furniture and became fashionable in clothing design, but plastics were later seen as cheap alternatives for higher-quality materials.

Popularity

Today plastics are commonly used in a wide range of applications. PET is mostly used to make soft drink and water bottles and is now much more widely used than glass because it is easy to manufacture, lightweight and is able to withstand knocks. **HDPE** has also become more popular and has replaced alternative methods of packaging. HDPE is suitable for the safe storage of food and drinks and so is used in milk bottles and ice cream tubs. It is also used to package liquids such as shampoos and detergents. PVC is also commonly used to produce window frames, pencil cases and shoe soles, but is less popular where the user wants quality items, such as wooden window frames and leather-soled shoes. Some mobile phone manufacturers choose not to use plastics as they consider the material not to have the aesthetic and sensory qualities of alternatives.

> **Key term**
>
> **HDPE (high-density polyethylene):** a thermoplastic with high impact resistance.

Cultural and ethical factors

Avoiding offence

It is important not to offend customers. If a company does offend customers, they will be unlikely to buy a particular product, and it may lead to none of a company's products being allowed in a particular region or country. It is important to understand different cultures and religions so that unintentional offence can be avoided.

Sometimes, a company could cause offence unintentionally. Dropping litter can have a negative effect on companies where branding is displayed on packaging.

Suitability for intended market

Understanding the intended market for a new product is very important; if it's unsuitable, it won't sell or could even cause injury. For example, if a designer has not fully considered how a child may use a plastic toy differently to how it was intended, it could lead to safety issues.

Use of colour and language

Research shows that colour can be used to express many meanings. Blue can be used to express wealth and security, whereas grey is often used to indicate strength and success. Researchers have found that there are similarities across cultures in the way in which people interpret the use of colour. Most consider blue to mean high quality, while red can be associated with love. However, there is less uniformity in the meaning attached to purple. In Japan and South Korea it is considered to represent luxury and expensive items, whereas in the United States it is considered to represent cheaper products. Black is the only colour that is considered to represent expensive products across cultures.

The consumer society

The development of computer and communications technology has made it much easier for consumers to research, compare and buy products. Consumers' expectations of getting things fast and efficiently have meant that it is difficult for some companies to keep up with demand, resulting in customers going elsewhere to buy their products. Companies now try to forecast sales to meet demands – when a large sporting event is to be broadcast on television, for example, TV, alcoholic drink and snack food sales increase. Similarly, when weather forecasters indicate hot weather is on the way, sales of barbecues, ice cream and sun tan lotion peak.

The effects of mass production

Mass production has enabled consumer goods to become much cheaper, making them accessible to groups who would not have been able to afford them in the past. However, mass production does not require as many unskilled workers, leading to loss of employment and a reduction in disposable income in the groups that used to be able to buy the cheaper mass-produced goods.

Built-in production obsolescence

When purchasing a product, you may not consider how long something will last before it needs to be replaced, but it is likely that this decision has already been made for you. Why do products only have limited guarantees or warranties? Products are designed to have a limited life so that they will need to be replaced. This is called **planned obsolescence**. Without this, companies would not sell enough items to stay in business.

Have you ever heard of a toothbrush that will last a lifetime or of a pair of running shoes that never wear out? The reason for this is that designers may make small adjustments to a design to increase renewed sales, or they will bring out a product where the technology supersedes existing products, making them redundant. The lifespan of a toothbrush is approximately 3–4 months as the bristles eventually wear out and become ineffective in cleaning teeth. Sports companies recommend renewing running shoes every 450 miles as they can lose grip and support. The technology in mobile phones soon becomes outdated as new operating systems require larger memory, more powerful batteries and faster transfer of data. When you purchase a new mobile phone, there is already another phone being developed to replace it.

> **Apply it**
>
> Research how many times a razor is used before it needs to be replaced. Is it more cost effective to buy a long-life razor or a disposable item?

> **Key term**
>
> **Planned obsolescence:** a strategy of designing a product with a limited life, so it will become outdated or fail after a period of time.

Summary

Key thing to remember:
- aesthetic considerations, environmental factors, availability factors, cost factors and social factors influence the selection of polymers.

Checkpoint

Strengthen

S1 Name an organisation that campaigns to reduce polymer waste.
S2 Describe how Biopol® is made.
S3 Describe how aesthetic properties of polymers can be changed.

Challenge

C1 Consider an application where plastic memory in polymers can be utilised.

4 Polymers

4.4 Impact of forces and stresses

> **Learning objectives**
>
> By the end of this section, you should know:
> - the forces and stresses that act on products made from polymers
> - contexts in which polymers need to be able to withstand forces and stresses
> - how items made from polymers are reinforced and stiffened.

Forces and stresses

Forces and stresses act by pushing or pulling on objects. This can be through gravity or due to different objects pushing and pulling against one another or the internal resistance to an applied force.

Compression

Polymers are used in scenarios that require them to be strong under compression. Traditional lead or concrete piping used in building houses and sewerage systems has been replaced with polymer-based alternatives, which are more cost effective to manufacture, lighter to transport and easier to install. The piping will need to withstand the weight of soil or concrete above it and retain its shape to allow water to flow freely. A smaller, more flexible type of this pipe is now used for underfloor heating systems.

A chair made from polymer can be made to withstand the forces applied by a person's body weight by creating angled or tubular legs.

Tension

Polymers are used as material alternatives for traditional products such as climbing ropes, kite strings and shopping bags. Polymers are high in tensile strength to prevent products stretching with load, but also offer elasticity to allow bags to change shape and climbers to have a smoother ride when abseiling down a cliff face. Polymers have an elastic limit and, if the load exceeds this, the polymer will be unable to return to its shape and size. If the elastic limit load is exceeded, the polymer will stretch until it fails. For instance, an abseiling rope needs to be high in tensile strength but also offer some elasticity to prevent shock to the climber on descent of the cliff face.

Shear

Shear forces are unaligned forces pushing against each other in different directions, such as in scissors or a guillotine. Currency made from polymers offers an advantage over paper-based alternatives: it can be washed without it being destroyed, it is more difficult to counterfeit and, most importantly, it is resistant to shear forces, where previously bank notes could be ripped.

Flexibility

Some polymers are flexible while others are stiff. These properties are useful when designing different products. An ice cream tub stored in the freezer needs a strong and stiff material for the container base, but the lid needs to be flexible so that it can be peeled from the packaging. This type of packaging needs to resist impact from being dropped and withstand a metal ice cream scoop being dragged around its edge. PVC-coated electrical

> **Apply it**
>
> Measure the distance between the legs on a plastic chair. Ask a friend to sit on the chair and measure the distance between the legs again. Record your measurements and consider why they have changed or stayed the same.

4.4 Impact of forces and stresses

cables need to be flexible for packaging purposes and for allowing products to be placed in different environments around the home or office. Flexible sheet takes up less space as it can be stored on a roll and plastic carrier bags can be folded away until they are used again.

Reinforcement and stiffening techniques

Frame structures
Polymer-based products can be strengthened using frame structures. Here parts are in tension and compression. For example, if designing and building a child's playhouse, a plastic tube construction could be used to make the item lightweight and easy to assemble. The structure needs to be stiff to retain its shape but also strong enough to hold the weight of the covering.

Triangulation
Using triangles to form the basis of structures provides strength, stiffness and rigidity to products.

> **Link it up**
>
> For information on suitable fabrication, assembly and construction processes, look at page 176. For information on the use of additives, look at Table 4.3.2 on page 177.

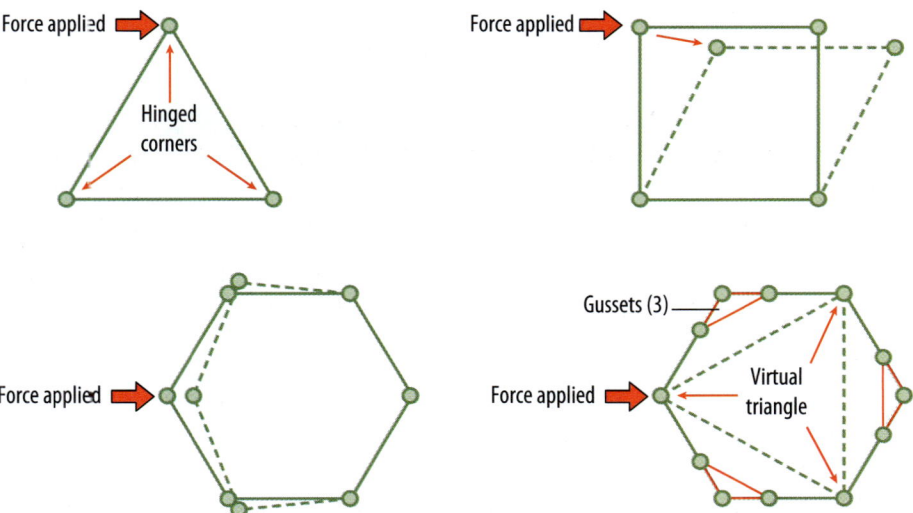

Figure 4.4.1 If built of stiff components with hinged corners, the triangle is the only shape that can retain its form. Other shapes can easily be misshaped unless gussets (brackets strengthening an angle or structure) or braces are added

Summary

Key points to remember:
- Triangular structures are very strong.
- They can be used to stiffen other shaped structures.
- Frame structures can easily be assembled to provide rigid forms.

Checkpoint

Strengthen
S1 Name three different forces or stresses that act on products made from polymers.

Challenge
C1 Explain how polymer based products can be strengthened using frame structures.

4 Polymers

4.5 Calculating quantity

> **Learning objectives**
>
> By the end of this section, you should know:
> - the range of forms and sizes of polymers available
> - how to calculate the cross-sectional area of different forms of polymer
> - how to calculate the diameter of materials.

Stock forms, types and sizes

Polymers are available in many forms and sizes. When designing products, you will need to consider the form and sizes available to you, as specifying non-stock items will be much more expensive, and require a specialist manufacturer to make the item. Polymers are available in round/square bars, mouldings, granules, as a sheet, tube, resin, powder and film. Round and square bars can be cut to length and machined to make more complex shapes. Sheet material and films can be cut to size and shape using traditional and modern processes, whereas granules and resins are used for forming and casting using moulds.

Stock form	Thickness	Cross-sectional area	Size (common in school)	Diameter	Advantages and disadvantages	Applications
Bar	3 mm, 5 mm, 6 mm, 8 mm, 10 mm, 12 mm, 15 mm, 20 mm, 25 mm, 30 mm, 40 mm, 50 mm Available as square and round bars	For square or round bar: width × thickness = area mm² For round bar: $\pi \times r^2$ = area mm²	1000 mm to 4000 mm in length	3 mm, 5 mm, 6 mm, 8 mm, 10 mm, 12 mm, 15 mm, 20 mm, 25 mm, 30 mm, 40 mm, 50 mm	• Easy to cut, drill and machine • Limited range of colours available • Long lengths difficult to store and transport	• Drawer runners and floor glides • Can be cut on a lathe or mill to make fittings
Sheet	1 mm, 1.5 mm, 2 mm, 3 mm, 5 mm, 6 mm, 8 mm, 10 mm	Width × height = area mm²	1000 × 600 mm Sheet sizes of 1220 × 2440 mm are available from specialist stockists	N/A	• Stable or flexible, allowing rigid structures to be formed or shape of structure to be followed • Easy to cut and drill • Thickness may be different due to allowed tolerances • Large sizes of sheet difficult to transport	• Shop and street signs • Cladding of buildings • Used to create vacuum mouldings
Pipe/tube	Wall thickness 3 mm	Outside area – inside area $\pi \times r_1^2 = (x)$ $\pi \times r_2^2 = (y)$ $x - y = z$ mm² (see the Maths in practice example on page 183)	300 mm, 500 mm and 1000 mm length Longer lengths of tube are available from specialist stockists	5 mm, 6 mm, 10 mm, 15 mm, 20 mm, 25 mm, 30 mm, 35 mm, 40 mm, 45 mm, 50 mm, 60 mm, 70 mm, 80 mm, 90 mm, 100 mm Larger-diameter tube is available from specialist stockists	• Available in rigid and flexible forms • Flexible tube can be supplied on a reel to reduce storage • Easy to cut and drill • Rigid tube length makes storage difficult	• Heating and plumbing piping

Table 4.5.1 Stock forms *Cont…*

4.5 Calculating quantity

Stock form	Thickness	Cross-sectional area	Size (common in school)	Diameter	Advantages and disadvantages	Applications
Mouldings	Mouldings come in many different shapes and sizes	Shape dependent	N/A	N/A	• Vast number of mouldings available to suit different applications • Specialist item, not available from all stockists • Limited range of colours	• Drain pipes, gutters, window and door frames, shower and bath trims
Resin	Sold by weight 1 kg, 2.5 kg, 5 kg and 10 kg	N/A	N/A	N/A	• Can be moulded to create many shapes and combined with glass fibres to create GRP • Needs a catalyst to harden resin • Messy to use • Needs to be stored in flammables cupboard	• Boat hulls, sports cars and trophies
Granules/powder	Sold by weight 1 kg, 2.5 kg, 5 kg and 10 kg	N/A	N/A	N/A	• Can be heated to create different forms or to coat and finish other materials • Needs to be heated to form shapes or be used as a finish • Can be messy to store	• Used in injection moulding applications and for plastic coating of metals
Film	0.076–7.62 mm	Length × width = mm²	• Roll width available 300 mm to 1000 mm • Length of roll normally 10–100 m	N/A	• Stored on a roll for easy storage and application • Can be difficult to tear/cut with a straight edge	• Food wrapping and vinyl stickers cut on a CNC plotter cutter

Table 4.5.1 Stock forms

Maths in practice
Cross-sectional area

To calculate the **cross-sectional area** of a tube, the area of the inner circle must be subtracted from the area of the outer circle. The equation for calculating the area of a circle is:

πr^2

where:
$\pi = 3.14$ (to two decimal places)
r = Radius

- Study the diagram opposite illustrating the end of an acrylic tube. Calculate the cross-sectional area of the tube. The tube has an outside diameter of 30 mm and a wall thickness of 3 mm.

Using the above equation to find the area of the **outside** circle, the answer is as follows.

πr^2 = Area of circle
r = Diameter ÷ 2 = 15
$3.14 \times 15 \times 15 = 706.5$ mm²

Note the tube has a wall thickness of 3 mm. This ultimately makes the inside circle 6 mm less in diameter and therefore the radius is given as 12 mm.

- Use the same equation for the **inner** circle to calculate how much material needs to be removed to calculate the area shaded brown.

πr^2 = Area of inner circle
$3.14 \times 12 \times 12 = $ **452.16 mm²**

- Finally you need to subtract the area of the inner circle from the area of the outer circle.

Area of outer circle − Area of inner circle = cross-sectional area of tube
$706.5 - 452.16 = 254.34$ mm²
The cross-sectional area of the acrylic tube surface = 254.34 mm²

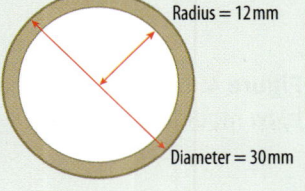

4 Polymers

4.6 Alternative manufacturing processes

> **Learning objectives**
>
> By the end of this section, you should know:
> - the processes used to manufacture different polymer products
> - the different scales of production
> - the techniques used for quantity production
> - quality control in production.

Processes

Polymers can be formed into many shapes using a wide range of manufacturing processes. Most of the techniques used are industrial and require expensive specialist equipment and moulds. The moulds for forming polymers can cost more than £10,000, so deciding on which technique to use depends on several factors, including complexity and volume of the product to be made.

Blow moulding

Blow moulding is a manufacturing process used to make a variety of complex hollow shapes, such as bottles for fizzy drinks, tablets or sun cream lotion. The process is:

1. A **parison** of material is extruded into an open mould.
2. The two halves of the mould close and pinch the parison so no air can escape.
3. Compressed air is blown into the parison until the material fills the shape of the mould.
4. The formed shape drops out of the blow moulding machine when the two halves of the mould open.
5. A new parison is extruded ready to start the procedure again.

This is a fast production method, although controlling wall thickness can be difficult. More expensive bottles use a more complicated technique known as injection blow moulding. This is a two-process technique where preforms are initially injection moulded and then blown into a hollow form. You can identify the way in which a bottle has been made by looking at its base. Where the base has a seam line, the bottle has been formed through blow moulding. Where the bottle has a central dimple, it will have been made by injection blow moulding.

> **Key term**
>
> **Parison:** the extruded material used as a basis on which to start the blow moulding process.

Figure 4.6.1 Cross-sectional view of blow moulding process

> **Exam-style question**
>
> Use notes and/or sketches to show the process of manufacturing the body of a plastic fizzy drinks bottle. **(4 marks)**

> **Exam tip**
>
> Use diagrams to describe the process. Split your answer into three different stages of the manufacturing process.

4.6 Alternative manufacturing processes

Press moulding

Press moulding is where two halves of a mould come together to compress the material into the shape of the void left between the two moulds. It is cheaper than injection moulding. This technique is usually used for thermosetting polymers, it is not suitable for complex mouldings. Typical products include electrical wall sockets and plugs. The process is:

1. Two halves of the mould are heated to a temperature that can soften the polymer.
2. A preform of the polymer is placed into the void at the bottom of the mould. The preform's volume is slightly bigger than that of the void it needs to fill.
3. The two halves of the mould are forced together using a hydraulic press.
4. The two halves of the mould remain together until cross-linking of molecules has completed.
5. The two halves of the mould open and the moulded product can be removed.

> **Key term**
>
> **Archimedes screw thread:** invented, or popularised, by the ancient Greek mathematician Archimedes, the screw thread is turned inside a hollow pipe to move liquid from one end of the pipe to the other.

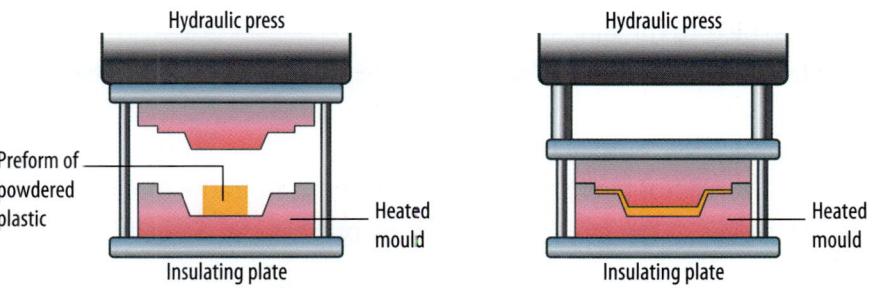

Figure 4.6.2 Cross-sectional view of compression moulding

Extrusion

Extrusion is used to create products with a fixed cross-section. This automated process can produce endless lengths of the same product. It usually cuts material to set lengths that fit within the factory constraints. Different dies are used at the end of the extrusion chamber to create shapes of different cross-sections. Producing new die for a new product line is relatively cheap. Molten polymer is pushed through the die using an **Archimedes screw thread**. On exiting the die, the polymer is quickly cooled in a water chamber so that it can retain the shape. Extrusion product requires further work, for example, cutting to length. Typical products made by this process include UPVC window frames and plastic pipes used by plumbers.

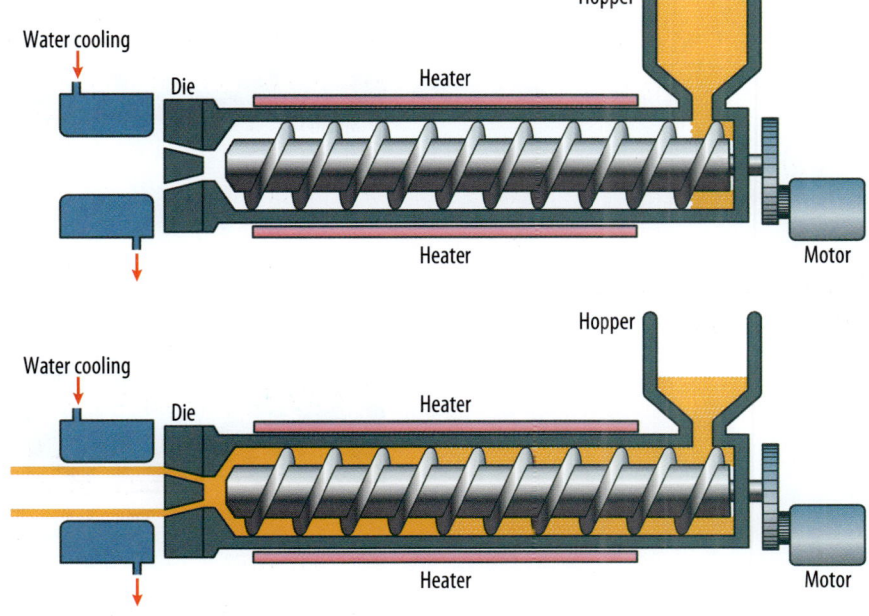

Figure 4.6.3 Cross-sectional view of the extrusion process

4 Polymers

Injection moulding

This process is very versatile and can be used to make a range of simple or complex products (such as very complex 3D shapes). It is used to make toothbrush handles, laptop casings, computer mice, car interior consoles, buckets and chairs. The moulds can be highly complicated and include many moving parts dependent on the item to be made. The moulds are expensive to manufacture but, where small objects are to be made, they can normally produce more than one part at a time. Injection moulding is commonly used to form thermoforming polymers but, if needed, can also form thermosetting polymers. The process is:

1. Granules of polymer are fed into a hopper. A pigment is added at this stage if a specific colour is required.
2. The granules are fed forwards towards the mould using an Archimedes screw.
3. The heat chamber that surrounds the screw gradually melts the polymer as it moves towards the mould.
4. The screw moves away from the mould as the volume of molten polymer builds up next to the mould.
5. A hydraulic system rams the screw towards the mould, pushing the molten polymer into the mould.
6. The polymer cools quickly in the mould. The two halves of the mould are opened. The ejector pins push the formed object from the mould.
7. The two halves of the mould close and the process starts again.

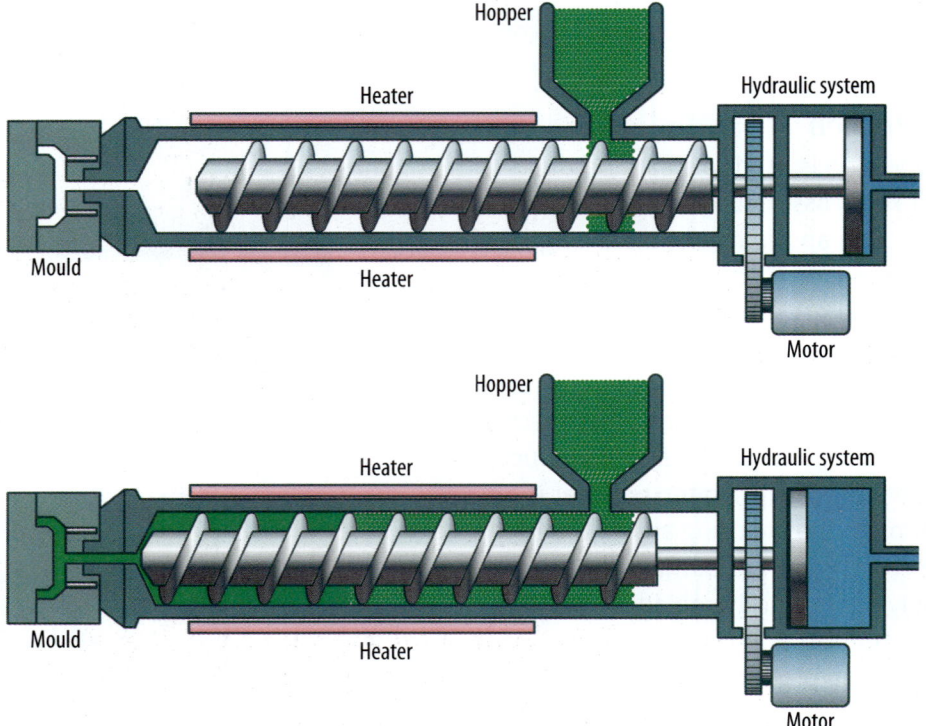

Figure 4.6.4 Cross-sectional view of the injection moulding process

Polymer welding

Polymers can be joined together using a range of techniques. Where the join is designed to be permanent, a form of welding can be used. It requires skill if done by hand and it is critical that the heat source is at the correct temperature.

Laser polymer welding can be used to give a high-quality finish joint. Firstly, the edges of the two objects to be joined must be prepared by ensuring they are smooth and clean. Heat is then applied by a high-precision laser while the two objects are pressed together. The heat from the laser softens the edges of the two objects together, bonding them while they cool.

When joining dissimilar polymer objects, a manufacturer may choose to use an ultrasonic welding process. This process involves the use of ultrasonic vibrations to cause friction between two objects held together. The friction creates heat, which melts the edges of touching objects, bonding the polymers together.

Hot gas welding is another process used for joining polymers. This technique doesn't require such specialist equipment and could be achieved in a school workshop, with practice. A heat gun with a specially designed nozzle is used to soften the two edges of the objects to be joined. A filler rod of the same polymer is also heated and pushed against the two parts to be joined. The quality of the finish is inferior to that of laser and ultrasonic welding, so it is usually used to repair broken items or on products such as chemical and water tanks.

> **Apply it**
>
> Design a toothbrush holder for a family of four to be made from sheet acrylic using line bending. Consider how squeezing a tube of toothpaste has similarities to the process of extrusion.

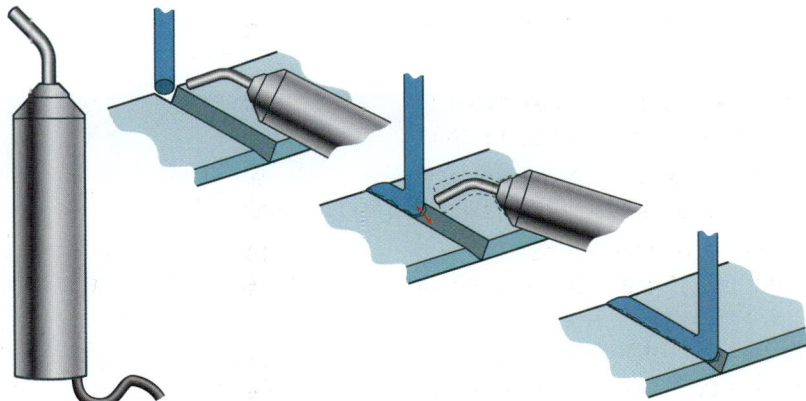

Figure 4.6.5 Thermoforming plastic welding process using hot gas and filler rod

Line bending

The equipment used for line bending is inexpensive and produces quick results. It is used to create a bend in sheet material by heating a strip of the material until it softens enough to form it into another shape. The polymer sheet is normally marked where the bend is required by the use of a chinagraph pencil. As the line will be straight, other marking-out tools, such as a try-square or ruler, are needed. The material is then placed over a heated wire strip at the point at which the bend is required, until it softens. Where thicker material is required, both sides of the material will need to be heated to prevent burning on one side of the material. Once softened and easy to bend, the material is put up against a former and left to cool. On cooling, the material will retain its new shape. A jig or former is required for multiples of the same product. Typical products include restaurant menu stands and leaflet holders.

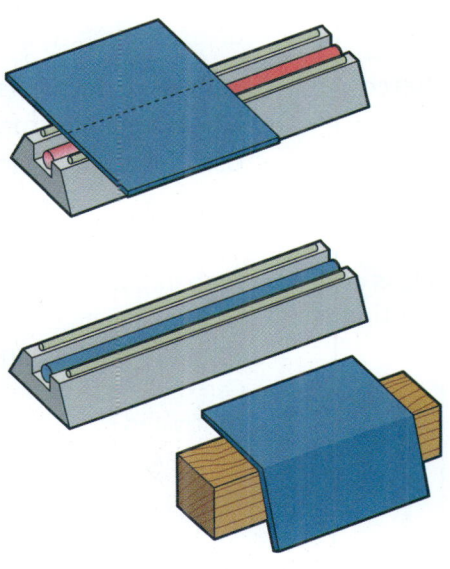

Figure 4.6.6 Line bending polymer sheet using a strip heater and a former

4 Polymers

Scales of production

The scale of production chosen to make items depends on many factors.

One-off

A product that is made using a one-off scale of production is usually commissioned by an individual client. It can also act as an exhibition piece that can be used to market the work of the designer or manufacturer. Making one-off items can be very labour intensive and generally requires skilled craftsmen. Items that can be made using this scale of production include shop frontage signage, specialist point-of-sale stands and racing yachts.

Batch

A product made using batch production will be one of a set of identical items. A batch of products can vary in number depending on the quantity required. Items such as biscuits and chocolate selection packs will be made using batch production processes as they are generally seasonal items and do not require continuous production throughout the year. Tools and machinery used for batch production are often considered to be flexible in that they can be used to make batches of different products.

Mass and continuous production

Mass production produces a high volume of products on a production line that makes use of automated procedures to cut costs. Mass production often involves assembly of sub-assemblies. Cars are often mass produced.

Continuous production produces a very high output of products that are in very high demand, for example soft drinks. Continuous production runs 24 hours a day, often for weeks and months on end.

There are some similar characteristics between mass and continuous production and these are detailed in Table 4.6.1.

> **Exam-style question**
>
> Name **two** methods that could be used to mass produce chocolate egg boxes. For each method, explain one advantage to the manufacturer. **(6 marks)**

Scale of production	Characteristics	Advantages and disadvantages
One-off	• High skill level required • Used for individual client needs • Labour intensive and time consuming • Used for items such as jewellery, wedding dresses and bespoke furniture	• Unique item tailored to individual needs • Expensive • Could be difficult to find a skilled person to complete the task • Could take a long time to make the product
Batch	• Semi-skilled workers • Flexible manufacturing systems • Use of jigs and templates to retain accuracy	• Quick response to meet customer demands at peak times of year • Flexibility in that other items can be made • A lot of time could be required to set up production of different products
Mass and continuous	• High initial investment in equipment • Can involve high maintenance costs to keep the production system running • Can make use of automated computer-controlled systems • Runs 24/7	• Affordable products • Quality control is high • Products are identical • Shift work is often needed to keep the production line in operation • Very high initial investment • Equipment not flexible, so is obsolete at the end of the production run • Can over-produce items if there is less demand

Table 4.6.1 Advantages and disadvantages of different scales of production

Techniques for quantity production

When making items in quantity, manufacturers use a number of techniques to make the process more efficient and retain accuracy. When designing and making, it is important to use the least amount of material necessary to produce the desired outcome. For all the methods listed below, efficient cutting to minimise waste must be kept in mind: this reduces costs, however, it does require careful planning.

Marking out

Marking out means drawing a guide on to material that is to be cut, shaped or bent, to make the process more accurate. It is cheap and relatively quick to do, but requires skill and mistakes are possible. There are different marking out tools for different materials. For example, a pencil should be used when marking out lines on to wood, but a scriber should be used if the material is made of metal.

Jigs

Drilling and cutting jigs are used to speed up production and ensure items are made to the same standard through easily repeated accurate positioning. They can help ensure drill holes are accurately placed and that lengths of material are cut to the same dimension. They reduce the time needed for marking out and prevent inaccuracies between different users. They are normally clamped to the material to prevent movement and avoid errors, but the jig must be positioned correctly.

Templates

Templates can be made from different materials. The simplest of templates can be a shaped piece of card or paper that is drawn around many times to nest items onto a sheet of material for cutting or for marking out where holes need to be drilled. They improve accuracy when cutting repetitive shapes but the template must be accurately produced and protected from damage. In industry templates are often made from plastics, wood and timber as these are more durable. They are used to make the process of marking out more efficient, especially where shapes are complex.

Patterns

Patterns are something from which a copy is made. For example, it could be a wooden pattern that is used to make a mould for a resin casting. One pattern can result in multiple accurate replicas, but the template must be accurately produced, which may be expensive.

Moulds

Moulds are designed for forming the same-shaped item many times. Where there is a limited production run, low-cost moulds can be made from wood and used for vacuum forming (plastic sheet) or hand layup of GRP. More durable materials are required where more parts are to be made and forming techniques such as injection moulding exert huge forces on the mould.

> **Apply it**
>
> Design an efficient method to make 100 paper cones measuring 100 mm high with a base diameter of 50 mm. You will need to mark out and cut the cones before using sticky tape to fix them in place. Consider how you will manage accuracy using jigs and templates.

4 Polymers

High-precision injection moulding moulds made from stainless steel

Injection moulding moulds are made of stainless steel, as it can be machined to a high level of accuracy and finish. Some moulds can cost £10,000 or more but, once made, can be used for many years and retain the same level of accuracy and quality. Designing moulds creates its own set of problems as it is not always possible to manufacture products as the designer has wished. Moulds create an identical outcome each time but they may be expensive to manufacture.

Computer-aided manufacture

Computer-aided manufacture (CAM) can be used to manufacture products in quantity and accurately. Computer-aided design (CAD) files are uploaded to CNC machines that are able to replicate objects with high precision. They are capable of working 24/7 and produce objects much faster than traditional methods, but they can be expensive to purchase and maintain with high initial costs and training required for programmer. CNC plotter cutters are able to cut card to make packaging nets or vinyl stickers for signage. Laser cutters use high-powered lasers to cut through materials, such as card and acrylic, while more specialist machines are needed to cut through metals. Designs can be nested together to reduce wastage and maximise efficiency of the machine. CNC lathes, routers and milling machines are able to cut complex 3D shapes from a variety of materials. A CNC lathe is capable of machining parts much faster and to a higher quality than traditional methods. More expensive machines have multi-turret machine heads that are able to store and change a range of tools that can perform different tasks.

Quality control

When making items in quantity, manufacturers need to have systems in place to monitor quality. This requires careful planning and implementation. Where few items are produced or where products need higher safety considerations, manufacturers may choose to inspect every item. In other circumstances, manufacturers may choose to inspect one in 10 or one in 1000 items, depending on the type of product being made. It is also usual for manufacturers to check the first item as mistakes made at this point could result in other products carrying similar defects reducing waste and improving likelihood of customer satisfaction. Visual checks can be made to ensure no parts are missing and that the finish of the product meets requirements. Objects can be taken from the production line and measured using calibrated high-precision equipment, or more simple tests which use Go/No gauges can be used.

Expensive automated cameras, lasers and computer systems are used to monitor quality control in mass production and continuous flow systems due to the high number of checks and speed needed to maintain flow rate.

Working within tolerance

Tolerance is the level of accuracy that a manufacturer sets on any product made. Tolerances on some products will be extremely high, such as in the manufacture of engines, but other products may have a wider tolerance without affecting quality. Careful application of tolerances ensures a product with several components will always fit together and that spare/replacement parts will fit too. This requires accurate machine set-up and checking systems, for example go, no-go gauges.

Summary

Key points to remember:
- Polymers are available in many forms and sizes.
- Polymers can be formed using a wide range of processes including blow moulding, extrusion, injection moulding, press moulding and line bending.
- Polymers can be joined together by using welding techniques.
- One-off production is for bespoke items, batch production is used where more than one product is needed and mass production is used where there is a continuous demand.
- Jigs and templates speed up production.
- Moulds are used to replicate the same form many times.
- Quality control processes ensure products made in quantity are the same.
- Polymers can be efficiently cut or moulded to minimise waste.

Checkpoint

Strengthen
S1 List four industrial processes that can be used for shaping polymers.
S2 List two processes that can be used to weld polymers.
S3 Describe the differences between one-off and batch production.

Challenge
C1 Discuss the advantages and disadvantages of mass production.

4.7 Specialist techniques for making prototypes and products

Learning objectives

By the end of this section, you should know:
- the techniques that can be used to shape and cut materials to form high-quality prototypes
- the tools and processes used to file and abrade polymers
- the techniques used to bend polymers
- the vacuum-forming technique used for shaping thermoforming polymers.

Shaping

Polymers can be used to shape, fabricate and assemble high-quality prototypes.

Link it up

For information on the tools and equipment used to shape and cut polymers, as well as digital design and manufacture, look at pages 184–87. For advantages and disadvantages, see Tables 2.7.1 and 7.7.3. For types of hand tools used, see Tables 2.6.2, 7.7.2 and 7.7.3.

Laser cutting and engraving

Laser cutting and engraving uses CAM CNC technology to melt or burn away material. The laser is focused on the area to be cut, through a series of mirrors and a lens. The distance between the lens and the material surface should be calibrated to ensure a clean cut that is able to pass through the material. Drawings are first created on a CAD program, with different colour lines and fills being used to indicate the type of cut and finish required.

4 Polymers

Advantages	Disadvantages
• High precision and able to repeat cut parts • Parts can be nested to reduce wastage • Can work 24/7 • Can be used with a rotary attachment to cut and engrave cylindrical objects	• Machine is expensive to purchase • Cutting emits gases that need extraction • Needs to meet local exhaust ventilation (LEV) guidelines • Laser bounces off mirrored finishes

Table 4.7.1 Advantages and disadvantages of laser cutting and engraving

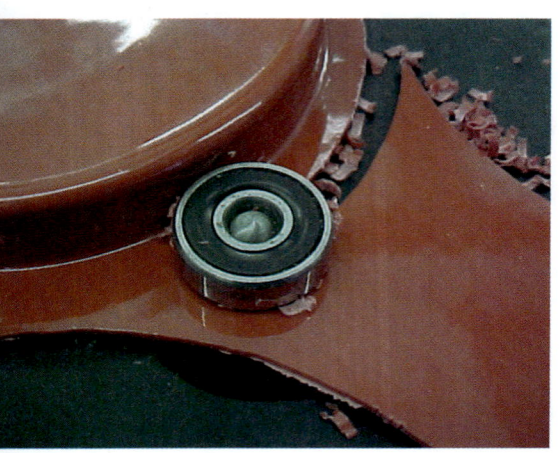

A gerbil cutter removes waste material from a vacuum-formed object

Cutting

Sheet, rod and tube polymers can be cut using a range of workshop tools. When marking out polymers for cutting and drilling you will need to use a chinagraph pencil, scribe or a fine-tip permanent marker as other methods of marking out are more difficult to see. Saws can be used to remove unwanted material. When cutting polymers, you need to ensure you use the correct saw. Saw blades with a finer tooth pattern are recommended as this helps to prevent chipping. Junior hacksaws, adjustable hacksaws and coping saws are all suitable when cutting plastics, but it is also possible to cut material using scroll saws, jigsaws, bandsaws and gerbil cutters. A gerbil cutter is a specialist tool used to remove unwanted material from vacuum-formed sheets with the use of an abrasive disc.

Filing

When finishing polymers, there are two main processes used in the workshop.

- Cross filing is used to remove uneven surfaces. The file is placed on the material and pushed forward with a downwards force. The file is then lifted and returned to a position where it can be pushed forward, as it should not be used in a back and forth motion.
- Draw filing is used to finish edges by removing marks left behind from cross filing. The file is placed at 90 degrees to the edge to be finished and held at either end with the material in the middle. It is moved back and forth with downwards pressure until a desired finish is achieved.

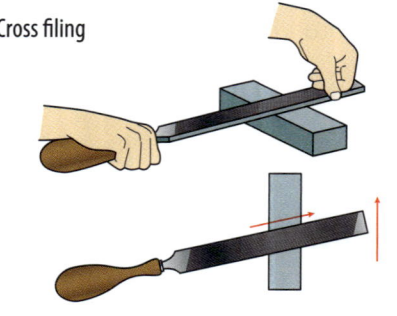

Figure 4.7.1 Cross filing and draw filing of materials

Bending

Heat is generally required to bend polymers and for them to retain a new shape. This can be achieved through the use of a strip heater. Polymers can also be bent using a hot air gun or oven. When using either of these techniques, care must be taken to avoid burns. A hot air gun can be used to bend rods, while an oven is normally used to heat a polymer sheet for drape forming, press forming and twisting. Time is needed to let the material cool before removing shapes from any moulds.

Abrading

A finer finish can be applied to the edge of polymers using abrasive emery cloth or wet and dry paper. This is usually wrapped around the edge of a file or sanding block to give a smoother, more even finish. The abrasive cloth/paper is used in increments to give a better finish. After filing, you should use a low-grade number paper, gradually working upwards until the desired finish is achieved. The final process is to apply and buff off a fine abrasive polish using a cloth.

Vacuum forming

A heated sheet of polymer is forced down over the mould by air pressure due to a temporary vacuum being created beneath the airtight seal around the sheet of polymer. It is used to make items such as yoghurt pots and fast-food containers. The process can be used to make casings for electronic products or point-of-sale shop displays. Moulds can be made from wood, metals and other plastics as long as surfaces are sealed and the materials do not melt together. The process is:

1. A specially designed mould is placed on the platen of the vacuum-form machine and lowered.
2. A sheet of thermoforming polymer is clamped into the machine and then heated.
3. When softened, compressed air is blown into the chamber, which stretches the material upwards.
4. The platen is raised and a vacuum pump removes air from the chamber, pulling the pliable sheet onto the mould.
5. The material is cooled and removed from the mould.

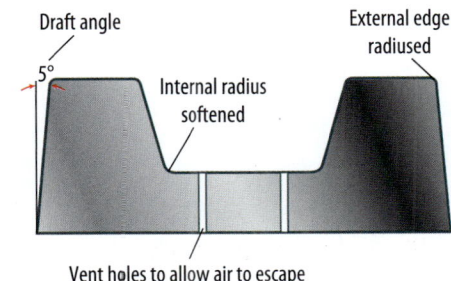

Figure 4.7.2 A vacuum-form mould

When designing moulds for vacuum forming, you will need to factor in some basic design features.

- The sides of the mould will need to be tapered (5 degrees) to allow the formed product to be removed from the mould.
- Corners and edges need to be rounded to prevent webbing and holes.
- Vent holes are required to prevent the material from failing to follow the shape of the mould.
- No undercuts are allowed in the design, otherwise you will not be able to remove the material from the mould.

Deforming

Polymers can be deformed using many methods. These include the use of a strip heater to bend material in a straight line, or a vacuum former where a sheet of polymer is heated and then sucked down onto a mould. Blow moulding and compression moulding are also used to deform the shape of polymers.

Reforming

Polymers can be reformed using many processes. The polymer is first heated into a viscous liquid before being reshaped using either extrusion, injection moulding or casting.

> **Apply it**
>
> Design and make a simple desk tidy that can be manufactured using a laser cutter. Include an engraved area in your design. Record the colours and settings needed for lines and areas to be cut and engraved.

4 Polymers

Fabrication, constructing and assembling

Products shaped from polymers can be formed so that no further fixings or fastenings are required. For manufacturing toys, casings for electronic products and components to be used alongside other materials, a range of fittings are needed. These are made up of temporary and permanent fixings.

Tapping and threading

Polymers can be threaded to create temporary fixings that can be removed to aid recycling and maintenance of components. It is possible to form threaded components through the process of injection moulding but, at school, you will need to carry out the process of creating threads by hand.

Tapping is the process of threading a hole using a tap and a tap wrench. A hole must be drilled slightly smaller than the tap size to be used, as this allows the tap to sit on top of the hole before being rotated into the hole to cut a thread. When tapping a hole, it is necessary to use a taper tap, followed by a plug and bottom to ensure the thread reaches the bottom of the hole. Care must be taken not to apply too much pressure and it is advisable to turn the tapping wrench in reverse for a quarter turn for every half a turn made clockwise to cut the thread.

Threading is the process of cutting an external round bar to create a screw thread. The screw thread could be designed to fit in the threaded hole or to manufacture a machine screw or bolt. A die and die stock holder are placed on the end section of a round bar. The end of the bar is usually slightly tapered to make the process easier to start. The die is held securely in the die stock holder and turned clockwise with pressure being exerted onto the bar until the start of a thread is cut. The die stock holder is turned half a turn clockwise and then a quarter turn in reverse to allow the cut material to break away.

> **Apply it**
>
> Thread a small section of a round bar using a split die and die stock holder. Record each stage of the process using sequence drawings.

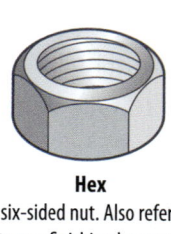

Hex
A six-sided nut. Also referred to as a finishing hex nut.

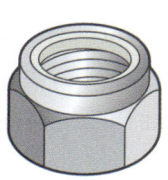

Nylon Insert Lock
A nut with a nylon insert to prevent backing off. Also referred to as a nyloc.

Wing
A nut with 'wings' for hand tightening.

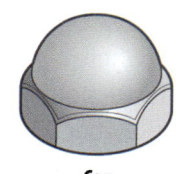

Cap
A nut with a domed top over the end of the fastener.

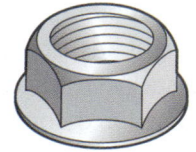

Flange
A nut with a built-in washer like a flange.

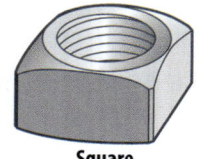

Square
A four-sided nut

Figure 4.7.3 A range of nuts

Fastening

Other forms of temporary fixings include nuts, bolts and washers. They can be used to secure parts of a product together, but can also be undone using spanners, or fingers, to allow for individual parts to be recycled, repaired and maintained. Nuts are available in different sizes and shapes that match bolts and threaded bars.

Bolts can be inserted into threaded holes in a part, or placed through a hole and tightened to a nut. They are mostly made of metal, but polymer alternatives used in electronic products are also available. They usually have a hexagonal head and a threaded section. A washer is placed between the head of the bolt and the part to prevent damage and spread loading. A washer is also placed over the protruding end of the bolt before tightening parts together with a nut. Lock washers and spring washers can be used to stop parts vibrating loose.

Use of adhesives

Adhesives are used where a permanent fixing is required.

- Contact adhesives are used for gluing large surfaces together or where it is difficult to clamp parts together. The adhesive is applied to both surfaces and left for 15 minutes until it is touch dry. When dry, the surfaces are brought together and bond on contact. Contact adhesive can be used where different materials need to be fastened together.
- Epoxy resin is supplied as a two-part adhesive, a resin and a hardener, that need to be mixed in equal quantities before it is used. It can fix a wide range of different materials together, but surfaces need to be clamped into position until fully bonded.
- Tensol® cement is used for gluing acrylic. It is clear in appearance and is usually applied to one surface with a small brush before the two objects are held together. Care needs to be taken not to accidentally get the cement on other areas, as it is difficult to remove and can spoil the appearance of a product.
- Liquid cement (dichloromethane) is a clear liquid that is applied between two polymer surfaces using a syringe when they are held together. The cement seeps between the two surfaces by capillary action and is fast acting. Any excess cement can cause surface damage to the product.

> **Link it up**
>
> You read about wastage in Section 4.2, see page 172.

Addition

Polymers are frequently used in the prototyping of products. Additive 3D printing machines replicate CAD drawings by building prototypes in very thin layers of polymer and fusing each together until the product is complete. The CAD drawing is sliced into very thin layers using specialist software, allowing intricate items to be made. Products are made from the base up, with the build platform moving one slice lower as each layer is replicated by extruding polymer in the areas where it is needed.

4 Polymers

Summary

Key points to remember:
- Polymers can be shaped using laser cutting and engraving, cutting with workshop tools, filing, bending, abrading, vacuum forming, deforming and reforming.
- Some polymer-based products do not need fixings or fastenings. However, those that do are often threaded or tapped.
- Adhesives are used where a permanent fixing is required.

Checkpoint

Strengthen

S1 Give one advantage and one disadvantage of laser cutting and engraving.

Challenge

C1 Explain the process of vacuum forming.

4.8 Surface treatments

Learning objectives

By the end of this section, you should know:
- the surface treatments that can be applied to thermoforming and thermosetting polymers
- the surface finishes that can be applied to thermoforming and thermosetting polymers.

> **Link it up**
>
> For more information about filing and abrading, look at pages 192–93.

Surface finishes and treatments

Polishing

The edges of acrylic can be polished to a high finish. A cut edge requires finishing where it will be seen or when it is to come into contact with a person. Rough edges can cause injury to the user and need to be finished to a safe standard. Where a high-quality finish is required, the surface will need to be filed and abraded before a polish can be applied.

A polish is a liquid or paste that contains very fine abrasives. It is applied to the edge with a cloth and buffed off, greatly improving the product's appearance. This is most useful when using transparent acrylic as a light shade, as light is diffracted (broken up) through the material to enhance the lighting effect on edges. The edge of acrylic can also be polished using a flame, although this requires skill and can destroy a product if used without great care. A fine-nozzle oxy-acetylene torch is passed over the edge of the material, melting the edge and creating a smooth finish.

Texture of moulds

Moulds are usually highly polished to give a high-standard finish to formed components, but a mould's surface can also be textured to change the surface pattern. Textures are applied to moulds to provide grip on products, define different parts of an assembly and to improve aesthetics. Texturing the surface of a mould can reduce the need for any finishing of components. Textures can be applied to a mould by machining or by etching. Etching is achieved by applying ferric chloride (iron) or nitric acid to the mould surface. Any parts where a texture isn't required are masked off. The mould can also be machined to add embossed text or patterns.

4.8 Surface treatments

Laser engraving

Materials such as acrylic can be engraved using a laser cutter, which is faster than using a hand engraving tool. The laser is set up to pass over the work at a high speed with low power to only engrave the surface. Multi-laminate polymer sheets allow the engraving through of one laminate colour to reveal another. This is mostly used when making small signs and tags. Engraving can be used to represent text, but can also be used to give a monochrome effect to the printing of photographs. There can be high initial equipment costs for laser engraving.

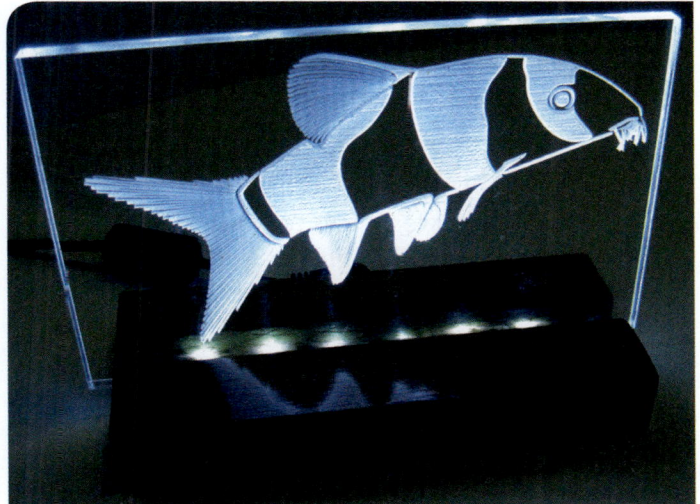

Laser-engraved acrylic, which has been illuminated

Vinyl stickers

A CNC plotter cutter can be used to make vinyl stickers. This is an easy method to add colour and text to a product. A roll or sheet of sticky-backed vinyl is fed into the machine. A file designed using a CAD program is sent to the machine. The force and speed needed to cut the vinyl away from the backing sheet is programmed into the machine. When a sticker is made from different colours, the process will need to be repeated on different-coloured vinyl and overlaid to make up the final design. It is also possible to print on vinyl sheet using special inks. These machines incorporate a printer and CNC cutter in one unit. Vinyl stickers are used for signage around school or in shops, as well as creating advertising wrap designs on buses and cars. Care needs to be taken when positioning stickers and they may peel off in some circumstances.

GRP pigments

Pigments can be added to polyester resin to colour products made from glass reinforced plastic (GRP). A small amount of pigment is mixed with the resin before adding a catalyst that hardens the resin and bonds the fibres of glass together. Pigments can be mixed like paint to make new colours, although multiple colours in the same GRP component are not possible. The coloured polyester resin gives a durable finish as it is often thicker than painted surfaces and scratched surfaces are often less noticeable.

Summary

Key points to remember:
- A laser cutter can be used to cut and engrave sheet material.
- Vacuum-formed moulds need to include draft angles, vent holes and rounded edges.
- Different finishes and textures can be applied to plastics to change their appearance.
- Parts can be joined with either temporary or permanent fixings.

Checkpoint

Strengthen

S1 List two techniques used for cutting a thread.
S2 Describe where and why you would use a washer.
S3 Describe the stages needed to finish an acrylic edge cut using a saw.

Challenge

C1 Draw a flow diagram to explain how a CAD file can be cut using a laser cutter.
C2 Use annotated sketches to explain the process of making and applying vinyl stickers to a product.

Preparing for your exam 4

Exam strategy

What to expect in the exam

Section B of the examination is designed to test your knowledge and understanding of the material category studied. You are advised to practise different styles of exam questions that require short and long answers, as well as some that require sketching and calculations. Throughout the course you will need to practise exam-style questions that will challenge you across all sections of the polymers category. Preparing carefully for your exams is important if you are to access all marking criteria.

Section B: Material category – Polymers

This section is worth 60 marks and contains a mixture of different question styles, including open-response, graphical, calculation and extended-open-response questions. This will include 5 marks for calculations.

In this polymer category, you should know about:

- its design contexts
- its sources, origins, physical and working properties, and their social and ecological footprints
- the way in which the selection of the material is influenced
- the impact of forces and stresses and how the material can be reinforced and stiffened
- stock forms, types and sizes to calculate and determine the quantity of the materials required
- alternative processes that can be used to manufacture the material to a different scale of production
- specialist techniques, tools, computer-aided manufacture, equipment and processes that can be used to shape, fabricate, construct and assemble a high-quality prototype
- appropriate surface treatments and finishes that can be applied to the material.

Revision tips

- Ensure you start revising in plenty of time before your exam. You will find it easier to remember facts you have revised several times over a few weeks than those you have tried to memorise at the last minute.
- Make clear and well-ordered notes about all the sections that relate to the core and your chosen material category.
- Test yourself at the end of each section. Work through the exam-style questions and complete activities to reinforce your knowledge and understanding.
- Work through all sample assessment materials and past papers available from Pearson.
- Identify the areas where you are likely to get mathematical questions and practise the sections on arithmetic and numerical computation, handling data, graphs, geometry and trigonometry.
- Discuss the course with your teacher and peers, as it will help your understanding.
- Work through corrections and identify areas where you may need further practice.
- Use online or other resources to extend your understanding of the design and technology context.

Exam tips

- You should plan to leave 60 minutes for answering questions in Section B.
- You must answer all the questions. If you are stuck on one, leave it and come back to it at the end.
- Although the questions will be different for each paper you sit, there is information on the page to help you answer the question. For example, the number of marks awarded for each question will tell you the number of separate points that need to be given in your answer.
- Pay attention to the command words used in the question as these will guide you how best to communicate your answers.
- Underline or highlight keywords in the question. After answering the question, read the question again to ensure you have done what was asked.
- If you have time available, plan the structure for long answers and make sure you give good examples where needed.
- Check through your answers at the end of the exam. Make sure you have included units and shown the workings for calculations.

Preparing for your exam 4

Sample answers with comments

The following questions give some examples of how the different command words should lead to certain answers.

Question 1: 'Explain' question

Polymers are made through the extraction and refining of oil. Oil is a non-renewable resource with its origin being mainly focused in certain parts of the world.

Explain **two** reasons why the cost of oil is unstable. (4 marks)

Student answer

A shortage in oil can cause the cost to rise as communities compete to buy what is available. When supply is high, the cost of oil reduces as there is surplus stock available. Conflicts and disputes between countries can also make it harder to transport oil, reducing supplies and ultimately increasing costs.

> **Exam tip**
>
> 'Explain' questions require an answer and a reason or set of reasons qualifying the answer, such as reasons why something can be considered to fulfil a need, provide a purpose, or communicate an intention. The answer must contain some element of reasoning/justification. It may be used to support a given statement.

Verdict

This is a detailed answer. The student would receive full marks for this question.

Question 2: 'Explain' question

Explain **three** reasons why Styrofoam™ is suitable for the modelling of prototypes in the school workshop. (6 marks)

Student answer

1. It can be shaped into complex forms with a hot wire cutter.
2. It is available in a range of thicknesses and can be glued together using PVA to give other thicknesses.
3. It is lightweight and easy to carry.

Verdict

Answers 1 and 2 are correct, as they both explain how Styrofoam™ is suitable for the modelling of prototypes in a school workshop. Answer 3 relates to the weight of the material, which is not relevant to this question as the prototype may need to be heavy. A better third answer could be 'Easy to shape using hand tools and can be sanded to give a smooth finish'.

Question 3: 'Explain' question

Explain **two** reasons for using urea formaldehyde rather than acrylic in the production of an electrical plug. (4 marks)

Student answer

Urea formaldehyde is a thermosetting polymer. Thermosetting polymers cannot be reformed once heated due to cross-linking between the molecular chains, making them safe to use in electrical products that can be exposed to heat or risk of fire. Acrylic is a thermoforming polymer. Thermoforming polymers have no cross-linking chains, allowing the polymer to be reshaped when exposed to high temperatures.

Verdict

The answer is correct, as it explains the main difference in structure between urea formaldehyde and acrylic. An excellent answer would also include reference to other material properties, such as strength and durability.

Preparing for your exam 4

Question 4: 'Explain' question

Explain two reasons why acrylic is an appropriate material for the manufacture of shop signs. **(6 marks)**

Student answer

1. *Acrylic is available in sheet form and a range of thicknesses. Different style text can be accurately cut using a laser cutter and edges need little or no finishing. It is available in many different colours, making it possible to match the brand image of the shop.*
2. *Acrylic has a high-quality finish and is easy to clean, maintaining the brand image of the shop. Acrylic is resistant to weathering and can be illuminated with back lighting to make the sign visible in the dark.*

Exam tips

Give an account of the main characteristics of the material or the steps in a process.

You should develop your answer but you do not need to include a justification or reason.

Verdict

Both parts of the answer are correct, as they explain a reason why acrylic is a suitable material for the manufacture of shop signs. The first part of the answer refers to material thickness, but does not say how this is useful in the manufacture of shop signs.

Question 5: 'Use notes and/or sketches to show' question

Use notes and/or sketches to show the vacuum forming manufacturing process of the paint palette. **(5 marks)**

Exam tip

Using graphical depiction with annotation, give an account of a process, showing its steps or stages in the correct order, or give an account of something, showing a series of features, points or trends. The number of points and the depth of answer required will be indicated by the mark allocation.

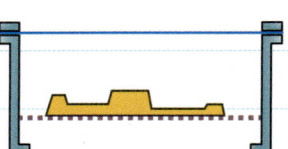
Mould placed on platen and material clamped in place

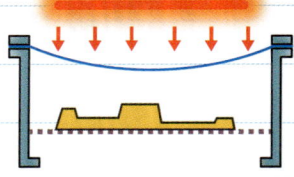
Thermoplastic sheet is heated

Student answer

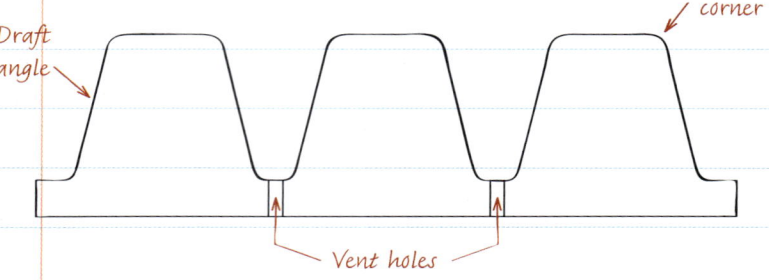

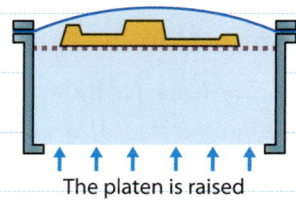
The platen is raised

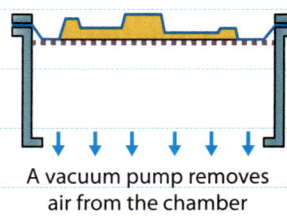
A vacuum pump removes air from the chamber

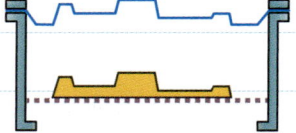
The platen is lowered and the moulding removed

Verdict

This is an excellent answer. Cross-sectional drawings clearly show each stage of the vacuum forming process and details of the mould. The annotations support this and such an answer would receive all marks available.

Preparing for your exam 4

Question 6: Calculation question

Calculate the amount of wastage from cutting three circles of 100 mm diameter from a sheet of acrylic measuring 320 mm × 120 mm, as shown in the diagram below. **(5 marks)**

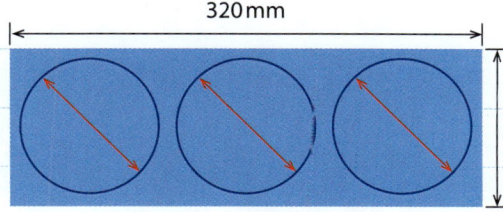

Each circle 100 mm in diameter

Exam tip

You will need to use your maths skills in the exam. The formula you need may be given in the question but it helps to be familiar with formulae that are likely to come up.

Student answer

Total area of acrylic sheet to cut = Width × height

320 mm × 120 mm = 38,400 mm²

Total area of three circles measuring 100 mm diameter = π × r² × 3

3.14 × 50² × 3 = 23,550 mm²

Verdict

This is an excellent answer. The workings of the calculation are clear. The surface area of the acrylic sheet is calculated, from which the area of the three circles is subtracted.

Question 7: 'Use notes and/or sketches to show' question

Use notes and/or sketches to show how the hand control for this games console is manufactured. **(5 marks)**

Exam tip

Using graphical depiction with annotation, give an account of a process, showing its steps or stages in the correct order, or give an account of something, showing a series of features, points or trends. The number of points and the depth of answer required will be indicated by the mark allocation.

Student answer

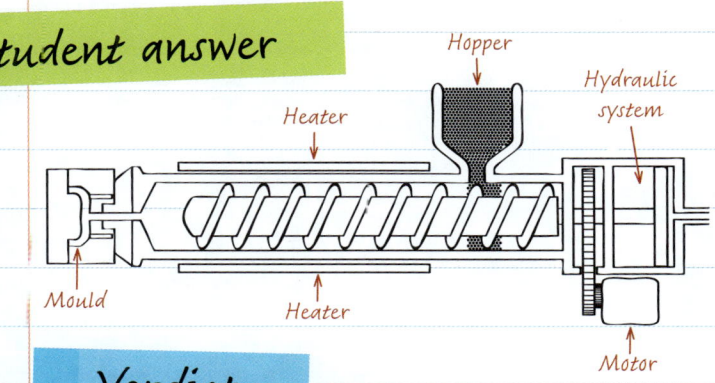

Verdict

The answer includes a detailed diagram and annotation of an injection moulding machine, but the process is not explained. The student would receive 4 marks for the answer given, but a better answer would include additional comments that refer to each stage of the process.

1. Granules of polymer and a colour pigment are fed into a hopper.
2. The granules are then fed forwards towards the mould using a screw. During this process they are heated until the granules melt.
3. The screw moves away from the mould as the volume of molten polymer builds up next to the mould.
4. A hydraulic rams pushes the molten polymer into the mould.
5. The two halves of the mould are opened and ejector pins push the formed object from the mould.

An excellent answer would also show the mould shaped like the product.

5 Systems

5.1 Design contexts

> **Getting started**
>
> Electronic systems have developed a lot, and have become an essential part of our everyday life. Think about where you live and consider the following questions:
> - Write a list of all of the electronic products you can think of.
> - If you could only keep one electronic product in your life what would it be and why?
>
> Think of an idea for an electronic product you would like that does not exist at the moment. What would you like the product to do? Why do you think it would be useful? What sort of people do you think would buy it?

Ever since electricity was first discovered, scientists and engineers have been designing new and better ways to use it to improve our lives. Modern electronic systems have developed very quickly in quite a short space of time, and the things they can do now would have seemed amazing 100 years ago.

The timeline opposite shows some of the important developments.

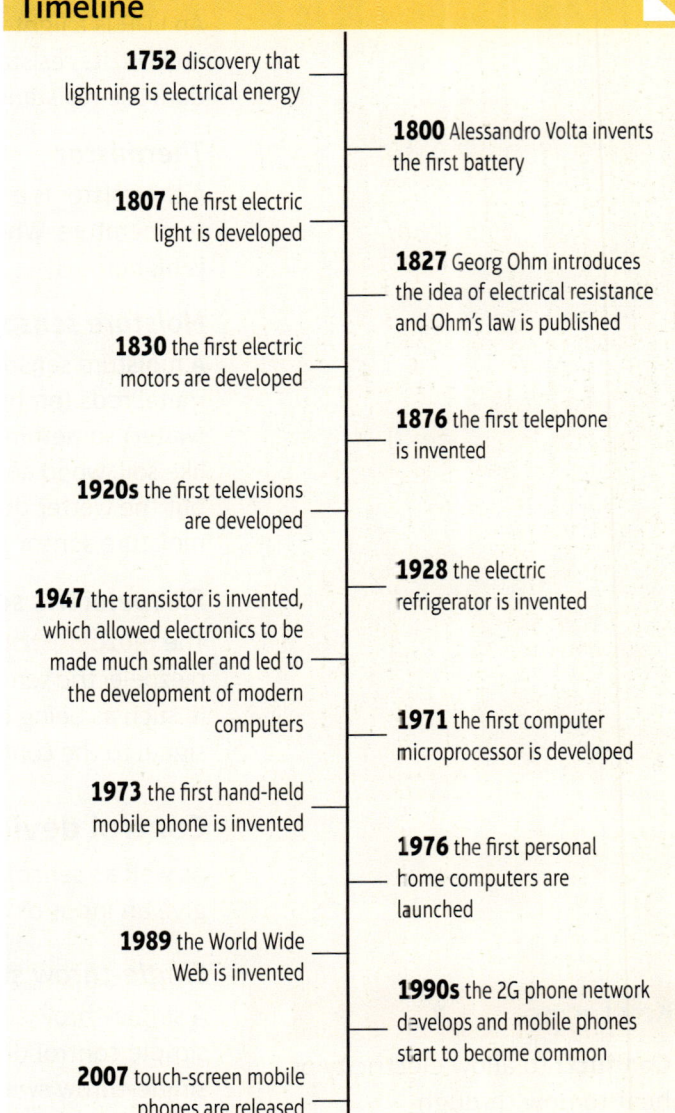

Timeline

- **1752** discovery that lightning is electrical energy
- **1800** Alessandro Volta invents the first battery
- **1807** the first electric light is developed
- **1827** Georg Ohm introduces the idea of electrical resistance and Ohm's law is published
- **1830** the first electric motors are developed
- **1876** the first telephone is invented
- **1920s** the first televisions are developed
- **1928** the electric refrigerator is invented
- **1947** the transistor is invented, which allowed electronics to be made much smaller and led to the development of modern computers
- **1971** the first computer microprocessor is developed
- **1973** the first hand-held mobile phone is invented
- **1976** the first personal home computers are launched
- **1989** the World Wide Web is invented
- **1990s** the 2G phone network develops and mobile phones start to become common
- **2007** touch-screen mobile phones are released

> **Summary**
>
> **Key point to remember:**
>
> Electronic systems have developed very rapidly over the last 100 years.

5 Systems

5.2 Properties and origins of components

> **Learning objectives**
>
> By the end of this section, you should know:
> - about a range of sensors, control devices and output devices that can be used to create electronic systems
> - where some of the materials used to make electronic products come from.

> **Link it up**
>
> For more information on sensors, see page 33.

Sensors

A sensor is affected by the conditions around it. A sensor can be used to give an input to an electronic system.

Light-dependent resistors

An LDR is a light-dependent resistor. When light falls on the sensing area of an LDR, its resistance changes. When it is light the resistance is low. When it is dark the resistance is higher.

Thermistor

A thermistor is a temperature-dependent resistor. Its resistance changes with temperature. When it is hot the resistance is low. When it is cold the resistance is higher.

Moisture sensor

A moisture sensor can be made by trying to pass electricity between two metal rods (probes). Water will **conduct** some electricity, so the more moisture (water) something contains the more electricity will pass through it. Things like soil, wood and plaster will not conduct much electricity when they are dry, but the wetter they get the more they will conduct electricity between the moisture sensor probes.

Piezoelectric sensor

The **piezoelectric** effect converts movement energy into electricity. A piezoelectric sensor creates a small electrical pulse when a force is put on it, such as being hit by something, or stood on. The electric pulse can give a signal to the controller, which decides what to do about it.

Control devices and components

As well as sensors there are some other components that can be used to give an input or control an electronic circuit.

Single-throw switch

A single-throw switch has a button that switches between on and off. It is a simple control device that the user can operate to turn a circuit on or off. A single-throw switch has two contacts, and can be on or off. A double-throw switch has three contacts. If you use the middle contact and one end contact it works like a single throw, and is on or off. If you use all three contacts you can have output A on one way, flick the switch and change to output B. It is also a useful way to make a motor go forwards or backwards.

> **Key terms**
>
> **Conduct:** to allow electricity or heat to flow through.
>
> **Piezoelectric:** pressure put on a crystal causing a small electrical pulse.

5.2 Properties and origins of components

Resistors
A resistor is a component that can be added to a circuit to change its resistance. This means it can limit the flow of electricity through part of the circuit. Resistors can be used to:
- protect delicate components by stopping too much electricity flowing through them
- help control the flow of electricity around a circuit.

Push to make switch
A push to make switch (PTM) has a button that can be pushed to bring contacts together and allow electricity to flow. Usually the contacts open again when the button is released. Some push switches 'latch on', so they stay on until pushed again. A push to make switch is **normally off**, and comes on when you push the button. You can also get **normally on** switches that are on all the time and go off when you push the button.

Micro switch
A micro switch is activated by a small movement of its arm or button. It is often used as a sensor. The switch is activated when something moves. For example, a micro switch can ensure that, if a door or guard is open, the machine will not run.

Reed switch
A reed switch is turned on or off by a magnetic field. The reeds are thin metal strips in a little glass tube that are pulled together (normally off) or pulled apart (normally on) by a magnet. A reed switch could be used as a sensor in an alarm system. When a door is opened, a magnet would move away from the reed switch, telling the controller the door was opened. The controller decides whether to sound the alarm.

Variable resistors
A variable resistor has a knob that can be turned to change its resistance. These can be very useful in a control circuit to change the sensitivity of a sensor. When paired with an LDR, the variable resistor makes a potential divider (see Figure 5.2.1 on page 206), which can be used to change the light level at which the output turns on.

> **Key terms**
>
> **Normally off:** the switch is off in its normal state, and turns on when it is activated.
>
> **Normally on:** the switch is on in its normal state, and turns off when it is activated.

> **Link it up**
>
> You can find out about transistors in the core content (Section 1) on page 34. A transistor is made of three layers of differently treated silicon semi-conductor. Most transistors are NPN, meaning a P layer sandwiched between two N layers. An N layer has extra electrons (Negative), while a P layer has electrons removed (Positive). Some transistors are PNP. When using transistors, make sure you know which pin is which on the type you have.

> **Apply it**
>
> Many outside automatic security lights have two variable resistors on them. They let you make changes to how the light operates. What things would it be useful to change?

5 Systems

Component	Symbol	Component	Symbol
LDR		Resistor	
Thermistor		Variable resistor	
Single-throw switch		Battery	
Double-throw switch		Power supply	9V / 0V
Push to make switch (normally off)		Buzzer	
Push to break switch (normally on)		LED	
Reed switch		Loudspeaker	
Transistor (NPN type)	collector, base, emitter	Motor	

Table 5.2.1 Circuit symbols

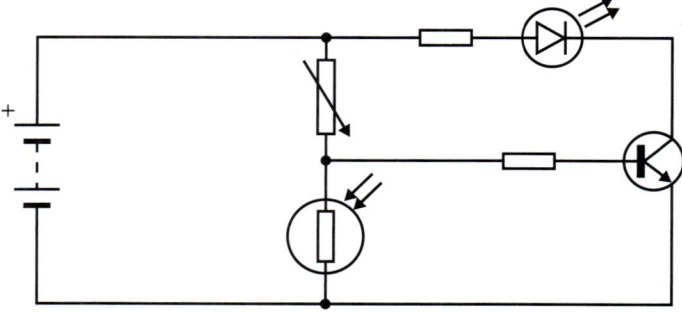

Figure 5.2.1 Example of a circuit diagram. The variable resistor and LDR make a potential divider. This divides the voltage (potential). As the light level falls, the voltage at the base of the transistor increases until it turns on the transistor, and the LED lights up. This method is used a lot to make sensing circuits

Apply it

Copy the circuit diagram and label the components. Draw a similar circuit with a thermistor that sounds a buzzer if the temperature gets too high.

Microprocessor

A microprocessor is an integrated circuit (IC) that contains thousands of tiny components (mostly transistors) etched onto a piece of silicon semi-conductor material. Microprocessors vary in size and complexity. They can perform a wide variety of tasks – think about a computer.

A microprocessor, showing 28 pins in a DIL (dual in line) arrangement (right) and 32 pins (left). There are more up to date versions of microprocessors in the market- research these and compare to picture shown here.

5.2 Properties and origins of components

Microcontrollers

A microcontroller, or programmable interface controller (PIC), is a chip that has a **flash memory**. That means a **program** can be written on a computer and loaded onto the chip. This gives the chip a huge range of possible functions because input and output devices can be connected to its pins and controlled by the program that has been loaded onto the chip. They provide greater flexibility as they can be reprogrammed to change function/task. Circuits can also be made smaller by replacing several discrete ICs. A disadvantage is that they are expensive.

These come in different sizes and layouts. One example is called a GENIE 08 – Figure 5.2.2 is just an example from one company. There are others that do the same thing, but have different pin layouts.

Relay

A relay does a similar job to a transistor – a small current triggers it to switch on. A transistor can only manage quite a small current. A relay is much bigger and has a mechanism in it that closes a switch, so it can handle a big current. A relay is used to allow a control circuit to turn on a larger output, such as a motor.

Outputs

In an electronic system, output devices are controlled by the system. They can be simple things like lights that are turned on and off or complex things like computer screens that output a lot of information.

Buzzers

A buzzer makes a sound. Some buzzers make quite a distinctive buzzing sound as they vibrate. There is a similar device called a piezo-sounder that makes a piercing single note sound. Some piezo-sounders can play different tones, so the controller could make them play a simple tune.

Light-emitting diodes

A light-emitting diode, LED, gives out light when electricity is passed through it. Small LEDs are used for things like indicator lights and the bars in light-up number displays. Modern LEDs are bright enough to light up a room in a house and, because they are more energy efficient, with a longer lifetime than other types of bulb, they are becoming increasingly popular. You can get LEDs in different colours, but it is worth noting that it is the different **semi-conductor** materials they are made from that make the colours, not the colour of the plastic case, although their colour can shift due to age and temperature.

> **Key terms**
>
> **Flash memory:** a memory that can store information, then be wiped clean and store different information repeatedly.
>
> **Progam:** a set of instructions that the controller follows to make the system work.
>
> **Semi-conductor:** a material that allows electricity to flow under certain conditions. It can behave as an insulator or conductor.

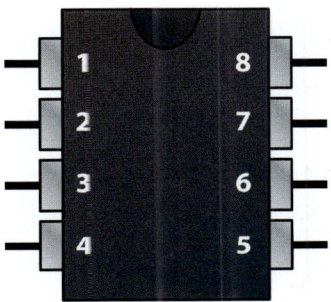

1	Power, +V (or positive)
2	Programming input
3	Analogue input or digital in/out
4	Digital input
5	Analogue input or digital in/out
6	Analogue input or digital in/out
7	Digital output
8	Power, 0V (or negative)

Figure 5.2.2 A GENIE 08

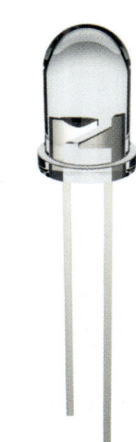

A typical small LED: the long leg is the + side (anode) and the short leg is the – side (cathode)

5 Systems

> **Key terms**
>
> **Electromagnet:** a coil of wire wrapped around an iron core that becomes magnetic when electricity goes through the coil.
>
> **Amplifier:** an electronic circuit that makes a small electrical signal more powerful, used to power a loudspeaker.
>
> **Ore:** rock that contains metals.

Loudspeakers

A loudspeaker is an output device that can be used to make sound. The controller uses pulses of electricity to send information to the loudspeaker. The electricity makes an **electromagnet** move, which vibrates a paper cone, and these vibrations travel through the air as sound waves. A large loudspeaker will need an **amplifier** to make the signal from the controller powerful enough to work the loudspeaker.

Motors

A motor is an output device that turns electricity into rotary motion. The controller can turn the motor on and off, make it go forwards or backwards and change the speed it turns at. The rotation of the motor spindle can be connected to many different types of machinery, wheels and gearboxes to make things move.

> **Exam-style question**
>
> Use notes and/or sketches to produce a circuit diagram that would allow you to change the direction of the motor. **(4 marks)**

> **Exam tip**
>
> Always make sure you use the correct circuit symbols in your diagram.

Sources of raw materials used in systems

Electronic products need a lot of materials, including several different metals. Most metals are found as an **ore** that has to be mined out of the ground and then processed to extract the metal from the ore.

Polymers made from crude oil

> **Link it up**
>
> For more information on polymers, look at page 43.

Plastic is a type of material called a polymer. Some plastics you might use in school are acrylic (polymethyl methacrylate), high-impact polystyrene (HIPS), acrylonitrile butadiene styrene (ABS) and polyvinyl chloride (PVC). Most plastics are made from the chemicals found in crude oil. Crude oil is found in many places around the world, including the UK, but the main countries that supply oil are Russia, Saudi Arabia and the United States.

Silicon

Silicon is the main material used to make silicon chips. A thin slice of it has chemical impurities added to it to make it a semi-conductor that partly conducts electricity, or conducts electricity sometimes. All our electronic gadgets rely on silicon. Some of the biggest silicon mines are in China, Russia and the USA.

> **Apply it**
>
> Why do you think the amount of silicon we use has increased over the last 30 years?

5.2 Properties and origins of components

Gold
Gold is a metal that is highly prized for jewellery because it does not **tarnish**. It is also one of the best conductors of electricity there is. Gold is sometimes used to make contacts in sensitive electronic products because the lack of tarnish makes a good electrical contact for a long time. Gold is very expensive because it is rare. Some of the biggest gold mines are in Australia, China and Russia.

Copper
Copper is a reddish-brown metal that is a good conductor of electricity. It is used a lot in electrical products, and is often used to make wires for electricity. It is quite soft, so it is easy to bend and stretch into wires. Copper is found in a lot of countries, but some of the biggest mines are found in Chile, China and Peru. Historically, the UK was a major producer of copper, particularly Cornwall and Wales. But there are currently no active copper mines in Britain.

Lithium
Lithium is quite an unusual metal. It is very lightweight and highly reactive. It has been used a lot in recent years to make lithium-ion batteries. Lithium-ion batteries are now the most popular type of rechargeable battery and are widely used in mobile phones, laptops, electric cars and power tools. Lithium is mined in Australia, Chile and Argentina.

Aluminium
Aluminium is a soft, lightweight metal that can be made into a strong, lightweight alloy used to make a lot of products such as aeroplane bodies, bicycle frames and car wheels. It is also used for the high-voltage power lines between electricity pylons. Most aluminium is extracted from an ore called bauxite, which is common in rocks all around the world. A lot of aluminium is produced in China, Russia and Canada. Although there is a lot of it, it can be quite expensive to extract the aluminium from the rocks.

Nickel
Nickel is a silvery-coloured metal that has a range of uses. It is used to make several alloys, including stainless steel, magnets and coins. Nickel is often used to **electroplate** other metals to protect them from **corrosion**. It is also used to make nickel cadmium rechargeable batteries (NiCad), which were common but are being replaced in a lot of things by lithium-ion. The largest nickel mines are in the Philippines, Indonesia, Russia, Canada and Australia.

Rare earth elements
Rare earth elements (REEs) are metals that can be found near the bottom of the periodic table, with unusual names like lanthanum, praseodymium, neodymium, promethium and lutetium. These are increasingly being used in modern technology, in things like electric car batteries, lasers, wind turbines, medical scanners and additives in specialist alloys. Most rare-earth elements are mined in China, with some also coming from Australia and the USA.

Physical characteristics

Resistor colour codes
A lot of electronic components come in different values. An important part of designing a circuit is choosing the right values for the components. Resistance is measured in a unit called an ohm, with the symbol Ω. Resistors come with many different values of resistance, from tens of ohms to millions of ohms, so it is important to have a way to read the resistance value. Resistors are quite small, so printing numbers on them is difficult. Instead of numbers resistors have a colour code on them (see Figure 5.2.3). Each number from 0 to 9 is assigned a colour. The first two stripes represent numbers, and the third stripe is a multiplier, or number of zeros. For example, 2 is red, so red, red, red would represent 2 2 (2 zeros) = 2200 Ω.

> **Key terms**
>
> **Tarnish:** a thin film that forms on the surface of a metal when it reacts with oxygen in the air. It often makes the metal look duller in colour.
>
> **Electroplate:** a metal object is dipped into a solution of the coating metal and electricity is passed through it. The metal object becomes coated with a thin film of the coating metal.
>
> **Corrosion:** the metal is eaten away as it reacts with oxygen and water in the air. Rust is formed through the corrosion of iron or steel.

5 Systems

Tolerance

The fourth stripe shows the **tolerance**. Tolerance is important when manufacturing something. A precise value is impossible to achieve; there will always be some inaccuracy. Tolerance says how much inaccuracy there is allowed to be.

- With a tolerance of ±10 per cent a 1000 Ω resistor could actually be between 900 Ω and 1100 Ω.
- With a tolerance of ±2 per cent a 100 Ω resistor would be between 980 Ω and 1020 Ω.

The 2 per cent resistor is higher quality because it is more accurate, but it is more expensive than the 10 per cent resistor.

Resistors also have a power rating. If a resistor is overloaded and its power rating is exceeded it will burn out and could catch fire. The power rating of a resistor is usually related to its physical size – the smaller the resistor, the faster it will heat up and overload. To identify the power rating of a resistor, hold it in your right hand with the tolerance band near to that hand, reading the resistor's colour bands from left to right.

Remember:

k = kilo (thousand) = 1000
M = Mega (million) = 1,000,000

Link it up

Resistors are only available in certain values called the E series. See page 219 for information on the E12 series of resistors.

Key term

Tolerance: sets an upper and lower acceptable limit for a measurement of something.

Apply it

1. What coloured stripes would be on a resistor with the following values?
   a. 1000 Ω ±10%
   b. 27 kΩ ±5%   (27 kΩ = 27,000 Ω)
   c. 68 MΩ ±10% (68 MΩ = 68,000,000 Ω)

2. What is the value of a resistor with the following coloured stripes on it?
   a. yellow, violet, red, gold
   b. red, red, brown, red
   c. green, blue, orange, silver

Answers:

1. a. brown, black, red, silver
   b. red, violet, orange, gold
   c. blue, grey, blue, silver

2. a. 4700 Ω ±5%
   b. 220 Ω ±2%
   c. 56,000 Ω or 56 kΩ ±10%

Resistor colour code

Band colour	Value
Black	0
Brown	1
Red	2
Orange	3
Yellow	4
Green	5
Blue	6
Violet	7
Grey	8
White	9
Gold	0.1
Silver	0.01

Tolerance colour code

Band colour	±%
Brown	1
Red	2
Gold	5
Silver	10
None	20

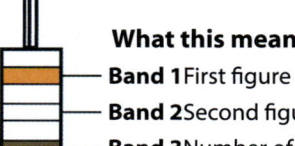

What this means
- Band 1 First figure of value
- Band 2 Second figure of value
- Band 3 Number of zeros/multiplier
- Band 4 Tolerance (±%) see below

Note that the bands are closer to one end than the other

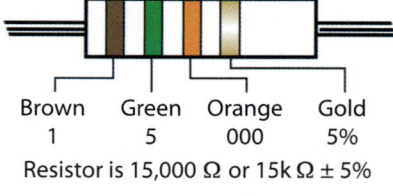

Brown 1 | Green 5 | Orange 000 | Gold 5%
Resistor is 15,000 Ω or 15k Ω ± 5%

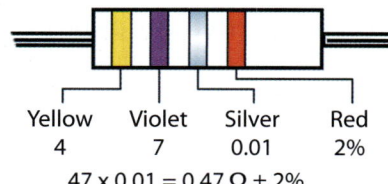

Yellow 4 | Violet 7 | Silver 0.01 | Red 2%
47 x 0.01 = 0.47 Ω ± 2%

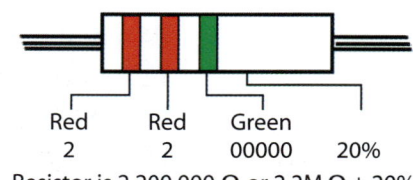

Red 2 | Red 2 | Green 00000 | 20%
Resistor is 2,200,000 Ω or 2.2M Ω ± 20%

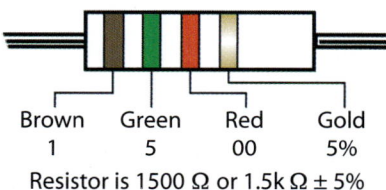

Brown 1 | Green 5 | Red 00 | Gold 5%
Resistor is 1500 Ω or 1.5k Ω ± 5%

Figure 5.2.3 How to use the resistor colour code

Material selection for case construction

The case for an electronic product could be made from hundreds of different materials: metals and their alloys, many different plastics, many types of wood and manufactured boards, or modern composites like carbon fibre.

None of these materials are perfect. All of them have a range of different properties that make them good for some things and not for others. The most technically brilliant material might not be used because a cheaper alternative is good enough. Some of the factors a designer needs to consider when choosing a material are:

- the purpose of the product
- how and where the product will be used
- how much the product will cost
- how many will be manufactured.

This helps to write a specification for the case. Then the designer needs to understand the properties of lots of different materials to work out which one will be the most suitable, so the product can be strong and durable enough, and so it can be manufactured for an acceptable cost. It is also important to choose materials that can be sourced sustainably, processed and disposed of without causing unacceptable environmental damage.

Working properties

A designer needs to understand the working properties of materials, so that they can choose a material that will work well for the job it needs to do.

Conductors and insulators

A material that lets energy travel through it is called a **conductor**. A thermal conductor lets heat travel through it while an electrical conductor lets electricity travel through it. Metals are good thermal and electrical conductors.

A material that does not let heat or electricity travel through it is called an insulator. Plastics, rubber and glass are all examples of good insulators.

> **Apply it**
>
> Electrical wires have a copper core and a plastic sheath around the core. Why do you think this is?

Polymers

A polymer is made up of long chain molecules, sometimes thousands of atoms long. A plastic is a man-made polymer.

> **Link it up**
>
> For more information on plastics, look at pages 163–197.

Plastic can be a good material to use for electronic products because plastic:

- is an insulator, so it will not interfere with the circuit and it helps protect the user from electric shock
- is cheap and easy to mould into very complex shapes
- is available in a range of colours and properties.

Plastics have different properties that make them good for different types of products.

- Most plastics are durable and are not damaged quickly by water or sunlight.
- Most plastics are not very hard, so they will scratch easily. Some are more hardwearing than others, so are better for things that may get a lot of surface abrasion wear.
- Some plastics are tough, so they withstand shocks and blows better, which makes them good for products that may get dropped or battered about in normal use.
- Some plastics are rigid, while some have more **elasticity**. A more elastic plastic is good for something that may need to stretch or absorb impact. A soft, rubbery handle on a product may make it safer and more comfortable to grip.

Social footprint

Relying on scarce elements

Some of the elements used in specialist electronic components are very rare. This means they can be expensive and if they are only found in a small number

> **Key terms**
>
> **Conductor:** lets energy flow through it easily. All metals are good electrical conductors.
>
> **Elasticity:** how easily the material can stretch and return to its original shape.

5 Systems

of places, any problems with supply can stop production of a product. Some examples are shown here.

- **Lithium**, which is used in rechargeable batteries. It is being used in much bigger quantities now it is in smartphones, laptops and electric cars. If the current mines start to run out, the price of lithium will go up, and we either need to find more of it or develop new batteries that do not need lithium.
- **Cobalt**, which is used in some high-performance alloys that are resistant to heat and temperature. It is important for turbine blades in jet engines. A lot of cobalt comes from a politically unstable part of Africa, and the supply can depend on what is happening in the region. Mining there is dangerous and uses child labour in very poor conditions.
- **Tantalum**, which is used in electronic components called capacitors and is important in miniature components used in mobile phones and laptops. Most tantalum comes from Australia now, but it is rare and some of it has come from central Africa, especially the Democratic Republic of Congo. Its sale provided some of the money that bought guns during a nasty civil war that lasted for many years and brought about the deaths of many people.

Effects of using modern systems

Modern electronic systems have made some big changes to the way we live our lives. Computers can store and process huge amounts of data and information. Vast amounts of information are quickly and easily available over the internet. Phone calls can now be made with a video link to the other side of the world. Social media has changed the way people socialise and keep in touch. Games consoles provide increasingly complex and vivid gaming experiences.

The internet provides a lot of convenience. We can buy things, order services, research things, communicate. All this connectivity also provides opportunities for criminals. Cybercrime is a huge problem, with people now finding they have had money stolen over the internet. Keeping computer networks and data secure is a major problem for all big companies.

Apply it

Some people think it is too easy to spend a lot of time using technology. Playing violent video games is less healthy than riding a bike or playing football. Using social media rather than going out and socialising face-to-face seems easy, but some argue it might not be good for people's happiness in the long term. What do you think?

Ecological footprint

The ecological footprint of a product is looking at how much effect it has on the natural environment. It includes the whole **product life cycle**, from mining and processing materials, to manufacturing, to use of the product, to disposal after use.

Effects of material extraction and processing of elements

Most metals are mined by digging ore out of the ground. The metal needs to be extracted from the ore, which can use lots of energy and often creates piles of waste. Some mining and processing creates toxic waste that is harmful if it gets into water supplies. If companies are not well regulated, their waste products can destroy the local environment. If the energy comes from fossil fuels it is contributing to global warming.

Effects of built-in obsolescence

A product becomes obsolete when technology has moved on and it is no longer useful or useable, or a part breaks that cannot be replaced so the whole product can no longer be used. Built-in obsolescence is designed in by manufacturers by ensuring that new products are no longer compatible with old ones, or parts wear out or only last for a certain time. Manufacturers rely on this built-in obsolescence because they can only make money if people keep buying new products. Because obsolete products are no longer any use, they are usually thrown away.

Effects of use

Some products have quite an obvious effect on the environment, such as motor vehicles that burn a lot of fuel and pump soot and gases into the air. The effect of using a lot of electrical goods is harder to see, but if the electricity comes from non-renewable sources like burning fossil fuels then it does have a negative effect on the environment.

Disposal of electronic products

When broken or obsolete products are finished with, they are thrown away. Most electronic products are very hard to recycle because they contain so many different components made from different materials. Electronics

Key term

Product life cycle: the life cycle of a product starts with obtaining raw materials, manufacturing the product, selling it, using it and finally disposing of it when it is finished with.

can be recycled. Products are dismantled and circuit boards are heated to extract the precious metals, for example gold. When products are not recycled they are often disposed of, and go to be buried in a landfill site. Electronic products often contain heavy metals that are toxic and hazardous to humans and wildlife. We have to be careful to make sure that, as these products degrade, the toxic metals are not washed into the ground, because they will get into water supplies and poison wildlife and possibly us. Polymers (plastics) take a long time to break down in the environment, so they will remain in the ground for a long time. Some polymers also contain toxic chemicals that are released if they are burnt or degrade in the ground.

> **Exam-style question**
>
> Explain **two** reasons why built-in obsolescence of products could be damaging to the environment.
>
> **(4 marks)**

Summary

Key points to remember:
- Sensors are a useful input device for a system. They tell the controller something has happened.
- Switches can be manually operated to give an input to a system.
- A range of output devices can be controlled by the system controller.
- The specialist metals used in electronic products come from mines around the world. Some are common, but some are found in only a small number of places.
- Metals are good conductors, so electricity can flow through them.
- Plastics are good insulators, so electricity cannot flow through them.

Checkpoint

Strengthen

S1 Name three output devices a system could have.
S2 What does tolerance mean?
S3 What is the ecological footprint of a product?

Challenge

C1 Explain how to use the resistor colour code.
C2 Explain why relying on scarce elements could be a problem for manufacturers.

5.3 Selection of components

Learning objectives

By the end of this section, you should know:
- the aesthetic factors to consider
- environmental legislation from the RoHS and WEEE directives
- material availability
- factors influencing cost
- social, cultural and ethical factors that can affect a product design.

There are many factors that influence the way a product is designed and the components that are used to make it. A designer needs to understand these factors to be able to design a product that will appeal to the consumer, be safe to use and cost effective to manufacture.

5 Systems

Aesthetic factors
Aesthetics are about how a product looks.

Form
The form of a product is how the overall shape and structure look. Some products are made as small as possible, some are designed to look good to the consumer. A poor appearance of the case for your systems project can lead to people making incorrect judgments about the quality of the whole project.

Colour
The colour of a product can influence who it appeals to and should be appropriate to the product. Sometimes bright colours are good, sometimes dull colours that blend in are preferred. Mobile phone cases are often black because it looks smart and inoffensive. Some mobile phones have different coloured clip-on cases, so the consumer can choose more interesting colours.

Texture
Most plastic products are smooth because that is easier to manufacture, but the surface of a product can be given a texture. A texture could be a pattern of little bumps or dimples. A different plastic could be used with a softer, rubbery feel. These textures are particularly good on the handle of a product where you need to get a good grip, for example a kettle.

Environmental factors

Restriction of Hazardous Substances Directive
The Restriction of Hazardous Substances (RoHS) Directive was developed by the European Union and is now UK law. Its full title is The Restriction of the Use of Certain Hazardous Substances in Electrical and Electronic Equipment Regulations. It aims to stop hazardous substances from being used in products and to keep them from causing damage when they are disposed of.

There is a list of banned substances, which includes lead, mercury and cadmium, that are toxic to fauna. Solder was made from lead and tin so new lead-free solder had to be developed for mass-produced products. Anyone who wishes to trade in the EU (regardless of where they are based) must comply with the RoHS directive, so designers must select their materials carefully.

Waste Electrical and Electronic Equipment Directive
The Waste Electrical and Electronic Equipment (WEEE) Directive is about waste electrical and electronic equipment recycling. WEEE covers products that have a plug or need a battery. About two million tonnes of WEEE is scrapped in the UK every year, which needs to be disposed of. The WEEE directive has rules about toxic substances and how they must be dealt with.

Fridges used to contain a coolant that is very bad for the atmosphere, and was damaging the ozone layer. This coolant is not used now, but old fridges that are being scrapped might contain it. It must be removed carefully so none of it leaks before the rest of the fridge can be disposed of. Fluorescent light tubes contain mercury, which is highly toxic. All mercury must be removed and disposed of safely so it cannot get into water supplies.

Availability factors

Use of stock materials
Materials are processed and sold in standard sizes, called stock materials. For example, acrylic sheet is readily available in 3 mm and 5 mm thick pieces. If you are making a case, you should design it using a standard thickness because if you wanted 4.2 mm thick acrylic you probably would not be able to get it, or it would be very expensive. Electronic components like resistors come in stock sizes. A designer would always use a stock size to keep costs down.

Use of specialist materials
Electronic products often contain specialist materials. This can make manufacturing more difficult, and manufacturers need to find a reliable supply of these materials because production would have to stop if they ran out.

Use of scarce elements
Electronic products contain a lot of rare earth elements, particularly within some of the components and in rechargeable batteries. Manufacturers need to find a reliable supply of these materials, because production would grind to a halt if they ran out. Some come from mines in only one or two countries, for example China.

Cost factors

Quality of components
When components are made, they will not be perfectly accurate. The manufacturer will state the tolerance of a component – this is an upper and a lower value that the component will fall between. The higher the tolerance needed, the more expensive the component will be, because the manufacturing processes will need to be more accurate. If a lower tolerance is good enough, the manufacturer will choose it to reduce costs.

Manufacturing processes necessary
The scale of manufacturing, and the processes needed to make a product, are big factors in the cost. Highly specialised factory equipment can cost a lot of money to set up. If a cheaper process can be used, the cost of the product can be reduced.

Social factors

Use for different social groups
Groups of people of different ages or interests will have different priorities. If a product designer can create a product that is appealing to a particular social group, the product may sell well to that group of people. However, it may be less appealing to other groups, so it can be a difficult balance between different customers' preferences, for example a mobile phone with a keypad will appeal more to one particular group than another.

Trends and fashion
If a product becomes fashionable it will sell well for a while, until the fashion changes and a different product becomes more popular. If a manufacturer can make their product the one everyone wants to have, they will become the market leader and sell well until the trend changes and something else takes over. As an example, 3D televisions were desirable in recent years and all major television manufacturers responded by offering 3D sets. However, their popularity has greatly declined so some manufacturers are no longer making them.

Popularity
The popularity of a product depends on a lot of factors. It has to work well, but it also has to look good and appeal to consumers. Sometimes clever products do not sell well because their appearance does not appeal to intended customers or the product does not have quite the right image. But sometimes a product can become very popular even if it is not the best that is available, simply because it became fashionable – for example celebrities could have been photographed using it.

> **Apply it**
>
> What electronic products can you think of that are fashionable at the moment? What is it about that particular product's use of materials or components that makes it seem desirable?

Cultural and ethical factors

Avoiding offence
It is fairly obvious that, if people find your product offensive, they are not going to buy it. It is less obvious that people in different parts of the world, or different cultures or religions, might be offended by something that is not offensive to the product designer. It is important to understand different cultures and religions so that you can avoid accidentally causing offence with a certain word, symbol or picture.

Suitability for intended market
It is important to understand the intended market for a product, so you can make sure a product is suitable for it. Different countries can use different technology, such as different voltages in their mains electricity, or differently shaped plugs. There is no point trying to sell a product in France with a British plug on it.

5 Systems

It is also important that a product designed for a particular age group is suitable for people of that age. If you are designing a product for teenagers, you need to understand the kind of things that appeal to them, so the product may have different features to a model aimed at their grandparents.

Use of colour and language

Colours often have significance to us and designers can use colour to give a particular feel to a product. However, it is important to remember that not all cultures give the same colours the same significance. For example, yellow is reserved for royalty in Malaysia; in China red is considered lucky and white is associated with death.

Language is important to understand, because the name you gave to your product in English might have a completely different meaning in another language. A product could be technically brilliant, but if it has a name people do not like, it will not sell very well.

The consumer society

In Britain, and much of the richer, developed world, we live in what has been called a consumer society. We are quite wealthy and products are quite cheap, so most people can afford to buy a lot of things they do not really need. There is nothing wrong with people having nice things or useful things if they are affordable, but some people can get themselves into debt buying too many consumer items. Also, we risk using up limited resources too quickly and damaging our environment.

The effects of mass production

Mass production has made products a lot cheaper than they used to be. This means they are more affordable and people can buy more things than they used to be able to. Mass production also means factories are more automated than before. Lots of people used to have jobs in factories making the same thing every day on a production line. Now machines do more of that work so there are fewer jobs. Instead there are jobs for small numbers of engineers and computer programmers to run the machinery.

Built-in product obsolescence

A lot of products have only a short lifespan. Manufacturers can withdraw support for products, making replacement parts unobtainable. This results in new purchases and increased use or rare resources. Manufacturers also deliberately make some products with parts that fail after a time and cannot be replaced.

Mobile phones keep improving, so many people want them for only a couple of years before upgrading to a newer model. A lot of phones now have built-in batteries, so they cannot be replaced. As the batteries lose power and a charge does not last as long, the phone becomes useless. People are expected to throw them away and get a new one, rather than replace the battery.

This process of making products with a short lifespan is called built-in obsolescence. Manufacturers like it because it means people buy new products more often. It is not a very environmentally friendly approach, however, because it means a lot more rubbish is created when people throw things away rather than mending them or just replacing a part.

Summary

Key points to remember:
- Product aesthetics are an important part of customer appeal.
- The RoHS and WEEE directives aim to keep hazardous substances that are used in products out of the environment.
- Manufacturers prefer to use materials that are easily available and will use stock sizes where possible.
- Different social groups have different needs and interests.

Checkpoint

Strengthen
S1 What does the word aesthetics mean?
S2 What is the purpose of the WEEE directive for disposal?
S3 Why is it important for a designer to have some understanding of other cultures?

Challenge
C1 Explain what built-in obsolescence is and the effect you think it might have on the environment.

5.4 The impact of forces and stresses on objects

Learning objectives
By the end of this section, you should know:
- the types of force that can act on a product
- how composite materials combine the properties of different materials.

Forces and stresses

There is a range of different forces and stresses that can act on materials. When designing a product it is important to understand the forces that will be put on it so you can choose the best materials and make the product strong enough.

Tension
A pulling force, like tugging on the ends of a rope.

Compression
A squashing force, like standing on something.

Torsion
A twisting or turning force, like turning a bolt with a spanner.

Shear
Forces in opposite directions, pushing one side up and the other side down, like the cutting action of scissors.

> **Link it up**
>
> For a visual representation of these forces, see page 140 (Figure 3.4.1).

5 Systems

Reinforcement/stiffening techniques

Some materials may need strengthening by the addition of extra materials or by shaping.

Using composite materials

A composite material is two or more different materials mixed together. Reinforced concrete is a composite material. Steel bars are laid into the concrete and make it stronger. Concrete has poor tensile strength, while steel has good tensile strength, so the steel works well to strengthen the concrete.

Some really useful composite materials are fibreglass and carbon fibre. These materials take a woven mat of high-tensile fibres made of either glass or carbon, lay them over a mould and cover them with a plastic resin that sets hard. Several layers of fibre mat and resin are built up. These composite materials are strong and lightweight, for example fibreglass has been used for things like canoe hulls because it is strong and lightweight. Carbon fibre is even stronger and more lightweight and is used for the body panels of high-performance cars. A similar material called Kevlar® is used for police and military equipment such as helmets and bullet-proof vests.

Ribbing to strengthen case structures

Manufacturers want to keep costs as low as possible, so the less material they can use the better. Designers have come up with clever ways to make products strong enough, but reduce the amount of material used. Plastic products, such as storage boxes, often have ribs added to them, so the plastic shell can be thinner and still be strong enough.

Summary

Key points to remember:
- A product needs to be strong enough to withstand the forces that might be put on it: tension (pulling); compression (squashing); torsion (twisting) or shear (opposite directions).
- Fibreglass and carbon fibre use a fibre mat and resin to make a strong, lightweight composite material.
- Intelligent design can increase strength and use less material.

Checkpoint

Strengthen

S1 Draw diagrams to show the following forces:
   a Tension
   b Compression
   c Torsion
   d Shear

S2 What is fibreglass made from?

Challenge

C1 Explain why carbon fibre is stronger than carbon fibre matting or plastic resin are on their own.

5.5 Stock forms of components

> ### Learning objectives
> By the end of this section, you should know:
> - the ways of mounting components onto a circuit board
> - the units used for important quantities
> - how to use Ohm's law
> - how to find the resistance of multiple resistors.

Stock forms/types

Tolerances, ratings and values

Many electronic components, such as resistors, are sold with a range of different values. Not every value of resistance is available, because there would be millions of different ones. Manufacturers decide what values to produce, and a designer will know what these stock sizes are and design a product to use a stock size. A common series of resistor values is the E12 standard. In each interval 1–10, 10–100, 100–1000 etc. the resistors are made in 12 stock values. For the interval 10–100 these are 10, 12, 15, 18, 22, 27, 33, 39, 47, 56, 68, 82. The next set is 100, 120 and so on. E12 resistors usually have a tolerance of ±10 per cent. Most values are catered for in the E12 series, especially when tolerances are considered. However, it is still necessary to use higher tolerance resistors in some instances so extra, more expensive resistors will occasionally be needed.

Most electronic components will also have a maximum rating that they must not exceed. This might be their maximum power or voltage. It is important to use a component with the correct ratings or it could overheat and catch fire. A component in a battery-powered circuit may be rated to 12V, while a component in a mains electricity-powered circuit needs to be rated to 240V.

Surface-mount technology

Surface-mount technology (SMT) is a way of fixing components onto a circuit board. The circuit board has copper tracks with a thin layer of solder on all of the connections. The components are all designed with legs that sit flat on the circuit board. All of the components are laid into place and the board is put in an oven and heated to melt the solder, fixing all of the components in place at the same time. It is faster to manufacture and no drilling is required for most components, but faults are harder to trace. This system works well in manufacturing where robots put the components on lots of circuits, which then go into the heater.

Surface-mount components on a printed circuit board (PCB): note the soldered joints on top of the board

Through-hole components

Through-hole components have wire legs on them that go through holes in a circuit board. The components are placed on the plain side of the board, and the legs go through a hole in the circuit board, where they are soldered onto the copper tracks on the other side. This is a useful method for making a small number of circuits by hand in a workshop and is easy to use for small-scale production or hobbyists. However it is easier to insert components incorrectly.

Through-hole components on a PCB: the legs go through the board and are soldered underneath

5 Systems

Sizes

It is important to know what units to use in calculations. Units are given a symbol that goes after the number. Units can also have a prefix that is a multiplier. The table on page 222 shows some common multiplier prefixes. An amp is a large unit in electronics and a smaller unit called a milliamp (mA) is used. 1 mA is one thousandth of an amp.

Unit of current

Current is a measure of the flow of electricity through a wire. The unit of current is the ampere, usually called the amp. It is given the symbol A.

Unit of resistance

Resistance measures how hard or easy it is for electricity to pass along a wire. The unit of resistance is called the ohm. It is given the symbol Ω (a Greek letter called omega).

Unit of potential difference

Potential difference is usually called voltage. It is the amount of force available to make electricity flow. The unit of voltage is called the volt. It is given the symbol V.

Quantity	Symbol in equation	Unit	Unit symbol
Current	I	amp	A
Resistance	R	ohm	Ω
Voltage (potential difference)	V	volt	V

Table 5.5.1 Unit symbols

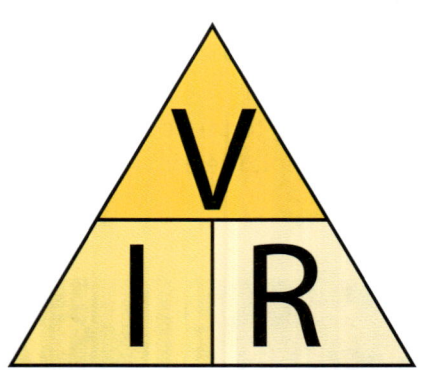

Figure 5.5.1 Ohm's law. This triangle can be a helpful reminder of the equation. Cover up the one you want to find and it shows you whether to multiply or divide the other two.

Ohm's law

There is a relationship between current, resistance and voltage:

- increase resistance and current decreases, because it is harder for the electricity to flow
- increase voltage and current increases, because there is more force to make the electricity flow.

Ohm's law states that voltage = current × resistance

$V = I \times R$

This is a very important equation in electronics, and you will use it a lot. If you know two of the quantities you can find the third by rearranging the equation:

- $V = IR$
- $I = V/R$
- $R = V/I$

5.5 Stock forms of components

> **Maths in practice 1**
> - You have a 9 V battery connected to a bulb. If 50 mA (0.05 A) is flowing through the bulb, what is the resistance of the bulb?
>
> So, we know that: $V = 9$ V and $I = 0.05$ A
>
> Find the right equation and put the numbers in: $R = V/I = 9/0.05 =$ **180 Ω**

> **Exam-style questions**
> 1. You have a 9 V battery and you connect it to a 1000 Ω resistor. Calculate the current that will flow through the resistor. **(3 marks)**
> 2. Mains electricity is 230 V and a lightbulb has 0.5 A flowing through it. Calculate the resistance of the lightbulb. **(3 marks)**
>
> Answers:
> 1. 9 mA
> 2. 460 Ω

> **Exam tip**
> Write down the facts you know. Find the equation that links what you know to what you want to know.

Resistors in series

All electronic components have a resistance, so an electronic circuit will have lots of resistances joined together. It is useful to be able to calculate the total resistance. The term 'in series' means the resistors are joined together one after the other. As the electricity goes through all of them, one after the other, the total resistance is the total of each one added together.

$$R_{total} = R_1 + R_2 + R_3$$

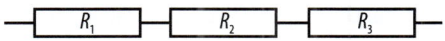

Figure 5.5.2 Resistors in series

Resistors in parallel

Joining resistors in parallel is more complicated. As the electricity can go through two or more resistors at the same time the total resistance is smaller than the individual resistors. You need to add the **reciprocals** of all of the resistors. See calculation on page 222.

$$\frac{1}{R_{total}} = \frac{1}{R_1} + \frac{1}{R_2} + \frac{1}{R_3}$$

$$R_{total} = \frac{1}{\left(\frac{1}{R_1} + \frac{1}{R_2} + \frac{1}{R_3}\right)}$$

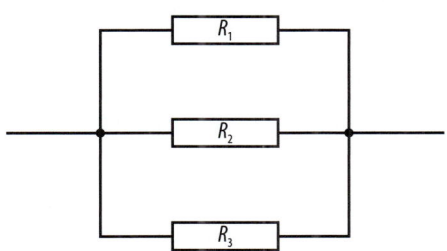

Figure 5.5.3 Resistors in parallel

Area

Area is the amount of space inside a flat shape. It is measured in m², or cm², or mm².

- Rectangle area = length × width
- Triangle area = ½ × width × height
- Circle area = **π** × radius²

π: 3.142

> **Key term**
> **Reciprocal:** 1 divided by the number; $1/x$ is the reciprocal of x.

Diameter

The diameter, Ø, measures the size of a circle, from one side to the other. It is double the radius, which goes from the centre to the edge.

5 Systems

Maths in practice 2

In systems you need to be able to do some maths.

Units

Units can have a prefix that is a multiplier. This is just a short way of writing lots of zeros. The table below shows some common multiplier prefixes.

Prefix	Multiplier	Example
Nano, n	1/1,000,000,000	1 nm = 0.000000001 m 1 m = 1,000,000,000 nm
Micro, µ	1/1,000,000	1 µm = 0.000 001 m 1 m = 1,000,000 µm
Milli, m	1/1000	1 mA = 0.001 A 1 A = 1000 mA
Centi, c	1/100	1 cm = 0.01 m 1 m = 100 cm
Kilo, k	×1000	1 kV = 1000 V
Mega, M	×1,000,000	1 MW = 1,000,000 W
Giga, G	×1,000,000,000	1 GB = 1,000,000,000 B

Table 5.5.2 Prefixes and multipliers

The table shows that 1 km = 1 × 1000 = 1000 m

Worked example

1 km = 1000 m
So 2 km = 2000 m
3.45 km = 3.450 km = 3450 m See how figures move three places to the left?
6789 m = 6789.0 m = 6.789 km See how figures move three places to the right?

Questions

- How many grams (g) are the following?

1 kg
1000 mg
0.275 kg

Answers

1 kg = 1000 g
1000 mg = 1 g
0.275 kg = 275 g

Rearranging an equation

If you have an equation, you can rearrange it to help you find the quantity you need.

E.g. Ohm's law is $V = IR$. So if you know I and R you can find V.

= means equals. Both sides are the same. You can rearrange the equation because if you do the same thing to both sides, the equation is still true.

We know that $6 = 3 \times 2$
Divide both sides by 2: $\frac{6}{2} = \frac{3 \times 2}{2}$
$\frac{2}{2} = 1$, so the 2s cancel: $\frac{6}{2} = \frac{3 \times \cancel{2}}{\cancel{2}}$
leaving us with: $\frac{6}{2} = 3$

We know this is also true. If this works with numbers it also works with letters!

Worked example

We know that: $V = I \times R$
Divide both sides by I: $\frac{V}{I} = \frac{I \times R}{I}$
$\frac{I}{I} = 1$, so the Is are cancelled: $\frac{V}{I} = R$
If $V = IR$, what does I equal?

Reciprocals

The reciprocal of a number is just 1 divided by it.
So the reciprocal of 2 is $\frac{1}{2}$
In the same way, the reciprocal of x is $\frac{1}{x}$
To add resistors in parallel you need to add the reciprocals $\frac{1}{R_{total}} = \frac{1}{R_1} + \frac{1}{R_2}$

Worked example

$R_1 = 400\,\Omega$ and $R_2 = 200\,\Omega$ are connected in parallel, what is R_{total}

We know $\frac{1}{R_{total}} = \frac{1}{R_1} + \frac{1}{R_2}$

So $\frac{1}{R_{total}} = \frac{1}{400} + \frac{1}{200}$

So $\frac{1}{R_{total}} = 0.0025 + 0.005 = 0.0075$

If $\frac{1}{R_{total}} = 0.0075$ we can work out that

$R_{total} = \frac{1}{0.0075} = 133\,\Omega$

Notice that R_{total} is less than the smallest resistor, which is sensible because the electricity had two paths to follow.

Questions

- If a circuit has resistors in parallel, work out R_{total} with resistances of:

1000 Ω and 500 Ω
250 Ω and 500 Ω
100 Ω, 100 Ω and 100 Ω

The formula for resistors in parallel can be rearranged to be easier to use.

$\frac{1}{R_{total}} = \frac{1}{R_1} + \frac{1}{R_2} = \frac{R_2 + R_1}{R_1 \times R_2}$

$R_{total} = \frac{R_1 \times R_2}{R_1 + R_2}$

This only works for two resistors, though.

Answers

$\frac{1}{R_{total}} = \frac{1}{1000} + \frac{1}{500} = 0.003$ $R_{total} = 333.3\,\Omega$

$\frac{1}{R_{total}} = \frac{1}{250} + \frac{1}{500} = 0.006$ $R_{total} = 166.7\,\Omega$

$\frac{1}{R_{total}} = \frac{1}{100} + \frac{1}{100} + \frac{1}{100} = 0.03$ $R_{total} = 33.3\,\Omega$

5.6 Manufacturing processes

> **Summary**
>
> **Key points to remember:**
> - Surface-mount technology solders components on top of the PCB. Through-hole soldering has the component legs going through holes where they are soldered onto the back of the PCB.
> - The unit of current is the amp (A); resistance is the ohm (Ω); voltage is the volt (V).
> - Ohm's law is $V = IR$.
> - Resistors can be joined in series or in parallel, with different ways to calculate the total resistance.

> **Checkpoint**
>
> **Strengthen**
>
> **S1** Does the E12 series of resistors include a resistor of 2700 Ω?
>
> **S2** What is the difference between surface-mount and through-hole soldering?
>
> **Challenge**
>
> **C1** Calculate R_{total} for the following resistors connected in series:
>   - **a** 270 Ω and 330 Ω
>   - **b** 100 Ω, 200 Ω and 300 Ω
>   - **c** 2500 Ω, 500 Ω, 100 Ω and 370 Ω
>
> **C2** Calculate R_{total} for the following resistors connected in parallel:
>   - **a** 100 Ω and 100 Ω
>   - **b** 270 Ω and 330 Ω
>
> Answers:
> 1 a 600 Ω
>   b 600 Ω
>   c 3470 Ω
> 2 a 50 Ω
>   b 148.5 Ω

5.6 Manufacturing processes

> **Learning objectives**
>
> By the end of this section, you should know:
> - how to make a PCB
> - the scales of production of manufacturing processes
> - some of the techniques used in mass production.

Processes

Photo etching

Photo etching is a method of producing printed circuit boards (PCBs). The board is an insulating plastic resin with a thin film of copper covering one side. The copper tracks are made by removing the unwanted copper, leaving just the tracks.

1. A 'mask' is printed onto clear film.
2. The clear film is placed over photosensitive copper board, placed in a light-box and exposed to ultra-violet light.
3. The exposed photo-board is placed in a developer solution that reacts with the unexposed areas of copper.
4. The board now goes into an etch tank, which can contain a solution of warm ferric chloride, or Fine Etch Solution, which is disodium peroxodisulphate hexahydrate.
5. The areas of copper that were exposed to UV light are eaten away in the etch tank, until only the areas of copper that were covered by the mask are left – creating copper tracks that match the original printed design.

Advantages are that it is suitable for school use and the mask can be used many times if stored safely. Disadvantages are that it is a slow process the mask must be correct and etchant becomes saturated with copper and must be treated before disposal.

5 Systems

PCB population

Once the PCB has been made, a hole needs to be drilled on each copper pad that a component leg will be passed through, ready for soldering. A small drill bit, usually about 1.0 mm, is used for the holes. The components are inserted from the blank side and soldered onto the copper pads. This is suitable for school use, but drilling must be accurate. All holes must be drilled in one go, otherwise it may be difficult to drill later once the soldering has commenced and the missing hole is noticed.

Scales of production

Choosing the right scale of production is very important when manufacturing a product. Investing in an expensive factory makes the product cheaper, but you need to sell a lot to pay for the factory. Alternatively, you could contract a supplier to do some of the work in their factory for you.

One-off prototyping

A prototype of a circuit can be made to test the idea to see if it works, before committing to the time and cost of making a PCB. A breadboard is the name given to a plastic block that has holes in, which are joined together in short rows. Components can be slotted into the holes to connect them together. The circuit can be experimented with and components changed until it is working correctly.

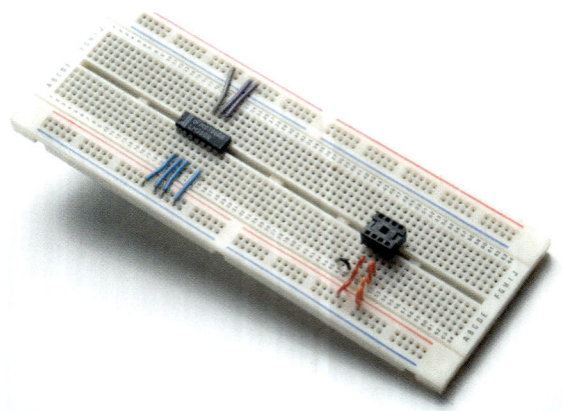

A breadboard for one-off prototyping of a circuit

Batch

A batch is a number of the same thing made at the same time. A simple batch production process might use a **jig** or a **template** to mark out or cut the same shape several times. Photo etching is a batch production method. A sheet of board can have several circuits on it, so, say, 20 could be made at the same time. Although it takes a while to set up, it is quicker than making each one individually. Vacuum forming is another batch production process. Once you have made the **mould** it can be used repeatedly to make lots of identical items. The vacuum former can be used again with a different mould to make other products.

Mass production

Mass production processes make the same product all the time. A factory is often set up to mass produce products. A plastic case might be injection moulded from plastic. The injection moulding machinery will be made for a particular part of a product and it will make that part all day long, day after day. Mass production processes are very expensive to set up, but once they are set up they can make the product cheaply.

> **Key terms**
>
> **Jig:** fits over a piece of material to guide accurate cutting or drilling without needing to mark out.
>
> **Template:** a cut-out of a shape that can be drawn around onto the material to mark out quickly and easily.
>
> **Mould:** a 3D block that material can be formed over or inside.

Continuous

Continuous production is a step up from mass production. Continuous production is used for products for which there is continuing high demand, so the factory will be highly automated and run 24 hours a day, seven days a week. Making and filling milk bottles would be continuous production processes.

Scale	Description	Advantages	Disadvantages
Batch	Several copies of the same product are made at the same time	Jigs, templates and moulds speed up the process and can be kept for future use – special machinery is not needed, so set-up cost is not high	Quite labour intensive, so it is quite expensive per product and it takes time to make jigs, moulds and templates
Mass	Factory machinery is set up to make lots of identical products	Can make a product quickly and cheaply	Machinery is very expensive to set up, so only worthwhile for making a lot of products
Continuous	Factory machinery making the same thing 24/7	Makes the product very quickly and cheaply	Machinery is very expensive to set up, so only worthwhile for making huge quantities of a product

Table 5.6.1 Scales of production

> **Exam-style question**
>
> Explain **one** reason why using jigs and templates makes it cheaper to batch produce products. **(2 marks)**

Techniques for quantity production

Pick and place technology

Components need to be placed on a circuit board in the correct places before soldering. People can do this, but they are slower than machinery. Automated systems called pick and place technology can pick up all of the components and place them in exactly the right place on a circuit board. It costs a lot to set up, but pick and place technology can do this quickly and accurately 24 hours a day. It works particularly well with surface-mount technology.

5 Systems

Surface-mount technology
Originally components went through a hole in the PCB and were soldered on the back by hand. This is still good for a one-off product. Industry now mostly uses surface-mount technology because it is better for mass production techniques, as it is quicker and increases reliability of circuit. The components are laid onto pre-soldered circuit boards with pick and place technology, then heated in an oven to melt the solder and fix the components on. The components need to be heat resistant enough to withstand the ovens used. This is not as suitable for schools and hobbyists.

Quality control
Quality control is a system for trying to ensure the products being manufactured are good enough for sale. It reduces waste and should help customers to receive a more reliable product. At stages through the manufacturing process a sample of the product is inspected to make sure it is correct. The more complex a product is, the more sampling is likely to take place. If the sampling finds a faulty product, the process might be stopped so it can be corrected before many more faulty ones are made. Disadvantages include planning and set-up costs of the system.

Marking-out methods
Marking out is transferring measurements onto material before it is cut, ensuring an accurate outcome. Sometimes manufacturing processes will not need to do marking out if machinery has been set up to process materials automatically. For one-off or batch production marking out is important. A reference point, the point on the material you start measuring from is essential. It could be the bottom left-hand corner, for example, and every measurement is taken from there. It could be any other known point on the material, as long as everything is correctly measured from that one reference point. Sometimes a particular line or surface of the material will be used as the known datum line or point that everything is measured from. This can be time consuming as it requires checks before cutting.

Templates
A template is a cut-out shape that you can draw around to mark out the shape you want to cut from a piece of material. A template might be made from paper or card for a single use, or it might be made from a thin sheet of wood or metal if it is going to be used a lot. A template is really useful in batch production, because it allows workers to mark out and cut the same shape quickly and accurately. It also reduces material waste; templates must be stored safely to prevent damage to its edges.

Patterns
A pattern is used to make an exact copy, for example to make a mould for a resin casting. This allows multiple copies to be made but the pattern must be stored safely to avoid damage to its surface.

Sub-assembly
A finished product has lots of parts that need assembly. A complex product will usually be made up of lots of sub-assemblies. These are parts of the product that

have been put together, often in one factory, then sent to another factory for the final product to be assembled from all of the sub-assemblies. For example, an electronic/digital musical keyboard may have a PCB produced in one factory, a power supply in another, and a case and keyboard in other factories, before all of these sub-assemblies are finally put together to create the finished product. Only sub-assemblies are likely to be available for repair purposes. For example, a broken key will require the replacement of the whole keyboard.

Working within tolerance

Manufactured parts always have a tolerance. It is the range of sizes within which the part is acceptable. Machining within tolerances ensures a high-quality item that will always fit other associated parts. The designer will need to specify a tolerance for a part. If you are cutting telegraph poles to length, a 100 mm error will not matter. If you are assembling the insides of a smartphone, however, a 1 mm error would be unacceptable. Building blocks are made to a tolerance ±0.04 mm (or +0.08 – 0.00). Manufacturing processes must be able to produce the right tolerance, and part of quality control is checking the parts are all within the required tolerance, which involves additional costs. Parts of a product are often made in different factories so stating the acceptable tolerance for every part is essential for the parts to fit together.

Efficient cutting to minimise waste

Material costs money, so it is important to use as little as possible when making products. This includes minimising waste to save money and resources. When cutting out materials, using a template to mark out shapes so they fit as close together as possible, rotating the template if necessary, can significantly reduce the amount of waste. This can increase initial costs with regard to the additional time required in the design and planning stages.

Summary

Key points to remember:
- A PCB is created using photo etching, by dissolving the unwanted copper to leave copper tracks behind.
- Production can be one-off, batch, mass or continuous.
- The scale of production chosen depends on how many products will be made.

Checkpoint

Strengthen

S1 What is a 'breadboard' used for?
S2 What is a template?
S3 Why is it important to specify the tolerance needed for a part?

Challenge

C1 If you wanted 50 of the same product what scale of production would probably be best? Why?
C2 If you wanted 10,000 of the same product what scale of production would probably be best? Why?

5 Systems

5.7 Processes for fabricating a prototype

> **Learning objectives**
>
> By the end of this section, you should know:
> - the hand tools that can be used to put together a circuit
> - some of the machinery that can help with making a circuit or a case prototype.

Tools and equipment

Hand tools

> **Link it up**
>
> There are many hand tools for working wood, metal and plastics covered in other chapters in this book, see pages 108–115, 192–94, 298–300.

Soldering iron

Solder is a metal alloy that melts at about 180 °C. A soldering iron has an electric heater that heats its tip up to about 300 °C. This will melt solder easily, but it will not damage the copper on the PCB, which melts at over 1000 °C. When soldering individual components by hand, the soldering iron is a good way to melt the solder to form the joints between components and the PCB.

Electric soldering iron and stand

Wire strippers

Electrical wire has a copper core that conducts electricity, covered with a plastic sheath for insulation. Where a wire is joined to a component, the plastic insulation needs to be removed to get to the bare copper. Wire strippers are a good tool for doing this. Put the wire in the jaws, close them to cut the insulation but not the copper core, and pull to remove the insulation.

Wire strippers

Side cutters

Side cutters are used to cut a wire, or cut the leg of a soldered component off, flat against the board. The cutting jaws are at one side of the cutting head, so they can cut flat against a PCB.

Side cutters

Needle nosed pliers

Needle nosed pliers are a useful tool for holding small components in place and bending pieces of wire.

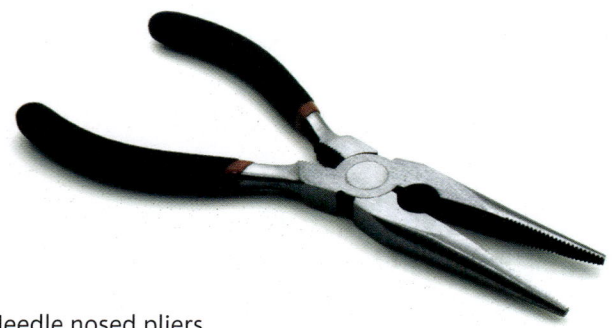

Needle nosed pliers

Solder sucker

If a component needs to be removed from a PCB a soldering iron can be used to heat the solder until it melts. It is usually possible to pull the component out when the solder is melted, but it is easier to remove the melted solder with a solder sucker. Depress the button on the end, then when you push the little release button the mechanism pops up and sucks through the nozzle, sucking up melted solder.

Screwdriver

A screwdriver is used to put screws in. They can have a flat head or a cross head, known as a Phillips screwdriver. Screwdrivers are useful for assembling parts of a product.

Machinery

CNC milling machine

A CNC milling machine has a cutting tool that can move left to right, forwards and backwards, and up and down. This can be used to engrave away the unwanted copper areas on a PCB to make the tracks. A PCB design can be drawn using a PCB design software package, and sent to the CNC mill to cut the tracks. It is a good way to make a one-off or a small batch, but it is slower than photo-etching for making lots.

PCB drill

A pillar drill can be used to drill the holes in a PCB, but a PCB drill is more convenient. The PCB drill is a small drill that has a stand to hold the drill and a handle to pull the drill tip down, just like the much bigger pillar drill.

Digital design and manufacture

Computers are a useful tool to help with the design and manufacture of products. Some uses are:

- simulate a circuit, to see if the idea works before making it
- draw the PCB, and print a mask for etching
- control a computer numerically controlled (CNC) milling machine to engrave a PCB
- draw a 3D model of the product casing to help develop the design
- control CNC equipment like a milling machine, laser cutter or 3D printer to make parts.

Advantages are that computer modelling can test ideas, which saves time making prototypes that do not work, and that CNC manufacture is faster and more accurate than hand processes.

Disadvantages are the cost of the equipment and that specialist training is often needed to use the software and equipment.

Solder sucker

A CNC mill

> **Apply it**
>
> Describe the correct technique for using a soldering iron to solder a component onto a circuit board.

5 Systems

Shaping

Vacuum forming

A heated sheet of polymer is forced down over the mould by air pressure due to a temporary vacuum being created beneath the air-tight seal around the sheet of polymer. The mould needs to be suitable. It should have tapered sides so it is easier to lift the plastic off the mould. It should also have rounded edges and corners so it does not tear the soft plastic.

It is quick to make once the mould has been made, so it is good for making a batch of identical products. It is possible to produce more complex shapes using vacuum forming, but the design of the mould is critical to ensure the plastic moulding can be released from the mould.

> **Link it up**
>
> For more information about vacuum forming, look at page 193.

CNC laser cutting

A laser cutter is a computer-controlled machine that uses a laser to cut through materials. The computer sends instructions to the machine, which guides the laser beam by moving mirrors to direct the laser beam along the coordinates given. Laser cutters are good for cutting wood and plastic as they cut quickly and accurately. However, there are also disadvantages: laser cutters can burn the edges of wood, they are expensive, they can cut only thin materials, they do not cut metals, the smoke is toxic and needs filtering, and the design needs to be drawn on a computer.

3D printing

A drawing is made in 3D software and converted into a .stl file that can be sent to the 3D printer. The 3D printer uses a nozzle that heats a thin plastic filament and moves the nozzle over the bed of the machine, building up the object a thin layer at a time. 3D printers can make complex 3D shapes and one-off products can be made that would need a complex mould to make any other way. They are a good way for making prototypes. Disadvantages include their slow speed, as it takes several hours to produce a product, and the fact that they can use only some types of plastic, which limits what they can be used for. 3D drawing software can also be quite complicated to use.

Drilling

Drilling makes a round hole in material. It is useful for making cases, to make holes to put screws in or wires through. Battery-powered cordless drills are useful to use by hand. Pillar drills are useful for accurate work, as they can get the hole at 90 degrees to the work surface easily. Drilling is quick and easy and lots of things can go through a round hole. While drilling is generally used to produce round holes, it is possible to use the machine to cut other apertures by drilling a series of holes (called chain drilling) inside a marked-out shape and then use saws and files to obtain the desired shape.

Fabricating, constructing and assembling

PCB mounting methods

A PCB with all of the components soldered onto it needs to be mounted in a case so that it is protected, to stop the board getting bent or the components getting damaged. It also looks neat and professional. Some mass-produced PCBs are mounted with a system that makes repair difficult or impossible. A PCB is often screwed onto a raised boss or has its legs moulded into part of the case, so that there is a gap between the board and case for the components. A range of ready-made mounts/pillars are available that fit through holes drilled into the PCB. Consideration should be given to where the mounts will be placed when designing the PCB and its case.

Cable management

A lot of components, particularly input and output devices and power supplies, are joined to the rest of the product with cables. It is important to manage cables to prevent them from getting damaged or tangled up. A wiring loom has a bundle of cables running through the product. These can be held together with cable ties, tape or by enclosing them in plastic sleeving. Correct cable management will contribute to the production of a reliable product. Time at the design stage is needed for this though. Where cables enter a device they must be secured so that the soldered joint is not put under strain, because a wire soldered onto a circuit can break off easily. Cable strain relief can be obtained by using commercial plugs/sockets and connectors. Threading a cable through an additional hole drilled in the PCB is a simple way to provide strain relief. The use of coloured cables can ensure accurate connections, for example coloured ribbon cable.

Wastage

Wastage is a process that starts with a piece of material and cuts material away to leave what is required for the product. Hand tools can be used to cut material away. A milling machine cuts material away from a block to leave the shape required for the product. The product is made from a solid piece of material with no joints or fixings needed, so it will be strong. A disadvantage is that a lot of material is wasted because it is not possible to use all the material that was cut away. However, in industry, waste material, for example waste metal cuttings (called swarf), are sold back to steel producers to be reused in new metal production, for example brass and steel.

Addition

Addition is a process that puts materials together to form the required shapes. Materials can be cut into shapes with hand tools and fixed together with joints, adhesives, mechanical fixings such as screws and rivets, and by heat, including soldering, brazing and welding. 3D printing is also an addition process, because plastic is added to build up the required design. Addition is an efficient use of material, as pieces are cut to the right size with little wastage. However, there are often lots of joins between pieces of material, so it is difficult to make the product strong.

Summary

Key points to remember:
- A soldering iron is used to melt solder for soldering components onto a PCB.
- CNC mills and laser cutters are a quick and accurate way to make parts of a product once the design is drawn in suitable software.
- Vacuum forming uses a mould to make a plastic shell.
- 3D printing makes complex shapes, but can be slow and hard to use.

Checkpoint

Strengthen

S1 Name three hand tools that might be useful to make circuit prototypes.
S2 Suggest two things a computer could help with when designing or making an electronic product.
S3 Give an example of a product that would be created using vacuum forming.

Challenge

C1 Find out the best technique for soldering a joint with a soldering iron and describe the process.
C2 Give an advantage of wastage processes and an advantage of addition processes.

5 Systems

5.8 Surface finishes and treatments

> **Learning objective**
>
> By the end of this section, you should know:
> - how to apply a range of surface finishes to products.

Surface finishes and treatments

There are a range of different surface finishes and treatments that can be applied to materials. Some are applied to protect the material. Some are applied for decoration. Some are good at doing both.

Metal plating

A metal product can have its surface plated with a thin layer of a different metal. This is often so most of the product is made with a cheap metal and then coated with a more expensive one to make it look better, to prevent corrosion or to improve its properties. Steel can rust, so it is often coated with chromium, which provides corrosion resistance, but ultimately will not stop rusting, although it does gives an aesthetically pleasing finish. Contacts in a high-performance electronic product might be made of copper plated with gold, because the gold surface does not tarnish and conducts electricity better.

Insulating coatings

Electrical wires need to transport electricity from one place to another. Copper wires are coated with an insulator, usually a plastic called PVC. This prevents wires touching each other or the case of the product by accident, causing what is known as a short circuit.

Some electrical products that use mains electricity have an insulating case, so that if there is a fault with the product the case does not conduct electricity.

Resistor colour codes

The resister codes we looked at earlier in the chapter are a way of using a finish on the surface of the resistor to create the colour bands that are used to identify its value.

Finishes applied to cases

Finishes are applied to the surface of a product. Some finishes are to protect the surface. Some finishes are for decoration. Most do a bit of both. Some examples of finishes that might be applied to the case of electronic products are shown in Table 5.8.1.

5.8 Surface finishes and treatments

Finish	Description	Advantages	Disadvantages
Anodising	• A piece of metal, often aluminium alloy, is dipped in acid and electricity passed through it • The acid reacts with the surface to form a thin surface layer that is resistant to corrosion • It can be dyed to make the product a bright colour	• Stops the surface from corroding • Can be coloured • Gives a very smooth finish	• Can be scratched away • Only works on some metals
Painting	• Paint is particles in a liquid that hardens as the liquid dries out • Applied to the surface of a material with a brush or spray	• Available in almost any colour • Protects a material from corrosion or rotting • Easy to apply to most materials	• Can fade in sunlight and wear away • Scratches and damages fairly easily
Screen printing	• The screen is a mask that goes over the surface • Paint is scraped over the surface, sticking to the exposed areas	• Can paint a complex design onto a surface • Can be done in full colour	• Only works on a flat surface • Full colour requires four separate screens

Table 5.8.1 Finishing for cases

Summary

Key points to remember:
- Electroplating puts a layer of a different metal onto a metal object.
- Electrical products need insulating coatings, which can be coloured plastic.
- Anodising is a surface treatment for some metals, usually for aluminium.
- Paint is a decorative coating that also provides some protection to the material.

Checkpoint

Strengthen

S1 What materials can electroplating and anodising be used on?
S2 Why are copper electrical cables covered with plastic?

Challenge

C1 Plastic is sometimes called self-finishing. What do you think this means?
C2 What finish would you use for the following products? Say why.
  a A steel light fitting
  b The plastic case of a cordless drill
  c The aluminium case of an expensive smartphone.

Preparing for your exam 5

Exam strategy

What to expect in the exam

Section B of the examination is designed to test your knowledge and understanding of the material studied. Throughout the course you should practise exam-style questions that will challenge your knowledge across all sections of the systems content. Different-style exam questions can require short answers, long answers, sketching and calculations. Preparing thoroughly for your exam is important if you are to achieve high marks.

Section B: Material category – Systems

This section is worth 60 marks and contains a mixture of different question styles, including short answer, sketching, calculation and extended open-response questions. This will include 5 marks for calculations.

In the systems category you should know about:

- some design contexts
- the sources, origins, physical and working properties of components and systems and their social and ecological footprint
- the way in which the selection of components and systems is influenced
- the impact of forces and stresses on objects and how they can be reinforced and stiffened
- stock forms, types and sizes to calculate and determine the quantity of components required
- alternative processes that can be used to manufacture components and systems to different scales of production
- specialist techniques and processes that can be used to shape, fabricate, construct and assemble a high-quality systems prototype
- appropriate surface treatments and finishes that can be applied to components and systems for functional and aesthetic purposes.

Revision tips

- Ensure you start revising in plenty of time before your exam. You will find it easier to remember facts you have revised several times over a few weeks than those you have tried to memorise at the last minute.
- Make clear and well-ordered notes about all the sections that relate to the core and your chosen material category.
- Test yourself at the end of each section. Work through the exam-style questions and complete activities to reinforce your knowledge and understanding.
- Work through all sample assessment materials, including past papers available from Pearson.
- Identify the areas where you are likely to get mathematical questions and practise the sections on numerical computation, handling data, rearranging and using equations.
- Discuss the course with your teacher and peers as it will help your understanding.
- Work through corrections and identify areas where you may need further practice.
- Use online or other resources to extend your understanding of the design and technology context.

Preparing for your exam 5

Exam tips

- You should plan to leave 60 minutes for answering questions in Section B.
- You must answer all the questions. If you are stuck on one, leave it and come back to it at the end.
- Although the questions will be different for each paper you sit, there is information on the page to help you answer the question. For example, the number of marks awarded for each question will tell you the number of separate points that need to be given in your answer.
- Pay attention to the command words used in the question as these will guide you in how best to communicate your answers.
- Underline or highlight keywords in the question. After answering the question, read the question again to ensure you have done what was asked.
- If you have time available, plan the structure for long answers and make sure you give good examples where needed.
- Check through your answers at the end of the exam. Make sure you have included units and shown the workings for calculations.

Sample answers with comments

The following questions give some examples of how to interpret the different command words.

Question 1: Explain

a) Figure PE5.1 shows a simple circuit for a safety night light to go on a child's rucksack. When it gets dark the LDR and transistor turn on the bulb.

The bag light needs to meet the following specifications:

- It must have an on/off switch.
- It must have an LED output.
- The light level it comes on at must be adjustable.

Use notes and/or sketches to show how the circuit could be modified to include these three specification points. **(6 marks)**

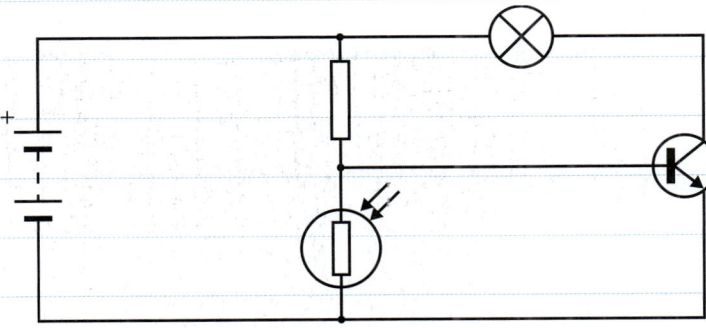

Figure PE5.1 A circuit for a safety night light on a child's rucksack

> **Exam tip**
>
> There are three separate changes to make to the circuit. Work out what they are, then try to draw the circuit using the correct circuit symbols.

Preparing for your exam 5

Student answer

a)

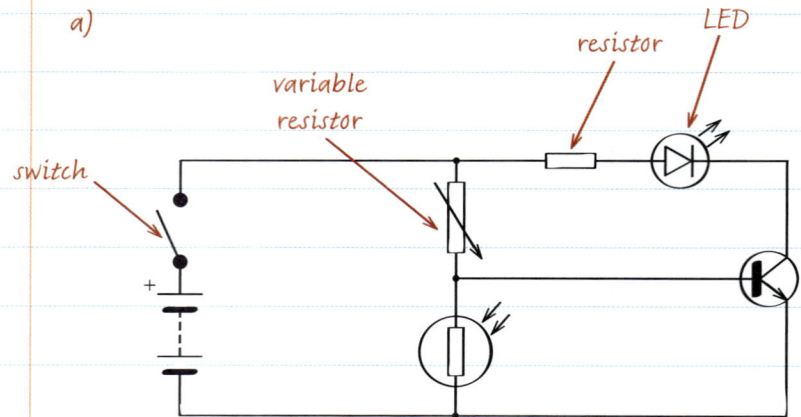

b) The transistor circuit could be replaced by a programmable interface controller (PIC). Explain one reason for using a PIC rather than a transistor. **(2 marks)**

Verdict

This answer is okay. The correct components have been added using the correct symbols, however, a resistor should be present at the base of the transistor. Although the labels are not really needed, it is a good idea to add them, so, for example, if a circuit symbol was wrong but correctly labelled you might get some marks.

Exam tip

Think about things a PIC can do that a transistor can't, and how the PIC could make the product more desirable.

Student answer

The PIC can be programmed, so LEDs could be made to flash or light up in different patterns or sequences. This would make the product more interesting, and a flashing light shows up better to motorists, so it would be safer.

c) Figure PE5.2 shows a child's rucksack with LEDs that light up and flash when it gets dark. The following list includes some specifications for the product.
  - The batteries must last at least four hours.
  - The lights automatically come on in the dark.
  - It must be water resistant.
  - It must have different flash patterns.
  - It must have adjustable sensitivity.
  - It must have an on/off switch.

Explain **two** ways the rucksack safety lights meet or fail to meet the criteria to keep children safer at night. **(4 marks)**

Verdict

This is detailed and thoughtful answer.

Figure PE5.2 A child's rucksack with LED lights

Exam tip

Decide which features of the product help to keep a child safer.

Student answer

It lights up.

Verdict

This is a poor answer. Although the answer is correct, this question needs two points, with well-explained reasons. A better answer would be:
1. The LED lights flash, which makes the child more visible to motorists at night.
2. The LED lights automatically come on when it gets dark, so the child cannot forget to turn them on.

Preparing for your exam 5

d) Explain one method of improving the product.
(2 marks)

Exam tip
Identify a potential problem with the product, then think of a way to solve that problem.

Student answer

There should be a warning when the batteries are getting low, so they can be changed or recharged before they go flat.

Verdict
This is a good answer. It would solve a problem with the product.

Question 2: Calculate

a) An LED output in a circuit will need a current limiting resistor.
Ohms law is $V = I \times R$
The battery supplies 9V
The LED used needs a maximum of 2V and a current of 20mA
Calculate the value of the resistor needed. (2 marks)

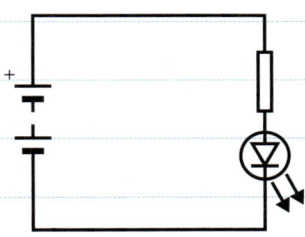

Figure PE5.3 A circuit diagram

Exam tip
Remember the current will be the same all around the circuit, while the voltage is split between the LED and the resistor.

Student answer

V across the resistor is 9 − 2 = 7V
I through resistor = 20mA = 0.02A
R = V/I = 7/0.02 = 350Ω

Verdict
This is correct. The student has shown how they worked it out, which is important. You should always show your working out in a calculation question.

b) Resistors have a tolerance. If the resistor chosen in part a) has a tolerance of ±10 per cent calculate the range of values the resistor could have. (2 marks)

Exam tip
Calculate the 10 per cent first.

Student answer

10% of 350Ω = 350 × 10/100 = 35Ω
The resistor is between 350 − 35 and 350 + 35 = 315Ω and 385Ω

Verdict
This is a good answer.

c) Explain one reason why a systems designer should use standard values for components.
(2 marks)

Exam tip
For two marks you need to give a good reason with a clear explanation of why it is important.

Student answer

Cheaper.

Verdict
This is a poor answer. Even though it is correct, more explanation must be given. For example, a company making resistors will make them in a range of set values because it is much cheaper than trying to make every value. So a system designer needs to use a resistor value that is readily available to keep costs down.

Preparing for your exam 5

Question 3: Discuss

Figure PE5.4 shows the circuit components for a simple mono amplifier.

a) Use notes and/or sketches to show a mould that could be used to vacuum form a suitable case for the amplifier. **(6 marks)**

Student answer

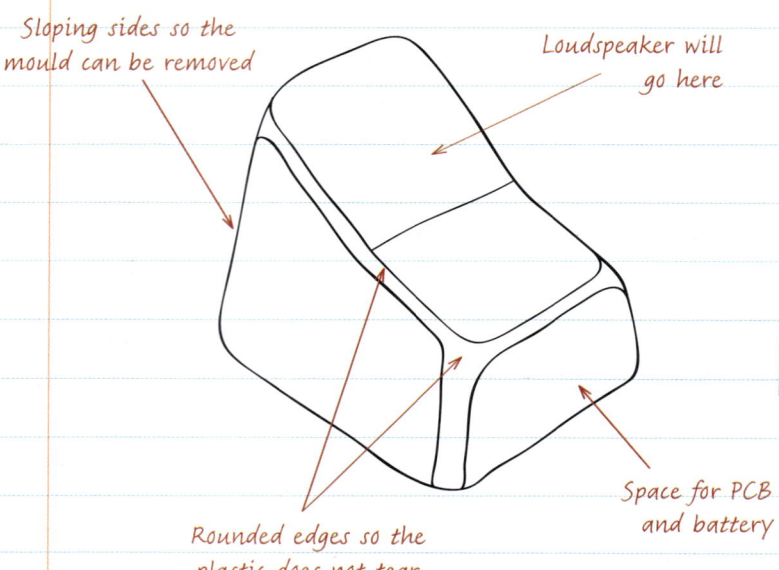

- Sloping sides so the mould can be removed
- Loudspeaker will go here
- Rounded edges so the plastic does not tear
- Space for PCB and battery

b) Explain **one** reason why vacuum forming is a good process to use to manufacture a batch of 50 identical cases. **(2 marks)**

Student answer

Once the mould has been made the vacuum former will make all of the cases the same because they are being formed over the same mould every time.

c) Explain **one** working property of high-impact polystyrene (HIPS) that makes it suitable for vacuum forming the case. **(2 marks)**

Student answer

HIPS is a thermoplastic that can be softened and moulded into a new shape by heating it and stretching it over a mould.

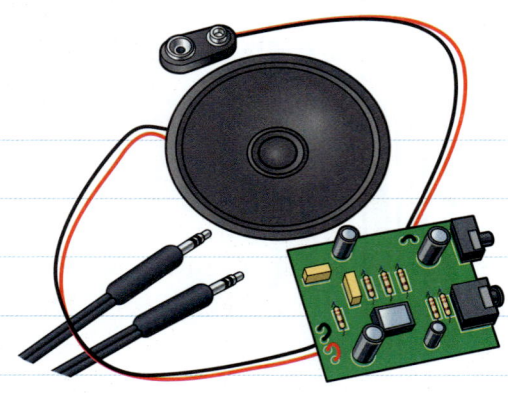

Figure PE5.4 The circuit components for a simple mono amplifier

Exam tip

There are two main points to consider: how the case can house the components and what the important features of a vacuum-forming mould are.

Verdict

This is a good answer. The student has drawn a design that is suitable for the product and suitable for a vacuum-forming mould. Notice how the labels are used to point out features of the design and explain them clearly.

Exam tip

State a reason and say why this is the case.

Verdict

This is a good answer.

Exam tip

Think what properties are needed for vacuum forming and what properties HIPS has.

Verdict

This is a good answer as it shows an understanding of the properties of the material. Saying it will take a high impact is not a good answer as it doesn't show much understanding of the material and is a guess based on the name. HIPS is just a denser form of polystyrene than the expanded polystyrene that is used to make packaging.

Preparing for your exam 5

d) Explain **two** quality control checks that could be carried out on the plastic case during the manufacturing process. (4 marks)

Exam tip

Quality control should make sure the product is being made correctly.

Student answer

Make sure there are no cracks and they are all the right colour.

Verdict

This a weak answer. The points are correct, but more explanation of the points is needed for four marks. The following would be a better answer.

1. Check that the plastic is fully moulded around the bottom edges of the mould. If it isn't, the plastic may not be getting hot enough.
2. Check that there are no blistered areas of plastic. If there are, the plastic is getting too hot before moulding.

Question 4: Evaluate

Figure PE5.5 shows a remote-controlled drone.

Some features of the drone include:
- lightweight construction
- rechargeable batteries.

Materials used are:
- some different types of plastic
- aluminium
- copper
- tin and traces of other metals in the electronics
- lithium in the batteries.

Evaluate the drone in terms of its ecological footprint. (9 marks)

Figure PE5.5 A remote-controlled drone

Exam tip

Spend a bit of time thinking through your answer before you start writing. It might help to make a list of points to include before you start writing your answer.

Student answer

The plastics used in the drone are made from crude oil, which comes out of the ground and has a limited supply. The metals used are mined and extracted from rock, which uses a lot of energy for processing and shipping around the world. None of the materials used are sustainable.

The drone uses a small amount of electricity to recharge its batteries.

When the drone comes to the end of its life it will be disposed of. The materials used make it very hard to recycle. There are different plastics used, mixed in with other materials, so they would be hard to separate for recycling. The metals used, such as the tin in the solder and lithium in the batteries, would be very hard to remove from the product. They can do environmental damage if they are thrown into landfill, where they can leech into the ground and get into water supplies.

The ecological footprint of the drone is high, because it uses a lot of different materials that are not sustainable and it cannot be recycled. How bad it is depends on how long it lasts. If it breaks quite quickly and gets thrown away and replaced, it is worse than if it lasted a long time.

Verdict

This is a good answer because it analyses the materials used for the main parts of the product lifecycle (manufacture, use, disposal). It finishes with a clear conclusion.

Pearson Education Ltd accepts no responsibility whatsoever for the accuracy or method of working in the answers given.

6 Fibres and textiles

6.1 Design contexts

Getting started
With so many fibres and fabrics to choose from, you need to look at the advantages and disadvantages of each before choosing the most suitable for your design projects. Look at what you are wearing today. Can you identify any of the fabrics? Do you know of any social or ecological implications relating to them?

While you are designing and developing or modifying your textile products you will have certain fabrics in mind. To make the right choices, you need to understand that the following factors affect the performance, look and cost of the finished product.

- **Fibre content:** should it be made of natural or synthetic fibres?
- **Fabric construction:** should it be woven, knitted or non-woven, for example?
- **The components:** are they available to you, to join the product and make it function – for example, zips and poppers?
- **Manufacturing processes:** should it be dyed, printed, mechanically finished or chemically finished?
- **The performance requirements:** how much wear will the product get?
- **The social and environmental impact:** does producing the fabric damage the environment or cause problems for nearby communities?

6.2 Properties of fibres and social implications

Learning objectives
By the end of this section, you should know:
- the properties and uses of a larger range of natural and synthetic fibres
- the origins of some fibres.

Natural fibres

Link it up
From Topic 1.11 (see page 47) you know that natural fibres are obtained from plant, animal and mineral sources.

Wool and cotton were covered in the core content section of this book. To remind yourself, see also page 47.

Fibres from plant sources include cotton, linen, hemp, sisal, jute and coconut. Fibres from animal sources include silk, wool and mohair.

6 Fibres and textiles

Table 6.2.1 looks more closely at silk, a natural fibre spun by a silkworm into a cocoon, which is carefully unravelled to make a long filament, and linen, a natural fibre that comes from the flax plant.

	Animal – silk	**Vegetable – linen**
Properties	Fibre is long, strong, smooth and has good light-reflective properties, which give the fibre lustre	Coarse, stiff fibre
Structure	*Diagram showing raw silk filament, sericin, fibroin strands, fibroin bundle, micro-fibrils, leaflet structure*	*Diagram showing cell wall, lumen, micro-fibrils, primary wall, secondary wall, orientation angle, middle lamella*
Advantages	• Excellent **drape** • Luxurious feel • Feels the correct temperature • Absorbent and dries quickly • Takes dye well	• More absorbent than cotton • Hardwearing • Strong especially when wet • Comfortable to wear
Disadvantages	• Difficult to care for • Expensive • Easily damaged by acids, bleach, perspiration and sunlight	• No drape • Poor elasticity and resilience • Creases easily, dull lustre
Example uses	Formal dresses, ties, luxury underwear	Tableware, bedding, clothing

Table 6.2.1 Properties and structure of two natural fibres – silk and linen

> **Apply it**
> Silk is stronger than steel, weight for weight. Find three uses of silk where this strength is utilised.

> **Key term**
> **Drape:** a fabric's ability to form waves or the desired shape as it is hung.

Synthetic fibres

In Section 1.11 you learned that **synthetic** fabrics are textiles made from artificial rather than natural fibres. Coal, oil and other petrol-based chemicals are their raw materials. Simple chemical molecules called monomers are joined to form polymers, using a process called polymerisation. The polymer chains are then spun into a **yarn**. Examples of synthetic fabrics include polyester, acrylic, polyamide (nylon), elastane and Kevlar®.

> ### Link it up
> Polyester and acrylic were covered in the core content (Section 1) of this book. To remind yourself, look at page 48.

Regenerated fibres are derived from wood pulp. A chemical is added to dissolve and extract the cellulose. The fibre is then reconstructed.

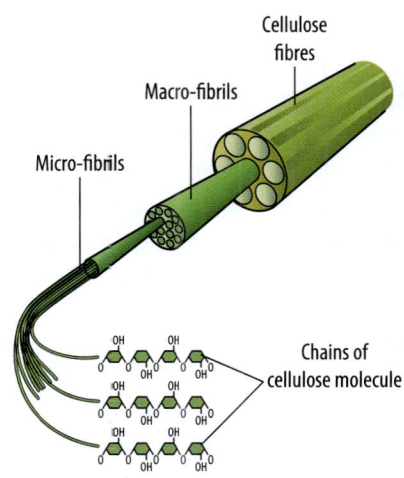

Figure 6.2.1 Structure of regenerated cellulose fibres

	Viscose	Acetate	Tencel® (lyocell)
Advantages	• Washes well, has low warmth, absorbent • Good drape	• Luxurious appearance, warm, resilient, crisp texture • Takes dye well	• Soft, absorbent and strong when wet or dry • Good drape, resilient, biodegradable, takes dye well
Disadvantages	• Not durable, creases easily	• Heat sensitive, poor abrasion resistance, dissolved by nail polish remover • More expensive than viscose	• More expensive than other environmentally friendly fabrics
Example uses	• Shirts, dresses, linings	• Dresses, linings, soft furnishings	• Dresses, trousers, jeans

Table 6.2.2 Advantages and disadvantages of regenerated cellulose textiles

	Polyamide (nylon)	Elastane
Advantages	Durable, inexpensive, strong, elastic, resists alkalis	Elastic, durable, keeps its shape, lightweight but strong
Disadvantages	Damaged by acids and sunlight, poor absorbency	Poor absorbency (an advantage when used for sports and swimwear)
Example uses	Carpets, ropes, outerwear, clothing, webbing straps	Sportswear, swimwear, blended with other fibres such as cotton to improve stretch, e.g. stretch denim jeans

Table 6.2.3 Advantages and disadvantages of synthetic textiles – polyamide (nylon) and elastane

> ### Key term
> **Yarn:** a twisted rope of fibres for knitting, weaving or sewing.

> ### Exam-style question
> Cycling shorts may contain 80 per cent polyamide and 20 per cent elastane. Explain **one** working property of polyamide that makes it suitable for use in cycling shorts. **(3 marks)**

6 Fibres and textiles

Woven fabrics

> **Link it up**
>
> From Topic 1.11 you know that weaving is the process of turning yarns into a fabric. You will have read about plain (calico) and twill (denim) woven fabrics on page 49. You can also remind yourself about warp- and weft-knitted fabrics in Topic 1.11 on page 49.

A loom is used to hold an arrangement of vertical threads or **warp** threads held under tension. The yarn that goes across horizontally is called the **weft**. The edges of the fabric where the weft threads loop back to form a non-fraying edge are known as the **selvedge**. Fabrics can also be constructed by knitting. There are two types of knitted fabrics: weft-knitted and warp-knitted.

> **Key terms**
>
> **Warp:** vertical threads in a fabric.
> **Weft:** horizontal threads in a fabric.
> **Selvedge:** edges of the fabric where the weft threads loop back to form a non-fraying edge.

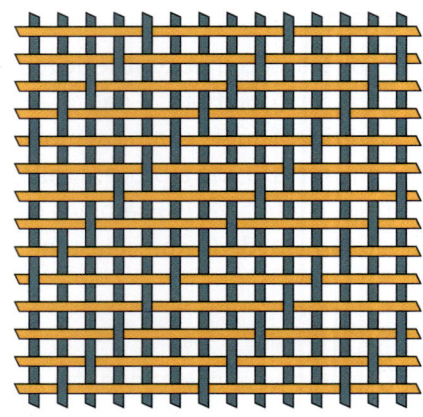

Figure 6.2.2 Satin weave

Satin-weave fabric

Satin weave has a shiny 'right' side and a matt 'wrong' side. On the shiny side, the weft threads go over more than four warp threads and under one.

The long 'float' threads mean the light falling on the yarn does not scatter and break up so the fabric appears shiny and lustrous.

Pile fabric

Pile fabric is woven in two thicknesses facing each other. After it comes off the loom, a knife cuts between the layers to create a cut pile.

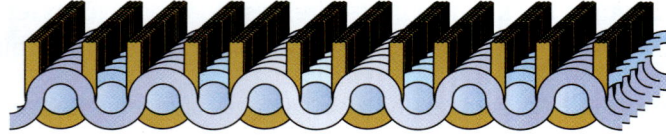

Figure 6.2.3 Pile weave

It can be made with a variety of fibres including cotton, silk or synthetics. Velvet is a pile fabric with a fibrous, tufted finish and a smooth feel. It is heavy and durable with a strong sheen. Silk velvet has a soft drape and shimmering surface, while synthetic velvets, such as those made from rayon and acetate, have a strong sheen but do not drape well.

	Satin – jacquard	Pile – velvet
Advantages	• Complex and textured patterns and colours possible • Strong and resilient	• Looks luxurious • Warm
Disadvantages	• Complex to set up • Firm fabric	• Heavy • The cut edges fray
Example uses	• Clothing (e.g. baseball jackets, sports shorts and lingerie) • Soft furnishings, ballet shoes and bed sheets	• Clothing • Outerwear • Soft furnishings

Table 6.2.4 Advantages and disadvantages of woven fabrics – jacquard and velvet

> **Apply it**
>
> To understand how jacquard fabric is constructed, cut a small piece of furnishing-style fabric, turn it over onto the reverse side and identify the number of colours used. It may help to start to fray it.

Non-woven textiles

Fibres can be turned into fabric without first spinning them into yarns. The fibres are layered at different angles to form a web held together by either felting or bonding.

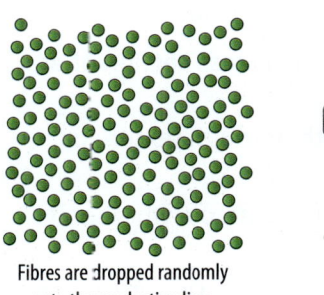
Fibres are dropped randomly onto the production line.

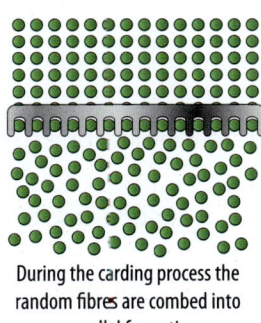
During the carding process the random fibres are combed into a parallel formation.

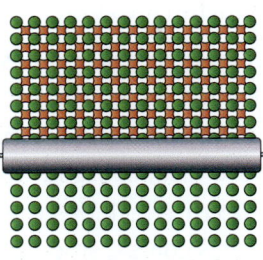
The combed fibres pass through high-pressure heated rollers and become thermally bonded.

Figure 6.2.4 Making a bonded web textile

Bonded fabrics were developed to make the first disposable nappies. Vilene®, in Table 6.2.5, is an example of a bonded non-woven fabric that you may have used in project work.

> **Link it up**
> For more information on fibres, see page 50.

> **Apply it**
> Collect a range of different types of Vilene® and create a sample board, suggesting uses for each.

Type	Bonded webs – Vilene®
Description	Iron-on Vilene® has a layer of adhesive on one side. It comes in a range of thicknesses from lightweight to firm.
Advantages	Easy and cheap to produce, little waste, no grain, will not fray, good insulator, range of weights
Disadvantages	No drape, distorted by stretching, quite weak, the surface can easily bobble
Example uses	Disposable clothing/overalls, interfacing used to stiffen fabrics

Table 6.2.5 Advantages and disadvantages of Vilene®

Fabric	Origin
Cotton	China, India, Pakistan, USA
Silk	China, India, Uzbekistan
Flax, linen	Belgium, Canada, France, Russia, Ukraine
Wool	Australia, China, New Zealand, United Kingdom, USA
Regenerated fibres	Alpine forests are a source of pine, spruce and hemlock trees used to make softwood pulp for producing cellulose
	European hardwood forests provide oak and birch wood pulp to make lyocell
	Cotton linters (the fibres removed from cotton seeds during the production process) can be processed to extract cellulose
Lyocell	European forests: oak and birch (hardwood)
Synthetic fibres, such as polyester, nylon, acrylic	Oil producers, including Russia, Saudi Arabia, UAE

Table 6.2.6 Origins of different textiles

6 Fibres and textiles

> **Key term**
>
> **Allergenic:** textile may irritate the skin due to its rough texture or chemical content.

> **Link it up**
>
> The working properties of elasticity, resilience and durability were covered in the core content section (Section 1.11) of this book. To remind yourself, look at page 51. Table 6.2.7 describes some more properties.

> **Exam-style question**
>
> Explain **two** reasons why nylon is used for parachute canopies.
> **(6 marks)**

Physical characteristics of textiles

The main physical characteristics of textiles are their **allergenic** characteristics, texture and density. Other physical characteristics include the fibre length, how long it takes to degrade and its fineness. Physical characteristics influence the choice of the material for specific tasks.

- **Fineness** determines how many fibres there are in a cross section of a yarn of given thickness.
- **Allergenic** textiles may irritate the skin, due to their rough texture or chemical content.
- **Texture** includes the tactile quality of a textile, for example whether it feels coarse, smooth or silky.
- **Density** measures weight in grams per cubic centimetre. Density affects physical properties like stiffness, impact strength and optical properties.

Working properties of textiles

Property	The ability of a textile to:
Tensile strength	resist pulling forces without stretching
Absorbency	absorb and hold liquid
Breathability	hold moisture on its surface, allowing it to evaporate
Electrical conductivity	conduct electricity
Heat conductivity	conduct heat
Insulation	prevent heat or electrical conductivity

Table 6.2.7 Working properties of textiles

> **Apply it**
>
> Collect 100 mm by 100 mm samples of a range of fabrics. Observe them under a microscope. Note the shape of the fibres and how the threads combine.
>
> Put a sample over a beaker and secure it with an elastic band. Use a pipette to drop 5 ml of water onto the surface. Wait for 1 minute. Observe how much water has been absorbed and how much has gone through to the beaker.
>
> Complete a copy of the table below to show the working properties of nylon, silk and wool. Then complete the properties for five more fabrics.

	Elasticity	Resilience	Durability	Tensile strength	Breathability/ absorbency	Electrical/heat conductivity
Nylon	Good	Excellent	Excellent	Good	Poor	Poor conductivity of heat if tightly constructed
Silk	Poor			Excellent when dry	Good	
Wool						Poor

Table 6.2.8 Working properties of specific textiles

Social footprint

Trend forecasting

Designers need to know what customers will buy months or even years ahead. Trend forecasters compile mood boards and colour palettes of emerging colour trends for fashion and interiors, and many brands subscribe to certain trend forecasting websites to gain information about what might be fashionable in the future. Trade shows showcase new developments in textiles technology or advancements in production or finishing techniques. Fashion used to change every season in high-street shops but now there may be new collections in every six weeks. Clothing retailers such as Zara have a turnaround time of two weeks due to frequent small batch production (see page 257).

Impact of material production on communities and wildlife

The following factors can have an impact on the communities where the factories are based.

- **Hazardous chemicals**, particularly in cotton production, may be released into waste water which may harm water-based life.

Common hazard symbols

- **Fibre dust** released when processing cotton can cause respiratory diseases.
- **Noise** may be a problem near factories, especially those associated with yarn manufacturing, knitting and weaving.
- **Waste disposal** needs to be dealt with responsibly.
- **Child labour** remains a challenge for the clothing industry because it is difficult to monitor sub-contractors and home workers.
- **Workers** in the clothing industry are often low skilled or unskilled. They may not know their rights as employees and may work in poor conditions for low wages. Some UK retailers are trying to impose ethical conditions on their suppliers.

Impact of farming and material production on communities and wildlife

Cotton growing and production is a good example of how the textile industry may have a negative impact on a local area.

Soil erosion and degradation

Cotton cultivation degrades soil quality. Most cotton is grown on fields that have previously been used for production, but their exhaustion leads to farmers expanding into new areas, which destroys habitats.

Pollution

Cotton production uses fertilisers and pesticides. These can run off the land and pollute rivers and drinking water, affecting local wildlife. Pesticides threaten the quality of soil too. Heavy use of pesticides also raises concerns for the health of farm workers and nearby populations.

Water

Cotton production and processing uses a lot of water, so rivers are often diverted to service the fields and factories. This has had severe impacts on ecosystems such as the Aral Sea in Central Asia, the Indus delta in Pakistan and the Murray River in Australia.

> **Apply it**
>
> 'The fashion industry is the reason why the Aral Sea in Central Asia has dried up.' Research this claim online. Is the fashion industry really to blame?

6 Fibres and textiles

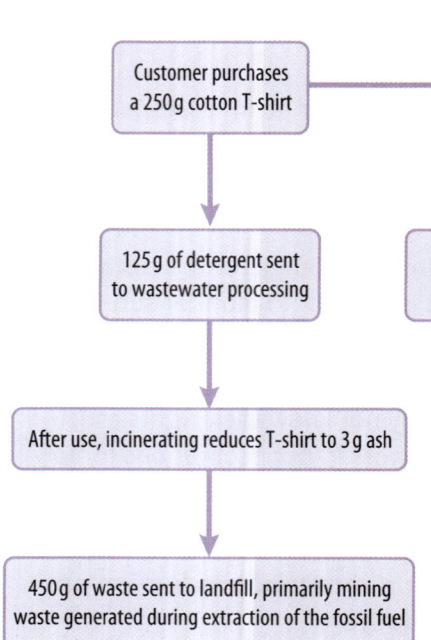

Figure 6.2.5 Potential waste from a T-shirt

Apply it

Create your own brand identity. First, collect examples of clothing brands. What makes a good logo? Now use these thoughts to design a company logo for your own fashion brand to appeal to your target audience.

Exam-style question

Explain **three** ways that a company can improve its social footprint.

(6 marks)

Recycling

According to the Department for Environment, Food and Rural Affairs (Defra) each year about 1 million tonnes of textiles go to landfill after use, while about 500,000 tonnes are collected to be reused or recycled (2007).

Consumers often wear garments for a short time before discarding them as they are no longer fashionable. Washing garments frequently at high temperatures can also shorten their life. The trend of 'fast fashion' means more garments are bought and thrown away. Both manufacturers and consumers have a responsibility to consider the ethics of generating all this waste and whether more could be done to make fashion more sustainable.

Reduction of chemical finishes – surface and aftercare treatments

Some chemical substances or mixtures that may be applied when processing textiles are hazardous and reducing their use would reduce pollution and other harmful side-effects.

Reduction of packaging materials

Textiles companies are trying to reduce packaging to be more environmentally friendly, by reducing waste, litter and energy use. For example, companies can reduce the number of plastic bags used when sending garments ordered online by post. They can also investigate the use of recyclable or biodegradable packaging materials.

Brand identity

A brand's identity is how a company wants customers to perceive it. This may cover its logo, messaging, customer service and reputation.

One element of this is how a company deals with consumerism. Businesses are dependent on customers for their income so they want customers to have the best experience of them and their products. However, consumerism can also relate to unnecessary consumption of products, so is associated with waste and greed. Companies need to balance these ideas within their brand identity. For example, they can promote the way that changes to their packaging have reduced waste in response to customer requests, making customers more likely to buy their products.

Ecological footprint

Human activities consume resources and produce waste. Sustainable development usually includes consideration of environmental, social and economic factors (see Figure 6.2.6).

6.2 Properties of fibres and social implications

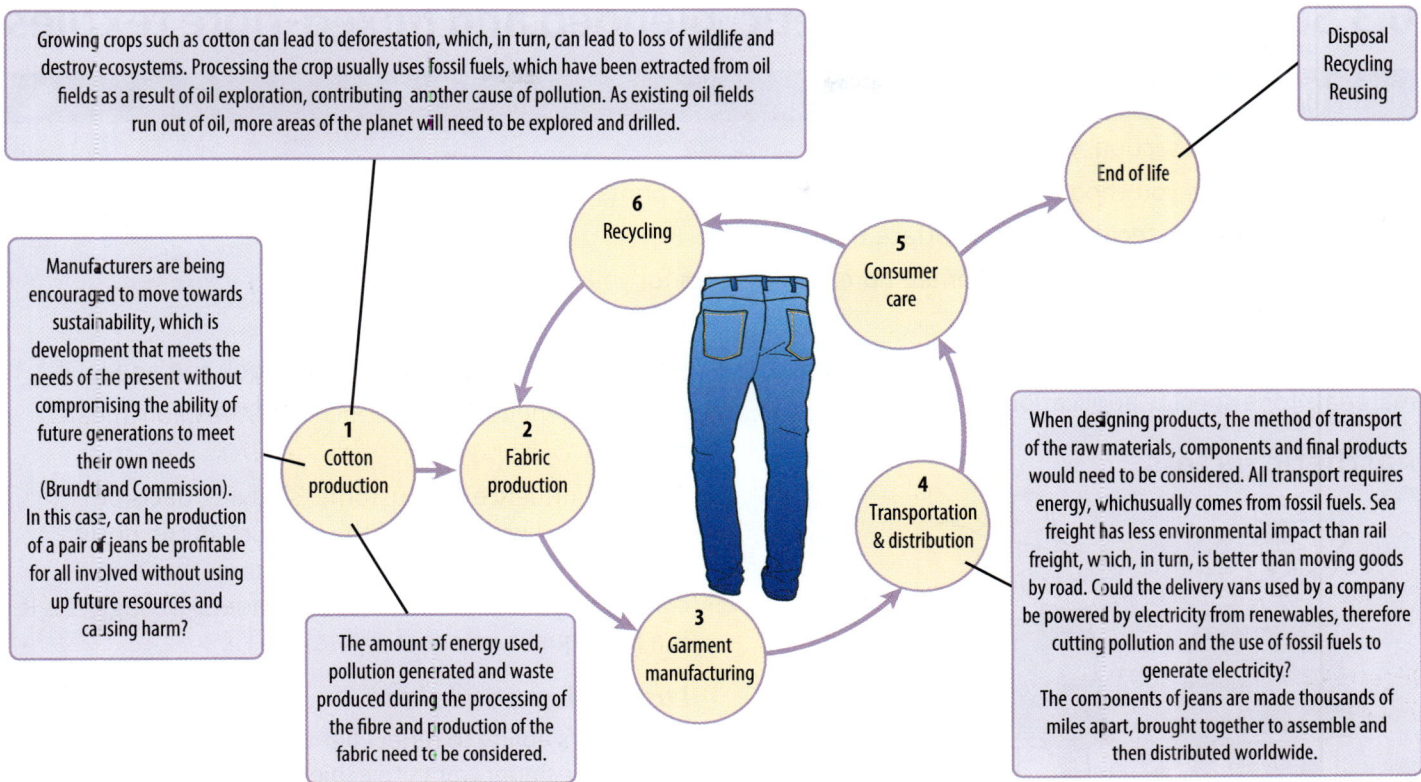

Figure 6.2.6 Environmental factors influencing the choice of fabrics

Maths in practice 1

- 33.4 kg of CO_2 are produced during the life cycle of a pair of jeans. 11% of this CO_2 is produced transporting the raw materials and final products. How many kg of CO_2 is this?

Worked example

11% of 33.4 kg = $\frac{11}{100}$ × 33.4 = **3.674 kg**

- 44% is from the growing and processing of cotton. How many kg of CO_2 is this?

Worked example

- 44% of 33.4 kg = 4 × 10% + 4 × 1% = 4 × 3.34 + 4 × 0.334 = **14.696 kg**

Summary

Key points to remember:

- Fabrics can be constructed by weaving, knitting, felting or bonding fibres together.
- Fibre production is a worldwide industry.
- The production of textiles has environmental and social impacts.

Checkpoint

Strengthen

S1 What is a synthetic fibre?

S2 How is a bonded web textile made?

Challenge

C1 Explain the environmental factors that could impact a manufacturer's choice of fabric.

6 Fibres and textiles

6.3 Selecting natural, synthetic, blended and mixed-fibre textiles

Learning objectives
By the end of this section, you should know:
- that the fabrics you choose have social and ecological footprints
- types of finishing techniques and surface treatments
- ways of selecting the most appropriate fibres and textiles for your project.

Many factors need to be considered when selecting materials for a specific application.

Aesthetic factors

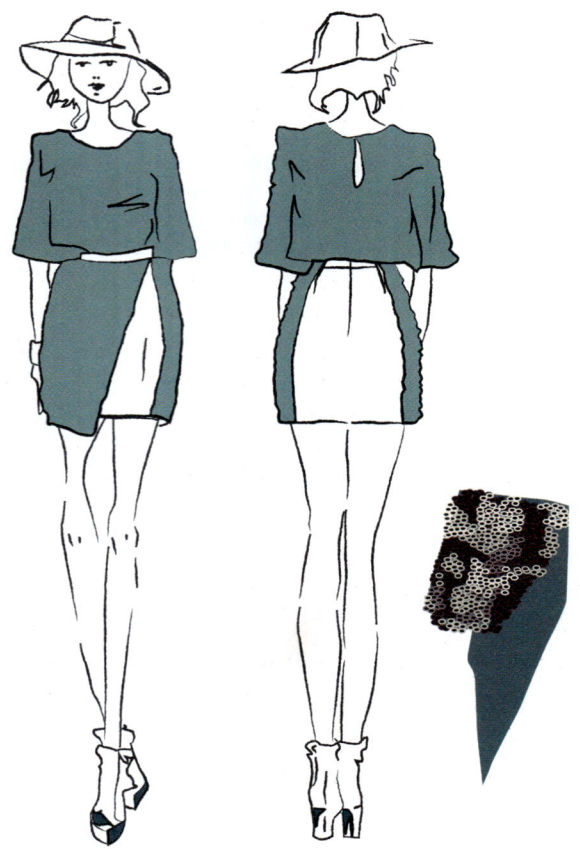

Figure 6.3.1 Design example influenced by aesthetic factors (how a product looks)

Form
The thickness, physical properties and size of the standard forms of the textile influence the designer.

Colour
Colours used will vary depending on the intended use of the product and the target customer. A garment with a muted colour palette of bronze, black and silver would have a completely different look and appeal if constructed in fluorescent crepe polyester.

Texture
This can influence the customer's buying decision and the market placing of the product. In the design example, the selection of heavy textures and a contrasting smooth fabric for the underskirt suggests it is a high-quality product.

Lustre, sheen and shine
The fabric's ability to reflect light has an impact on the look the designer wants to achieve. High-lustre fabrics such as silk convey quality. Some have a highly reflective surface, making them suitable for party wear. Matt fabric is more suitable for workwear as it conveys a more serious and professional image.

Environmental factors
Ecological thinker and writer Edwin Datschefski describes the 'hidden ugliness' of everyday objects: the hidden pollution and waste behind products and materials. Does a product become more attractive to a customer if its environmental impact is minimised?

An outfit made from recycled materials

Sustainability

The production and use of a fabric should harm the environment as little as possible, provide a fair income for the producers of the raw materials, and disposal should not harm wildlife or create pollution. Materials derived from plant sources (such as bamboo) are more sustainable than those from crude oil (such as nylon). It is difficult to assess the sustainability of a material without knowing its entire history.

Pollution

The designer should try to choose the textile that causes the least pollution in its production, use and disposal.

Upcycling

This is using the material from one product to make a new, higher-value, product. Livia Firth, creative director of Eco-Age, wore a dress on the red carpet made from recycled plastic bottles and started the Green Carpet Challenge, which aims to promote sustainable fashion at red-carpet events.

Availability factors

Use of stock materials

Stock materials are easy to source and come in standard widths (90 cm, 137 cm and 154 cm) and weights.

These are easy to order, readily available and are ready for immediate use, saving time and costs. Manufacturers can guarantee a good-quality finish with stock materials, as their properties, sizes and quality are consistent.

Specialist materials are more difficult to source and may be made to a designer's specific requirements. They may come in non-standard widths and weights.

Designers need to research how specialist materials could, for example, take print and join. Their thickness or finish may not fit in standard machinery, so a bespoke setting may need to be applied. An example of a specialist material would be uniquely patterned gold sequinned silk chiffon for a one-off evening dress.

Specialist materials

Designers need to research how specialist material could, for example, take print and join. Their thickness or finish may not fit in standard machinery, so a bespoke setting may need to be applied. An example of a specialist material would be gold sequinned silk chiffon for an evening dress.

Cost factors

Every process has an associated cost. Here are some examples.

Quality of material

The higher the quality of the materials, the higher the cost of producing the product. For example, calico is cheap while heavyweight silk is expensive.

Manufacturing processes

Processes such as cutting, seaming, overlocking (oversewing of an edge to prevent it from fraying) and assembling have associated labour and machine costs. The more processes, the higher the cost.

Treatments

Treatments such as **fire proofing**, **stain resistance** and **waterproofing** involve applying chemicals, specialist machinery and additional labour.

Transportation

The costs of transporting raw materials to the processing site and then transporting the finished fabric, perhaps around the world, including hiring or buying vehicles, fuel and drivers, are significant. The choice of delivery method depends on time, the distance to be travelled, and budget.

Road: providers generally charge a 'per mile' rate. This varies according to distance, weight, type of product and service times.

Rail: not as flexible as road transport but can be cheaper and more energy efficient over long distances.

Sea: this is a commonly used method, though can take a long time. However, it is often the cheapest method for large deliveries.

Air: goods can be moved quickly but this is more expensive and less environmentally friendly. Costs are often determined by weight.

Social factors

Fashion and trends within different social groups may popularise a particular fabric, colour or fashion. Street fashion also has an influence on demand for styles, fabrics and patterns leading to items becoming more popular, such as a particular brand of trainers. Different materials and fashion will also appeal to different social groups. Younger people tend to be more interested in trying new trends and fabrics than older people, who may have different priorities, such as durability or warmth.

6 Fibres and textiles

Cultural and ethical factors

Avoiding offence
Fashionable clothing can sometimes be designed to provoke a reaction, even if it is not intended to offend. However, using fur, leather or other animal products is likely to offend many people.

Also, different cultures may find certain fashion choices unacceptable. For example, in Uganda it is an offence to wear mini-skirts.

Suitability for intended market
The market should be researched early on, considering the wants, needs and priorities of those likely to buy the product. Some customers may prioritise sustainability while others are motivated by cost.

Use of colour and language
Different colours have different associations in the world, for example blue in Europe and America suggests peace and calm, whereas in Korea and Mexico it represents mourning. Phrases printed on clothing should be carefully checked to ensure they are not mistranslations, ungrammatical or offensive.

The consumer society
Many customers want products quickly. This demand has an impact on the people producing the clothes, particularly in factories in developing countries where conditions and pay are poor.

The effect of mass production
Mass production is often the most cost-effective approach for producing a lot of identical products, however, it does use large amounts of energy and creates pollution. The textile industry is allegedly the second largest polluting industry after the oil industry.

Factories make mass production cheaper by employing a large number of workers in less developed countries. However, this has led to the decline of the UK industry, mass redundancies and, in some cases, exploitation of some of the world's poorest workers.

> **Link it up**
>
> There is more about mass production in the core content section (Section 1) of this book. To remind yourself, look at page 10.

Built-in product obsolescence
A product becomes obsolete when it is no longer considered fashionable or useable, or it wears out. New trends become popular within the fashion industry quickly, with new 'seasons' of styles of clothes. Cheaper, high-street fashion could be said to have built-in product obsolescence as the materials tend to be cheaper and therefore less durable than more expensive brands. The idea of 'fast fashion' creates a natural product obsolescence in the fashion industry.

> **Exam-style question**
>
> Explain **two** reasons why built-in product obsolescence can contribute to social and environmental problems.
>
> **(4 marks)**

Summary

Key points to remember:
- Different types of fibres and fabrics have different working characteristics and physical properties which influence their use.
- Designers and manufacturers must balance the social, cultural and environmental impact of the textiles that form their products with customer requirements.

Checkpoint

Strengthen

S1 Compare the properties of felted wool with a knitted fabric.

S2 Explain why businesses care about reducing packaging materials.

Challenge

C1 Evaluate the impact of cotton farming on neighbouring communities.

C2 Investigate the term 'fast fashion'. How does our desire to wear the latest fashions have an environmental impact?

6.4 The impact of forces and stresses on textiles and the process of reinforcing or stiffening

> **Learning objectives**
>
> By the end of this section, you should know:
> - the different forces and stresses textiles could be subjected to when used
> - the ways textiles could be reinforced.

Forces and stresses

Fabrics are subjected to many forces when used in products. A fabric's ability to withstand these forces determines if it is a successful choice.

Force/stress	Definition	Application to textiles
Compression	A force that tries to squash or shorten	Decreases the thickness of a material by increasing the pressure, e.g. by sitting on a cushion. A fabric that compresses easily feels soft, warm and comfortable. Surface changes such as singeing, milling or pressing (see page 268) influence compressibility.
Tension	A force that tries to stretch or lengthen	Fabrics are tested to determine how much force is needed to break them (tensile strength). New fabrics are given a minimum tensile strength for use.
Shear	A force that acts in opposite directions	Tearing a fabric exerts a shearing force. The tearing strength is the force needed to continue to rip an existing tear. After several tests, the average is taken. Tear strength can be improved by blending in fibres resilient to tearing or by improving the construction of the product to prevent weak spots.
Flexibility	A force that bends without breaking	This is the ability of a fabric to stretch and recover. Comfort stretch fabrics stretch and recover for a 25% extension, whereas power stretch fabrics can recover from being stretched by 200%.

Table 6.4.1 Types of force and stress on textiles

In addition, natural fibres are subjected to forces within the fibre as it grows, which affects their strength and shape. Linen fibres are subjected to the push and pull forces of the wind, which can affect the shape of the plant. Slight breezes help young plants grow sturdier but gale force winds can damage or even break them. Plants are also affected by gravity.

> **Link it up**
>
> For a visual representation of types of force and stress, see page 92.

Reinforcement and stiffening techniques

Textiles often need to be reinforced or stiffened if they are going to be used in certain clothes, upholstery or outdoor products, such as tents that will be subjected to stress or force.

Ribs and boning

Ribs and boning support fabrics to make a more rigid shape. For example, they are used in strapless gowns to make the bodice stay up. Modern boning is made not of bones but of a strip of nylon cut to size and sewn into the fabric.

> **Exam-style question**
>
> Explain **one** reason why boning might be added to a corset.
>
> **(2 marks)**

6 Fibres and textiles

Fabrication, assembly and construction processes
The method of construction can affect the product's ability to resist forces when worn or used. Extra care is needed at high stress points, such as underarm or back seams on a suit jacket. French seams (see Table 6.7.2) are suitable for an item that it going to be washed often, such as pillow cases or duvet covers, as they are stronger and resist fraying. Extra stitching at the top corners can reinforce patch pockets.

Lamination
A laminated fabric combines the properties of several layers of different materials. For example, fabric that might tear under tension could be layered with one that can withstand more force to improve the fabric's performance. The designer has the confidence of knowing the laminate's properties should be consistent. Stock forms for laminated textiles use the same sizes as standard materials.

Embedding composite materials
D3O® is an example of a textile that uses embedded composite materials. It is flexible with shock-absorbing properties, so is used in protective wear like motorcycle jackets. In its raw form, the material's molecules flow freely and it behaves like a thick liquid, allowing it to be soft and flexible like putty, but on impact the molecules lock together to dissipate impact energy and reduce force.

Stay stitching
This is where a row of stitches is sewn on a single piece of fabric to help it keep its shape before it is constructed, for example on curved edges that may stretch during sewing. Stay stitching is also used on folds of fabric, such as darts and pleats, to help hold them in place while you attach other pieces.

6.5 Typical stock forms, types and sizes used for textiles

Learning objectives
By the end of this section, you should know:
- about typical stock forms, types and sizes in order to calculate quantities.

	Description	Advantages	Disadvantages
Rolls or bolts	- The most common stock form - Up to 91 m of fabric on a full roll - Comes in standard widths of 90 cm, 137 cm and 154 cm	Easy to calculate how much fabric you need	Wide or semicircular shapes need to use joined pieces of fabric
Blocks	- Furnishing foams come in blocks - Foams for applications such as sound insulation come in sheets 200 cm × 100 cm	Easily cut to size	Can be fragile
Denier	- A unit equal to the weight in grams of 9000 m of yarn (silk would weigh 1 gram) - Used to describe the thickness of hosiery (tights)	Industry standard so that you know what weight of fibre to expect	Specific denier weights may not be available
Single and double weights	- The weight of woven fabrics is measured in grams per square metre (gsm) – a lightweight fabric (chiffon, linen, organza) is typically 30–150 gsm, medium weight (satin, taffeta) 150–350 gsm and heavyweight (upholstery fabric, canvas, denim) 350+ gsm - A double-weight jersey fabric is two single jerseys knitted together to leave the two flat sides on the outside of the fabric, making it heavier, with less stretch	You know the weight and thickness to order	The two weights may be too thin or too thick

Table 6.5.1 Stock forms, types and sizes of textiles

Yarn weight

Knitting yarn weights are labelled as 'chunky' down to 2 ply (very fine) and are sold in balls of 25 g to 100 g.

Yarn can be measured by looking at its weight per unit of length. The tex system expresses this in grams per metre. The coarser the yarn, the greater its tex value.

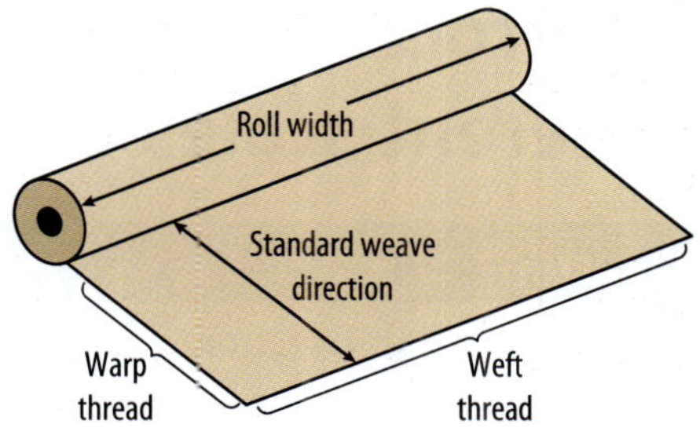

> **Maths in practice 2**
>
> Use these formulae to work out the sizes of fabric you need for your product.
>
> **Area** of a square or rectangle = length × width
>
> **Worked example:** length 100 cm × width 200 cm = 20,000 cm²
>
> **Diameter** is the measurement through the centre of a circle from edge to edge. To calculate the diameter of a circle from the radius multiply its radius (distance to its centre) by 2.
>
> Diameter = 2 × radius
>
> The **area of a circle** is calculated using the formula
>
> $A = \pi r^2$ (i.e. 3.142 × radius × radius)
>
> **Worked example**
>
> Calculate the area of a circle with a radius of 5 cm.
>
> $A = \pi r^2 = 3.14 \times 5\,cm \times 5\,cm = $ **78.5 cm²**
>
> **Answer:** 78.55 cm²
>
> To calculate the circumference of a circle (distance around its outside) use either $2\pi r$ or πD.
>
> **Worked example**
> - Calculate the diameter of a circle with a radius of 25 cm
>
> $D = 2 \times r$
>
> $D = 2 \times 25\,cm = $ **50 cm**

Figure 6.5.1 Structure of a fabric roll or bolt

Link it up

For information about laminates, see page 129.

Summary

Key points to remember:
- A fabric's ability to withstand stress and forces determines if it is a successful choice.
- Fabrics and products can be reinforced to withstand these forces.
- Fabrics come in stock forms, weights and sizes.

Checkpoint

Strengthen

S1 State the difference between tension and shear.
S2 Name three reinforcing techniques.
S3 Explain one advantage of using a stock form of fabric.

Challenge

C1 Evaluate the flexibility of three fabrics and suggest a use for each.

6 Fibres and textiles

6.6 Processes used to manufacture typical products to different scales of production

Learning objectives
By the end of this section, you should know:
- the different manufacturing processes available, depending on the quality and scale of production.

Processes used to cut and shape materials

	Description	Advantages	Disadvantages
Shears	Sharp scissor-like blades	Easy to use, clean edge	Requires skill for accuracy
Stamp/die cutting	Sharp blades stamp out shapes	Precise, can cut identical multiple pieces	Bespoke dies are expensive; ready-made dies could limit design
Laser cutting	A computer-controlled laser melts or burns through the material	Quick, easy to set up	Burnt edge on fabric, not all fabrics are suitable
Heating element – soldering iron	A hot blade melts and seals the edges of synthetic fabrics	Quick, easy to set up	Burnt edge on fabric, imprecise, only effective on synthetics
Extrusion	A high-pressure punch	Long lengths of precise sections	Needs specialist equipment, expensive

Table 6.6.1 Methods of cutting and shaping materials

Scales of production

Link it up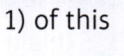
Scales of production were covered in the core content (Section 1) of this book. To remind yourself, look at pages 9–10.

6.6 Processes used to manufacture typical products to different scales of production

Table 6.6.2 summarises four methods as they apply to textiles.

	Definition/application	Advantages	Disadvantages
One off	A high-quality, expensive item made once for a specialist market or clientele, e.g. wedding dresses, theatre costumes and haute couture garments	High-quality, exclusive garments	• Expensive to make and buy • Needs highly trained workforce • Labour intensive
Batch	Produces up to 20,000 identical products before production moves to a different product, e.g. T-shirts for film merchandise	Cheaper production costs	• Needs design, pattern making and sampling skills • Repetitive tasks • Requires training • Lost time changing production line after each run
Mass production	Produces a high volume of identical products, usually on a production line, e.g. plain T-shirts, sheets, socks	• Materials bought cheaply in bulk, keeping costs low • Can be automated, requiring only a small semi-skilled and unskilled workforce	• Expensive to set up • Needs a large storage area • Jobs taken by machines
Continuous	Constantly produces a high volume of identical products, e.g. fabric and tights	• Low unit costs • A small workforce is needed	• Expensive to set up and restart production if something goes wrong • Only suitable for simple products with few components

Table 6.6.2 Scales of textile production

> **Link it up**
>
> See page 224 for more information about scales of production.

> **Exam-style question**
>
> Give **one** textile item likely to be made by one-off production. **(1 mark)**

6 Fibres and textiles

Techniques for quantity production
Larger quantities of products can be made by hand or using a larger-scale manufacturing process.

	Description	Advantages	Disadvantages
Marking out	• Using reference points, lines and surfaces to mark a pattern on fabric • A datum point in the bottom left corner is used to mark from • Tools include tailor's chalk, washable pens and tracing wheels	• Quick to do	• Requires some skill and accuracy
Templates	• Pre-cut plastic or cardboard shapes to trace multiple shapes on fabric • Produced by hand or commercially • Examples are patchwork shape templates	• Improves accuracy when cutting multiple shapes	• Takes time to produce or source templates
Patterns	• Paper templates with markings indicating grain direction, component placement and seam allowances • Produced commercially or by hand, by taking products apart to trace	• Tested commercial patterns will be accurate	• Commercial patterns do not cover all sizes • Knowledge of pattern markings needed
Sub-assembly	• A production cell away from the main line that produces parts of the product, e.g. handles and pockets for a denim shoulder bag	• Speeds up production	• Production may stop if sub-assembly line stops
Computer-aided manufacturing (CAM)	• A programmable machine attached to a computer, e.g. digital printers, dye sublimation printers, computerised sewing machines, cutting machines	• Accurate • Can operate 24/7 • Easy to make changes	• Equipment is expensive • Training needed to learn software • Jobs taken by machines
Quality control	• A system of quality checks during the product manufacture, e.g. checking seam allowances, correct component insertion and stitch quality	• Produces high-quality products	• Extra time taken • Cost of quality control staff • Wastage if pieces are rejected
Working within tolerance	• A measure of accuracy – how much larger or smaller you can cut patterns or sew seam allowances • A tolerance of + or – is set in mm for each size	• Accurate sizing	• Takes care and skill • Wastage if badly cut pieces are rejected
Efficient cutting to minimise waste	• Commercial patterns include a diagram showing the layout of the pattern pieces to make best use of the fabric and minimise waste	• Saves materials and costs	• Takes time and consideration

Table 6.6.3 Techniques for quantity production

6.7 Specialist techniques used for high-quality textile prototypes

> **Learning objectives**
>
> By the end of this section, you should know:
> - the different specialist techniques used when assembling high-quality prototypes.

Tools and equipment

Hand tools

Common hand tools found in most school textiles areas include: fabric scissors; sewing needles and sewing machine needles; pins, safety pins and pin cushions; all-purpose thread; bobbins; seam rippers; measuring tapes. Other useful equipment includes tracing wheels, cutting wheels and marking-out pens or chalks. Fabric scissors should be carefully looked after and used only to cut fabrics.

Hand tools are generally cheap and easy to buy and have immediate results, if used with skill. As with all tools, they should be used with care.

Machinery

Using machinery achieves professional results more quickly. However, machinery may be expensive and users need training to operate it effectively and safely. Individuals normally use a sewing machine, possibly with an overlocker. Sophisticated industrial machines include a laser flatbed cutting table and huge jacquard looms.

Digital design and manufacture

Specialised software can design patterns or whole products, which are then downloaded to a digital machine. This can range from a simple set-up – like a computer attached to a sublimation printer with specialist inks and papers for printing a T-shirt design – to more complex lay plan software and large-scale cutting machines.

While designs can be quickly and accurately transferred to textiles in large quantities, the process can be expensive to buy and maintain, so the investment needs to be calculated as worthwhile beforehand.

Shaping

Whether used for clothes or another product, fabric needs to be shaped to fit its purpose. The methods depend on the end use.

Large-scale digital heat transfer printing

6 Fibres and textiles

Adding and reducing fullness

Method	Description	Details
Pleats and tucks	• Pleats are folds of fabric held in place by stitches, then pressed flat. Used on skirts and trousers: small pleats on shirt front panels are called pin tucks • Advantages: creates desired shaping. Disadvantages: costs more for added fabric, more work, time consuming	(Diagram showing fronts of fabrics facing each other, seam allowance, machine stitching)
Gathering	• Reducing fabric width by sewing two parallel lines of stitching at the top edge, knotting one end and pulling the other end gently • Used for puff sleeves, gathered skirts and ruffles • Advantages: creates full shape. Disadvantages: costs more for added fabric, more work, time consuming	
Darts	• Triangular folds or tucks that go to a point • Straight, curved or double ended • Used for shaping garments around the back, waist and bust • Advantages: creates a more fitted shape. Disadvantages: more work, time consuming, needs care	
Shirring	• Sewing with thin elastic that gathers the fabric to create a stretchy panel • Used to create a snugly fitting bodice • Advantages: creates a closely fitting garment. Disadvantages: costs more for added fabric and elastic, more work, time consuming	(Photograph of woman wearing shirred bodice top)
Ease	• Written instruction on sewing patterns, e.g. fitting a constructed sleeve into an armhole – by careful pinning, or with basting stitches, the bigger piece is reduced to fit the smaller one • The negative or positive amount of room in a garment is also called ease: a loosely fitting garment has positive ease; a stretch-rib polo neck top has negative ease and is smaller unworn than worn • Advantages: creates a closely fitting garment. Disadvantages: some may not like the close fit.	
Godet	• A piece of curved fabric, which is inserted into a garment to add fullness • Used in skirts and dresses • Advantages: creates desired shaping, such as flared shape to a skirt. Disadvantages: costs more for added fabric, more work, time consuming	
Under stitching	• When a seam is pressed and folded in two it can roll back again, especially if it is a neck facing • Under stitching prevents this roll and makes a neater, sharper edge • Advantages: creates a better quality garment that keeps its shape. Facings are kept in place. Disadvantages: time consuming	

Table 6.7.1 Methods of changing fullness

6.7 Specialist techniques used for high-quality textile prototypes

> **Exam-style question**
>
> Explain **one** reason why pleats would be used in the manufacture of trousers. **(2 marks)**

Moulding

Textiles may need to be moulded into a 3D shape to fit the design. Moulding can achieve this without the need for seams. For example, wool felt was traditionally moulded into bowler and top hats by being placed over a mould and treated with heat and steam. The use of heat and steam means that health and safety must be considered. Cotton sleeves may also retain their shape when pressed with heat and steam.

Most other textiles need to be stiffened by dipping in a dilute solution of PVA adhesive. The wet fabric is draped over a mould and should retain the shape when dry.

Adding structure

Interfacing adds an extra rigid layer to parts of garments that need to retain their structure, for example the collar, cuffs, pockets and shoulder seams of shirts. This may be an extra layer of the same fabric where it does not show, or a bonded web that comes in various weights with a fusible glue on one side to make it easy to apply. The weight of the interfacing is determined by the weight of the fabric. The wrong weight makes the area too stiff or not stiff enough. Adding structure can be time-consuming and extra costs may be involved when using boning and specialist machinery.

> **Link it up**
>
> For information on boning, look at page 253.

Fabricating, constructing and assembling

Various techniques and considerations are needed to assemble the parts into a finished product. The methods influence important aspects, such as drape, which is the fabric's ability to form waves as it is hung. The fabric's stiffness, weight and rigidity will affect its ability to form shapes well.

Seams

Joining two pieces of fabric creates a seam. This is a weak point and sometimes a feature, so the most suitable type of seam should be chosen.

Method	Description	Details
Plain or flat	<ul><li>The most common seam</li><li>When completed, it is pressed open and raw edges should be neatened to prevent fraying</li><li>Advantages: straightforward to achieve. Disadvantages: the raw edges of the fabric will need overlocking or zig zag stitch applying to prevent fraying</li></ul>	
Felled	<ul><li>An overlapping seam sewn flat to be strong, durable and neat, most often seen on jeans</li><li>Time consuming to achieve</li><li>Advantages: very strong seam. Disadvantages: takes more time to achieve</li></ul>	Step 1, Step 2, Stitch here, Step 3
French seam	<ul><li>Used on delicate fabrics such as chiffon</li><li>The raw edges are contained inside a double-stitched seam</li><li>Advantages: very neat finish; raw edges are enclosed so don't need finishing. Disadvantages: takes a little longer</li></ul>	Step 1: Sew wrong sides together and trim seam allowance. Step 2: Turn so right sides are facing and stitch close to the seam.

Table 6.7.2 Types of seam *Cont…*

6 Fibres and textiles

Method	Description	Details
Double stitching	• Stitching a plain seam as normal and then stitching again 5 mm away from the stitch line within the seam allowance • Prevents seams on lightweight or stretchy fabrics from unravelling • Advantages: stronger than a plain seam. Disadvantages: takes twice as long as a plain seam; edges still need finishing	
Topstitching	• Stitching a plain hem, pressing it open, reversing it and stitching a line of stitches close to the crease • A decorative effect that also keeps the seam flat • Used for patch pockets • Advantages: looks attractive. Disadvantages: needs great precision to look professional	

Table 6.7.2 Types of seam

> **Exam-style question**
> Use notes and/or sketches to show the process of making a French seam. **(4 marks)**

Finishing raw edges

Although it takes time, finishing raw edges makes the garment last longer as it prevents fraying and improves the neatness of the finished product.

- **Zig zag stitching** along the raw edge strengthens it, but adds bulk. A sewing-machine overlocking foot can make it neater.
- **Bound seams** use bias binding, which encases raw edges on both sides.
- **Rolled hems** are narrow hems on delicate fabrics such as chiffon. A row of straight stitching is sewn 6 mm from the raw edge and pressed under with an iron. The fabric is turned over, and a row 6 mm from the edge is sewn again close to the pressed edge.
- **Turned under and sewn:** the raw edges are turned under and a row of straight stitches is made close to the fold.

- **Blind hemming** neatens a hem without visible stitches, by hand or using a sewing machine and a special presser foot. The hem is doubled over and pressed. Tiny stitches catch the hem material to the main body.
- **Invisible (slip or ladder) stitching** is useful for seam repairs and involves the needle entering the folded edge directly opposite the last stitch.

Fusing

Normally, needle puncture holes would allow water through seams. In waterproof garments and outdoor textile products such as tents, seam tape covers the seams and heat-fusing is used to bond the inside of the product to form a waterproof sealed seam. Three-layer seam-sealing tapes are applied by a hot-air machine to sewn seams of a garment to prevent water leaving through the seam. Seam tape is expensive so another method is sealing the seams with a brush-on plastic adhesive.

Component linkage

Two pieces, or ends, of material often need to be joined temporarily, for example while a garment is worn or a bag is closed. A huge number of options are available.

6.7 Specialist techniques used for high-quality textile prototypes

Type of component	Description	Advantages	Disadvantages
Button	A decorative fastening to join two pieces of material	• Readily available in different sizes and colours	• If insecurely fastened can be lost from the garment • Tricky for those with arthritis or young children to operate
Toggle	A long wooden button which fits through a loop on the other side, traditionally used in duffle coats	• Easy to apply • Readily available	• Sometimes made from wood • Not very water resistant
Zip	Joins two pieces of fabric using interlocking teeth	• Quick way of undoing garments	• Quite tricky to fit • Requires a specialist foot on the machine
Hook and loop fastener	• A strip of tiny hooks on one side of the fabric attach to loops on the other side • Suitable for children as it is safe and easy to open and close	• Easy to apply • Readily available • Good for children's shoes and bags as easy to operate	• Makes a loud noise when undoing it
Press studs/poppers	• Two-part interlocking pieces: one with a dome, one with a recess so that they clip together • Made of plastic or metal • Used on duvets and children's clothing	• Readily available • Easy to sew on	• Hard for those without fine motor skills to locate the two parts of the popper
Magnetic clasps	Two magnetic parts, often used on handbags	• Quick method of closure • Easy to operate	• Not readily available • Would need specialist tools to affix • Not very secure
Buckle	Used to adjust belts or straps to the right length	• Secure fastening • Usually plastic or metal	• Cost • Belt buckles are riveted onto leather requiring specialist tools
Frog buttons	A button made from a knotted cord which is pushed through a loop	• Look very attractive	• Not readily available • Need to find right colour for garment or make your own
Safety buckles/clips	Plastic two-part clips used on rucksacks	• Secure fitting	• Small parts sometimes break off
Hook and eye	• A hook links to an eye on the opposite side of the fabric • Used at the top of dress/skirt zips	• Cheap • Readily available • Easy to apply	• Can be difficult to sew on • Can bend in use
Rouleau loops	Decorative button and loop closure often seen on wedding dresses	• Can look very attractive in vertical rows	• Very difficult to make consistently the same
Rivets	Copper two-part components used to reinforce pockets on jeans or to attach other components, such as buckles, to bags	• Attractive look	• Need strength and skills to apply to heavy fabrics
Upholstery tacks	Used to neaten edges of upholstery and provide a decorative finish	• Look attractive on the edge of the upholstered item	• Need to be applied carefully to look professional • Could be considered an 'old-fashioned' style
Staples	Used to attach upholstery fabric to backing boards	• Very easy to use • Readily available	• Don't look attractive if the piece is on show (usually used on hidden undersides of seat pads)
D-rings	Used to loop handles to bags, sometimes made of brass	• Widely available • Easy to put on	• Not very secure • The tape holding them on can wear and break
Cord toggle	• A plastic clip with an internal spring that keeps cords in place. Used on fleeces and waterproof coats	• Easy to adjust the cords to make a garment fit	• Need to find the right toggle to fit the cord and work well

Table 6.7.3 Types of linking components and fasteners

6 Fibres and textiles

Overlocking

Overlock stitches sew over the edge of one or more pieces of material to form a strong barrier against fraying. Overlocking machines or attachments generally use two-, three- or four-thread arrangements.

- **Two-thread** stitches are used for edging and seaming, neatening seam edges, stitching elastic and lace to underwear, and hemming.
- **Three-thread** stitches are used on narrow rolled hems, neatening edges and creating seams on knitted or woven fabrics.
- **Four-thread** stitches are the strongest, so are used for potentially high-stress areas that need to stay flexible, such as the seat of workwear trousers.

Pressing

Pressing is ironing the seams open as you create the product and then setting the position using heat or steam. It helps to press all seams open before joining subsequent sections. Additional shaping, such as darts, should be pressed to one side before assembling other parts. When the garment is complete, it is pressed again to set the shape and remove creases, ready to be worn or sold.

> **Link it up**
>
> For information on moulding, look at page 224.

Wastage and addition

Fabric may need to be reduced (such as by a dart, see page 260) or added to (such as with a godet, see page 260).

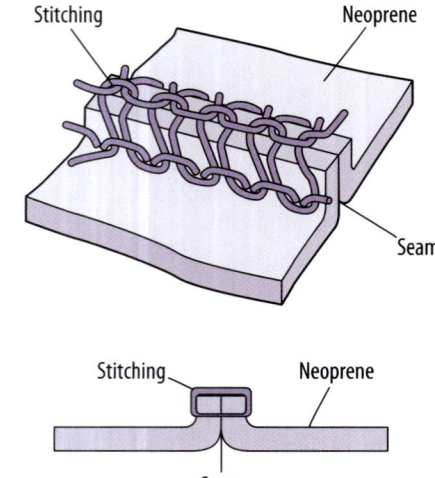

Figure 6.7.1 Overlocking

Summary

Key points to remember:
- Textiles are cut, shaped and produced in several ways.
- Additional techniques help to produce several identical products or components quickly.
- Hand tools, machinery and digital design aid production.
- Shaping and assembling techniques include changing fullness, moulding, adding structure, seaming, fusing and using linking components.

Checkpoint

Strengthen

S1 Describe the purpose of an overlocker.

Challenge

C1 Investigate fusing techniques for waterproofing external fabrics.

C2 Justify the use of batch production for school uniforms.

6.8 Surface treatments/finishes

> **Learning objectives**
> By the end of this section, you should know:
> - the types of finishing techniques and surface treatments.

Before or after the product is assembled, it may need to be decorated or finished for functional and aesthetic purposes. Here are some common techniques.

Decorations

Surface treatment	Application	Advantages	Disadvantages
Fabric painting	- Used in handmade one-off pieces - Created using fabric paints directly on fabric - Applied with a paintbrush, with a stencil, by spraying, sponging or marbling - Fixed by ironing	- Only brushes, paints and stencils required - Low cost - Interesting effects, e.g. using salt on silk paintings makes mottled light and dark textural areas	- Requires skill - Errors are hard to rectify - Fabric becomes stiffer
Batik	Used for decorative pieces: 1. Hot wax is drawn onto fabric and allowed to cool 2. Cloth is cold-dyed 3. The parts covered in wax resist the dye and remain the original colour 4. After the final dyeing the wax is removed by ironing or boiling	Interesting effects created simply	- Requires specialist equipment, e.g. tjantings (tool used to apply wax to fabric), beeswax pellets and a wax melting pot - Hot wax is a health and safety risk
Laminating	- Creates a fabric of two or more layers to combine their properties - Used in luggage and accessories, waterproof breathable textiles and for creating textured looks such as high-shine or wet-look PVC	Better properties than single fabric	Can come apart, darts are stiff and creases are not sharp
Couching	A decorative embroidery technique involving laying threads onto fabric and securing them with small stitches across the threads	Easy to do	Time consuming
Embroidery	- Used for decorating fabric using a needle and thread or machine stitches - Decorative stitches include French knots and satin stitch	Only requires embroidery threads, a hoop and embroidery needles	- Requires knowledge and skill to achieve high-quality results - Time consuming if done by hand
Appliqué	Creates textures and interesting effects by sewing smaller pieces of fabric onto larger pieces to create a pattern or motif	Able to create textures and effects	- Time consuming, so costly - Requires skill

Table 6.8.1 Types of decorative technique *Cont...*

6 Fibres and textiles

Surface treatment	Application	Advantages	Disadvantages
Block printing	Dye is applied to the carved surface of a wooden block and then pressed onto fabric repeatedly to make a pattern	Easy to do	• Time consuming, so costly in an industrial setting • Requires skill to create a regular pattern
Screen printing	The most common method of printing onto fabric: 1. Fine mesh is stretched over a wooden frame and a stencil is made from paper or chemicals using a photographic method 2. The dye is moved over the mesh with a squeegee and forced through it onto the fabric to produce a pattern	• Can make multiple prints with the same screen • The colour is bonded with the fibre and resists washing and friction	• Needs a separate screen for each colour • Multi-coloured patterns are costly
Digital printing	• Inkjet prints onto fabric, onto a product or onto large rolls of fabric • Often used for customised banners, signs, retail graphics and silk scarves	• Short run reduces wastage • Immediate • No restriction on number of colours • Low set-up costs	Not cost effective for long runs
Sublimation	• Printing a pattern onto special paper, which transfers it to polyester using heated rollers or plates and heat-sensitive inks • Suitable for detailed, intricate designs	• Fairly quick • Cheap once set up as only printed paper needs to be changed to change pattern	• Expensive equipment • Can only be used with polyester • Limited to size of printer and press
Resist dyeing	• Creates richly decorated fabrics by making areas of cloth that will not dye by either painting on a paste or folding, twisting or bunching and binding the fabric, then dipping it in indigo dye (shibori) • Batik (see above) is an example of resist dyeing	Unique patterns and rich colours	• Labour intensive, slow • Resist is difficult to remove
Patchwork	• A traditional technique for making quilts and furnishings, involving sewing together small pieces of fabric to make a larger design • Formed of simple squares or more complex patterns	A good way of recycling fabric or using offcuts	Time consuming
Quilting	Sewing together two or more layers of fabric with padding between them to make a thicker quilt or garment	• Creates a soft, strong fabric • Attractive designs possible	• Labour intensive • Time consuming to correct errors • Requires a lot of fabric

Table 6.8.1 Types of decorative technique

6.8 Surface treatments and finishes for functional and aesthetic purposes

Blocking technique of painting

Batik technique of painting

Chemical treatments

The advantage of using chemical treatments is that they improve properties of fabrics, but this adds to the cost of the final product. The disadvantages are listed in table 6.8.2.

Treatment	Description	Advantages	Disadvantages
Bleaching	Chemicals remove natural colour from cotton and linen. The fabric can be weaker.	The lighter shade may make printing clearer.	The fabric can be weakened; bleaching uses large amounts of chemicals, water and energy.
Easy care	Resin is applied to cotton and viscose to reduce creasing and shrinkage, giving them some properties of synthetic fibres.		Eventually washes out; hard to handle; loss of tensile strength.
Mercerising	Cotton fabric is soaked in sodium hydroxide to straighten the fibres	Gives the fabric strength and lustre.	Adds cost to the fabric.
Carbonising	Acid removes grease and impurities from wool.	This help it to hold dye.	Uses sulphuric acid which needs careful storage and could harm the environment; can break the fibres.
Fire proofing	Flame resistant chemicals are applied to yarn or fabric.		Stiffens fabric; needs careful washing.
Stain resistance	Silicon or resin is sprayed onto the fabric's surface to repel stains.		Uses fluorocarbons.
Shrink resistance	Wool-fibre scales are removed using chlorine or coated in resin to prevent felting.		Shrinking may still occur in washing.
Water-repellence	Silicon is sprayed onto the fabric surface or the finished product to reduce absorbency.		Wears off.
Anti-static	Permanent or semi-durable chemicals are applied to synthetic fabrics to make the surface of the material slightly conductive by upping the moisture content. They can also reduce frictional forces by providing lubrication. This also improves the finish and feel.	This reduces their conductivity and increases their moisture content to improve their finish and feel.	Eventually washes out.

Table 6.8.2 Types of chemical surface treatments and finishes

6 Fibres and textiles

Physical treatments

Treatment	Description	Advantage	Disadvantages
Calendering	Heavy rollers press down on the fabric to create a polished surface.	• Improved sheen • Feels smoother and softer	Cost of equipment
Raising	The fabric is passed between hooked rollers to bring end fibres to the surface and create a raised, fuzzy surface	Increases thermal insulation	Cost of equipment
Heat-setting	Heat and pressure make the surface of the fabric smooth	• Better handle • Smoother surface	Cost of labour and power
Brushing	• The fabric is passed between wire rollers which pull the fibres and raise them • It may also be briskly brushed by hand	• Feels softer • Provides a raised surface	Cost of equipment
Desizing	Size, a chemical agent applied to strengthen warp yarns during weaving, is removed	Improves the fabric's absorbency and ability to take dye	Cost of labour and equipment
Singeing	Loose yarn ends are burnt off	Creates a smooth surface that is printed on clearly	Health and safety risks of heat and flames
Emerising	The fabric is passed between rough, emery-covered rollers to create a suede-look finish	• Feels softer • No animal products used • Increased water, crease and stain resistance	Cost of equipment
Milling, fulling (walking)	• Traditional method of cleansing and thickening woollen cloth • First it is pounded and then milled (felted)	Does not need expensive equipment	• Does not work for all wools • Labour intensive

Table 6.8.3 Types of physical surface treatments and finishes

Biological techniques

These use enzymes (catalysts made by living cells) to get the desired finish, but the cost of purchasing the enzymes and equipment can be high.

Treatment	Description
Biostoning	This creates a stonewashed finish on denim without pumice stones, which damage hems and waistbands. Instead, denim is washed with enzymes, which are milder than stones and chemical agents, and achieves an even finish. An advantage of biostoning is that it uses less harsh chemicals, does not damage the products, and gives a more even finish. However, there is a cost to purchase the enzymes and equipment.
Biopolishing	This one-time enzyme treatment decreases the pilling (bobbling) tendency of cotton and knitted fabrics. It removes fibres above the surface so it feels smoother and softer, and looks better for longer. An advantage of biopolishing is the improved wearing properties and the fabric looks better for longer However, again, there is a cost to purchase the enzymes and equipment.

Table 6.8.4 Types of biological treatments

6.8 Surface treatments and finishes for functional and aesthetic purposes

Smart techniques

In this context, smart materials react to a stimulus like heat or light. Many are based on **microencapsulation**. Microcapsules are embedded in the fabric and are like tiny bubbles filled with solids, such as anti-bacterial compounds or mosquito repellents. These containers release their contents under controlled conditions to create otherwise impossible properties in a fabric. The effects are reversible, which is useful, but the cost of dyes and the microencapsulation process is high.

Treatment	Description
Thermochromic dyes	Based on mixtures of leuco dyes that change between colourless and coloured depending on temperature
Photochromic	Change colour in response to the UV level in light: microcapsules are usually added to textiles by screen printing
Solvation chromism	Change colour in response to moisture, for example in nappies
Electrochromic	Change colour in response to an applied electrical current

Table 6.8.5 Types of smart material treatments and finishes

Summary

Key points to remember:
- Surface treatments and finishes are applied to textiles for decorative purposes or to change their properties.
- These treatments may be physical, chemical, biological or smart.

Checkpoint

Strengthen

S1 Name a way to add colour to plain fabric.
S2 Explain why embroidery might affect the cost of producing a garment.

Challenge

C1 Describe and compare the different ways of adding a chemical finish to fabrics.
C2 Investigate different smart material treatments and design two products that could use them.

Preparing for your exam 6

Exam strategy

What to expect in the exam

The examination is designed to test your knowledge and understanding of textiles. Throughout the course you will need to practise exam-style questions in all areas. Preparing carefully for your exams is important to enable you to get as many marks as you can.

Section B: Material category – Textiles

This section is worth 60 marks and contains a mixture of different question styles, including open-response, graphical, calculation and extended-open-response questions. Five marks are allocated to calculation questions in Section B.

For textiles, you should understand design contexts. You should also know about natural, synthetic, woven and non-woven, knitted, blended and mixed-fibre textiles in relation to:

- the sources, origins, physical and working properties of each one, and their social and ecological footprints
- the way in which their selection is influenced
- the impact of forces and stresses and how each one can be reinforced and stiffened
- typical stock forms, types and sizes used in order to calculate and determine the required quantity
- alternative processes that can be used to manufacture typical products to different scales of production
- specialist techniques, tools, equipment and processes that can be used to shape, fabricate, construct and assemble a high-quality prototype
- appropriate surface treatments and finishes that can be applied to each one for functional and aesthetic purposes.

Revision tips

- Ensure you start revising in plenty of time. You will find it easier to remember facts you have revised several times over a few weeks than those you have tried to memorise at the last minute.
- Make clear and well-ordered notes about all the sections.
- Work through all sample assessment materials, past papers and textbook questions available from Pearson.
- Identify the areas where you are likely to get mathematical questions and practise arithmetic and numerical computation, handling data, graphs, geometry and trigonometry.
- Discuss the course with your teacher and peers as it will help your understanding.
- Use online or other resources to extend your understanding of the design and technology context.

Preparing for your exam 6

Sample answers with comments

The following questions give some examples of how to interpret the different command words.

Question 1: 'Calculation' question

Figure PE6.1 shows the dimensions for a pattern for a circular bag made of denim.

Calculate how much fabric is wasted when the piece is cut from a square of fabric measuring 160 mm by 160 mm. **(5 marks)**

Formula for the area of a circle, or radius r:

Area of a circle = $\pi \times r^2$

$\pi = 3.14$

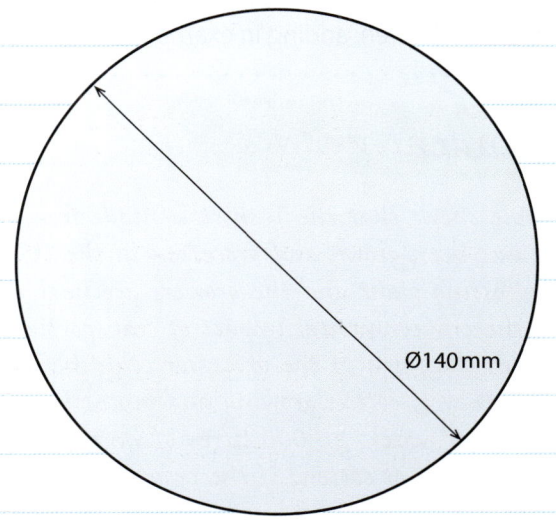

Figure PE6.1

Student answer

a) Area of a circle = $\pi \times r^2$

   d = 140 mm π = 3.14

   Area = 3.14 × 70 mm × 70 mm

   = 3.14 × 4900 mm^2

   = 15,386 mm^2

   Area of fabric = length × width

   = 160 mm × 160 mm

   = 25,600 mm^2

   Area of fabric wasted = 25,600 mm^2 − 15,386 mm^2

   = 10,214 mm^2

Exam tip

You will need to use your maths skills in the exam. The formula you need may be given in the question but it helps to be familiar with formulae that are likely to come up

Verdict

Although the student has the correct answer they have not explained that they have divided the diameter by 2 to get the radius. Read questions carefully as they may give further instructions as to the units the answer would need to be expressed in, for example mm^2, cm^2 or m^2, and to how many decimal places.

Preparing for your exam 6

Question 2: 'Explain' question

Explain *two* reasons why farming and material production may impact on communities and wildlife. **(4 marks)**

Student answer

1. Local opportunities for employment but some workers possibly on very low pay.
2. Possible pollution and soil erosion caused by processing and growing fibres.

Exam tip

'Explain' answers need to be fairly detailed, exploring aspects of the situation by reasoning or argument.

Verdict

The student has given two reasonable answers that explore aspects of the concept. Care needs to be taken to consider both the positive and negative effects of farming and material production on local communities. The student could expand on the answers given, adding in examples.

Question 3: 'Evaluate' question

The product above is a cotton T-shirt with a screen-printed design. The table below gives information about the T-shirt. Evaluate the T-shirt with reference to its ecological impact. **(9 marks)**

Material	Cotton
Source of material	USA
Manufactured	Los Angeles, USA
Decoration	Screen printed using plastisol inks (derived from crude oil)

Verdict

This is a good answer. The student has made several well-balanced evaluations drawing on the impacts of growing, transporting and processing the material to make the T-shirt. They have also considered what might happen to the T-shirt once the user has finished wearing it.

Student answer

The table shows that the T-shirt is made from cotton which has been grown and processed in the USA. If the processing plant and the growers are near each other, the environmental impact of transporting the crop from the farm to the processor could be quite small. However, cotton growing and processing uses a great deal of water: 20,000 litres of water are needed to produce 1 kg of cotton. If the crop is not grown organically then pesticides are likely to be used, which could leak into water courses causing pollution. Cotton growing needs lots of water and has been linked to the drying of river basins in the Rio Grande area of the USA. This has an impact on the surrounding ecosystems. Cotton is a recyclable material or the T-shirt could be reused when the user has finished wearing it. The T-shirt has been screen printed with inks that are derived from crude oil. These could be replaced with vegetable-based inks, which would make the environmental impact of the T-shirt less harmful.

Overall I think that the T-shirt has quite a large environmental impact, which could be reduced if the crop is grown with careful management to prevent damage to the environment. Many cotton clothing items are discarded when they go out of fashion, ending up in landfill.

Exam tip

'Evaluate' answers need to look at the strengths and weaknesses of a proposition and then draw a conclusion.

Preparing for your exam 6

Question 4: 'Explain' question

The cushions below are made of linen and have a flame-retardant finish applied to the surface.

Linen cushions

1. Give **one** method of increasing the strength of the cushion. (1 mark)
2. Explain **two** reasons why linen is an appropriate material for a cushion. (4 marks)

Exam tip

This is a combination of a 'Give' question and an 'Explain' question.

'Explain' questions require you to give reasons why you have chosen your answers.

Student answer

1. Reinforce the seam with a second line of stitching in the seam allowance.
2. It is strong and it looks smart.

Verdict

In part 1, the student has correctly identified a suitable method.

In part 2, the student does not give the full justification required. They could have written the answer in the following way.

2a) Linen is a hardwearing fibre meaning that it will withstand abrasions and washing. This will be a useful property for cushions as they are often rubbed against other fabrics. They can be abraded by the chair covering or the user's clothing, resulting in uneven wear on each side.

2b) Linen is a strong, stiff and smooth fibre, which means that the cushion will keep its shape even after being deformed in use and will not pick up dirt due to its smooth surface.

Question 5: 'Give'/'name' (short answer) question

The materials that products are made from are chosen because of their characteristics. The picture opposite shows a one-piece swimming costume.

The swimwear is made from 62 per cent polyamide and 38 per cent elastane. Give **one** reason why elastane is used in the manufacture of swimwear. (1 mark)

Student answer

1. Elastane is a suitable material as it keeps it its shape even when wet.

Verdict

The student has answered the question as required.

Exam tip

This type of question requires specific information, but it does not need to be clarified further.

Preparing for your exam 6

Question 6: 'Give' (short answer) question

Figure PE6.2 is a pie chart showing the amounts of water used during the various production stages of making a pair of jeans.

Give **one** reason why cotton cultivation uses the most water.
(2 marks)

> **Exam tip**
> This type of question requires you to find the answer from key information displayed in a certain format.

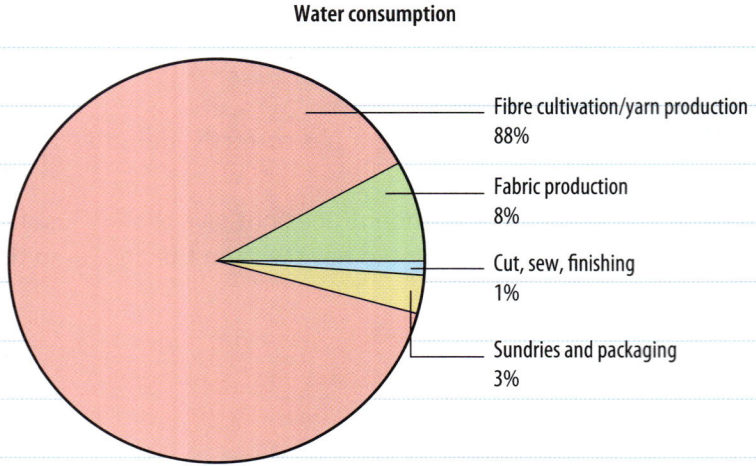

Figure PE6.2 Graph to show the amounts of water used during the various production stages of making a pair of

> **Student answer**
> Cotton plants need water to grow. This is done by irrigating the land.

> **Verdict**
> The student has answered this question well.

Question 7: 'Use notes and/or sketches to show' question

Figure PE6.3 shows a solution for hanging storage in a student bedroom. It is made from cotton and folds flat when not in use.

The design needs to be improved to:

- provide more pockets to store items
- be part of a new children's nursery range
- have some sections that can be fastened shut.

Use notes and/or sketches to show how the design could be modified to include these points.
(6 marks)

> **Exam tip**
> It is important to annotate (label) sketches as the detail is not always clear in a sketch and the marks awarded can also come from written or drawn information.

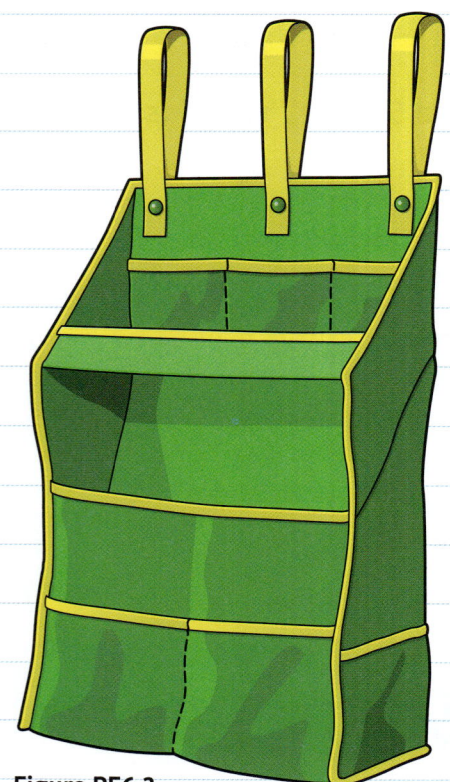

Figure PE6.3

Preparing for your exam 6

Student answer

My design has now been made bright and colourful for a nursery with many more pockets added to all sides

One pocket has a zip fastening

Some pockets have flaps with press studs that can be closed

Verdict

This is a good answer. The annotation states that the design has now been made bright and colourful for a nursery with many more pockets added to all sides. Some of the pockets have flaps with press studs that can be closed, and one has a zip fastening.

Pearson Education Ltd accepts no responsibility whatsoever for the accuracy or method of working in the answers given.

7 Timbers

7.1 Design contexts

> **Getting started**
>
> Timber has a variety of uses in everyday life. Think about where you live and consider the following questions:
> - How many objects can you think of that are made of wood?
> - How many types of wood can you name?
>
> Trees are an important part of the natural world. Describe some of the ways in which trees are important to animals, birds and humans.

Timber is wood that has come from tree trunks and been dried and cut into usable planks or boards.

Timber has been used for thousands of years. There is evidence of Stone Age people making houses with timber frames. Imagine how long it took to cut up a tree with a stone axe! Large areas of Britain that are now fields and cities used to be forest. As the population grew more and more, trees were cut down to build houses and boats and the land was used for agriculture instead of trees.

Timber is still used today, even though we have developed many new materials. Timber is a strong, lightweight material and it looks attractive, so it is used for construction, furniture and many other things. Some traditional hand craft techniques have not changed much for hundreds of years, but manufacturing processes can prepare timber and make products at a speed that would have been unimaginable 100 years ago.

People used to use whatever timber grew near where they lived. As transport got cheaper and easier, people were able to use different timbers from all around the world. Oak used to be used in Britain, because it grew here naturally and it is a good, strong wood to make things from. Now most of the oak has gone, the majority of the timber we use is pine, with a lot of it imported from other countries. Some timbers, such as mahogany, used to be imported from tropical rainforests in South America, Africa and Indonesia. Nowadays less tropical hardwood is imported because of concerns about damage to the rainforests.

7.2 Sources of timber

> **Learning objectives**
>
> By the end of this section, you should know:
> - some of the different hardwoods, softwoods and manufactured boards available
> - the advantages and disadvantages of some timbers, and the kind of products they are often used for
> - some of the physical characteristics of timber
> - some of the social issues raised by the use of timber.

Natural timbers – hardwoods

A hardwood comes from a tree with broad leaves and its seed in a fruit. Many hardwood trees are **deciduous**, meaning they lose their leaves in winter. Hardwood trees grow quite slowly, often taking more than 100 years to be big enough to use for timber. There used to be a lot of hardwood trees in Britain, but most of our natural forests were cut down a long time ago.

> **Key term**
>
> **Deciduous:** a tree that loses its leaves in the winter.

7 Timbers

There are many types of hardwood. Some common ones are shown below.

Oak, mahogany, beech and balsa

> **Link it up**
>
> The advantages and disadvantages of using **oak**, **mahogany**, **beech** and **balsa** were covered in the core content section (Section 1) of this book. To remind yourself, look at page 52.

Jelutong, birch and ash

Type	Appearance	Advantages	Disadvantages	Common uses
Jelutong		Even, close grain is easy to cut and shape	Soft and not very strong, so not good for structural uses	Model making, moulds for casting or vacuum forming
Birch		Regular, even grain and easy to work	Low resistance to rot and insect attack	Veneers: to make plywood and to surface cheaper materials that are used for interior door and furniture
Ash		Strong, tough, flexible and finishes well	Low resistance to rot and insect attack	Handles for tools, sports equipment, ladders

Table 7.2.1 Properties of jelutong, birch and ash

Natural timbers – softwoods

A softwood comes from a tree with needle-like leaves and seeds in a cone, like a Christmas tree. Most softwood trees are evergreen, meaning they have leaves on all year. Larch is an unusual softwood because it does lose its leaves in winter. Softwood trees grow quite quickly, and can be used for timber after about 30 years. This means they can be grown commercially, so most forests planted for timber are softwoods. That is why softwood timber is a lot cheaper than hardwood timber.

> **Link it up**
>
> The advantages and disadvantages of using **pine** and **cedar** were covered in the core content section (Section 1) of this book. To remind yourself, look at page 53.

Type	Appearance	Advantages	Disadvantages	Common uses
Larch		• Tough, durable and resistant to water • It can be used outside untreated, and fades to a silvery grey	Costs more than some other softwoods	Small boats, yachts, exterior cladding on buildings

Table 7.2.2 Properties of larch

Manufactured timber

Natural timber is a useful material, but because of the size of a tree trunk it is only available in fairly narrow planks. Also, the grain lines in timber are what give it strength and they only go in one direction, so timber is strong lengthways but not across its width. Manufactured boards use timber to manufacture a board that has different properties to plain timber. If you want a large, thin sheet of wooden material you need a manufactured board.

> **Link it up**
>
> **Plywood** and **MDF** were covered in the core content section (Section 1) of this book. To remind yourself, look at page 53.

Type	Description	Advantages	Disadvantages	Common uses
Chipboard	Wood chips are mixed with glue and pressed into flat sheets	Uses waste materials so is cheap to produce	• Not much structural strength, especially in damp conditions • Surface is very rough, so usually plastic coated	Desktops, kitchen worktops, cheap flatpack furniture

Table 7.2.3 Properties of chipboard

Sources and origins of timber

Different types of tree grow naturally in different parts of the world, due to different climates. In the past, this influenced which timbers were used in manufacturing, but globalisation means timber and goods are moved around the world. Most softwoods naturally grow in colder regions. Some hardwoods grow in temperate climates, such as Europe, while others grow in tropical rainforests.

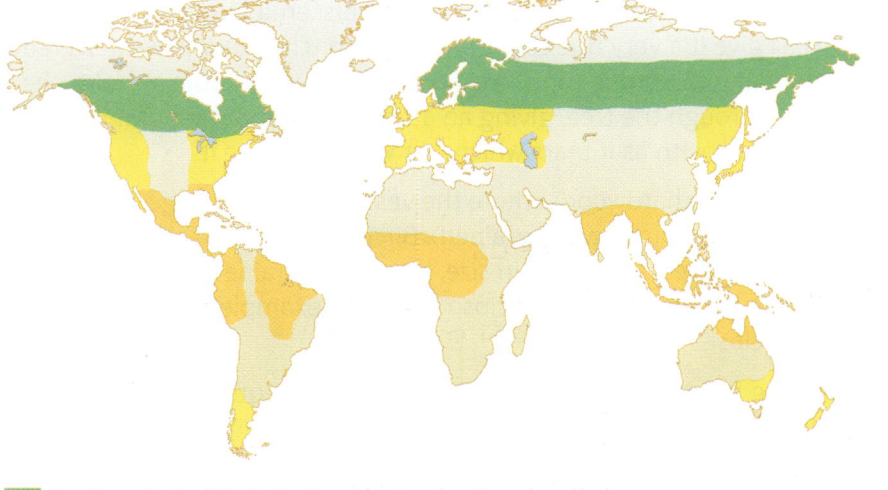

■ Cold climates (such as Alpine) with softwood forests, such as pine, cedar and larch.
■ Temperate climates (such as European) with a mix of softwoods and temperate hardwoods, such as oak, beech, ash and birch.
■ Tropical climates (such as Amazonian) with rainforests of tropical hardwoods, such as mahogany and jelutong.

Figure 7.2.1 Where different types of timber can be found in the world

> **Exam tip**
>
> Sometimes there is more than one material you could choose. Make sure you justify why you have chosen it by mentioning the properties of each material and explaining why that makes it suitable.

> **Exam-style question**
>
> Give **one** type of timber you would use to make a table top for a children's nursery.
> **(1 mark)**

7 Timbers

The physical characteristics of timber

Because of the way trees grow, all timbers have a similar set of physical characteristics.

Knots

A knot in timber appears where a branch grew out of the tree: the grain swirls around and the wood can be harder, so a knot can make that part of the timber harder to cut with saws and chisels. Knots also fall out, leaving a hole, so it is good to use timber that is free from them. However, knots can also make timber visually appealing, but if timber is to be painted, knots should be treated with knotting (shellac dissolved in methylated spirits) to prevent resin in the knot from staining the painted surface.

Colour

Different woods have different colours, from the pale colours of pine to the rich, dark reddish browns of mahogany. But trees are living organisms and their colours will vary from tree to tree and within the tree itself. This means that when buying timber it's important to remember that colour may vary from plank to plank.

Grain structure and density

Timbers are split into hardwoods and softwoods. Hardwoods have two types of long vessels, known as fibres and pores, which run the length of the tree. Softwoods have one main cell called tracheids. Both have annual rings, produced as growth is added under the bark each year. These give timber its grain. Slow growth and narrow annual rings is sometimes called close grained. Birch and holly do not have clear growth rings but they can be seen by staining. Parana pine has almost no discernible growth rings and its small cells give it a very fine texture, whereas pitch pine and western red cedar have clear growth rings. In some hardwoods such as utile or iroko, the vessels spiral through the tree, giving an attractive interlocking grain, which is difficult to work with as it tears whichever way you plane it.

Open grain refers to hardwoods where the vessels are quite large and show at the surface (also called coarse grained). Birch and holly are close grained timbers with small vessels similar in size, hence fine grained. All hardwoods are somewhere between open and close grain. For example, red oak is very open, birch is close.

When applying finishes to grain, softwoods generally require sanding first. With most hardwoods, grain filler is needed before painting or polishing, otherwise the vessels will show through. Even very dense hardwoods like rosewood need grain filler.

Density varies from timber to timber; balsa wood has a density of 60 kg per cubic metre, while oak has a density of 750 kg.

Working properties

When talking about materials, you must use the correct meaning of the words that describe the properties of materials. It is helpful to compare properties of materials when describing them. For example, rubber is more elastic than metal.

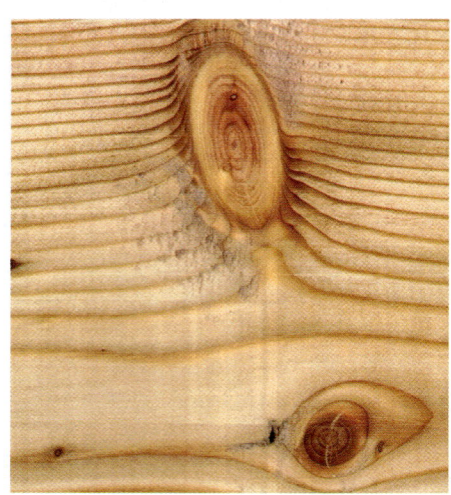

Knots in timber

> **Key terms**
>
> **Grain:** fibres run the length of a tree trunk, which give it its strength and make the distinctive patterns you see on timber.
>
> **Density:** weight in grams per cubic centimetre or kilograms per cubic metre. Density is the compactness of a substance or material. Wood is often said to have a high strength to weight ratio because of its low density and good structural strength.

Elasticity

The elasticity of a material is its ability to stretch and return to its original length or shape. Rubber is an elastic material. Wood is not very elastic, although some woods are a little more elastic than others. Yew is excellent for making bows (archery).

Tensile strength

The tensile strength of a material is the amount of force it can withstand when being pulled. The tensile strength of most timbers is three to four times the compressive strength. Ash and oak have high tensile strength, more than double that of western red cedar.

Compressive strength

The compressive strength of a material is the amount of force it can withstand from a crushing force. The denser the wood, the more likely it is to have good compressive strength. Hickory has approximately double the compressive strength of western red cedar.

Social footprint

Trend forecasting

Manufacturers and retailers try to forecast the trends there will be in a year or two, so they can invest in designing and making products people will want in the future.

One current trend is the increase in the use of softwoods from sustainable sources. Tropical hardwoods are being used much less, partly because of the damage their loss causes to rainforest areas and the impact that has on the people and wildlife that rely on those rainforests.

Another current trend is towards greater use of manufactured timbers in construction, with builders using manufactured I shaped beams for joists instead of the traditional solid timber.

Impact of logging on communities

Sometimes logging (cutting trees for timber), an industry, brings jobs and money to an area. However, in many poorer regions, such as the Amazon rainforest, logging is badly managed and large companies log in areas where indigenous people live. Logging activity often pushes them out of their ancestral homes, leaving them with nowhere to go, and destroys their traditional way of life and the wildlife they depend on for food.

Recycling and disposal

Timber is a natural material that will biodegrade and rot away in time. Composite materials, such as chipboard covered with plastic, are much harder to dispose of. Timber cannot be recycled by melting it down and re-moulding it like plastics and metals can. Sometimes timber can be reused for something else, e.g. by cleaning it up and sawing it into smaller pieces. Timber can be disposed of by burning to create heat, which can be useful if it is well managed, and biomass boilers generate electricity from burning wood. 'Clean' timber – meaning a supply of timber that is not mixed with manufactured boards and other rubbish – is sometimes turned into boards such as chipboard or MDF. Timber can be disposed of by burning to create heat, which is useful if it is well managed.

Ecological footprint

At its simplest, it is the amount of the environment required to produce the goods and services necessary to support a particular lifestyle. It includes the whole product life cycle, from cutting the trees down and seasoning the timber, to manufacturing, use of the product and disposal after use.

Sustainability

Sustainability of timber is the idea that there are always trees available to be used. Hardwood trees take a long time to grow, so are rarely replanted once cut down. Softwood trees grow more quickly and are often planted in large areas of forestry. Some forests now are sustainably managed, which means that trees are being replanted as soon as others are cut down, so that there is always an area of the forest that is mature enough to be cut down.

The Forest Stewardship Council lets timber producers use its logo on their timber if that timber comes from forests that are shown to be sustainably managed. Schemes like this help consumers make informed choices

7 Timbers

Deforestation

Deforestation is a global problem, with trees being cut down faster than they grow. Most of Europe was deforested hundreds of years ago and deforestation is now a major problem for areas of the developing world, such as South America and West Africa. Deforestation can cause a lot of accompanying environmental issues such as soil erosion. For example, in Nepal deforestation has caused problems with landslides. Worldwide about 46,000–58,000 square miles of forest are lost each year. That is an area the size of England every year, or equivalent to 48 football fields every minute.

Because trees absorb carbon dioxide from the air, scientists think that having fewer trees will make the greenhouse effect worse, which will warm the Earth and affect the climate and sea levels for the whole world.

Habitat destruction and loss

When an area of forest is destroyed, the animals that live there lose their habitat, and they usually have nowhere else to go. Some well-known animals including tigers, gorillas, orangutans and elephants are in danger due to loss of habitat, and there are hundreds more species of animals, birds and insects that are at risk of extinction if deforestation continues.

This photo shows a large area of forest cut down: the land is likely to be used to grow crops or keep cattle, not replanted with trees

Processing

When a tree is cut down it needs to be processed to make usable timber. A tree trunk will be sawn into planks and then dried out in a process called seasoning (natural or kiln-drying). These processes, particularly kiln-drying, use energy which adds to the ecological footprint of the timber. Waste material such as leaves and small branches are no use, so are often burnt or left to rot.

Transportation

When a tree is cut down in a forest, it must be taken out of the forest to go for processing, either on lorries or sometimes by being floated down a suitable river. Most of the timber used in Britain has been imported. As most transport burns fossil fuels this increases the carbon footprint of the timber.

Wastage

The trunk of a tree will be used for planks, but other parts of the tree such as small branches and leaves that are not useful will be left to rot or burnt if the l and is being cleared for farming. Larger branches and the waste from the trunk after cutting into useful planks may be turned into chipboard or MDF. As timber has become scarcer it has become more expensive. It is also becoming increasingly important to reduce wastage. It is important to note that many of these timbers and manufactured timbers (such as MDF) appear on the toxic wood list. When prolonged turning and routing take place, the exposure to toxicity can be high and can cause health problems such as skin, nose and eye irritation, and respiratory issues such as asthma. The Health and Safety Executive produces Woodworking Information Sheet Number 30, which covers how to reduce negative effects. This includes ensuring that work areas are well ventilated and that protective equipment, such as gloves and masks, are used.

Pollution

Trees absorb carbon dioxide from the atmosphere and release oxygen, so living trees are very good for the environment. When wood is burnt for firewood, or to clear land, it releases carbon dioxide into the air, which increases the greenhouse effect. The other pollution from timber comes from the transportation of it around the world.

Summary

Key points to remember:
- There are many different types of timber and manufactured boards. Learn some of their properties and the things they are good for.
- Timber is a natural material with a grain structure that affects its strength and how it is used.
- Managing forestry is an important global issue for the sustainability of timber sources and to preserve the natural environment.

Checkpoint

Strengthen
S1 What is the difference between hardwoods and softwoods?
S2 Give three examples of manufactured boards.
S3 In what parts of the world are you most likely to find oak and beech trees?

Challenge
C1 Describe what impact deforestation can have on local communities and habitats.
C2 Explain how large-scale deforestation can affect the atmosphere around the world.

7.3 Selection of timber

Learning objectives

By the end of this section, you should know:
- the aesthetic, cultural and social factors affecting product design
- the environmental factors involved in the use of timber
- how cost and availability affect product design
- how to use this information to select the most appropriate materials.

Aesthetic factors

Aesthetics is about how a product looks.

Form
The form of a product is the way that the overall shape and structure looks. Some products are designed to be purely functional; some are designed to look good to the consumer. A good product manages to do both. Timber's flowing, sometimes twisting grain patterns make it particularly attractive.

Colour and texture
Timber can vary in colour from light yellowish brown to dark browns, even to almost black. Lighter timber, such as pine, is sometimes stained to make it look like a darker wood, keeping the distinctive grain pattern that gives natural wood its characteristic look. The texture of wood can be quite rough, but it finishes to a smooth surface that feels quite warm to the touch. Ash is light brown; western red cedar is dark brown/red; sycamore is white; beech is pinkish-brown to white.

7 Timbers

> **Link it up**
>
> For more information on sustainability, look at page 281.

> **Exam-style question**
>
> Explain **one** benefit for the environment of using upcycled material to make a bookend.
>
> **(2 marks)**

Environmental factors

Designers and manufacturers need to consider certain environmental factors in order to choose the most suitable material for their product/chosen application.

Sustainability

If timber from sustainable sources is used, it does less damage to the environment. This is better for the long-term health of local ecosystems and global climate.

Genetic engineering

Genetic engineering allows scientists to make changes to the DNA of a tree. If they can work out how to change the right parts of DNA in the right way they can create a tree that is different from natural trees. It is possible to make a tree resistant to particular diseases. Scientists are also trying to develop trees that grow faster than they do naturally. This would mean timber could be grown more quickly.

Campaigners against genetic engineering of plants are concerned that we do not know enough about the long-term effects of releasing genetically engineered plants into the environment.

Seasoning

A freshly cut tree is about 85 per cent water, so it's very wet. It must be dried out to below 18 per cent water, and is often dried to 10–12 per cent water for indoor use. Drying timber is called **seasoning**.

Seasoned timber has increased strength, resistance to decay, and stability, meaning it is less likely to **warp** (bend).

Air seasoning stacks the planks outside and after a few years they have dried out to about 18 per cent water. This is a slow process, and does not get the timber dry enough to use indoors. Kiln seasoning stacks the planks in a room and pumps first steam then warm dry air around them. This dries them to the required level in a few weeks. Kiln-drying is much quicker, it kills insect eggs in the timber, and it can dry the wood to the 10 per cent needed for use in our warm, dry, centrally heated houses. A designer will select timbers that have been correctly and appropriately seasoned for their intended purpose. This ensures that the final product, for example a wooden window frame, will not warp in use.

Upcycling

A timber product can sometimes be given a new lease of life by upcycling. A designer may specify used timber to create a particular style, such as rustic or shabby chic. A piece of old furniture might be repaired and then painted to make it look more modern and stylish. Old pallets can be turned into a product such as a garden table. This continued use of the timber is better than burning it.

> **Key terms**
>
> **Seasoning:** reducing the water content of timber to 10–18%.
>
> **Warping:** bending or twisting that happens to timber as it dries out.

Availability factors

Use of stock materials
Materials are processed and sold in standard sizes, called stock materials. A sawmill cuts timber into standard sizes. If a designer uses stock sizes it saves time cutting the wood again to make it smaller, and saves a lot of wasted timber.

Use of specialist materials
There are some specialist timber products that can be used for specific purposes, for example:

- marine plywood is waterproofed for outdoor use
- expensive hardwood veneers can be laminated on the outside of cheaper timber
- structural house timbers can be treated with flame retardant chemicals to slow the spread of fire.

Hurricanes, storms and disease
Trees can be affected by naturally occurring events. Hurricanes and severe storms can blow trees over. It can take a long time for trees to grow again.

Disease can kill trees. If a new disease arrives in a country it can spread and kill off a particular type of tree. In Britain a lot of elm trees were killed by a disease called Dutch elm disease. More recently ash trees have died from a disease called ash dieback, and about 126 million trees in British woods are at risk from this disease.

Cost factors

Quality of material
Timber is a natural material, and trees grow with variations and defects. Sometimes timber can warp (bend), depending on how it is cut and seasoned. Some pieces of timber have more knots than others; some develop splits as they dry. Timber is sorted, graded and sold for different purposes.

Constructional carcassing timber is used for structural applications, such as joists, roof trusses (the wooden frames that support roofs) and stud walls (plasterboard walls supported by a wooden frame), where it will not be seen. It is graded for strength. For softwood C16 is the most common grade. C24 is also quite common and is a bit stronger.

Joinery timber comprises the better-looking pieces of timber, and is used for products where the timber will be seen, e.g. window frames and doors. It has low knot content, straight grain and a smooth finish.

Manufacturing processes necessary
The manufacturing processes required affect the cost of the product. The scale of production chosen will depend on how many products are to be made. The scale of production needed will also affect the choice of manufacturing processes. The designer will use stock sizes and standard components bought in, so that their company does not need the specialist equipment to prepare timber or make parts that can be bought ready made.

> **Link it up**
> For more information on sizes of timber, see pages 290-291.

> **Apply it**
> Find out what thicknesses of MDF and plywood your school has in stock.

7 Timbers

Treatments

Timber will burn and rot quite easily and quickly. It can be treated with chemicals to reduce this.

Timber can be pressure treated with a preservative. The pressure treatment forces the preservative chemicals deep into the wood, and makes it resistant to rotting. Pressure treated timber can be used outside for years. A common chemical used is called Tanalith E, and the treated timber is called tanalised timber.

Timber can be treated with fire proofing chemicals that make it burn less well. Correctly treated wood can slow the spread of flames, allowing more time for people to escape, reducing damage to the wooden structure and giving more time to extinguish the blaze.

Social factors

Use for different social groups

Groups of people of different ages or interests will like different things. If a product designer can create a product that is appealing to a particular social group the product may sell well to that group of people. That product may be less appealing to other groups, so it can be a difficult balance between making it acceptable to everyone or desirable to only some people.

Cheaper materials, such as chipboard and MDF, are more likely to be used in the mass-consumer market, such as for flat-pack furniture. Bespoke furniture made by a local carpenter for a wealthier clientele is more likely to be made of more expensive hardwood, such as oak.

Trends, fashion and popularity

Trends and fashions come and go. The popularity of a product depends on lots of factors. It has to work well, but it also has to look good and appeal to consumers.

> **Apply it**
>
> Consider the difference between furniture made from oak and that made from chipboard. What are the advantages and disadvantages of each as a material?

Solid timber was used more in the past as newer, cheaper materials were not available. A hundred years ago children's toys would often be made of wood, but now such products are usually made of plastic. Bespoke wooden toys are still very popular, for example wooden rocking horses, but they are often very expensive. Most furniture was made of solid wood and people expected it to last their lifetime. But the trend now is using chipboard, or veneered chipboard, and many people only expect furniture to last for a few years.

Cultural and ethical factors

Avoiding offence

It is obvious that if people find your product offensive they are not going to buy it. It is less obvious that people in different parts of the world, or other cultures and religions, might be offended by something that is not offensive to the product designer. It is important to have some understanding of different cultures and religions so that you can avoid accidentally causing offence with a word, symbol or picture that has a different significance to other people.

Suitability for intended market

It is important to understand the intended market for a product, so you can make sure a product is suitable.

It is also important that a product designed for a user of a particular age, or with a particular need, is suitable for people of that age or need. If you understand the needs of your user, you can make sure they can use the product and that it is safe for them.

The consumer society

In Britain, and much of the richer developed world, we live in a consumer society. We are relatively wealthy and products are quite cheap, so some people can afford to buy a lot of things they do not really need. There are lots of companies advertising products to try to sell us these things we do not actually need.

There is nothing wrong with people having nice things or useful things if they are affordable, but some people can go so far as to get themselves into debt consuming too much. From an environmental point of view, some people think that as a society we are using up limited resources too quickly and damaging our environment.

7.3 Selection of timber

The effects of mass production
Carpenters used to make products one at a time. Now products tend to be mass produced. Mass production and manufactured boards have made products a lot cheaper than they used to be. This means they are more affordable and people can buy more things than they used to be able to.

Mass production also means factories are more automated than before. Lots of people used to have jobs in factories making the same thing every day. Now machines do more of that work, so there are fewer low-skilled jobs. These have been replaced by jobs for smaller numbers of engineers and computer programmers to run the machinery that has taken the jobs of the manual workers.

Built-in product obsolescence
A lot of products only have a short lifespan. Manufacturers deliberately make some products with parts that fail after a time and cannot be replaced. This process of making products with a short lifespan – that are intended to be thrown away and replaced – is called built-in obsolescence. Manufacturers like it because it means people buy new products more often. For example, using lower quality boards such as chipboard will lead to early product failure. It is not very environmentally friendly because it means a lot more rubbish is created when people dispose of things rather than mending them or replacing a part.

> **Apply it**
> What are the advantages and disadvantages to a society of increasing the mass production of products?

Summary
Key points to remember:
- Timber may be selected for its strength, cost or appearance.
- Seasoning is drying timber to make it stronger and more stable.
- Timber is graded and used for different purposes.
- Timber can be treated to improve its resistance to rot and fire.
- Furniture manufacture increasingly uses cheap laminated chipboard instead of solid timber.

Checkpoint
Strengthen
S1 Why is it important to season timber?
S2 How could you make a piece of timber better for use outdoors?

Challenge
C1 What are the advantages and disadvantages of using plastic-coated chipboard for furniture instead of solid oak?
C2 Is the genetic engineering of trees a good thing? Explain your answer.

7 Timbers

7.4 Strengthening timber

> **Learning objectives**
>
> By the end of this section, you should know:
> - the types of forces that can act on timber
> - some ways to strengthen timber beams and frames.

Forces and stresses

There is a range of different forces and stresses that can act on materials. When designing a product, it is important to understand the forces that will be put on it so you can choose the best material and make the product strong enough.

- **Compression** is a squashing force, like standing on something.
- **Tension** is a pulling force, like tugging on the ends of a rope.
- **Shear** forces act in opposite directions, pushing one side up and the other side down, like the cutting action of scissors.

> **Link it up**
>
> For a visual representation of the types of forces and stresses, see pages 137–142.

Natural forces within the timber as it grows

When a tree grows, branches grow out of it, the wind blows at it and it can lean to one side. The weight of the tree leaning over a bit or supporting big branches stresses the wood. This does not matter to the tree, but when it is cut down and sawn into planks, the stress is released from the wood and it can bend and crack.

Pre-stressed construction beams

When a beam is loaded, it tries to bend and the bottom of it is in tension. If you pre-stress the beam by putting the bottom rail in tension (stretching it) when the beam is made, it will stretch less when the beam is loaded. This means the beam will bend less and be stronger.

Reinforcement and stiffening techniques

Frame structures

A square or rectangle is a useful shape to make things from, but it is not very strong. The corners can twist and the square easily turns into a diamond shape.

Figure 7.4.1 A rectangle can easily collapse under force

A rectangle can be strengthened in several ways:

- by putting a thin panel inside the frame
- by adding a diagonal strut or triangle across each of the corners
- by adding a strut corner to corner to make two triangles.

Figure 7.4.2 A diagonal strut used to prevent collapses

Fabrication, assembly and construction processes

Fabrication processes are the processes used to make the parts for something. Assembly processes are the processes used to put the parts together.

> **Link it up**
>
> For more information on fabrication processes, look at page 301.

7.4 Strengthening timber

Lamination

A laminate is a thin layer of material. **Lamination** can be useful to make curved shapes from timber. The thin layers are glued and bent into shape. When the glue is dry, the layers are fixed together in the bent shape. Timber can be bent a little bit by steaming it, but laminating can achieve much larger bends. Lamination can also greatly increase the strength of material such as plywood. Lamination is used to increase the strength of wooden beams, for example Glulam and Laminated Veneer Lumber (LVL).

Braces and tie bars

A brace is a bar added to a frame to strengthen it. They are usually diagonal, to make triangle shapes. A tie bar is similar, but is a rod that is good in tension. Steel is often used. The rod is fixed across the frame like a brace and, because it cannot stretch, it holds the frame in shape.

Embedding composite materials

A composite material is made of different materials bonded together. Sometimes adding other materials to a timber product can improve its properties. GRP (fibreglass) can be used to make a strong, hardwearing, waterproof shell around a wooden beam. Steel strips fixed on a timber beam strengthen it because of the high tensile strength of the steel. Fibres can be laminated into timber to greatly improve strength. For example, a Japanese company is developing a wooden beam that has laminated carbon fibre called Carbon Fibre Reinforced Wood (CFRW). Stiffer and stronger laminated beams will result in smaller cross section, reducing the amount of timber needed in a project.

The seat and back of this chair have been made by laminating thin layers of wood

> **Key term**
>
> **Lamination:** bonding several thin layers together to make a thicker material.

> **Summary**
>
> **Key points to remember:**
> - Learn the meaning of tension, compression and shear.
> - Pre-stressing components of a beam during manufacture can strengthen the beam.
> - Braces and ties go diagonally across a rectangular frame and make it a lot stronger.
> - Laminating joins thin layers together and can be used to make bent wooden parts.

> **Checkpoint**
>
> **Strengthen**
>
> **S1** Draw diagrams to show tension and compression acting on a piece of timber.
> **S2** Draw a rectangle and add a cross brace that would strengthen it.
> **S3** What is laminating?
>
> **Challenge**
>
> **C1** Draw a beam that is bending. Add arrows to show where it is in tension and where it is in compression.

7 Timbers

7.5 Stock forms and sizes

> **Learning objectives**
>
> By the end of this section, you should know:
> - the stock shapes timber comes in
> - the standard stock sizes timber comes in
> - how to use this information to select the appropriate timber.

Stock forms/types

Timber is available in a variety of stock forms.

Name	Availability	Picture	
Regular sections	• Timber is sold in a standard range of cross-sectional shapes and sizes – sawmills do this for convenience, so there is a limited range of sizes to cut • Designers can use the standard sizes when designing products		Commonly available sizes and shapes of timber
Mouldings	• Lengths of timber cut into decorative shapes • There are lots of shapes available for different purposes, such as skirting boards or decorative edging • Saves time but can be relatively expensive		Common moulding shapes
Dowels	• Wooden rods that are round in cross-section • Have a variety of uses, from model making to furniture construction – can be used to strengthen simple joints • Short lengths of dowel are used to join pieces of wood with a dowel joint • Requires accurate drilling of holes		Different-sized dowels
Sheets	• Manufactured boards come in standard-sized sheets in a range of thicknesses • Available in large sizes but large sheets are relatively difficult to cut and edges may splinter		A stack of manufactured boards in a warehouse

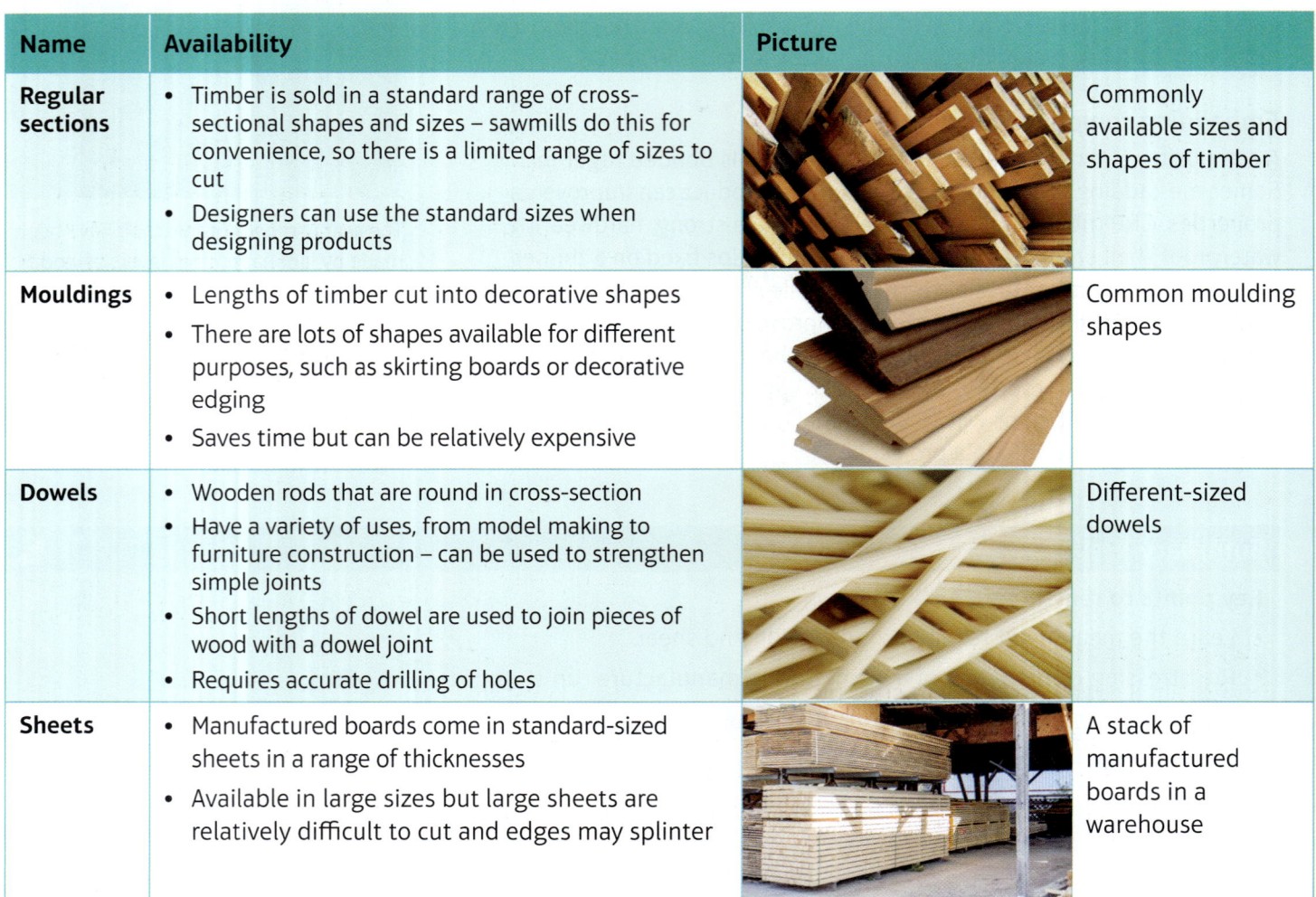

Table 7.5.1 Standard sizes of timber

Sizes

Imperial and metric

Understanding imperial sizes can help to understand why timber comes in the sizes it does. Although wood is sold in metric sizes today, it is still the equivalent of the nearest old imperial size. For instance, 100 mm × 50 mm used to be 4 inches × 2 inches, and many carpenters will still call it two-by-four.

One inch is roughly 25 mm, so timber sizes usually increase in 25 mm steps. Manufactured boards generally go in 3 mm steps: 12.7 mm is half an inch and 6.35 mm is a quarter of an inch.

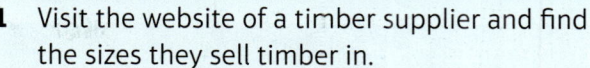

PAR and PSE

PAR stands for 'planed all round'. This means all four surfaces have been planed, and it will have slightly rounded edges to make handling easier and safer. Constructional timber, such as for studwork (frames for interior walls) is usually PAR.

PSE is 'planed square edge'. All four surfaces are planed, but the edges are left square. Joinery timber is usually PSE. PAR and PSE are planed and ready to use. They are often only available in long lengths (1.8 m). The timber may be warped or twisted so check before use.

It is worth knowing that timber is usually sold by the sawn size. The planed size is a few millimetres smaller. So, the 100 mm × 50 mm standard size is the rough sawn size. If you buy 100 × 50 PSE, it will actually measure about 96 mm × 47 mm.

Cross-sectional area

The price of timber will depend on its cross-sectional area (width by thickness), although it will always be sold by its width and thickness as these are the important sizes.

A few common sizes of timber are:
- 15 mm × 75 mm
- 15 mm × 100 mm
- 15 mm × 150 mm
- 50 mm × 50 mm
- 50 mm × 100 mm
- 75 mm × 75 mm
- 100 mm × 100 mm

There are many more sizes available.

Apply it

1. Visit the website of a timber supplier and find the sizes they sell timber in.
2. Find out what sizes of timber your school usually stocks.

Diameter

The diameter is the measurement across a circle from one side to the other. A dowel has a circular cross-section, and comes in a range of sizes. A few common sizes are 4 mm, 5 mm, 6 mm, 8 mm, 10 mm, 12 mm and 25 mm.

Board sizes

Manufactured boards are usually sold in a sheet measuring 2440 mm × 1220 mm. In imperial this was 8 feet by 4 feet. DIY stores sometimes sell part sheets, such as 1220 mm × 610 mm, because they are easier for customers to handle.

Manufactured boards are sold in standard thicknesses. Plywood and MDF thicknesses include 3 mm, 6 mm, 9 mm, 12 mm, 15 mm, 18 mm and 25 mm. Chipboard commonly comes as 15 mm or 18 mm thick.

Summary

Key points to remember:
- Timber is sawn into standard sizes by sawmills.
- PAR and PSE are planed timber, which has smooth surfaces.
- Mouldings can be used to add decorative trim to products.
- Manufactured boards come in standard-sized sheets, in a range of thicknesses.

Checkpoint

Strengthen

S1 What do PAR and PSE mean?
S2 Why is most timber sold in multiples of 25 mm?
S3 What is a dowel?

Challenge

C1 Why is it important for a product designer to use standard-sized timber wherever possible?

7 Timbers

7.6 Manufacturing processes

Learning objectives
By the end of this section, you should know:
- some of the machinery used to process timber
- the different scales of production in manufacturing
- how manufacturing aids can be used in production processes.

Processes to cut and shape materials

Routing
A router contains a rotating cutter. It can be used with lots of different-shaped cutters. It can be used to make a straight slot in wood, it can be used with a jig to cut shapes or it can be used with a bearing-guided cutter to profile the edge. Routing can also be carried out with a computer-controlled router/milling machine. It removes material quickly and there are a wide range of cutters available. Large cuts may burn/blacken timber so must be used with extreme care.

Sawing
Sawing machines are used to prepare timber quickly, with the circular saw and bandsaw being the most common. Small ones are used in a workshop to cut timber to the required size and shape. Sawmills use much larger versions to cut whole tree trunks into planks. Cutting thicker timber on a bandsaw may result in edges not being square.

A hand-held router being used to cut a decorative shape into the edge of a piece of timber. The man in the picture above is not following correct health and safety procedures. What is he doing wrong?

A table circular saw used to cut timber to size: the circular blade makes straight cuts in timber

A bandsaw: the blade is one long band with teeth that can make straight and curved cuts in timber. What's wrong in this photo?

Use of a mortiser

A mortiser makes a square hole. It gets its name from the mortise (slot) half of a mortise and tenon joint. The round centre of the chisel drills a round hole, and the square chisel around it cuts the corners out to make a square. Produces mortises quickly and accurately, but requires requires accurate marking out and care to get the exact size mortise required.

Use of a bag press

A bag press is a bag that can be sealed and have the air sucked out of it. A mould and laminates are put inside it. When the air is sucked out of the bag, the laminates are forced into the mould, and are held there while the glue dries. Presses equally on all surface areas but may not work with thicker laminates.

> **Apply it**
>
> Find out which of these pieces of equipment your school has. Which ones would you be allowed to use in school?

A bench-top mortiser

Scales of production

Choosing the right scale of production is very important when manufacturing a product. Investing in an expensive factory makes the product cheaper, but you need to sell a lot to pay for the factory.

One-off

A one-off product can be made in a workshop by a craftsperson. A one-off might be made for an individual client who wants something unique.

A prototype of a product can be made as a one-off to test a design, before the time and cost of setting up machinery for mass production.

Batch

A batch is a number of the same thing made at the same time. A batch production process might use a jig, a template or a mould to mark out or cut the same shape several times.

For example, 20 chair legs of the same shape could be made by drawing around a template. Screw holes in the chair legs could be made in the right place by putting a jig over the end of the leg to guide the drill. Curved chair backs and seats could be made the same by laminating them over the same mould in a bag press.

7 Timbers

Mass production

Mass production processes make the same product all the time. A factory is often set up to mass produce products. The chipboard pieces for flat-pack furniture will be cut to the correct size by automated saws. Holes for the fittings will be drilled in exactly the right place by computer-controlled drills.

Machinery will be set up to make a particular part of a product and it will make that part all day long, day after day. Mass production processes are very expensive to set up, but once they are set up they can make the product cheaply.

Continuous

Continuous production is a step up from mass production. Continuous production is used for products that have a high demand all the time. The factory will be highly automated and running 24 hours a day, 7 days a week.

Scale	Description	Advantages	Disadvantages
One-off	One product made at a time, either for a specialist product or to test an idea	• No set-up cost • Made with existing equipment • Product can be customised to the user's needs	Slow, so expensive to make several
Batch	Several copies of the same product are made at the same time	• Jigs, templates and moulds speed up the process and can be kept for future use • Special machinery is not needed, so set-up cost is not high	• Labour intensive, so it is quite expensive per product • Takes time to make jigs, moulds and templates
Mass	Factory machinery set up to make lots of identical products	Can make a product quickly and cheaply	Machinery expensive to set up, so only worthwhile for making a lot of products
Continuous	Factory machinery making the same thing 24/7	Makes the product very quickly and cheaply	Machinery very expensive to set up, so only worthwhile for making huge quantities of a product

Table 7.6.1 Scales of production

> ### Exam-style question
> A company has been batch producing coffee tables. A large retailer has just ordered 3000 of its tables. Explain **two** reasons why the directors should change to mass production. **(4 marks)**

> ### Exam tip
> With a question like this, it is important to show the examiner you understand the batch and mass production processes. Start by explaining the advantages and disadvantages of both processes. Then say why mass production is the preferred choice.

Techniques for quantity production
Marking-out methods

Marking out is transferring measurements onto material before it is cut. Sometimes manufacturing processes will not need to mark out if machinery has been set up to process materials automatically. But for one-off or batch production, marking out is important. A reference point is essential. This is the point on the material you start measuring from. It could be the bottom left-hand corner, and every measurement is taken from there. Sometimes, a particular line or surface of the material will be used as the known starting point that everything is measured from.

When preparing a piece of timber, get one face flat. This is called the face side. Then, using the face side, get one edge square with it. This is now called the face edge. Mark the timber as shown, and make all measurements from these surfaces.

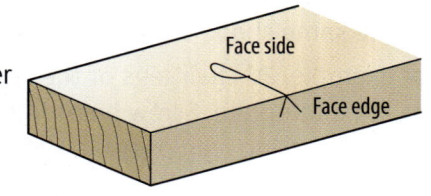

Figure 7.6.1 The marks used to indicate the face side and face edge

Jigs

A jig can be put over a piece of work and guide a drill or a saw to cut in the required place. It is a quick and accurate way to make lots of holes or cuts in exactly the right place, as long as the jig is positioned correctly. Jigs are very useful for batch production because once you have the jig you can keep using it.

Figure 7.6.2 A drilling jig that has been clamped to the corner of the workpiece to get the holes in the correct place

Fixtures

A fixture holds the workpiece in place while it is being cut or shaped. This speeds up processes but a range of fixtures may be required, adding to initial costs.

Templates

A template is a cut-out shape that you can draw around to mark out the shape you want to cut from a piece of material. A template might be made from paper or card for a single use, or it might be made from a thin sheet of wood or metal if it is going to be used a lot. A template is really useful in batch production because it allows workers to mark out the same shape quickly and accurately. Templates must be accurately produced and protected from damage.

Patterns

A pattern is similar to a template, but the term is sometimes used to refer to a collection of templates used to make the complete product. The pattern for a product might include several individual templates needed to make the whole product. One pattern can result in multiple accurate replicas but the template must be accurately produced, which may be expensive.

Sub-assembly

Sub-assemblies are components that have been assembled and used as an individual component in a larger product. The sub-assembly is built to a uniform specification, quality tested in its own right and can be entirely replaced. An example is a standard DVD module inserted into different desktop computers.

Computer-aided manufacturing

Computer-aided manufacturing (CAM) uses a computer to guide the cutters on a computer numerically controlled (CNC) machine. The product outline will be drawn on a computer-aided design package (CAD). The computer sends cutting instructions to the CNC machine, which has cutters moved around by electric motors. This is very accurate and can operate 24/7. It has high initial costs and training is required for programmer.

CNC routers, milling machines and laser cutters can all be used in a workshop to make one of a product or a batch of lots of the same products. Factories use large machinery controlled by computers.

Quality control

Quality control is a system for trying to make sure the products being manufactured are good enough for sale. It reduces waste and should help customers to receive a more reliable product. At stages through the manufacturing, a sample of the product is inspected to make sure it is correct. The more complex a product is, the more sampling is likely to take place. Careful planning and implementation is required. If the sampling finds a faulty product, the process might be stopped so it can be corrected before many more faulty ones are made.

Working within tolerance

Manufactured parts will always have a tolerance. That is the range of sizes within which the part is acceptable. The designer will need to specify a tolerance for a part. If the holes on a flat-pack cupboard are the wrong size the fittings will not work. If the holes are 2 mm out of line, the pieces will not go together properly. Careful application of tolerances ensures a product with several components will always fit together and that spare/replacement parts will fit too. Manufacturing processes must be able to produce the right tolerance, and part of quality control is checking the parts are all within the required tolerance. Parts of a product are often made and assembled in different factories, so stating the acceptable tolerance for every part is essential for the parts to fit together. It requires accurate machine set-up and checking systems, for example go, no-go gauges.

Efficient cutting to minimise waste

Material costs money, so it is important to use as little as possible when making products. This includes minimising waste to reduce costs and better use finite resources. When cutting out materials, the way shapes are marked out can make a big difference to waste. Using a template to mark out shapes so they are as close together as possible, and designing the part to ensure the closest possible fit to the next one, can make a big difference to the amount of material wasted, although this requires careful planning.

7 Timbers

Summary

Key points to remember:
- Machinery like circular saws and bandsaws is used to prepare timber.
- The different scales of production, and some of their advantages and disadvantages.
- How jigs, moulds and templates can be used to assist batch production.
- Computers can be used to control machinery quickly and accurately.
- Ensuring good quality control and correct tolerances of components are important parts of manufacturing processes.

Checkpoint

Strengthen

S1 List the four scales of production.
S2 What is a template used for?
S3 Draw a jig that could be used to drill a line of four holes equally spaced along the edge of a piece of MDF 200 mm wide.

Challenge

C1 Explain why it can be a big risk for a company to invest in mass production facilities.

7.7 Equipment and processes used to make prototypes

Learning objectives

By the end of this section, you should know:
- the purpose of a range of hand tools used for working wood
- the purpose of some of the machinery that can be used to work wood
- the fixtures and fittings that can be used to join wood together.

Tools and equipment

Hand tools

There is a variety of useful hand tools for marking out, cutting and shaping wood.

Tools for marking out accurately are important. If you mark out your work accurately you can cut it accurately too.

A try square is used to mark a line at 90° to an edge and check if something is square – versatile, may be damaged if dropped

A marking gauge used to mark a line parallel to an edge – can mark out several pieces of timber at the same measurement, the scribing point (spur) scratches the timber so it is vital the gauge is set correctly

7.7 Equipment and processes used to make prototypes

Machinery
The first woodworkers had to do everything with hand tools, which could be quite time consuming. Nowadays we have a lot of electrically operated machinery that makes woodwork much quicker and easier. The circular saw and bandsaw in Section 7.6 on page 292 are very useful machines for cutting timber to the required size.

Digital design and manufacture
Computer-aided design software is useful for drawing parts of a product accurately. It is essential if the work is going to be cut out with computer-aided manufacture, as the computer sends information from the drawing to the machine, such as a CNC router or a laser cutter. The big advantage of computer-aided design and manufacture is the speed and accuracy with which it can cut.

Shaping
Drilling
A drill makes a round hole in material. There are different types which all have their advantages and disadvantages.

A pillar drill: in a workshop work is held flat on the table and the drill makes accurate 90° vertical holes. It requires various clamping methods depending on the shape and thickness of the material to be drilled

A hand-held 'cordless' battery-operated drill is very useful on site or for big pieces of work that are hard to move – no power lead so it can work away from a power source, but requires a charged battery to work

Name	Appearance	Use	Advantages	Disadvantages
Twist drill		• Drilling smaller-sized holes in most materials • The **flutes** lift the swarf out of the hole	Readily available in a wide range of sizes from very small up	• Usually only up to 13 mm diameter • Deep holes can block up the flutes
Flat bit		Drilling larger holes in wood	• Centre spur gives an accurate starting point • Drills quickly	Cannot be used to make an existing hole bigger
Forstner bit		Drilling flat-bottomed holes in wood	Small centre spur can make a blind hole with a flat base	Slower than a flat bit
Auger		Drilling deep holes in wood	Can bore deep holes	Needs to be used at a slow speed
Hole saw		Cutting large holes	Can make a large hole in a sheet of manufactured board	• Only good for quite thin materials • Limited range of sizes available

Table 7.7.1 Types of drill bit

> **Key term**
>
> **Flutes:** the twisted spirals along a drill bit that remove the swarf (fine pieces of stone).

7 Timbers

Cutting

Timber is cut with a saw. A saw has teeth on it that cut the wood as the saw is pushed over the wood. There are different types of saw, but they all use the same principle.

Name	Appearance	Use	Advantages	Disadvantages
Hand saw		Used to cut larger pieces of wood	Can cut long, deep cuts through big planks	• Blade can bend, so it's important to saw straight • Harder work than a power saw
Tenon saw		Used to cut smaller pieces of wood and accurate detail like joints	Stiffened blade makes it easier to make precise, straight cuts	Stiffened blade back means it cannot cut deeper than the blade, as the spine that keeps the blade stiff is thicker than the blade
Coping saw		Used to cut shapes out of thin wood and manufactured boards	• Thin blade can go around curves • Blade can be taken out and put through a hole to cut internal shapes	• Blade snaps quite easily • Small teeth saw slowly
Scroll saw		Used to cut shapes out of thin wood and manufactured boards	Can cut fine, accurate details	Large pieces of wood cannot be cut with it
Jigsaw		• The blade goes up and down • Used to cut large thin pieces of wood clamped to a bench	• Can cut quite quickly • Thin blade can cut curved shapes	• Difficult to cut straight lines • Blade can wander in thicker materials

Table 7.7.2 Types of saw

Planing

A plane has a sharp blade, which must be kept sharp, protruding from a flat base plate. It is used to remove wood from the edge of a piece of timber, and is good for getting a crooked edge straight. Planes are available in different lengths and it is easy to adjust depth of cut.

A planer/thicknesser is a useful machine for preparing timber. A rotating cutter block planes the wood. The top of the table planes it to get flat, square faces and edges. Under the table the thicknesser draws the wood in and planes it to the set thickness.

A jack plane, good for making a long flat surface or edge: smoothing plane is shorter, and easier to handle on small pieces of timber

Chiselling

A wood chisel is used for paring wood, that is, slicing between the grains. A mortise chisel has a much thicker blade and a heavier duty handle. It is used for cutting slots in wood, so it is hammered with a mallet a lot. Chisels are hard to use across end grain. A sharp chisel is easier and safer to use.

A bevel-edge chisel, available in a range of widths. It is good for general-purpose woodworking

Turning

A wood-turning lathe holds a piece of wood and spins it. The operator holds a chisel on a rest and guides it over the spinning wood to chisel wood away. It requires careful preparation of material and setting up of the lathe.

Maths in practice 1
Calculating wastage

Materials cost money, so it is important to keep waste to a minimum. To work out how much material is going to be wasted, you need to be able to calculate the area of shapes.

Rectangle
area = width × length
E.g. area = 10 × 20 = 200 mm²

Triangle
area = $\frac{1}{2}$ base × height
E.g. area = $\frac{1}{2}$ × 10 × 10 = 50 mm²

Or area = $\frac{1}{2}$ × 20 × 20 = 200 mm²

Circle
area = πr²
- π = 3.14
- r = radius
- r² = radius squared = r × r
- r = $\frac{1}{2}$ diameter e.g. diameter

e.g. radius
area = πr² = 3.14 × 10 × 10 = 314 mm²

r = $\frac{1}{2}$D = $\frac{20}{2}$ = 10
area = πr² = 3.14 × 10 × 10 = 314 mm²

- Figure 7.7.1 shows a shape that is being cut out of 3 mm thick plywood. Calculate the area of plywood that is wasted.
  All dimensions are in mm.
  Hint: work out the area of the waste pieces and add them together.
  area of 1 triangle = $\frac{1}{2}$ base × height = $\frac{1}{2}$ × 20 × 20 = 200 mm²
  area of circle = πr²
  = 3.14 × ($\frac{30}{2}$)² = 3.14 × 15 × 15 = 706.5 mm²
  wasted area = (4 × 200) + 706.5 = **1506.5 mm²**

Figure 7.7.1

cont...

A thicknesser with a lower table

A wood lathe turning between centres: a long piece of timber is held and spun, so the operator can chisel away the edges to create complex designs, such as a decorative table leg

A piece of timber on a face plate: the face plate spins the wood and the operator can chisel away the middle and the edges to shape and hollow it out, making a bowl shape

7 Timbers

- Figure 7.7.2 shows a shape that is being cut out of 6 mm thick MDF. Calculate the area of MDF that is wasted. All dimensions are in mm.

Hint: sometimes it is easier to work out the area of the piece of material you want and subtract it from the rectangle it is cut from to find the waste. Remember it is important to show your working in any calculation question. The shape fits in a rectangle area = 60 × 160 = 9600 mm²

The cut out shape is a rectangle and two half circles, making a whole circle.
- rectangle area = 100 × 60 = 6000 mm²
- circle area = 3.14 × 30 × 30 = 2826 mm²
- shape area = 6000 + 2826 = 8826 mm²
- area wasted = 9600 − 8826 = **774 mm²**

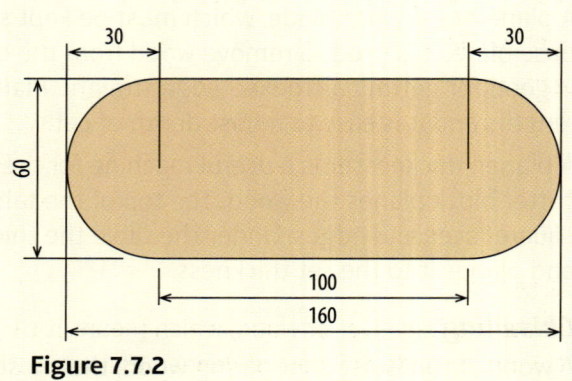

Figure 7.7.2

Abrading

Abrasive paper has a rough grit bonded on a paper or cloth backing. The first abrasive used was sand, hence the name sandpaper. Glass grit is more commonly used now.

Abrasive paper is measured by the number of pieces of grit in a square inch, so the bigger the number the smaller the grit. P80 is a coarse grit that is good for the initial removal of material on a rough surface. P120 gets a smoother finish, and P240 gets a really smooth finish on wood. You can get finer grits, but there is little need for them when working with wood.

When sanding wood, it is best to sand in line with the grain. Going across the grain can tear the grains and leave it rougher.

Electric sanders are useful tools for abrading wood to shape it and smooth it.

Carving

Woodcarving uses shaped chisels to cut away the wood. It is a skilled art form that takes a long time, but can create very detailed decorative pieces of work. It was once used a lot, but traditional woodcarving has mostly been replaced by CNC machinery, as it is much faster.

Files, rasps and surforms

Files, rasps and surforms have teeth on them that can be used to abrade away wood. They all come in a range of shapes. Flat ones are good for flat surfaces and external curves. Round and half-round shapes are good for internal curves.

Name	Appearance	Use	Advantages	Disadvantages
File		A range of tooth sizes and shapes available	Good for smoothing and shaping the sawn edges of manufactured boards	Small teeth are quite slow on wood
Rasp		• Large individual teeth • Available in different shapes, usually flat, half-round and round	• Big teeth cut soft woods quickly • Good for rough shaping	Big teeth leave marks in the wood that need removing with a file or sandpaper
Surform		A frame holds the blade with pressed metal teeth, rather like a cheese grater	• Good for rough shaping of soft materials • Blade can be removed from frame and replaced	• Leaves a rough surface • Hard work on harder woods

Table 7.7.3 Tools to abrade wood

Fabricating and constructing

Lamination
Laminating is joining layers together. Plywood is laminated, it is layers of veneer glued together. Laminate flooring is made up of layers. Laminating is useful in the workshop because thin layers can be bent and glued together, and they stay in the bent shape when the glue has dried. The bag press on page 293 is helpful for this.

Veneering
Veneer is a thin layer of wood, which means it can be more prone to damage. Plywood is made of layers of veneer laminated together. Veneer can be glued onto the surface of a cheaper material, such as MDF, to make the surface look like more expensive wood. MDF can be bought covered with hardwood veneer.

Use of screws
Screws are a very useful fixing for joining pieces of wood together. They create a tight fit to make a strong joint, and they can be unscrewed and removed if necessary.

There are two main head designs: slotted (also known as flat) and Phillips (a cross shape). You need the right screwdriver tip to fit the screw head.

A countersunk screw is useful in wood, because you can make the head of the screw fit flat with the surface of the wood. A clearance hole must be drilled first to accommodate the screw head. Drilling a pilot hole as well, which must be narrower than the screw thread, will make it easier for the screw to go in.

Nailing
Nails come in a range of shapes and sizes. Nails are hammered into the wood grain, which pinches tight onto them so they are hard to pull out. It is quick and nails can be driven below the surface and covered over to improve appearance. However, holes may need to be drilled to prevent wood from splitting.

- **Round wire nails** usually have a large flat head so they do not pull through thin materials.
- **Oval nails** spread the grain less, so are less likely to split the wood when hammered in.
- **Panel pins** are small nails for small workpieces and for holding thin boards onto timber.

Adhesives
PVA (polyvinyl acetate) is a commonly used wood glue. It is a thick white liquid, but becomes clear when it dries. It makes a strong joint in wood as long as the pieces are clamped tightly together while the glue dries. It is almost impossible to disassemble a joint without destroying it when PVA has set.

Contact adhesive is good for sticking a flat piece of a different material onto wood. Spread a thin film onto both surfaces, wait until it is nearly dry, then press the two parts firmly together. It is fast but there is little or no opportunity to reposition the pieces and it gives off solvent fumes.

> **Link it up**
> For more information on lamination, see page 289.

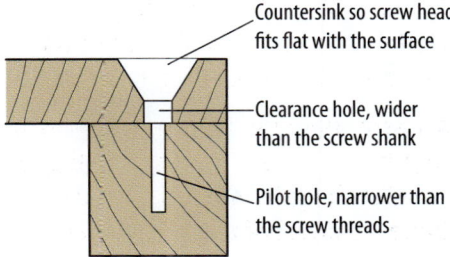

Figure 7.7.3 Drilling timber parts ready for a countersunk screw

7 Timbers

Wood joints

Name	Appearance	Advantages	Disadvantages
Butt		Easy to make, it is just square ends glued together	• Weak: there is no mechanical strength, just the glue • Not aesthetically pleasing
Dowel		Automated machines can drill the dowel holes quickly and accurately	Hard to line up the dowels accurately by hand
Lap		Quite easy to cut	Not very strong
Housing		• Holds a shelf or divider securely in the middle of a carcass (frame) • Pairs well with corner lap joints	• Can be tricky to cut neatly on a wide board • Very accurate marking out and cutting required to ensure a shelf is exactly level
Mitre		• Looks good because no end grain shows • Good for picture frames	Weak, it is only a butt joint at 45°
Mortise and tenon		• A strong joint • Good for joining a table or chair frame to legs	Time consuming to cut by hand
Dovetail		• A very strong joint – the dovetails lock together securely • Good for a drawer front that will get pulled hard	Very tricky to cut accurately by hand

Table 7.7.4 Types of joint

Wastage

Wastage processes cut material away and waste it. This is usually the fastest way to obtain the required shape with sheet materials. Most woodworking processes are wastage processes: sawing, planing, filing and sanding all remove material that is wasted and leave the required shape behind. Waste can be minimised by careful planning and use of stock sizes or off-cuts. Waste material adds to the cost of the product so should be reused wherever possible.

Addition

Addition processes add pieces of material together. Assembling parts, by making joints, gluing, screwing and nailing pieces together are addition processes. This is a fast method of producing 3D shapes but often requires a range of joining techniques, which may be time consuming.

Assembling

Knock-down fittings

Knock-down fittings are a useful range of blocks and fittings that are easy to use to fix the pieces of a product together. They are used a lot for flat-pack furniture and cupboards because they are easy for the customer to fit themselves.

Ironmongery

Ironmongery is a name for a range of parts that can be bought to go onto products. Items include:

- hinges
- handles
- knobs
- hooks
- drawer runners
- locks.

Hinges

Name	Appearance	Use	Advantages	Disadvantages
Butt hinge		Used to fit doors	Hidden from sight when door is closed	Hard to fit as an accurate slot needs to be cut on both sides
Flush hinge		Used for small cupboard doors	Easy to fit as no slots to cut	Leaves a gap between the door and frame
Butterfly hinge		Screws onto the surface, often a decorative shape	Easy to fit, as it screws onto the surface with the parts lined up	The whole hinge shows on the surface
T hinge		Used for gates and shed doors	Long bar good for supporting the weight of a gate	Sits on the surface, so shows on the front of the gate or door

Table 7.7.5 Types of hinge

7 Timbers

> **Summary**
>
> Key points to remember:
> - The name and purpose of the hand tools.
> - The name and purpose of woodworking machines.
> - The advantages and disadvantages of the different types of wood joints.
> - The advantages and disadvantages of the different types of fixtures, fittings and hinges that can be used.

> **Checkpoint**
>
> **Strengthen**
>
> **S1** What type of drill bit makes a flat-bottomed hole in wood?
> **S2** Why are knock-down fittings used a lot for flat-pack furniture?
> **S3** Why is a mitre joint good for the corner of a picture frame?
>
> **Challenge**
>
> **C1** Explain why knock-down fittings are good for flat-pack furniture.
> **C2** List the steps in preparing and screwing two pieces of timber together with a countersunk screw.

7.8 Surface treatments and finishes for functional and aesthetic purposes

> **Learning objective**
>
> By the end of this section, you should know:
> - the advantages and disadvantages of a range of surface finishes that can be applied to timber.

Surface finishes and treatments

There are many surface finishes and treatments that can be applied to wood. Wood is porous, so it will absorb water and grease and quickly look dirty and damaged. A surface finish fills the pores and makes it water resistant and easy to wipe clean. A finish can also make a product look better.

> **Link it up**
>
> You need to remember to consider health and safety implications when treating and finishing timber.

7.8 Surface treatments and finishes for functional and aesthetic purposes

	Description	Advantages	Disadvantages
Painting	• A coloured pigment in liquid that dries out	• Available in a range of colours	• Covers up the natural wood grain
Staining	• A coloured liquid that soaks into the wood surface	• Makes a pale-coloured wood like pine a darker colour to mimic more expensive woods like oak or mahogany	• Does not look quite like another wood as the pine grain still shows
Varnishing	• A clear coating that dries to a shine	• Gives a hardwearing finish that shows the grain of the wood • Can be a high gloss or a matt finish	• Can scratch or chip and expose the wood
Wax	• A soft solid that is rubbed into the surface with a cloth	• Easy to apply • Gives a plain, natural look	• Rubs away and needs reapplying • Not a glossy finish
Oil	• Is rubbed onto the surface and soaks in	• Good waterproofing for timber • Vegetable oil on kitchen ware is non-toxic	• Surface feels oily
Shellac	• A cloudy liquid made from a resin secreted by a beetle • Lots of layers are rubbed on and polished to create a finish called French polish	• Traditionally used on expensive furniture for its glossy lustre	• Easily damaged by water and heat
Veneering	• A thin layer of wood glued onto the surface	• An expensive, decorative wood like mahogany can be put onto a cheaper wood like pine or chipboard	• The veneer is natural wood, so it still needs a finish applied

Table 7.8.1 Treatments and finishes for wood

Summary

Key point to remember:
- the advantages and disadvantages of the different finishes.

Checkpoint

Strengthen

S1 Why is it important to apply a finish to a wooden product?
S2 What is an advantage of using varnish?
S3 Why is stain used?

Challenge

C1 What finish would you use on a dining table? Explain your choice.

Preparing for your exam 7

Exam strategy

What to expect in the exam

Section B of the examination is designed to test your knowledge and understanding of the material studied. Throughout the course you should practise exam-style questions that will challenge your knowledge across all sections of the timbers content. Different styles of exam questions can require short answers, long answers, sketching and calculations. Preparing thoroughly for your exam is important if you are to achieve high marks.

Section B: Material category – Timbers
This section is worth 60 marks and contains a mixture of different question styles, including short answer, sketching, calculation and extended-open response questions. This will include five marks for calculations.

In the timbers category you should know about:

- some design contexts
- the sources, origins, physical and working properties of natural and manufactured timbers, and their social and ecological footprints
- the way in which the selection of each natural and manufactured timber is influenced
- the impact of forces and stresses on timber and how it can be reinforced and stiffened
- stock forms, types and sizes to calculate the required quantity of timber
- processes that can be used to manufacture typical timber products to different scales of production
- specialist techniques and processes that can be used on timber to shape, fabricate, construct and assemble a high-quality prototype
- appropriate surface treatments and finishes that can be applied to timber for functional and aesthetic purposes.

Revision tips

- Ensure you start revising in plenty of time before your exam. You will find it easier to remember facts you have revised several times over a few weeks than those you have tried to memorise at the last minute.
- Make clear and well-ordered notes about all the sections that relate to the core and your chosen material category.
- Test yourself at the end of each section. Work through the exam-style questions and complete activities to reinforce your knowledge and understanding.
- Work through all sample assessment materials, including past papers available from Pearson.

Preparing for your exam 7

- Identify the areas where you are likely to get mathematical questions and practise the sections on numerical computation, handling data, rearranging and using equations.
- Discuss the course with your teacher and peers, as it will help your understanding.
- Work through corrections and identify areas where you may need further practice.
- Use online or other resources to extend your understanding of the design and technology context.

Exam tips

- You should plan to leave 60 minutes for answering questions in Section B.
- You must answer all the questions. If you are stuck on one, leave it and come back to it at the end.
- Although the questions will be different for each paper you sit, there is information on the page to help you answer the question. For example, the number of marks awarded for each question will tell you the number of separate points that need to be given in your answer.
- Pay attention to the command words used in the question, as these will guide you in how best to communicate your answers.
- Underline or highlight keywords in the question. After answering the question, read the question again to ensure you have done what was asked.
- If you have time available, plan the structure for long answers and make sure you give good examples where needed.
- Check through your answers at the end of the exam. Make sure you have included units and shown the workings for calculations.

Preparing for your exam 7

Sample answers with comments

Question 1: Give/state/name (short answer question)

a) Figure PE7.1 shows a design for a chair.
The chair must be:
- comfortable to sit on
- strong enough if the user rocks back on it
- easy to pick up and carry.

Use notes and sketches to show how the chair could be modified to include these three specification points. **(6 marks)**

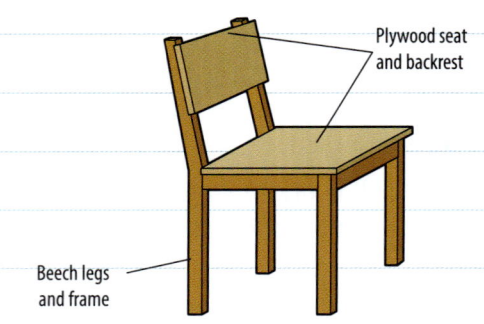

Figure PE7.1 Design for a chair

> **Exam tip**
>
> There are three changes to make to the chair. Work out what they are, then sketch the chair with your changes.
>
> Use notes to explain things that are not obvious in your sketch, and give reasons for your changes.

b) Explain **one** reason why beech is a good choice for the chair legs/frame. **(2 marks)**

> **Exam tip**
>
> Think about the properties of beech compared to other woods.

c) Figure PE7.2 shows a modified design for the back of the chair with all of the dimensions.

All dimensions are in millimetres.

Calculate the area of wood that is wasted. **(5 marks)**

Area of a circle = π × r²
Area of a triangle = ½ × base × height
π = 3.142

Figure PE7.2 Design for the back of the chair

> **Exam tip**
>
> Divide the wasted portions into simple shapes.

d) Explain **two** different methods that could be used to manufacture the re-designed chair back. **(6 marks)**

> **Exam tip**
>
> Consider different methods: hand tools, batch production, CAD/CAM etc.

Student answer

a)

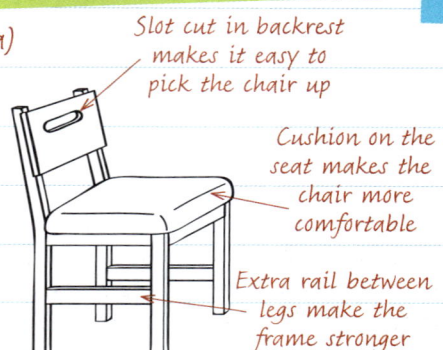

- Slot cut in backrest makes it easy to pick the chair up
- Cushion on the seat makes the chair more comfortable
- Extra rail between legs make the frame stronger

Figure PE7.3 Modified chair design

Verdict

This is a good answer. The changes made would meet the specifications better than the original design.

b) It is strong.

Verdict

This is a poor answer. Beech is quite a strong wood, but the answer needs to be more specific. For example: Beech has a close, even grain that makes it stronger and tougher than many other woods, so beech would withstand the stresses put on a chair frame better than many other woods.

Preparing for your exam 7

c) Area of each corner = ½ × 80 × 60 = 2400 mm²
Area of 4 corners = 4 × 2400 = 9600 mm²
The slot is two half circles (a whole circle) and a rectangle
Slot = (π × 30²) + (60 × 160) = 2827.8 + 9600 = 12,427.8 mm²
Wood wasted = 9600 + 12,427.8 = 22,027.8 mm²

> **Verdict**
> This is a correct answer. All working out is clear – it is important to show your working out in a calculation question.

d) 1. The chair back could be batch produced by marking the shape out with a template, drilling holes at each end of the slot and sawing out with a jigsaw. The corners could be cut off with the jigsaw or a bandsaw; finish with a sander.
2. The chair back could be cut with a computer-controlled router: draw the shape with suitable software on a computer; tessellate several together – as many as will fit in the machine; place the plywood plank in a computer-controlled router and cut out.

> **Verdict**
> This is a good answer – it describes two different methods in enough detail.

Question 2: 'Discuss' question

2 a) Figure PE7.4 shows a design for a simple wooden candle holder. The candle holder must:
- have a stable base so the candle is not knocked over
- have an attractive appearance
- be easy to pick up and carry the candle safely.

Explain **two** ways in which the candle holder meets or fails to meet the design criteria. (4 marks)

Figure PE7.4 Design for a wooden candle holder

> **Exam tip**
> Decide which features are good or need improving. Make it clear if your points are meeting or failing to meet the criteria.

b) A Forstner bit is used to drill the blind hole. Explain **one** reason why a Forstner bit would be used to drill the hole. (2 marks)

> **Exam tip**
> Think about what makes a Forstner bit different from other types of drill bit.

c) Use notes and sketches to show the process of drilling the blind hole safely and accurately.
You will be marked on how you apply your understanding of design and technology, not on your graphical skills. (4 marks)

> **Exam tip**
> Use a sketch to show the main points of your answer. You might not need to show the whole machine.
> Add notes to explain the main points or anything that is not obvious from your sketch.

Student answer

a) 1. The candle holder meets the criterion of a stable base. The base is a large flat-bottomed square that would be quite hard to knock over.
2. The candle holder does not meet the criteria of an attractive appearance well. It is a plain square shape with no interesting design features to make it stand out or appeal to the consumer.

> **Verdict**
> This is a good answer. Two sensible points are made and clearly explained.

b) A Forstner bit makes a round hole.

> **Verdict**
> This is a poor answer. It is a correct statement, but it has no value because all types of drill bit make a round hole. A Forstner bit would be used because it is designed to make a large round hole with a flat bottom, so it is best for a blind hole.

Preparing for your exam 7

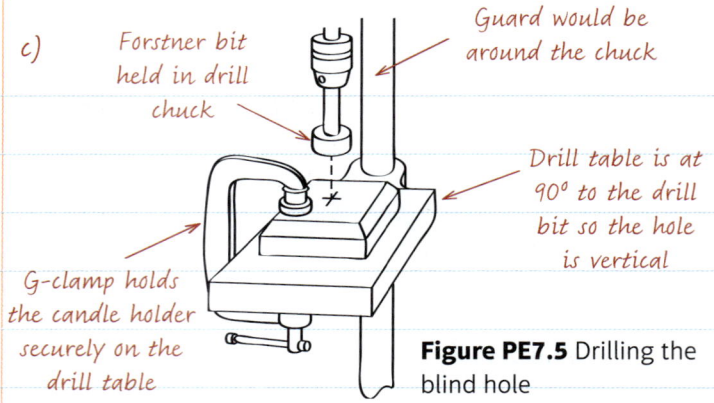

c) Forstner bit held in drill chuck
Guard would be around the chuck
Drill table is at 90° to the drill bit so the hole is vertical
G-clamp holds the candle holder securely on the drill table

Figure PE7.5 Drilling the blind hole

Verdict

This is a good answer. Notice the student has only sketched part of the pillar drill to explain their point, and has used labels to make the key points clear. A good addition to the answer would be to include use of a depth stop to get the hole the right depth.

Question 3: 'Explain'

Figure PE7.6 shows a design for a picture frame. The frame is to be made from decorative moulding.

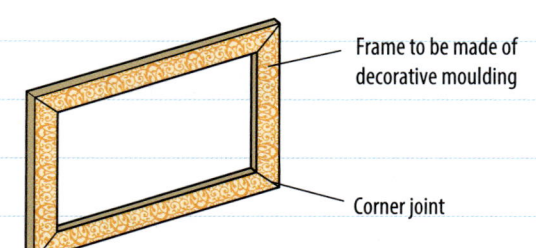

Figure PE.7.6 Design for a picture frame

Frame to be made of decorative moulding
Corner joint

a) To batch produce 20 picture frames, a ready-made decorative moulding has been bought in long lengths. Explain **one** reason why buying ready-made moulding might be a good idea. **(2 marks)**

> **Exam tip**
> State your reason and explain why it is good for the company making the frames.

b) (i) Name a good joint to use in the corner of the picture frame. **(1 mark)**
   (ii) Explain **one** reason for your choice. **(2 marks)**

> **Exam tip**
> Make sure your reason matches the joint chosen.

c) Explain **two** quality control checks that could be carried out on the frame during the manufacturing process. **(4 marks)**

> **Exam tip**
> Quality control should make sure the product is being made correctly.

d) Table PE7.1 shows some information about the picture frame.

Raw material	Mahogany
Source	South American rainforests
Growth rate/lifespan	25–100 years
From sustainably managed sources	no

Table.PE7.1 Information about a picture frame

> **Exam tip**
> Spend a bit of time thinking through your answer before you start writing. It might help to make a list of points to include before you start writing.

Analyse the information in Table PE7.1.
Evaluate the picture frame with reference to its ecological footprint.
(9 marks)

Preparing for your exam 7

Student answer

(a) Although plain wood is cheaper to buy than moulding, it would be expensive to buy and set up the equipment needed to make the moulding, so for the small number needed it is cheaper to buy it ready-made from a specialist supplier.

Verdict

This is a good answer. Remember, this is about scales of production. If the company was going to manufacture 20,000 picture frames every year they would probably buy the equipment to make the moulding themselves.

(b) (i) A mitre joint.
(ii) A mitre joint has both ends cut at 45°. It looks good because it hides the end grain and the moulding pattern would join up neatly in the corner.

Verdict

This is a good answer. The student has correctly identified that the joint used will need to look good.

(c) Make sure they are all the right size.

Verdict

This a weak answer. It is a true statement, but more explanation of specific checks is needed for four marks. A better answer would be:

1. Check that sawn pieces are exactly the right length before cutting joints.
2. Check that each joint is cut at exactly 45°, so the two angles fit together to make square corners.

(d) Mahogany is a tropical hardwood from rainforest. This mahogany has come from a South American rainforest that is not sustainably managed, so new mahogany trees are not being planted. The cleared land might be used for agriculture afterwards, so the forest is being lost forever.

Even if the forest areas were being re-planted after cutting down the mahogany trees, it would take at least 25 years for them to grow big enough to harvest again, and the other plants and animals that lived in the forest areas before would have been lost.

South America is a long way away. The trees have been transported to the coast on lorries or boats, then shipped to the UK. This is a lot of transport, using fossil fuels and doing damage to the environment.

The mahogany is being used to make moulding, which can be quite wasteful because a lot of the wood is machined away to dust to create the shape and patterns in the moulding.

The ecological footprint of using mahogany is high because of the environmental damage caused by destroying the forest and the impact of transporting it around the world. The picture frames could be made from pine from sustainably managed forests in Northern Europe and stained a darker colour. This would have less environmental impact.

Verdict

This is a good answer. Notice how the student has explained a list of four different factual points and finished with a clear conclusion.

Pearson Education Ltd accepts no responsibility whatsoever for the accuracy or method of working in the answers given.

Component 2: Controlled Assessment

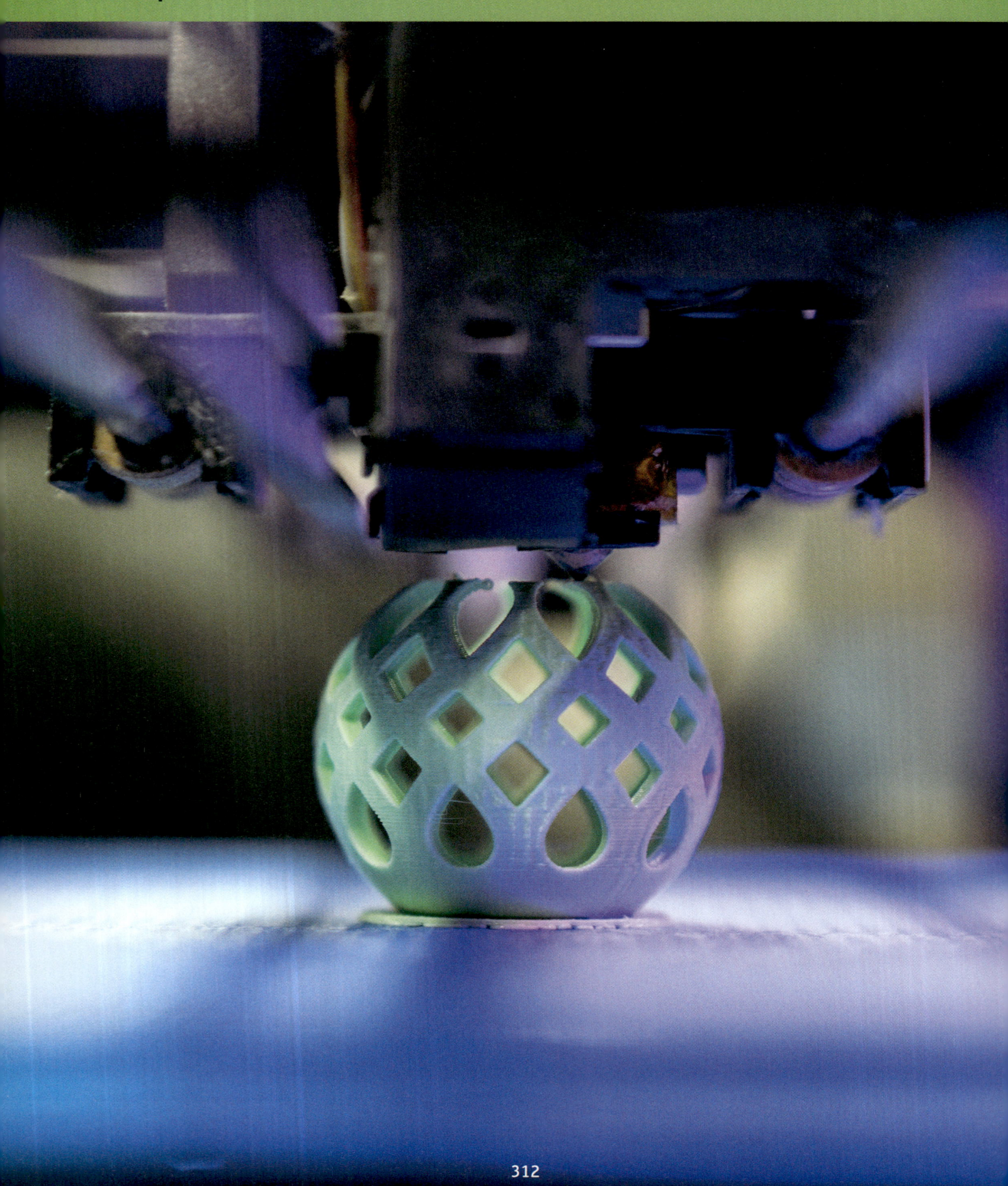

Introduction

Everything in our world is designed: from the big things, such as houses and cars, to the little things, such as paper clips, plug holes and matches. Some of these things are so common that we tend to forget that they were ever designed.

Some things, on the other hand, are more obvious, due to their technical design or humour. You will have the challenge in Component 2 to design either a product from scratch or redesign an existing product from a set of scenarios.

Design scenarios

Throughout our lives we come across problems, annoyances or things we don't like. Designers love to work out these problems to create solutions and ultimately to make money. However, the problems that we face in our own lives might be very different to those faced by our neighbours or people in other countries. Designers need to identify their customer clearly and understand their needs, wants, dislikes and values.

What am I expected to do in Component 2?

A year before your exams, your teacher will introduce you to Component 2, the non-examined assessment, which does not include an examination. Each year, three different exciting scenarios are set by Edexcel; each one provides a challenge with limitless possibilities for you to respond to through a design and make activity. This is your chance to show off your developed Design and Technology skills by identifying and meeting a user's needs and wants in a certain scenario. You will present your ideas through the following stages:

- investigate
- design
- make
- evaluate.

These sections are all covered separately in this section.

> ### Apply it
>
> **The scenario:** In 1978, James Dyson found that he could not get his vacuum cleaner to suck up dirt properly from the carpet. His frustration led him to open up the vacuum cleaner, where he was surprised to find that the vacuum bag was nearly empty, not full as he had imagined. On further investigation, he realised that a thin layer of dust had coated the inside of the bag, blocking the bag's pores. This had caused the vacuum to lose suction power.
>
> The identification of this problem led to many hours of brainstorming, design thinking, and hundreds of models and prototypes until he released the first Dyson vacuum cleaner. Today Dyson is a leading brand in a range of products. Where could your ideas lead you?

Component 2: Controlled Assessment

> **Apply it**
>
> An example scenario could be: Improving working spaces both inside and outside of the home (environments and objects)
>
> - How can work spaces be made more environmentally friendly?
> - How can workspaces encourage students to revise more for their exams?

Each design scenario will include two questions to help stimulate your imagination. Think carefully about the scenarios, but remember it is not compulsory to follow one of the questions. Instead, you may generate your own questions. You need to pick a scenario that will sustain your interest over a few months and one that sets off your imagination. It might be that you want to analyse each scenario by brainstorming your first thoughts and carrying out some initial research to help you make your decision. It may also be worth reading ahead so that you can see what is expected of you, however, you don't need to have a solution all ready as this will come through the **iterative design process**.

What does controlled assessment mean?

Component 2 is a controlled assessment task. This means that the work you submit must be your own and must be completed in your classroom. You can ask your friends for their opinions and their feedback but you cannot submit work done by anyone else.

How much of my GCSE is it worth?

Component 2 is worth 50 per cent of your Design and Technology GCSE, so you need to try your best at every stage of the creative process.

How will I be marked?

There are 100 marks for the project and you will submit it to your teacher as a portfolio and **prototype**. Your portfolio will be approximately 20–30 sides of A3 paper. You may also submit models (using mediums such as paper/card/foam) alongside your finished prototype. You will either submit your work electronically or as a printed project, depending on your teacher and school – a selection of these will then be passed on to an **external moderator**. You will use your knowledge, skills and understanding that you have gained throughout KS3 and KS4 to complete your project.

The moderator may not see your actual prototype in the flesh. Therefore, it is really important that you take pictures at every stage of the manufacturing process to show that it was you who made it and not your friend, the teacher or the technician!

Can my teacher help me?

Your teacher will be there to guide you through the process, discuss your ideas with you, ensure that you are working safely and provide general feedback to your group. Your teacher is not allowed to give you individual feedback on how to meet the assessment criteria or allow you to re-work your portfolio after it has been marked. Therefore, you need to make sure that you listen carefully to any whole group feedback and apply this to your own work.

> **Key terms**
>
> **Iterative design process:** where you continually test, evaluate and refine your ideas, meaning that you will do work on different stages at a variety of points through your project.
>
> **Prototype:** either a scale model or an actual finished product. For example, if you are designing an interior, you would not have time to make this full size, so a scale model would be appropriate.
>
> **External moderator:** someone who will check that your teacher has given your non-examination assessment the correct mark.

Component 2: Controlled Assessment

Investigation

Getting started

Your teacher will tell you the three scenarios for your controlled assessment. These will be available in June during the year before your final exams. Think carefully about:
- which scenario sounds the most interesting to you
- which scenario sparks your design imagination.

Learning objectives

By the end of this section, you should know:
- how to identify and fully investigate a design question that you would like to solve
- how to research your users' needs and wants with full reference to form and function
- how to use your research to write a design brief and comprehensive specification.

Identifying a design problem

Once you have chosen your design scenario, you are then on to the exciting and limitless task of identifying a design question within it. When exploring the context, you may discover a need or opportunity that you hadn't thought of. Brainstorming and carrying out market research such as speaking to users, trying out products and doing some internet research could help you to narrow down your area.

Identifying user requirements

Hopefully you now have a question that you would like to explore and solve. The next step is to identify your users' needs and wants. This could be done through observations, interviewing a particular user or user group and then assessing whether form or function is more important to a user.

Observations

As part of your observations, you could:
- watch someone's routine (for example, getting a child to go to sleep)
- watch someone use, or wear, a product, system or service.

Identifying User Requirements

Name – Alan George
Age – 56
What is your occupation?
I am the postman for Duporth in St Austell and I have done this job for the last 36 years. I empty all the postboxes in the local area each day.

How has your job changed in the past 36 years?
I have noticed a real decline in the amount of letters being posted each day over the past 36 years. I used to empty lots of postboxes twice a day and now the amount of postboxes has been reduced and the collections have been minimised.

How do you think people could be encouraged to use the postal system?
I think it would be interesting to see postboxes where they work in more of an electronic way. Perhaps you could weigh your parcel and put the correct postage on at the actual postbox, rather than going to a post office where you are restricted with times. In a few years' time, I wonder whether postboxes might start to look more like the Amazon lockers that are cropping up around the place.

What problems do you find with the actual postbox?
I often find that inconsiderate people have put litter inside of them and sometimes this can be dangerous things, such as used needles. I also find that they could all do with a good WD40 to stop them creaking so much!

It is amazing to see how weathered the paint looks in such a short space of time – I love how they look when they are freshly painted!

Overall conclusions:
It was really interesting speaking to Alan the postman and hear his experience in his job over the past 36 years and his thoughts on the future of the postal system. From this I am going to do the following things to help meet my users' needs and wants:
- Research into other postal methods, such as the Amazon lockers, and look at some self-serving systems such as self-serve at the library for library books and ATMs, as these could influence some of my design thoughts and increase the use of the postal system.
- Research into how to make the postal method that I choose user friendly, as from my observations of him emptying the postbox, I could hear the squeaks of the metal inside and it was obvious that Alan had to use a bit of force to open it up.
- Research into methods that could stop people selfishly dropping litter in them while protecting our postmen and -ladies

Positive – This student has provided clear primary research

Things to improve – It would be useful for this student to include an interview with someone who regularly/irregularly uses postboxes for their valued opinions, too.

Student coursework example page (1):
This student's design problem revolves around the declining use of the postal system. She has observed how a postman empties the postbox and interviewed him with carefully worded questions. Who would you observe to understand your user?

Component 2: Controlled Assessment

Ergonomic research

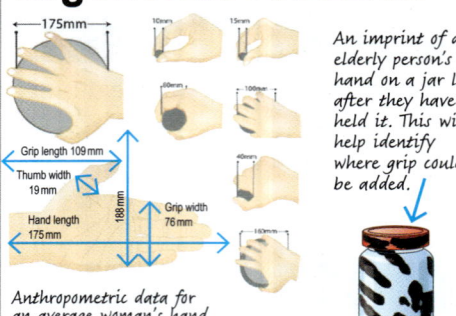

Anthropometric data for an average woman's hand

My Granny Tilly suffers from arthritis. She agreed to try to open jars with different sized lids to help my design research – 55mm, 70mm and 85mm in diameter. The photo above shows her trying to open an 85mm jar. She found the very small jar very difficult to open as it was fiddly. The large jar was also difficult as she could not grip it very well. I need to aim around the 70mm diameter for my product to enable the elderly to open them easily.

An imprint of an elderly person's hand on a jar lid after they have held it. This will help identify where grip could be added.

Products that use effective grip

Some information about arthritis
- There are many common symptoms of arthritis. They include **swelling, pain, stiffness and a loss of motion in the joints.**
- **1 in 5 people have arthritis over the age of 18. It is the UK's number one cause of disability.**
- The Arthritis Foundation have an **'Ease of Use'** mark that can be placed on products. Companies that develop products designed for people with arthritis can apply for their product to be tested by a team of scientists to see if it meets the requirements of a person with arthritis.
- **Each product is evaluated against a number of 'pass' or 'fail' requirements.**
- The scientists assess and establish user tasks based on how someone with arthritis might use a product. This includes the point from which from the product is purchased- how might they remove the product from the packaging?

Conclusion from the page:
Having researched the average measurements of a female adult hand, I have found out that:
- My user has a roughly average-sized grip circumference of 189 mm. Using that data, and having seen how my user interacts with different sized jar lids, I now know that the maximum diameter of the lid needs to be 70 mm for my user to comfortably open. This is smaller than for people without arthritis as I have found out that arthritis causes joints to swell and, therefore, the full grip circumference will be harder to achieve.
- Much smaller jar lids, such as the example in the first diagram, were too uncomfortable to open..
- It is also amazing to see the vast amount of people who suffer from arthritis, which shows the huge impact that a solution to my design problem could have.
- I need to start to think about products that successfully use grips, such as bike handles, and consider how I may incorporate this into my design solutions. I therefore want to research materials that enable a hand to grip in more detail.
- The Arthritis Foundation has an 'Ease of Use' mark – this has provided a good place to test my product once it has been manufactured. I will try this with my gran who suffers from arthritis.

Positive – this student has found out useful information about their users' arthritis condition and started to research essential anthropometric measurements that will help design a comfortable product.

Things to improve – it would be useful to repeat the jar opening exercise with differer shaped lids and a variety of elderly people as perhaps she might have come across certain shapes that would be easier for people suffering from arthritis to twist.

Student coursework example page (2): This student's design problem revolved around creating a set of storage units for items in the kitchen that could be opened and closed easily by elderly people suffering from arthritis

Interviewing a particular user or user group
Before interviewing, think carefully about what you would like to find out and what would be beneficial to know or understand in order for you to generate ideas and solutions. Use these thoughts to help you carefully word pre-prepared questions but also be ready to improvise depending on the responses from the interview.

Is form or function more important?
Some people think that **form** (how a product looks) is more important than **function** (how a product works), some people think the other way around and some people think that they carry equal weighting.

For example, the gold-plated version of the Alessi lemon squeezer called the Juicy Salif corroded with lemon juice – Philippe Starck (an Alessi designer) was quoted saying that 'it was not meant to squeeze lemons' but 'to start conversations'. The Juicy Salif costs approximately £50, whereas, in contrast, a plastic lemon squeezer can be bought from a pound shop. The £1 lemon squeezer would squeeze lemons perfectly, while not corroding, could be seen as inferior with regard to aesthetics. Is form or function more important to your user/s?

User research
You may need to research conditions that affect your user, such as arthritis, disabilities, colour blindness or allergic reactions.

These will all vary depending on the problem that you are trying to solve. Remember to record these findings, as it shows that you are understanding the problem through your users' eyes and consequently helps you to design and make your product according to their needs.

Investigating existing products
Think of your mobile phone. There are many competitor mobile devices on the market today, differing in size, camera capability, apps, storage and so on. Brands such as Apple, Samsung and Motorola constantly look at each other's products to try to make their own products more appealing than their competitors'. It is important for them to know what is already out there, their prices, functions, customer opinions and so on. You need to do exactly the same. Ask yourself these questions:

- What have designers done in the past that was successful/unsuccessful?
- What products do current designers have on the market/who is your competition?
- What are the current trends, such as vintage fashion?
- What are their prices? Are they good value for money?
- What is good/bad about their products?
- What are their customer reviews like?
- What other products could also influence your design? For instance, one that uses a similar mechanism that could apply to your design solution.

Investigation

Try to look at as many existing products in the flesh as possible. Picking up the products, feeling them and testing them will give you the hands-on feel that your user will experience. As you work through these questions, keep in mind who your user is and what their opinion would be on each of these points – if you don't know then ask them. Record this through images and words.

Product disassembly

It is always fascinating to have a look inside a product, as you can learn a lot about materials, components and fixings. Try to find a product that could be useful to your scenario to take apart. Ask yourself:

- What components/fixings would you need to include in your solution? What constraints will they give you on size?
  - Essential internal components and their relevant sizes, e.g. bulb, battery.
- What options/limitations will you have?
  - Different options, such as choices of switches – slide/push/toggle
  - Different fastenings, for example hook and look fasteners, poppers or zips.
- How has the product been assembled, for example use of linings or bias binding?
- What materials have been used and could this influence your design ideas?
- What could you learn from this product for your design ideas?

Research strategies

Depending on your chosen scenario and design question, your design research may go in different directions compared with others in your class. This is perfectly normal and makes the whole process more interesting. The following table provides possible suggestions, but you may find other things/routes that you could also find out more about, such as market research (see page 315).

Investigating existing products

INTRODUCTION
I am investigating the design scenario of 'creating alternative play spaces for young children'. I have found three different products that I would like to look into with more depth and gain my customer's opinion from. My customer is Leanne Ashworth, mother to two-year-old Michael Ashworth.

This tepee costs £129.99 and is sold on the teepeeeforfun website. It is similar to many sold on websites such as Not on the High Street or Etsy. The average price is £100 for them but they go up to £250+. I personally feel that this is extortionate, however, some customers are prepared to pay this for a customised tepee. As shown by the customer review, 59% of people have rated it as 5/5 and 34% as 4/5, therefore customers do seem happy with it. The lights look really effective in the dark and this could be a lovely little hideout for young children. I would definitely consider using lights in one of my design solutions, although I will need to be careful with the batteries around children and the potential heat from bulbs/LEDs. The five poles make the space inside larger for play, however, this might limit people with smaller rooms.

CUSTOMER OPINION *'I like the look of it, however, with tepees like this, I have found that they often fall over, especially if Michael pushes/runs into/knocks one of the poles. I would not be happy going out of the room and leaving him in there just to nip to the toilet in case it fell on top of him. I also think Michael would appreciate it being more "boyish" and ideally I would like it to have a base.'*

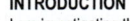
59% of people have rated this 5/5 and 34% have rated it 4/5.

The child's teepee cost £30 and is sold in a large toy superstore. Rather than the fabric tepee above, it is made using polyester material. This is a good idea, as it means that it can be wiped clean easily, but I do not like the feel of the plastic and personally feel that it makes it look cheap. I like the native-American inspired pattern and I think that a theme is important to include for the child.

CUSTOMER OPINION *'I love the colours and I think Michael really would too. I understand the polyester material can be wiped clean, I liked how the poles could be taken off the tepee and the fabric popped in the wash for a thorough cleaning.'*

The Eden Project has inspired to think about a play place/den for a young boy. The domes allow a large amount of light in and create a warm atmosphere inside while aesthetically they look amazing. I am thinking that perhaps a blow-up play place could be created. This would allow it to be deflated and stored when not in use, but it could also be transported easily into different rooms and the garden. It would also be wiped clean.

CUSTOMER OPINION *'Although I have not been to the Eden Project with Michael, I have been with my husband Adam and we were equally amazed about the fantastic spaces created. I think that this would be a great idea although it would be harder to incorporate a theme into it, which I know Michael would love. I think we would be more likely to use it inside than outside, due to our limited garden space. So being able to deflate/inflate it would not be a huge selling point to myself.'*

OVERALL FINDINGS
Having looked carefully at three different products from my own perspective and my customer's perspective, I have come to the following conclusions for my design requirements:
- Must be capable of being disassembled and put in the washing machine
- Must incorporate a theme suitable to my user (I need to do some investigation into potential themes)
- Must not topple over if the child accidentally or non-accidentally walks/pushes into it.

Positive – this student has managed to analyse three different products and consider how they would appeal to her customer. This has informed her design requirements.

Improvements – it would have been good to see three completely different products actually tested out by Michael rather than using images from the Internet. This would make the page stronger. As well as this, two of the products are very similar- they should all be different. From the design/manufacture side, it would be useful to also disassemble and photograph some of the products to see how they have been made.

Student coursework example page (3): This student's design scenario revolved around creating alternative play spaces for young children

Component 2: Controlled Assessment

	Things you may need to research
Material choices	• Suitable materials for different parts and purposes, for example rubber for grips on handles and blackout linings • Smart materials, including thermochromic and glow in the dark materials
Different technologies	• Fingerprint sensor, password or eye retina recognition
Aesthetics	• Colours that appeal to certain user groups, like primary colours for children • Colours for dangers/warnings/hazards • Textures
Biomimicry	• Inspiring mechanisms found in nature, such as the pitcher plant that eats insects
Sustainability issues	• Energy sources: solar power, wind-up power or rechargeable batteries • Recycled materials • How could the product be repaired/recycled/reused at the end of its life?
Sizes	• Dimensions of existing products/related products/components • Size constraints of places for the product to be stored
Laws that may be relevant	• Safety standards, flammable/toxic materials
Packaging	• How does the product reach its user? • How is the product protected from damage? • How is the product marketed to its user? • How can you reduce the ecological footprint of the product?

Table CA2.1 Areas to research

> **Key term**
>
> **Biomimicry:** how products/materials take inspiration from nature. For instance, Velcro® was developed from the tiny little hooks found at the end of the cocklebur flowering plant after the inventor George de Mestral found them attached to his dog following a hunting trip.

Design brief

You will need to write a design brief based on the findings of your investigation. This is a short statement that identifies what you plan to do, for whom, where it will be used and why you have chosen to follow this route.

> *I am designing a working space for some teenagers' bedrooms to encourage them to revise and help them to achieve high marks in their exams.*

Product specification

Your specification is a list of design requirements from your research that are realistic, technical, measurable and justified. The requirements will focus on what your product has to do to be successful. You will use them to assess and re-work your ideas throughout the iterative design process and to evaluate the success of your final prototype.

To strengthen your specification, you will need to justify your requirements with reasons and ideas from your research. For example:

The requirement to hold three AA batteries is a measurable part – if one of your designs is only big enough to hold two batteries then it will not be fulfilling your specification.

The student example below refers to their product disassembly and their user interview.

> *My product must be able to hold three AA batteries as shown from my product disassembly. These must be securely contained in a screwed compartment as my user's mother told me that he likes to try to take his toys apart.*

Apply it

Have a go at finishing these sentences:
- My design must enable a child to play, interact, create movement and create sound because…
- My design must appeal to a 3- to 6-year-old and a parent…
- My design should be no bigger than 150 mm × 150 mm…

Writing your own specification

Use the ideas bank below to help you write your design requirements. Your product specification needs to consider the points in Table CA2.2. It is sometimes useful to start off the sentences using 'my product must/should/could':

Key terms

Function: relates to the way in which something works.
Ergonomics: how anthropometric data is used to make a product more comfortable for its user.
Form: relates to the way that something looks.

	Considerations	My product must/should/could:
Function and performance	• What are you designing and why? • What will your product do that makes it different from others on the market? • Where will the product be used and how will it endure the conditions?	Example: *My product must be able to be seen clearly in the dark so that users can tell the time when they wake up in the middle of the night.*
Customer/ user	• Who are you designing your product for (age range/size of customer/customer likes/dislikes/ ergonomics) and why? • User/buyer: Is the person who is going to buy it different to the person going to use it? What do they both require from this product and how can you meet their needs?	Example: *My product must appeal to elderly people aged 70+ who suffer from arthritis and movement restrictions.* *It should help them to open jars easily and efficiently.*
Form/ aesthetics	• What could your product look like/represent? • Think about colour/pattern/texture/smell/taste/ design style/era.	Example: *My product could represent a cartoon animal to appeal to the 8-year-old child.* *It must not look scary so that the child is not scared of being alone in their room.*

Table CA2.2 Developing your product *Cont…*

Component 2: Controlled Assessment

	Considerations	My product must/should/could:
Cost/scale of production	• How much should your product cost to make? Why? Think about scale of production: batch/mass/one-off. • How much should your product cost to sell? Why? Think about affordability/value/profit margins. • Where would it be sold? High street store, specialist shop or internet site.	*Example:* My product should cost no more than £20 otherwise it will be unaffordable to a typical average family, as shown in my user research. It will be sold in mainstream toyshops, such as Toys R Us, that attract families to the store.
Environment/ sustainability	• Is it refillable? For example with batteries/liquid – are these easy to access? • Can the product change with the customer's age or needs (for example some highchairs convert into a toddler chair)? • How could it be disposed of or recycled at the end of its life? Is it easy to disassemble to then sort for recycling?	*Example:* My product must have the batteries easily accessible so that my customer can change the batteries without having to replace the whole product.
Safety precautions	• What do you need to consider in the design of your product? (For example sharp edges/loose parts/choking hazards/accessible electronic parts/allergic reactions/non-toxic paint for children's toys/flammable textiles/parts that produce heat and therefore shouldn't be covered.) • What do you need to consider in the use of your product? Think about age limits or instructions to prevent harm.	*Example:* My product must have all of its electronics hidden away and not accessible to small children, so that they do not harm themselves.
Size	• Dimensions – cm/mm/m/weight/storage capacity (for example, to hold 12 pencils) • Anthropometrics and ergonomics: is the size appropriate to the client? Can it be held easily? Will it fit your customer? • Is it foldaway/expandable? Where can it be stored?	*Example:* My product must fold away to half the size to fit in the cupboard underneath a bedside cabinet (540 × 400 × 450 mm) so that it can be stored easily in my customer's cluttered room.
Materials and components	• What materials will you use and why? Polymers/metals/woods/ceramics/fabrics • Will your materials need protecting? Varnishing/dip coating/painting? • Where will your product be used? Waterproof, sturdy, ability to be wiped/cleaned/washed. • **BOP** parts (bought-out parts, such as nuts, bolts, zips, poppers, buttons)	*Example:* My product will be used outside so must be waterproof and be able to withstand all weather conditions without ageing. It should be easy to clean due to animals in the garden and birds flying over.

Table CA2.2 Developing your product

> **Key term**
>
> **BOP:** bought-out parts from a supplier, e.g. screws, nuts and bolts.

Summary

Key points to remember:
- Identify a clear problem to solve and sum this up in your design brief.
- Research your users' needs and wants.
- Analyse existing products and carry out any other relevant research.
- Use your research to write a justified specification.

Checkpoint

Strengthen

S1 Is your research specifically relevant to your design scenario and design question?

S2 Have you found out something about your design scenario or question that you did not know before?

S3 Is there anything that you found out from your research that you could use to strengthen your design requirements in your specification, for example, it needs to include a grip on the lid, as my user said that they most often use the product in the kitchen after washing their hands.

Challenge

C1 Have you included measurable user and design requirements that can be easily tested?

C2 Have you justified your user and design requirements against your research?

Component 2: Controlled Assessment

Design

Getting started

This is the creative part of the project where you have the wonderful opportunity to solve your user's problems through creative ideas. Think carefully about:

- What would your user like?
- How can you respond to your user and design requirements from your design brief and specification?

Investigate a variety of design approaches that designers might use when coming up with design ideas. To support your investigation, refer to Section 1.16.

Learning objectives

By the end of this section, you should know:

- how to use your research to help you come up with a range of creative design ideas
- how to address your design and user requirements from your specification at all stages
- how to use a range of communication techniques to model and develop your ideas into a tested and modified final concept.

Design ideas

'If you **always do** what you **always did** then you'll **always get** what you **always got**…' **Henry Ford, industrial designer and founder of the Ford Motor Company**

Let your imagination take over and do not let the issue of 'how' constrain your initial thoughts – some ideas might seem a little far-fetched but what you learn from these may help you to build stronger ideas later on. You will consider the detail and practicality in more depth when you start to develop your ideas.

How can I communicate my ideas?

There are many strategies that you can use to communicate your design ideas, your development and your final concept such as:

- freehand sketching (2D and/or 3D)
- cut and paste techniques
- digital photography/media
- 3D models
- isometric and oblique projection
- perspective drawing
- orthographic and exploded views
- systems and schematic diagrams
- computer-aided design (CAD) and computer-aided manufacture, such as laser cutting/3D printing
- exploded views to show how things fit together.

Try to use a mixture of communication techniques. However, you may feel that either your own personal strengths or the style of your project will suit certain strategies more than others.

Link it up

For more information on how to communicate your design ideas, see page 68–76.

Annotations

To get top marks for communicating your design ideas, you will need to add lots of annotations. The annotations will help you to explain your ideas and will enable anyone looking at your work to understand your ideas without the need to speak to you. Always respond to your design brief, address the design requirements from your specification and refer to your research. The table on page 323 gives a list of things to think about including when communicating and annotating your designs.

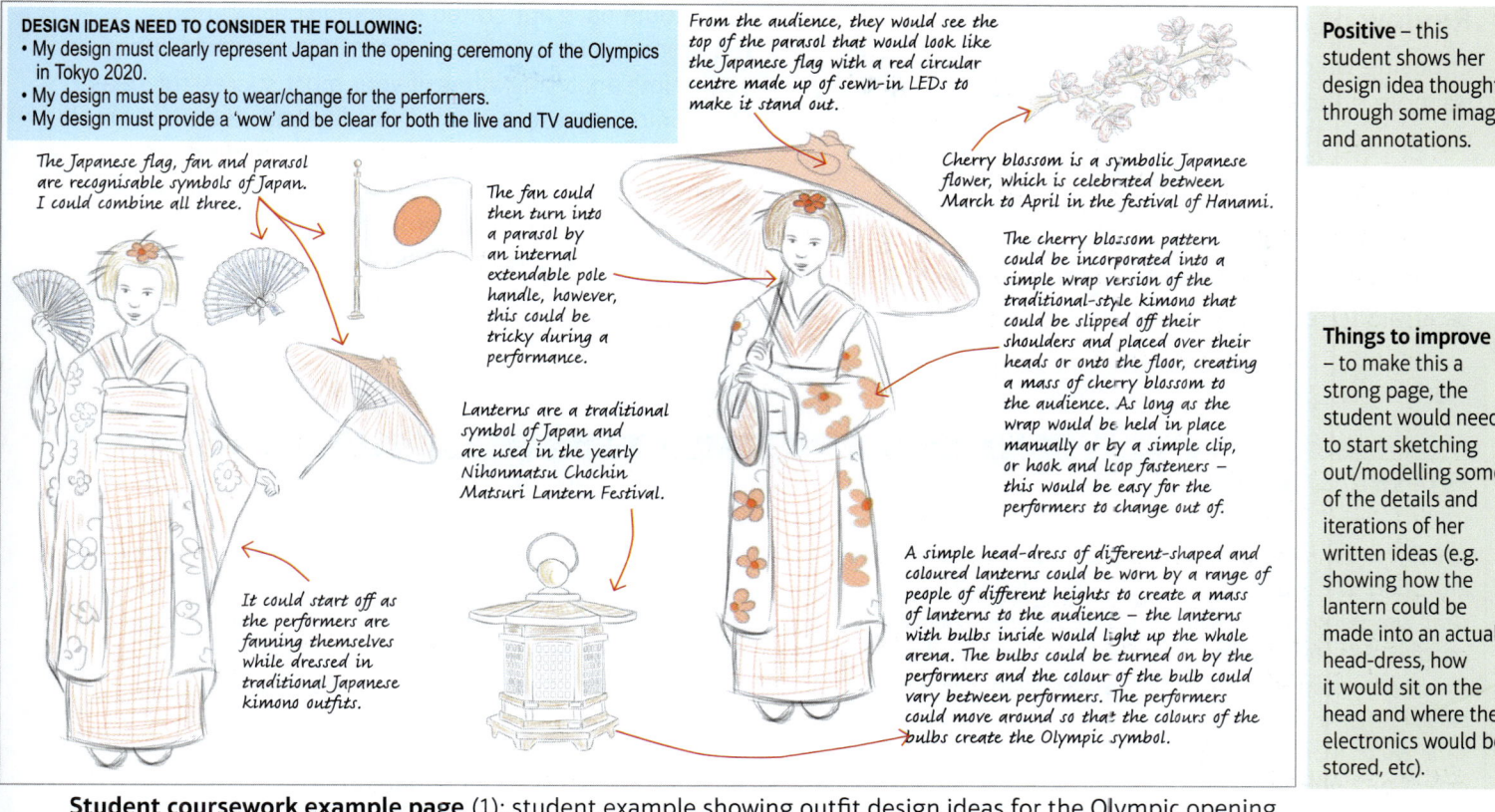

Student coursework example page (1): student example showing outfit design ideas for the Olympic opening ceremony in Tokyo 2020

Checklist
☐ How does it respond to your design brief?
☐ How does it meet the points in your specification? If it does not, then why and how could you modify it?
☐ How would it achieve the function(s) that you intended?
☐ What are the positives/negatives of each design?
☐ Does it appeal to your user/customer? ☐ • Ergonomics: would your user be able to use/operate/wear it comfortably? ☐ • Does it appeal to your user's cultural values?
☐ Would it be possible within the budget that you have set yourself/the price that you would like it to be sold at?
☐ What are your thoughts on potential materials/components/processes and techniques?
☐ Would it be sustainable? ☐ • Materials ☐ • Sustainable sources of energy (solar/wind-up) ☐ • Could it be recycled? Easily dismantled?
☐ Is it an idea to take forward? Or would part of it be an idea to take forward?

Table CA2.3 Checklist of things to show/consider when communicating your ideas

Component 2: Controlled Assessment

Review of initial ideas

Choosing which design to take forward can sometimes be more difficult than coming up with the design ideas themselves. This is where you will need to take feedback and advice from your **user**, reflect on your design brief and be objective on the design requirements decisions that you made in your **design specification**. Try to do this throughout the whole designing process and do not be afraid to rethink at any stage.

You should have annotated user and specification requirements in your design ideas, but you could spend some time analysing a few of your most successful ideas. This could be presented in a table like the student example. You may be surprised at which ideas come out more positively measured against your design requirements or you might notice that elements of each design could be used to make one really successful idea. These design decisions will then help you to modify both your ideas and thought process when you go on to develop your design.

Specification points	Design 3 – The alert cone	Design 7 – The buzzing watch	Design 10 – The pre-recording
FUNCTION – My product must be able to detect noise from a baby's room and alert the parents so that the parents can feel comfortable doing their own thing (for example a dinner party), in the knowledge that their monitor will detect any problems.	This design idea has a large red LED that flashes ON/OFF ten times every time a noise is received through the monitor. It will also relay the noise made from the baby.	The receiver to this design idea is a small buzzer that can either be worn as a watch or can go in your pocket. The vibration would alert you to a noise from the baby's room.	This idea detects the sound of the baby, but sets off a pre-recorded sound saying something like: 'Henry is awake and needs feeding!' This could help put a light-hearted side to the baby waking up, especially with being able to customise the recording.
AESTHETICS – My product must be easily seen and found in a messy, child-friendly house so that it does not get lost.	The vacuum-formed case represents a large red alert button. This will stand out in most rooms and is unlikely to get lost in the surroundings.	This design would not be seen easily but would be hard to lose if attached to the parent. It is discreet if other people are around.	This design looks like a little cartoon baby with the sound coming from the baby's mouth. It can be customised by the slot behind the see-through baby's head where a picture of your baby can be included.
USER OPINION	I think this design will stand out in my house, especially with the flashing LEDs, but I feel that it is a bit of an eyesore.	I like this idea as I am less likely to leave it around the house, although I would like to know how much the baby is crying – is it just a whimper or a distressed cry? This design would not enable me to do this.	I like this idea as we could change the recording and have a bit of a giggle with it, although again I would like to hear the type of cry too.

Table CA2.4 Part of a student example page where the student is creating an electronic product to detect noise from a baby's room

Positive – This is a strong page as the student has analysed three of their designs against the design requirements in their specification alongside feedback.

Things to improve – The student goes on to talk about each requirement from their specification, however, including a row about the positives that they want to take forward from each design could help to strengthen their analysis.

Developing your design

Apply it

Dyson has always encouraged his designers to think of the design process as a cycle, rather than a straight line. When designing the DC01 vacuum cleaner, Dyson produced 5,127 different prototypes that didn't work, but rather than giving up, he used his findings to help him with the next model. Try to take the same approach with your ideas – don't be afraid to keep going back to the drawing board!

Many of the prototypes for the later DC22 Dyson vacuum were made from a mixture of card and existing parts from previous machines – this allowed Dyson to experiment with certain set sizes/components

Considering user group needs and preferences

You now arrive at the exciting part of developing and experimenting with one or several parts of your ideas so to develop a working prototype. You will start to ask yourself questions about the practicalities of your designs and this will highlight new problems/obstacles/opportunities that you will need to research. Use a variety of methods such as drawing, modelling and CAD alongside additional research to allow you to explore, modify and strengthen your ideas just like Dyson.

It is really important that you incorporate the valuable user feedback from your design decisions and continually use them to help you generate and evaluate your new developmental ideas – the more you do this, the more successful your design will be.

Do not be afraid to 'go back to the drawing board' as this is part of the iterative design process as we talked about in the introduction to Component 2. Have a think about what your developmental research should involve.

Checklist for developmental research

- Does your design respond correctly to your design brief?
- What design requirements from your specification does your design not meet?
- What do you need to do/find out to enable all the requirements to be met?
- Could you merge successful features from other design ideas?
- How will it actually work? Think about:
  - Mechanisms
  - Ways of opening
  - Ways of moving/spraying
  - What electronic parts will you will need?
  - Joining/assembly, such as glue, fixings, hook and loop fasteners, clips, hooks
  - Components – which ones would you buy (BOP)? Examples could include timers, bulbs, hook and loop fasteners, poppers
  - Internal sketches, such as hollow parts to contain certain parts, hidden seams
  - Specific materials.
- How would it be manufactured? Think about:
  - Processes – for example CAM
  - Techniques – such as jigs, templates or patterns.
- How could it appeal to your user more?
  - Aesthetics
  - Is there anything else that you need to find out about your user?
  - Ergonomics – could it be made easier to pick up, for example?
  - Positioning and fitting: where to place handles, zips, buttons.
- Sustainability issues
- Safety/BSI standards.

Component 2: Controlled Assessment

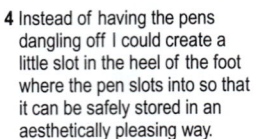

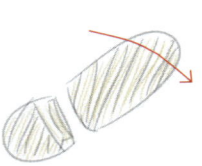
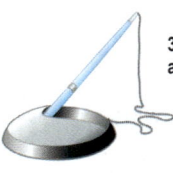

1 This is where people will queue up to pay in the shoe shop. I have added footprints for the children who are bored in the queue to doodle on. My initial thoughts were to use ordinary marker pens on a whiteboard or chalks on a chalk board, however, my user suggested that their children might end up drawing on things that they shouldn't.

2 After conducting some further research into clean and creative children's toys, I came across the Doodle Mat. It meets many of my user and design requirements as it allows children to draw with pens that are filled only with water, meaning that they are non-toxic so not harmful to the kids or the products in the store! The marks disappear after 5–10 minutes so the mat does not need to be wiped or cleaned after.

4 Instead of having the pens dangling off I could create a little slot in the heel of the foot where the pen slots into so that it can be safely stored in an aesthetically pleasing way.

3
a These pens are often found in places such as banks to ensure that people do not run off with the pens. I need to do something like this to ensure that the water pens are not taken by the children. It would also meet my user requirement about not creating extra work or cleaning for employees.

b I could use something like elastic or a chain or a shoe lace to attach to the water pens. I will need to research into suitable lengths so that I meet my design requirement of being safe for children in case of cords causing strangulation.

Positive – this student has clearly looked at other products/methods that could provide useful ideas for developments and iterations to her design scenario whilst referring to the design and user requirements.

Improvements – this student could include research about suitable and safe lengths of cord/shoe lace for the pens to be attached to. More detail could be added to show the design iterations made, such as a zoom in showing the slot for the pen. Could the student be more creative in the design of the pen?

Student coursework example page (2): a student example showing ways to develop a concept for a shoe shop store counter that helps prevent queuing children becoming bored and misbehaving in a shop

Testing

A successful way to develop your ideas is to model and test them out as prototypes. Prototyping could be through materials such as paper, fabric, cardboard, Styrofoam, high-impact polystyrene and other traditional materials, or through computer modelling, 3D printer models and simulations. Sometimes seeing the idea in full size and 3D allows you and your user to interact with the model. For example, is it easy enough to pick up/open/fit/move around or is it a little awkward? Remember to take pictures of your model at each stage as proof of your thinking. Record your user's responses and use this feedback to adapt your model or draw the adjustments on top of one of the photographs – both are great examples of further development. Remember to annotate your pictures and your adaptations to clearly show your thinking.

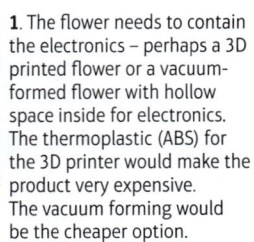
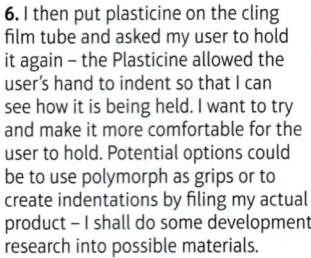

2. At first, I used a toilet roll tube as the handle. However, I replaced this with a cling film tube – the diameter is narrower and my user found it easier to hold on to, so I need to think about the diameter of the material I choose to use here – options could be acrylic tubing or a wooden dowel/pole.

3. The toilet tube does not hold the cling film pole straight inside the flower pot.

4. I tried a hook and loop fastener at the bottom, however, my user disliked the noise it made when removing the flower torch from the pot and it doesn't seem very secure.

5. So, I created a slot-in section in MDF using the forstner drill and this works better – I then added a supporting Styrofoam rim and this works well. Perhaps I could use a magnet at the bottom, too.

1. The flower needs to contain the electronics – perhaps a 3D printed flower or a vacuum-formed flower with hollow space inside for electronics. The thermoplastic (ABS) for the 3D printer would make the product very expensive. The vacuum forming would be the cheaper option.

6. I then put plasticine on the cling film tube and asked my user to hold it again – the Plasticine allowed the user's hand to indent so that I can see how it is being held. I want to try and make it more comfortable for the user to hold. Potential options could be to use polymorph as grips or to create indentations by filing my actual product – I shall do some developmental research into possible materials.

Positive – This student has created a physical model to explore sizes/joints/materials and asked for user feedback to develop it further.

Improvements – It would be good to see a picture of the model in the environment (for example, a bedside cabinet in a child's room). Modelling using the vacuum former for the flower would show further development.

Student coursework example page (3a): student example showing the developmental model of a nightlight/lamp that turns into a torch to help stop children being scared of the dark and enabling them to navigate to the toilet in the middle of the night

Design

Final concept

Once you have modified your design, taking into account your user feedback, you will have a finalised design. This will have evolved from your design brief, user and design requirements.

You now need to present your final concept using a mixture of the communication techniques discussed on page 322. You will also need to show clear details of the following:

- materials
  - mathematical calculations of quantities
  - technical details of materials
- processes/manufacturing techniques
- components.

To allow your final concept to gain a strong mark, you will need to evaluate your final concept effectively and review the modifications that you made to it including feedback from your user(s).

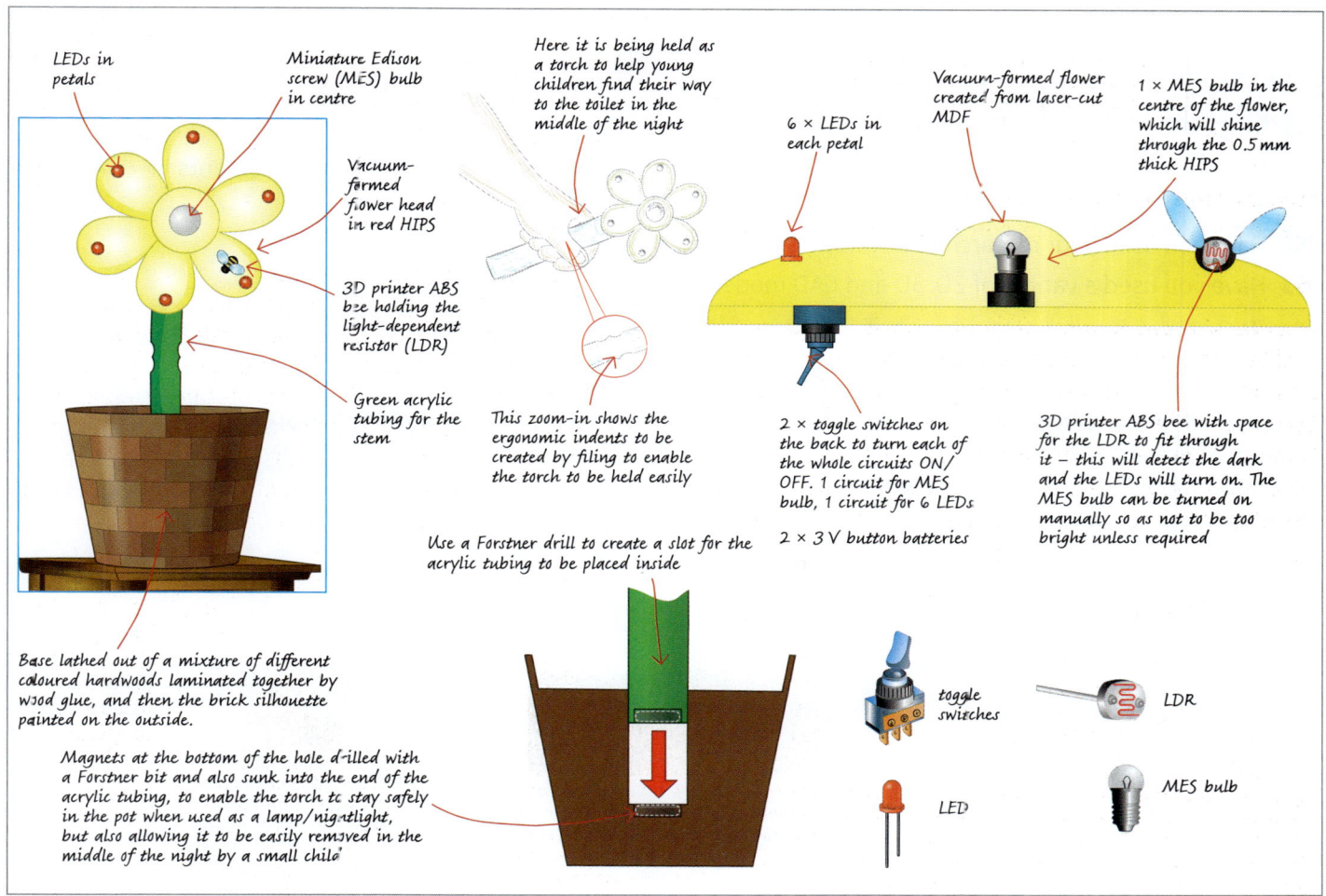

Student coursework example page (3b): student example showing the final concept for a bedside light

Positive – following the example in the prototyping, this student has gone on to produce their final concept through annotated drawings and CAD models.

Improvements – this student needs to ensure that they detail all calculations for quantities of materials and provide an effective analysis against their specification and user requirements. This would need to be done on an additional page due to the extent of their drawings and CAD models.

Component 2: Controlled Assessment

Summary

Key points to remember:
- Come up with lots of design ideas creatively and communicate them in a variety of ways.
- Always refer back to your user and design requirements from your design brief and specification through annotations.
- Use added research to help you to modify and develop your design ideas.
- Test your ideas using 3D models and simulations.
- Present a final concept with details of materials, components and plans for manufacture.
- Do not be afraid to rework your ideas throughout the iterative design process.

Checkpoint

Strengthen

S1 Have you fully considered the design brief, user requirements and the specification requirements in your designs?

S2 Have you used your research to develop your designs?

S3 Have you used a variety of 2D, 3D and CAD modelling techniques to develop your design?

Challenge

C1 Is it clear how your product could be made in terms of materials and manufacturing processes?

C2 Could anyone understand your ideas from your portfolio without the need to speak to you in person?

Component 2: Controlled Assessment

Make

> ### Getting started
> This is the hands-on part of the project where you have the opportunity to manufacture the design that you have developed. Think carefully about:
> - what materials and processes will be the most suitable for your project
> - how you can ensure that you manufacture a quality prototype.
>
> Have a look around your school workshop. Do you know what every machine does? If not, then find out – perhaps it could help you to develop how your design is going to be made.

> ### Learning objectives
> By the end of this section, you should know:
> - how to manufacture a successful and working prototype that meets your user and design requirements
> - how to carefully select suitable materials and processes
> - how to demonstrate accuracy and how to stay safe throughout the manufacturing process
> - how to present all of the above using photos and annotations.

Manufacturing

This is your opportunity to produce either a full-sized product, scaled working model(s) or a functioning system. This will depend on the problem you are solving and the design development that you have produced. It will need to be fully functioning and meet your user needs and design requirements from your specification. You will need to use a wide range of competent making skills with precision and accuracy to carefully assemble and then finish your prototype to a high quality. You will go on to use this product/prototype to test and evaluate your ideas against your user and design requirements.

Material selection

You can use a range of materials such as:
- woods
- metals
- plastics
- fabrics
- electronic components
- papers and boards.

You must select which materials to use that are fully appropriate for your chosen prototype. You need to show your understanding of material properties clearly when choosing your materials, to make it clear why you think it is the most suitable material for your design, and you must demonstrate your mathematical skills when deciding on the quantities you will require. Talk through your plans with your teacher before going ahead to ensure that you have access to the appropriate materials and manufacturing processes.

Manufacturing processes

While selecting your materials you need to think about the following:
- marking-out tools/hand tools/machinery
- techniques
- fixtures, templates, jigs, patterns
- components
- surface treatments and finishes
- assembly
- quality.

Each material will require different considerations. Use the information specific to the material you are using (see core section, pages 2–77) to help you select appropriately for your prototype.

Planning your manufacture

Using your final concept, you may wish to plan your manufacture before commencing. Have a think about the timescale that your teacher has given you – would

Component 2: Controlled Assessment

it be possible to manufacture your prototype? Consider the following:

- What processes will you use?
- Which rooms/facilities will you be able to use in which lessons?
- Will you need to allow time for things to dry/set? For example paints, epoxy resins.
- Will you need to allow order and delivery times for any materials?
- Will you need to build/make any jigs/templates/patterns to enable you to make your prototype accurately?
- How much time will you need to assemble it?
- Have you factored in enough time to get the accurate and quality finish that you would like?

Plan your time wisely; for example, do not paint your prototype at the start of the lesson if it means that you have nothing else to do for the rest of the lesson because you are waiting for it to dry. Could you do something else first?

Manufacture log

You must remember to take photographs at every single stage of the manufacture of your product. This is evidence that you have made the product by yourself and will also show your understanding of materials, manufacturing processes, accuracy and safety. Try to ensure that all photographs are well lit and of a high resolution. These photographs will need to be presented in the correct order in your portfolio accompanied by short explanations:

> **Photo explanations checklist:**
>
> ☐ What are you doing in the photo/what stage are you at?
> ☐ What materials have you selected and why?
> ☐ What processes/tools are you using and why?
> ☐ What CAD/CAM have you chosen to use and why?
> ☐ How are you being accurate, for example using a drilling jig to help you drill in exactly the same place in every piece of material (jigs/templates/fixtures/patterns)?
> ☐ How are you ensuring that you are staying safe?
> ☐ What have you selected in terms of components and fittings/surface treatments/finishes?
> ☐ How have you been sustainable in your manufacture?
> ☐ How is each stage helping to meet your user and design requirements from your **specification**?

Safe manufacture

Your teacher and technician can advise you on safe working practices at any time in your manufacture – do not be afraid to ask them. Through your manufacture log, you should be able to demonstrate how you are staying safe, this could be through a mixture of safety precautions such as:

- wearing goggles/aprons/heatproof gloves when appropriate
- tying back hair/loose clothing
- using extraction/ventilation with certain machines/tools/processes
- using guards with certain machines/tools
- setting up your area safely; for example, keeping wires out of the way from soldering irons.

Quality assurance

Quality checks help to ensure that you produce a functioning and successful prototype. Examples could be:

- Accuracy in terms of
  - aesthetics
  - correct assembly
  - consistency between parts
- surface finishes
- is it going to function as intended?
- choice of materials
- testing components using **multimeters** or **logic probes** to check that they produce the correct outputs within a circuit.

While carrying out your quality checks, we would be surprised if you did not encounter problems throughout the manufacture. This does not mean that you have failed, but might mean that you need to re-look at your ideas/materials/processes and make modifications. This is all part of the iterative design process, just make sure that it is recorded in your manufacturing log.

> **Key terms**
>
> **Multimeters:** an electronic measuring instrument that can measure voltage, current and resistance. It is often used to find faults within circuits.
>
> **Logic probes:** an electronic measuring instrument that tests the logical states of a digital circuit to see whether a circuit is working correctly or not.

Make

Meeting the user's requirements from the specification highlighted in blue.

Making Log

RED comments = how I am staying safe
BLUE comments = meeting my user requirements

  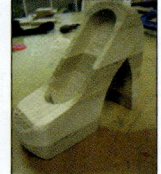

Accurate marking out.

Effective selection of materials for the prototype.

Safe working practices highlighted in red.

Economic use of materials.

Experimentation to create an effective outcome, while considering material properties.

1. I laminated an individual block of wood by gluing scrap pieces of ash and oak together to create a block 160 mm high and 175 mm wide. I chose to use two hardwoods as I want to route a hole in it later. I then drew the shoe outline.

2. I cut the main outline of the shoe using a tenon saw, however my teacher helped cut some of the internal curves on the band saw which I am unable to use due to Health and Safety laws.

3. To create as much space as possible for jewellery, I drew an outline on the front surface of the shoe. With help from my teacher due to Health and Safety, I routed the sole creating a space 2.5 cm in depth and 14 cm long.

4. In order to get a quality finish and to make my product look more realistic, I used the hand-held palm sander. I held it flat on each of the surfaces of the shoe and evenly moved it over it while the sand paper vibrated. I tied my hair up, wore an apron and used a vacuum bag to extract all the dust into. I also used the vertical sander for the front of the shoe and then finally glass paper to achieve a high-quality smooth finish.

5. I used a coping saw to cut off the heel from the shoe and began experimenting with creating a mould for the heel that I could pour crystal resin into to make a unique one-off heel.
I created a silicon mould by mixing the white and blue clay like materials together, however, when this was set, it was really difficult to take the wooden heel out and the mould broke.
I then tried a tester mould (so as not to waste the crystal resin) in 2 mm thick HIPS (High-Impact polystyrene). This worked well, however, the blue HIPS left a slight tinge on the crystal resin and was very difficult to remove, being so thick. From this I decided to vacuum form my heel using 1 mm thick white HIPS.
I also tried another sample piece in a plastic cup with dolly mixtures in to see if the crystal resin would still set and they would keep their colour – they did!

6. In order to vacuum form the mould for my shoe's heel successfully, I have added to the heel's original slanted base using plasterine to give it a flat base and ensure that the heel can stand upright when being vacuum formed and the HIPS can mould over the whole shape.

7. The teacher poured the crystal resin into the mould for me due to the fumes and it was left in a well-ventilated area to dry for 24 hours. I watched wearing a face mask.

8. After the 24 hours I ripped away the mould and the heel was set and strong. It had a quality finish with a clear, smooth surface and after cutting the top fits perfectly onto my shoe. I am really pleased as it has created a unique heel that could not be exactly replicated.

Positives – this student has provided good explanations as to how the product was made accurately and safely, whilst referring to the user requirements.

Things to improve – the student would need to add more photos as evidence to how it was made, such as the handmade silicon mould and the vacuum formed mould.

Competent use of a variety of different machines and hand tools to create a quality finish.

Student coursework example page (1): A design and technology student designed and made a bespoke jewellery stand for a young woman who loves shoes and jewellery. This is a page of their Making Log, with clear annotated evidence of the skills that were used. Teacher comments are included to show the type of feedback this coursework example would get.

Final outcome

You will also need to show photographs of your final prototype/product to show that it is accurately assembled and finished to a high quality. Remember, your portfolio will be sent to a moderator so be sure to take photographs from a range of angles showing details of all sides and features of your 3D outcome. You should include detailed annotations against your user and design requirements will clearly show that you have fulfilled your specification.

My Final Product

Front view closed.

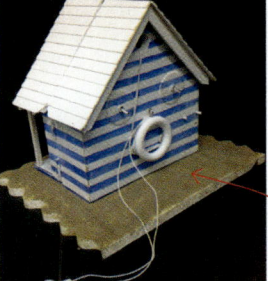

Real sand from the beach.

Front view open and front view with outside lights off.

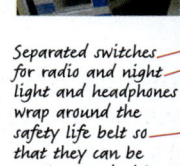

Electronics hidden in the rafters.

Chiselled slots for the hinge.

Internal view showing sublimation printing for interior and clock face with mechanism behind. Clock can be seen with doors open or closed for my user to tell the time when it is on their bedside cabinet.

Separated switches for radio and night light and headphones wrap around the safety life belt so that they can be neatly stored without getting tangled.

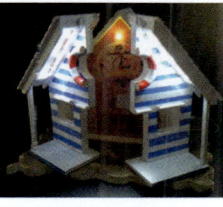

Colour-changing LED's as a nightlight to create a relaxed atmosphere for going to sleep.

Positives – The range of photos and annotations show clearly how the student has met their user requirements, including the effect of the product in the dark.

Things to improve – A picture of the product being used by the user themselves and in the home environment would have strengthened this page.

Student coursework example page (2): A design and technology student designed and made a beach hut night light, clock and radio, with a headphones port, for a child who has trouble getting to sleep. They used a wide range of skills, including dowel joints, laser cutting, sublimation printing, electronics, painting and chiselling.

Component 2: Controlled Assessment

Summary

Key points to remember:
- Carefully select your materials and manufacuring processes according to your user and design requirements.
- Plan your manufacturing so that you finish on time.
- Stay safe and check the quality of your product/prototype throughout manufacture.
- Record your manufacture processes and decisions through annotated photographs.
- Do not be afraid to rework your ideas throughout the iterative design process.

Checkpoint

Strengthen

S1 Have you fully considered your user and design requirements throughout your manufacture?

S2 Have you clearly shown your decision making and modifications through your manufacturing log?

S3 Have you taken high-quality photos of every angle of your prototype, showing clearly how it functions?

Challenge

C1 Is your manufacturing log clear enough for a stranger to follow?

C2 Re-read your manufacturing log – have you gone into enough detail and depth?

C3 Have you used the correct terminology for different materials, tools and machinery? For example, HIPS instead of plastic.

C4 Have you clearly shown how you have been accurate? For example, confident use of drilling jigs, measuring depths of holes and so on.

Component 2: Controlled Assessment

Evaluate

Getting started

You will need to be creative in generating individual ways to test and evaluate your product throughout the whole iterative design process. Have a think about the following:
- Who could you ask to provide useful comments to evaluate your product?
- What creative ways could you come up with to test your product?

Investigate the difference in how designers test the following products:
- car scraper
- lava lamp
- wet suit
- pop-up book.

Learning objectives

By the end of this section, you should know:
- how to conduct suitable tests to evaluate your product
- how to evaluate your product/prototype against your user and design requirements
- how to assess the impact of your final prototype(s) on the environment.

Evaluation is not just a 'tick the box' exercise at the end. Evaluation should have been continually carried out and used to modify your ideas throughout the whole iterative design process. As we approach the close of your project, it is now your opportunity to evaluate your final product/prototype extensively and make suggestions for any future developments. Different designers have different approaches to evaluation and testing depending on the product that they manufacture, and this will be the same between you and others in your class. Be sure to provide evidence of your testing, this could be through photographs, quotes and written techniques.

Apply it

Dyson carries out a variety of tests on its products such as:

Obstacle course

To ensure that Dyson vacuum cleaners can endure the bumps and bashes of real life, Dyson have set up an all-day, all-week obstacle course. Machines are knocked over, bashed into doors and skirting boards, and pushed down stairs!

Drop test

Dyson engineers drop their vacuum cleaners over and over again to test whether the finished product will still work, if dropped on the floor by future users.

Life test

Dyson uses a process called highly accelerated life testing (HALT) over several days to test how its vacuum cleaners will perform over their expected lifetime. One such test has a machine that pushes and pulls the prototypes at a walking pace. This piece of equipment operates for more than 2 weeks, 24 hours a day, allowing the vacuum cleaners to travel more than 1,300 km. This enables Dyson engineers to decide on future improvements and calculate a realistic lifetime for each product, which affects other decisions, such as length of guarantees.

You are unlikely to test your product/prototype to the extent that Dyson does with its vacuum cleaners. Think about what creative tests you could do at school/home to see whether your product achieves what you set out to do in your specification.

Component 2: Controlled Assessment

Analysing against your specification

Using both your user and design requirements from your specification, you need to carefully analyse and evaluate your product/prototype to make sure that it meets the specification.

User requirements

You now have a physical product or prototype to present to your user for them to use/wear/interact with. Use your user and design requirements to shape questions to either ask your user or user group.

My product must appeal to elderly people aged 70+ who suffer from arthritis and movement restrictions, it should help them to open jars easily and efficiently.

You could gather a collection of different-sized jars and ask the user to open them a) firstly using without your product and b) with your product. You could time each one and then compare times, their thoughts and your observations.

The dance outfit should fit a 10-year-old girl comfortably and enable them to move freely while performing a Latin-style dance. It should catch the light using embellishments and electronics so as to stand out in a dance competition.

You could ask the user to perform a Latin-style dance routine while wearing the outfit. Record your observations through photographs and written techniques with regard to fit and the impact of the embellishments/electronics in the dance show lighting. Ask for their thoughts on comfort and their dance teacher's thoughts on the suitability at a dance competition.

Pockets to hold batteries for fairy lights

Loops inside the top of the tepee to feed fairy lights through

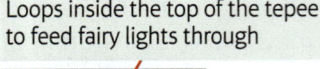

Fabric matches curtains and 'H' for Henry.

Pockets at the bottom to store books and sensory toys

OBSERVATIONS
I gave the tepee to my auntie and her 15-month-old son Henry to keep for a week and to test it out. I also watched Henry play in the tepee at the start of the week and the end of the week. His confidence had really grown by the end of the week and he was confidently exploring/playing with it independently. I felt really bad taking it away from Henry to bring back to school and have promised he can have it back soon! From watching him – he seemed really proud to be playing in it and proud to be reading his books inside. He loved the fact that I could also fit inside with him so we could play together. As you can see from the pictures, he was fascinated by the fairy lights when we turned off his bedroom lights – luckily the battery pocket meant that he could not get to the batteries.

QUESTIONS TO PARENT (THE BUYER):

Does Henry enjoy playing in the tepee?
Yes, Henry loves to go into his tepee and play with his toys in there. His favourite things are dinosaurs, so we love the fabric that you managed to find.

How often does Henry play in the tepee?
We put the tepee upstairs in his new bedroom for a week and he played in there every time we were upstairs while I was doing jobs like sorting the washing. This was great for me as it allowed me to get some jobs done.

How does Henry play in the tepee?
We put some of his books and cuddly toys in the tepee and he goes in and plays with them. He also loves it when I hide inside and boo him! He loves running around the outside of it too!

What do you think about the lights?
As above I love them but also like the fact that the batteries are hidden away in the secret pocket and the loops enable the lights to not fall down but stay in place.

What do you personally like about the tepee?
I love the way that you listened to my views about other tepees on the market as they all seem to fall down every time Henry bashes into them – whereas the way you have created a structured base with bamboo canes is brilliant as it does not fall over or topple over. I love the inside pockets with the different textures and the fairy lights – he likes looking at them from inside but also loves to be held up so that he can see them from above. I also love the way that you have incorporated the curtain fabric into the tepee as it goes so nicely with his new big boy room.

What would you change about the tepee?
I would like you to add a peep window with a roll curtain over.

How much would you be prepared to pay for this tepee?
Custom-made ones in the shop start at around £100 – I would be happy to pay this as I personally feel that it is so much better than the current ones around, due to the structured base. I also like the fact that it has an inbuilt fabric base and that the bamboo canes can come out easily so that it can be washed.

Positive – This student has managed to observe their user (who is too young to talk) while he plays with the product, alongside receiving feedback from their potential buyer – the parent.

OVERALL FINDINGS/CONCLUSIONS
I am really happy with the feedback from my targeted buyer and from the observations of my user Henry playing with it. This interview clearly shows that I have met so many of my user and design requirements. I agree that a window would have been a good addition to have and I think that I will make one before I give Henry the actual tepee.

Student coursework example page: this student has carried out an effective user requirements analysis by carefully wording questions to both the customer (the parent) and the child (the user). They have also taken pictures of the user interacting with the product while noting down personal observations

Things to improve – To get more reliable results it would be good to see a few different users interacting with the tepee. The student could have considered taking the tepee to a children's playgroup to provide a range of different users and views.

Evaluate

Testing to ensure fitness for purpose

Just like Dyson, you will need to conduct a variety of tests under realistic conditions to ensure that your product is fit for its purpose and meets both your user and design requirements. Think about what these tests could be:

My product should use an LDR to respond to the natural light fading so that a child does not become scared of the dark.

Does the LDR work? Could you test this by putting the product in a dark cupboard to see whether the lights or LEDs switch on by themselves? Take pictures as your evidence.

My product must fold up easily and fit underneath a standard single bed when not in use so that it can be stored easily.

Take your product to a home with a standard single bed. Does it fit underneath? Take a picture of it folded out, in the process of it being folded, fully folded and then underneath the bed as evidence. Did your user find it easy to fold? Observe, photograph and record their thoughts.

Specification points	Evaluation of my finished product	User feedback/testing	Evidence
FUNCTION – My product must help the user to comfortably hang and store a range of jewellery (such as rings/necklaces and bracelets) to prevent them from becoming tangled and/or broken.	My product has fulfilled this specification requirement through three wire hangers that allow you to hook necklaces and bracelets on and prevent them from getting tangled. The hangers are also high enough for the jewellery to hang and not touch whatever surface the product is on. Rings are also able to be stored as there is a large ring cushion inside the shoe.	• Could fit four of her rings onto the ring holder with space still left for more if she adds to her collection. • Could hang four bracelets and four necklaces, still with space for more. • Commented, 'I found it easy to hang and then remove the jewellery from the stand without them tangling up'.	Testing a bracelet and ring on the finished product.
SIZE – My product should fit onto a bedside table or desk, therefore it should not be too large or take up too much room. It should be no taller than 40 cm high, which would enable the majority of necklaces to hang from it freely, without touching the surface of the table or desk.	My product is 38 cm tall from the base of the shoe to the top of the hanging wires, enabling the majority of necklaces to be hung without touching the surface, but also without being excessively big. *For future development, I would add a row within the shoe which is slightly narrower so as to hold earrings easily without them falling out.*	When tested, the jewellery holder was placed on a desk in her bedroom. It didn't take up too much room but held enough storage space for all of her jewellery. Only one particularly long necklace had to be looped over twice so it did not touch the desk.	

Table CA2.5 This student designed a jewellery storage product in the shape of a shoe. This is an extract of their evaluation against their specification where they have analysed against each design and user requirement while referring to the evidence from the testing. The comments in red show areas for future development. Additional pictures in the evidence column would make this page stronger.

Sustainability

You will also need to evaluate the impact that your final product/prototype has on the environment through carrying out a life-cycle analysis (LCA).

Link it up

For more information on LCA, see page 61.

Component 2: Controlled Assessment

Think about the energies used and released in the following stages from **cradle to grave** for each part of your product to assess its impact on the environment:

- **Raw materials** – Where have your materials originated from? For example certain plastics will have come from crude oil.
- **Material processing** – How were your raw materials made into the actual material that you used? For example, extrusion of PVC.
- **Manufacture** – How did you shape/join/finish/embellish your raw materials? For example CAM embroidery of designs.
- **Distribution** – If you were to make this product on a larger scale, how would you distribute it to the retailers?
- **Product in use** – Having observed your user interacting with your product, what impact could it have? For example, using batteries/mains/renewable sources of energy to power your product.
- **Repair and maintenance of the product** – Thinking ahead like Dyson does with its highly accelerated life test, how would your product be maintained or repaired? For example, does it have the ability to use rechargeable batteries that are easily accessible by the user so that the product can continue working?
- **Disposal or recycling** – Thinking ahead, what would happen to your product at the end of its life? Could it be easily disassembled and sorted for recycling? Have you included recycling symbols to make this process easier for your user?

Think carefully about each stage from cradle to grave of your product. Where has your product/prototype had a small or large environmental impact? If you could reduce your environmental impact through the energies used or released, which stage(s) would be the most appropriate?

Key term

Cradle to grave: the life cycle of the product from the design stage to the disposal or recycling of the product (i.e. from raw materials through materials processing, manufacture, distribution, use, repair and maintenance, and disposal or recycling).

Summary

Key points to remember:
- Test and evaluate against all your user and design requirements.
- Provide evidence for each test and evalution that you carry out on your product/prototype – this could be through photographs, quotes, observations etc.
- Your testing and evaluation might be very different to others in your class. This is a good sign as it shows that you have adapted your evaluation to suit your own product.
- Use LCA to evaluate the impact of your product/protoype on the environment.

Checkpoint

Strengthen

S1 Think carefully about the tests that you have carried out on your product/prototype. Are there any other rigorous tests that could provide useful information for you to be able to evaluate?
S2 Have you thoroughly evaluated against each user and design requirement?
S3 Have you provided clear evidence in your portfolio from each of your tests?

Challenge

C1 Have you carefully considered the current and future impacts that your product/prototype has and could have on the environment?
C2 Have you provided some mathematical data/results/measurements for some of your testing?

Index

Page numbers in **bold** indicate key term definitions.

3D
   drawing 70
   modelling 70, 75
   printing 75, 195, 230

abrading 115, 193, 300
adhesives 120, 195, 301
aesthetic factors 91, 136, 174, 214, 250, 283
allergenic **246**
alloy **38**
aluminium 88, 209
amplifier **208**
analogue **36**
annotated sketches 76, 322–3
anthropometric data **67**
apprenticeships 6
Archimedes screw thread **185**
areas, calculating 144, 221
   cross-sectional 97, 183
assembly drawings 74
automation **6**
availability factors 91, 137, 175, 215, 251, 285

Bakelite **163**
batches 9, 103, 148, 188, 224, 225, 257, 293, 294
beam types 94
belts and pulleys 29
bending 114, 192
binding 153
biodiversity **133**
biomimicry **318**
bioplastics **169**
blow moulding 184
board **41** see also paper and board
bonded fabrics 245
BOP **320**
brand identity 133–4, 248
brazing 116
breadboard/stripboard **70**, 224
buzzers 34, 207

CAM **75**, 106, 149, 190, 258, 295
cams **27**–8
cantilever **94**
carbon dioxide calculation 249
carbon footprint **14**, 59

carving 300
casting 96, 99
challenges 58–61
chemical treatments 267
chiselling 299
chuck **112**
circuit **34**
   symbols 206
cloud (or crowd) funding **4**
CNC **75**
   machines 106, 113, 190, 191, 197, 229, 230, 295, 300
collaboration 66
colour bars 149, **150**
command words 80
communication techniques 68–77
components **34**
   programmable 35–7
   properties and origins 204–13
   selection 213–17
   stock forms/types 219–23
composite material 21–2, **166**, 218, 254, 289
compressive strength **21**, 89, 139, 140, 281
computer-aided design (CAD) 75–6, 108, 151, 191, 195, 229, 259, 297
computer-aided manufacture (CAM) see CAM
computer modelling **70**, 229
conduct **204**
conductor **211**
construction lines **71**, 72
consumer society 138, 178–9, 216, 252, 286
consumerism **134**
consumers **5**
contexts which inform outcomes 55–8
continuous production 10, 103, 148, 188, 224, 225, 257, 294
control devices and components 34, 204–7
controlled assessment 312–36
   design 322–8
   evaluate 333–6
   introduction 313–14
   investigation 315–21
   make 329–32
copper 209

corrosion **209**
cost factors 60, 91, 137, 176–7, 215, 251, 285–6
cotton production 247
cradle to grave **336**
cranks and sliders 30
critical evaluation **11**–12
crop marks 149, **150**
cross-sectional areas 97, 183
cultural and ethical factors 91, 138, 178–9, 215–16, 252, 286–7
culture **6**–7
current **34**, 220
cut and paste 69
cutting 110–11, 147, 150, 192, 256, 258, 298

deciduous **277**
decorative techniques 265–7
deforestation **135**, 282
demographic movement **3**
density 89, **131**, 168, 280
design
   brief 318–19
   constraint **164**
   controlled assessment 322–8, 335
   strategies 66–8
designers and companies, work of 64–5
diameter 144, 221
digital photography/media 69
disassemble **74**
drape **242**
drawing programs 75–6
drilling 111, 230, 297
ductile **87**
ductility **39**
durable **54**, **168**

ecological footprint
   fibres and textiles 248–9
   metals 89–90
   paper and board 134–5
   polymers 171–3
   systems 212
   timbers 281–2
efficiency 27
elastic **211**
electromagnet **208**

Index

electroplate **209**
encapsulation **141**
energy 15–18
engraving 191–2
enterprise **4**
environmental factors 59–60
    fibres and textiles 249, 250–1
    metals 91
    paper and board 136–7
    polymers 174–5
    systems 214, 255
    timbers 284
environmental impact
    energy sources 18
    logging 281
    new technologies 8
    polymers 169–70
    systems 212–13
environmental perspectives 13–14
equations 220, 221, 222
ergonomics **319**
ethics **13**
evaluate, controlled assessment 333–6
evergreen **53**
exam questions and answers
    command words 80
    core section 81–5
    fibres and textiles 271–5
    metals 125–7
    paper and board 157–61
    polymers 199–201
    systems 235–9
    timbers 308–11
exam tips 79, 170, 198, 235, 307
existing products, investigating 316–17
exploded views 74
external moderator **314**
extrusion 96, 100, 185, 256

fabric **47** *see also* fibres and textiles
fabricating/constructing
    fibre and textile 261–4
    metals 116–18
    paper and board 152–3
    polymer 194–6
    systems 230–1
    timber 288–9, 301–4
feedback loop **36**
fibres and textiles **47**, 240–69
    calculating size 255
    categorization 47–50
    cutting and shaping 256
    design contexts 241
    ecological footprint 248–9
    exams 270–5
    fabricating/constructing 261–4
    fasteners and links 262–3
    forces and stresses 253
    manufacturing processes 256–8
    moulding 261
    origins 245
    properties and social implications 51, 241–9
    prototypes 259–64
    quantity production 258
    reinforcement/stiffening 253–4
    scales of production 256–7
    seams 261–2
    selection 250–2
    shaping 256, 259–61
    smart 19–20, 269
    social footprint 247–8
    stock forms/types/sizes 254–5
    surface finishes 265–9
    tools and equipment 259
    working properties 246
filing 108–9, 192
fixtures 105, 149, 295
flange **94**
flash material **172**
flash memory **207**
flexible packaging **169**
flowcharts 35
flutes **297**
followers **27**, 28
forces and stresses **25**
    fibres and textiles 253
    metals 92–3
    paper and board 139–41
    polymers 180–1
    systems 217
    timber 288
forging 98
form **319**
freehand sketching 69
friction **28**
fullness 260
function **319**
fusing 262

gears 30–2
glass reinforced plastic (GRP) **45**, 166
global warming **13**, 59
gold 209
grain **52**, 280
'green designs' 59–60

hard **54**
hardening metals 93, 102–3
hardness **39**
hardwoods **52**, 277–8
HDPE (high-density polyethylene) **178**
hinges 303
HIPS (high-impact polystyrene) **43**, 44
hydrocarbons **167**

industry 3
injection moulding 186, 189
input device **33**
input signal **33**
insulators **46**, 211
internet of things (IoT) 7
investigating work of others 62–5
investigation, controlled assessment 315–21
ironmongery 303
isometric projections 71
iterative design process **314**

jigs 105, 149, 189, **224**, 295
joints, wood 302

knitted textiles 50

laminating **141**
    fibres and textiles 254, 265
    paper 141, 142, 153
    timbers **289**, 301
laser
    cutting 147, 191–2, 230, 256
    engraving 197
    printing **137**
lettering 153
levers **25**–7
life-cycle analysis (LCA) **14**, 61
light-dependent resistors (LDRs) 33, 204
light-emitting diodes (LEDs) 34, 207
lignin **137**
line bending 187
linkages 27
lithium 209, 212
logic probes **330**
loudspeakers 208

make, controlled assessment 329–32
malleability **39**

Index

malleable **88**
manufacturing, controlled assessment 329–32
manufacturing processes 60–1
  advantages and disadvantages 57
  fibres and textiles 256–8
  justifying 57
  metals 98–107
  paper and board 145–7
  polymers 184–91
  production techniques and systems 9–10
  systems 223–7
  timbers 292–6
marking-out methods 104–5, 148, 189, 192, 226, 258, 294, 296
mass production 10, 103, 148, 188, 224, 225, 257, 294
  effects of 138, 179, 216, 287
mechanical advantage 26
mechanical properties **55**
metals 86–123
  assembling 118–20
  beam types 94
  calculating waste 106
  categorization 37–9
  design context 87
  ecological footprint 89–90
  exam 124–7
  fabricating/constructing 116–18
  forces and stresses 92–3
  manufacturing processes 98–107
  marking-out methods 104–5
  properties 39, 87–8, 89
  prototypes 107–20
  quantity production 105–6
  reinforcement/stiffening 93
  scales of production 103–6
  selection 90–2
  shaping 108–15
  sizes 96–7
  social footprint 89
  sources and origins 88
  stock forms/types 95–6
  surface finishes 121–3
  tools and equipment 104–5, 108, 110, 111
  working properties 89
microcontrollers 207
microprocessors 206
milling 113
modern materials 19–20
modular **61**

monoculture **135**
monomer **48**
motors 208
moulds 105, 189–90, 193, 196, **224**
movement, mechanical devices to produce 25–32
  cams **27**–8
  cranks and sliders 30
  followers **27**, 28
  gear types 30–2
  levers **25**–7
  linkages 27
  pulleys and belts 29
movement, types of 25
multimeters **330**

nails 301
natural fibres 47, 241–2
natural resources 5
new and emerging technologies
  evaluating 11–14
  impact 3–10
nickel 209
non-renewable resource 5, 15, **163**
non-woven textiles 50, 245
normally off/on **205**
nuts 119, 194

oblique projections 71
offset lithography **137**
Ohm's law 220–1
oil 170, 171, 176
one-off production 10, 103, 148, 188, 224, 225, 257, 293, 294
ore **208**
origins *see* sources and origins
orthographic views 73
output devices **33**, 207–8
output signal **33**
overlocking 264

packaging
  brand 134, 137
  disposable cups 138
  flexible **169**
  laminate 130, 131, 141, 154
  reduction in 133, 248
  rigid **169**
  trends 169
paper and board **40**, **41**, 128–55
  design contexts 129
  ecological footprint 134–5
  exam 156–61

  fabricating/constructing 152–3
  forces and stresses 139–41
  manufacturing processes 145–7
  properties and structure 40–2, 130, 131, 132
  prototypes 151–3
  quantity production 148–50
  reinforcement/stiffening 140–1, 152
  scales of production 148
  selection 136–9
  shaping 151
  sizes 142–4
  social footprint 132–4
  sources and origins 131
  stock forms/types 142
  surface finishes 154–5
  tools and equipment 151
  working properties 41, 132
PAR and PSE 291
parison **184**
patent **74**
patterns 105, 189, 226, 258, 295
PEEL 170
people 5–6
perspective drawing 72–3
photo etching 223
photovoltaics **16**
physical properties **55**
piezoelectric **204**
planing 299
planned obsolescence 91, 138, **179**, 212, 216, 252, 287
pollution **5**
  fibres and textiles 247, 251
  metals 90
  new technologies and 5, 8
  paper and board 133, 135, 137
  polymers 172–3, 175
  timber 282
polymers **43**, 162–97
  biodegradable 175
  calculating quantity 182–3
  design contexts 163–4
  ecological footprint 171–3
  in electronic systems 208, 211
  exam 198–201
  fabrication and construction 194–6
  forces and stresses 180–1
  manufacturing processes 184–91
  oil processing 171–3
  oil supply and price 176
  properties 44–6, 164–5, 167–8
  prototypes 191–6

Index

quantity production 189–91
reinforcement/stiffening 181
scales of production 188
selection 174–9
shaping 191–3
social footprint 169–70
sources and origins 166–7
specialist materials 175
stock forms, types and sizes 175, 182–3
surface finishes 196–7
symbols 170
thermoforming **43**–4, 45, 164–6
thermosetting **43**, 44–5, 166
treatments and additives 177–8
working properties 44–5, 168
powder metallurgy 96, 100
powering systems 17
press moulding 185
printing 145–6
product disassembly 59, 317
product life cycle **212**
program **33**, 207
properties
    fibres and textiles 51, 241–9
    materials and components 55–6
    mechanical **55**
    metals 39, 87–8, 89
    paper and board 40–2, 130, 131, 132
    physical **55**
    polymers 44–6, 164–5, 167–8
    systems 204–13
    timber 54, 280–1
prototypes **57**
    controlled assessment **314**, 326, 329–31
    fibres and textiles 259–64
    metals 107–20
    paper and board 151–3
    polymers 191–6
    systems 228–31
    timbers 296–304
pulleys and belts 29
punching 116
PVC (polyvinyl chloride) **46**, 177, 178

qualitative **167**
quality control 106, 149, 190, 226, 258, 295
quantity production techniques
    fibres and textiles 258
    metals 105–6
    paper and board 148–50
    polymers 189–91
    systems 225–7
    timbers 294–6

rack and pinion 31
rare earth elements 209
raw edges 262
reciprocals **221**, 222
recycling **5**, 59, 60
    electronic products 212, 214
    fibres and textiles 248, 250, 251
    metals 89
    paper and board 133, 134, 137
    polymers 170, 171, 172
    timbers 281
regenerated cellulose textiles 243
registration mark 149, **150**
reinforcement/stiffening techniques
    fibres and textiles 253–4
    metals 93
    paper and board 140–1, 152
    polymers 181
    systems 218
    timber 288
relays 207
renewable energy 16, 18
research strategies 317–18
resistance **33**, 34, 220, 221
resistors 34, 205, 219, 221
    colour codes 209–11, 232
respect for different groups 58
Restriction of Hazardous Substances (RoHS) Directive 214
reusing products and materials 5, 59, 60
revision tips 79, 124, 156, 198, 234, 270, 306–7
revolutions per minute 31
rigid packaging **169**
riveting 117
routing 292

sandwich construction **141**
saws 292, 298
scales of production
    fibres and textiles 256–7
    metals 103–6
    paper and board 148
    polymers 188
    systems 224–5
    timbers 293–4
SCAMPER 66
schematic diagrams 74–5
screws 120, 301
seams 261–2
seasoning **284**
selection
    fibres and textiles 250–2
    metals 90–2
    paper and board 136–9
    polymers 174–9
    systems 213–17
    timbers 283–7
selvedge **244**
semi-conductors **34**, 207
sensors 33, 204
shaping
    fibres and textiles 256, 259–61
    metals 108–15
    paper and board 151
    polymers 191–3
    systems 230
    timbers 297–300
silicon 208
simulations **70**
sliders and cranks 30
smart materials 19–20, 269
social factors 91, 137, 177–8, 215, 251, 286
social footprint
    fibres and textiles 247–8
    metals 89
    paper and board 132–4
    polymers 169–70
    systems 211–12
    timbers 281
society 7–8
softwoods **53**, 278–9
soldering, hard 116
sources and origins
    electronic products 208–9
    fibres and textiles 245
    metals 88
    paper and board 131
    polymers 166–7
    timbers 277–83
specification criteria 62–3, 334–6
specification, writing a 319–20
stamping 100
staple **47**
stock forms/types/sizes
    electronic components 219–23
    fibres and textiles 254–5
    metals 95–6
    paper and board 142

Index

polymers 182–3
timbers 290
stripboard/breadboard **70**, 224
Styrofoam **70**, 165, 168
sub-assembly 105–6, 226–7, 258, 295
surface finishes and treatments
  fibres and textiles 265–9
  metal 121–3
  paper and board 154–5
  polymers 196–7
  systems 232–3
  timbers 304–5
surface-mount technology (SMT) 219, 226
sustainability **63**
  controlled assessment 335–6
  fibres and textiles 251
  metals 90
  new technologies 4–5
  paper and board 134–5, 136
  polymers 174
  timbers 281, 284
switches 34, 204, 205
synthetic fibres 48, 243
system diagrams 74–5
systems 33–5, 202–33
  case construction 211
  control devices and components 34, 204–7
  design contexts 203
  ecological footprint 212
  exams 234–9
  forces and stresses 217
  machinery 229
  manufacturing processes 223–7
  maths 222
  outputs 207–8
  PCB population 224
  programmable components 35–7
  properties and origins of components 204–13
  prototypes 228–31
  quantity production 225–7
  rare earth elements 209
  raw materials 208–9
  reinforcement/stiffening 218
  resistor colour codes 209–11, 232
  scales of production 224–5
  selection 213–17

shaping 230
sizes 220–3
social footprint 211–12
stock forms/types 219–23
surface finishes 232–3
tools and equipment 228–9
working properties 211
systems thinking 67–8

tapping 118, 194
tarnish **209**
technical textiles 23–4
templates 105, 149, 189, **224**, 226, 258, 295
tensile strength **21**, 89, 180, 246, 281
textiles *see* fibres and textiles
texture **131**, 136, 154, 174, 196, 214, 250, 283
thermistors 33, 204
thermoforming polymers **43**–4, 45, 164–6
thermosetting polymers **43**, 44–5, 166
threading 118, 119, 194
through-hole components 219
timbers 276–305
  design contexts 277
  ecological footprint 281–2
  exam 306–11
  fabrication, assembly and construction 288–9
  joints 302
  manufactured 53, 279
  manufacturing processes 292–6
  natural 52–3, 277–9
  origins 279
  properties 54, 280
  prototypes 296–304
  quantity production 294–6
  scales of production 293–4
  selection 283–7
  shaping 297–300
  sizes 290–1
  social footprint 281
  sources 277–83
  stock forms/types 290
  strengthening 288–9
  surface finishes 304–5
  tools and equipment 296–7, 300
  working properties 280–1

tolerance 106, 149, 190, **210**, 227, 258, 295
tooling **176**
tools and equipment
  fibres and textiles 259
  metals 104–5, 108, 110, 111
  paper and board 151
  systems 228–9
  timbers 296–7, 300
torque **31**
toughness 46, **54**
transistors 34, 205
transparency **131**
transportation 4, 8, 14, 90, 135, 172, 251, 282
trend forecasting 89, 132, 169, 247, 281
tungsten carbide **112**
turning 112, 299

user-centred design 67
user requirements 315–16, 334

vacuum forming 193, 230
vanishing point **72**
velocity ratio 26, 29, 30
veneers **21**, 53, 301
voltage **34**, 220

warp **244**
warping **284**
waste 5, 8, 59
  fibres and textiles 248
  metals 90, 106, 118
  minimising 106, 150, 227, 258, 295
  paper 135
  polymers 169, 170, 172, 175
  systems 212–13, 214, 231
  timber 282, 299–300, 303
Waste Electrical and Electronic Equipment (WEEE) Directive 214
web **94**
weft **244**
weight calculation 129
welding 101, 187
wildlife 89, 133, 170, 247
woven fabrics 49, 244

yarn **243**, 255

Acknowledgements

The publisher would like to thank the following for their kind permission to reproduce their photographs:

(Key: b-bottom; c-centre; l-left; r-right; t-top)

123RF.com: 297tr; **Alamy Stock Photo:** Ajotte 219b, Art Directors & Trip 12, Claudia Rehm 278tl, 279, Cultura Creative RF 259, David Bleeker Photography 104t, David J Green tools 105, Design Pics Inc 166, foodfolio 65, Glasshouse Images 292br, Ian Davidson Photography 299br, India Picture 267l, JuniArt 290 (d), Kevin Whitehouse 206, Krys Bailey 228l, Magdalelena Rohova 72, Naoki Kim 53b, National Geographic Creative 22, Panther Media GmbH 162, razorpix 201, Richard McDowell 219t, Simon Balson 273b, Solostock Industrial 299c, Tetra Images 86, Tewin Kijthamrongworakul 52 (d), Theerapol Pongkangsananan 70; **ArtiFacture:** 197; **(c) Percy Marin:** 229b; **Forest Stewardship Council:** 281; **Fotolia.com:** 122248337 131, Africa Studio 273t, alexmx 119b, 120t, 126, amphotolt 297 (d), cristis180884 228cr, csproductions23 119t, danishch 297 (c), deetshana 53t, design56 120l, 120r, 155, goodween123 52 (a), hafizismail 267r, Henk Jacobs 228br, ironstealth 280, kuarmagadd 229t, lucag_g 317c, miroslavmisiura 52 (b), musa_smsk 2, nonillion 115t, PETRA 317b, pilotl39 119c, pongans68 52 (c), Raftel 145, scaliger 278bl, sergey0506 299cl, Sociologas 278c, srki66 172, stoleg 115c, 115b, Tiler84 49, Will Thomas 83b, Zerophoto 152b; **Getty Images:** Boston Globe 71, Carlos Orario 250, Carol Yepes 317t, dejan Jekic 190, Fotonoticias 260, In Communicado 293, malerapaso 128, Martin Harvey 170, 290 (c), Science & Society Picture Library 289, Vincenzo Pinto 140, Zoran Milch 312; **Greenpeace UK:** Kemal Jefri 282; **HL Studios:** HL Studios 210; **Jenny Dhami:** 326 (all), 331 (all), 334 (a), 334 (b), 334 (c), 334 (d), 334 (e), 334 (f), 334 (g); **Pearson Education Ltd:** Gareth Boden 224, 292bl, 296r, 297 (b), 299tr, 299cr, 300b, 303 (a), 303 (b), 303 (d), Rob Judges 298 (d), Jules Selmes 228tr, Coleman Yuen. Pearson Education Asia Ltd 271, Studio 8 200, Trevor Clifford 296l, 297 (a), 297 (e), 298 (b), 298 (c), 300t, 300c; **RJH Finishing:** 192; **Shutterstock.com:** 257923 138, anaken2012 202, Andrei Kuzmik 298 (a), arek_malang 136t, Bardodz Peter 247, Bill McKelvie 104b, Chilli Productions 290 (b), ervstock 83t, Hermann 207, Lamarinx 292tr, Mega Pixel 42, Nagy-Bagoly Arpad 298 (e), Peteri 17, Pincasso 290 (a), Route66 152t, Ruslan Semichev 297cr, Stehen Bonk 303 (c), Sufi 240, Taina Sohlman 276, Zakharchenko Anna 272; **The Allandale Group/http://www.machine-dro.co.uk/:** 104c; **Thrace Synthetic:** 24; **Vegware:** 136b

Cover images: *Front:* **Getty Images:** Yagi Studio

All other images © Pearson Education